CW01646115

Iron Age and Roman Occupation in the West Bridge Area, Leicester

Excavations 1962-1971

Patrick Clay and Richard Pollard

with contributions by
David J. Smith, Brenda M. Dickinson, Geoffrey B. Dannell, Kay Hartley, Mark Hassall, C. Carreras, David F. Williams, Deborah Sawday, Richard Buckley, Andrew P. Fitzpatrick, Robert A. Rutland, D.F. Mackreth, Sarnia Butcher, Louise Monk, John Lucas, Anthony J. Gouldwell, Ann Stirland and G.C. Morgan.

LEICESTERSHIRE MUSEUMS
ARTS & RECORDS SERVICE

1994

ISBN 0850 223555

Published by Leicestershire Archaeological Unit,
Leicestershire Council Council Museums, Arts and Records Service
116 Humberstone Drive,
Leicester
LE5 0RD
Tel: (0533) 765534; Fax (0533) 760202

LEICESTERSHIRE
COUNTY COUNCIL

Acknowledgements

The authors would like to thank the original site directors for their assistance and co-operation in the preparation of these reports. The sites were excavated with the help of grants from the the Ministry of Works and Leicester City Council. Post excavation work was funded by Leicestershire County Council and some grant aid provided by English Heritage. Thanks also go to the many individual developers who provided access for the work to be undertaken.
The site reports and plans were prepared by Patrick Clay. All other illustrations were undertaken by the individual specialists except for the brooches which were prepared by James Allison (1-19) and David Neal (20-31) with some additional drawings by David Hopkins and Sally Warren. Students from the University of Leicester, School of Archaeological Studies Post Excavation Studies Course assisted Richard Pollard with some pottery sorting. The reports were prepared between 1985 and 1989 and the typescripts produced by central typing at Leicestershire County Council, County Hall and Leicestershire Museums, Arts and Records Service. Much helpful advice and comment was provided by colleagues at Leicestershire Museums; any errors however remain the responsibility of the authors.

Cover: Central panel (reconstructed), Peacock Mosaic Pavement now in the Jewry Wall Museum.

Designed and typeset by Dr Alan McWhirr, Leicester University Archaeological Research Centre, and produced by the Reprographic Unit of Leicester University.
1994

Contents

Figures

Plates at the end of the volume

Tables

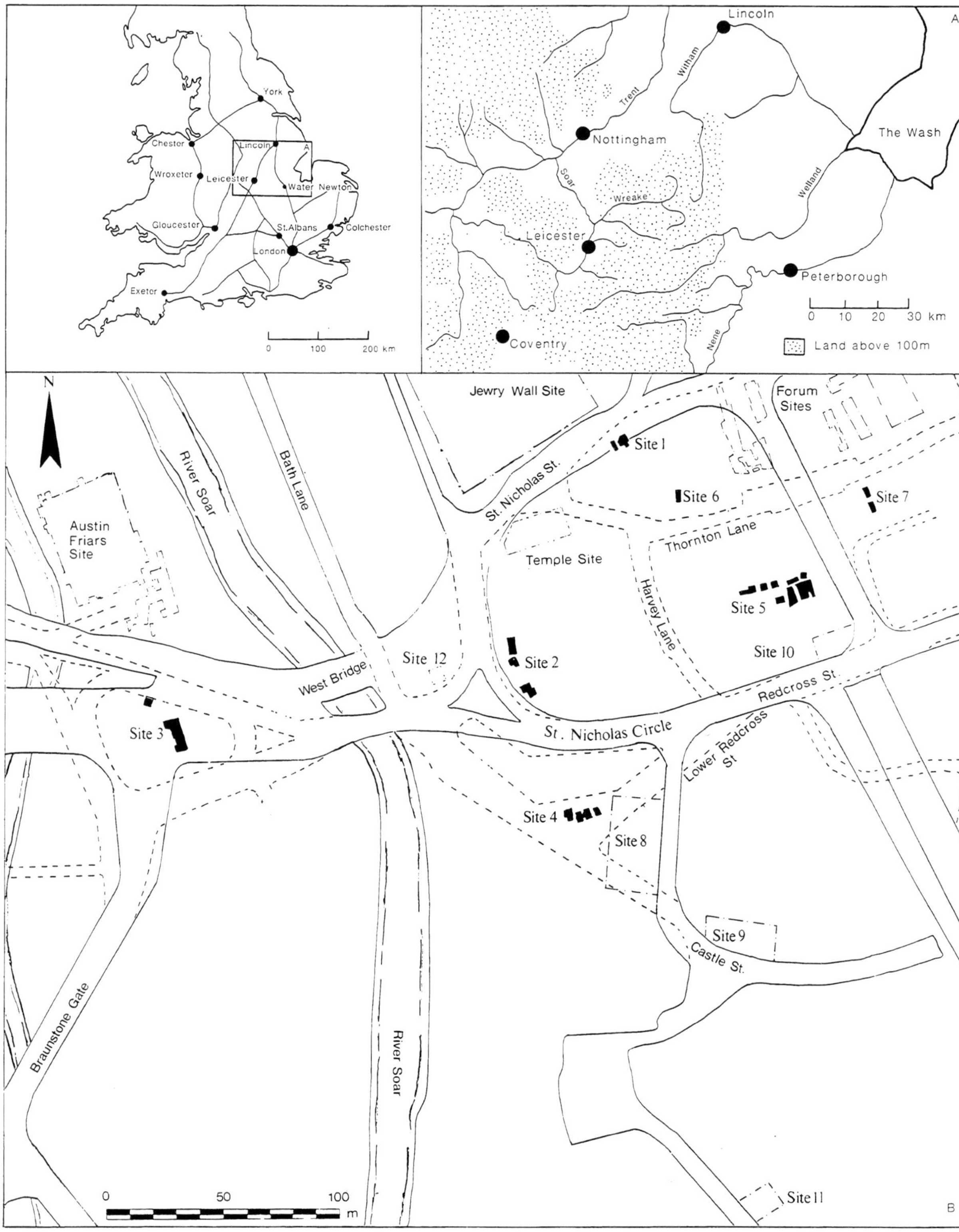

Fig. 1 Location of sites (see also Fig 43). Site 1 51-2, St Nicholas Street (Peacock Pavement) (A653.1965); Site 2 St Nicholas Circle (A163.1969); Site 3 West Bridge (A568.1967WB); Site 4 Lower Redcross St (A568.1967RC); Site 5 Redcross St (A316.1962; A174.1963); Site 6 51, Thornton Lane (A305.1963); Site 7 28, Thornton Lane (306.1963); Site 8 Castle St (Townhouses Site; A124.1970); Site 9 Castle St (Everards Brewery; A622.1966); Site 10 St Nicholas Circle (Garage Site; A471/6.1971); Site 11 Newarke Houses Garden (20.1939; 253.1951); Site 12 Applegate St (366.1965).

Introduction

Between 1961 and 1973 various excavations were undertaken in Leicester in advance of redevelopment directed by M H Hebditch and Jean E Mellor, successive Field Archaeologists with Leicester City Museums. Within the overall aim of recovering further information on the Roman and medieval town, specific work was carried out in the area of the Roman forum (Hebditch and Mellor, 1973; Mellor forthcoming(a)) and the town defences (Buckley and Lucas 1987). In addition areas to the east of the River Soar centred on Bath Lane have been examined (Clay and Mellor, 1985), which have provided information on the Iron Age and early Roman aspects of Leicester's development. It is these aspects which are the dominant feature of the sites in the West Bridge area (Fig. 1) which are discussed in this report. Seven excavations are considered consisting of sites at 51-52 St. Nicholas Street (Peacock Pavement) (Site 1), St. Nicholas Circle (Site 2), West Bridge (Site 3), Lower Redcross Street (Site 4), Redcross Street (Site 5), 51 Thornton Lane (Site 6) and 28 Thornton Lane (Site 7). In addition four watching briefs and a small scale excavation are included at Castle Street (Townhouses Site) (Site 8), Castle Street (Everards Brewery) (Site 9), St. Nicholas Circle (Garage Site) (Site 10) and Applegate Street (Site 12). A re-examination of part of the excavation at Newarke Houses (Clarke, 1952) is also included (Site 11). Many of the site names are of streets that no longer exist following road developments in 1969. Sites 1, 2, 4-7, 10 and 12 are all now part of St. Nicholas Circle. These were all small excavations, the areas opened constrained by the extent of development, finances and time. Individually the value of these sites is limited due to their restricted size and the nature of later disturbances. However, if treated as a sample of this area of Leicester they do provide some important information and indicate where further work would be profitable.

The Iron Age and Roman occupation within these sites is discussed in full together with various medieval pit groups encountered. However the medieval aspects of Sites 4, 8 and 9 include activity connected with the development of Leicester Castle and these will be discussed in Buckley (forthcoming). The medieval phases on Site 3 should also be considered in relation to the nearby excavations of the Augustinian Friary (Mellor and Pearce, 1981).

The Excavations

All the excavations and watching briefs considered in this report were recorded using conventional free hand site notes with plans and sections recorded on imperial graph paper. No appreciable shrinkage was discernible when these plans were copied in 1984 and 1985. Each site was given a unique museum accession number e.g. A163.1969 (Site 2). Sites 3 and 4 however share the same accession number (A568.1967) but are separated using the suffixes WB (Site 3) and RC (Site 4). Finds from these two sites share the same number sequence - the context numbers however are separate for each site. Each individual context is divided into an area (Roman numerals) and context number (Arabic numerals) e.g. I 18. The context number is incomplete without the Area prefix. The only exceptions to this are Site 6 where no Area number is used as only one area was examined and Sites 7 and 8 where sequential numbers were used regardless of areas. Feature numbers are allocated to all negative features but only to make-up, floor or road deposits where a separate activity is discernible (e.g. Site 1 Phase 1C F51). Occasionally separate feature numbers were allocated to different parts of one feature. Only one feature number is now used, the duplicate number appearing in brackets e.g. Site 1 F73 (F75) for archive reference. Day book letter codes were used on Sites 5-8 but are not included in this report. The features and contexts are listed at the beginning of each phase. Missing context numbers usually denote modern intrusions or unstratified contexts. Where phasing has been impossible unphased contexts are listed separately. An example of this is from Site 5 where Area V (ext.) was dug in spits owing to time considerations. These spits cannot be related to the phased deposits and are considered separately (p. 36). Plans of all features are included where possible; where the plan of the feature is in doubt this is shown by hatched lines. This is used where, for example, a feature is apparent in the section but not in plan e.g. Site 1 Phase 9B F57 and F58 (Figs. 9 and 11). Sections were usually drawn of the baulks separating areas or the extent of the site and these are included where possible. Levels are included with the sections where this information is recorded. Although the plans were originally recorded in imperial measurement only metric measurement is now included.

The Phase descriptions include brief details of the finds, when present, with further details in the individual finds sections. Modern disturbance, medieval pit digging, worm action and human error may all have contributed to the presence of some intrusive material. Where material is probably intrusive this is noted in the phase description.

As was the practice with many excavations at this time some material believed to be residual or intrusive was discarded. This must be borne in mind when considering the finds reports (lists of material discarded, where available, are included in the archive). All finds (or occasionally groups of finds) are allocated a unique number within the site accession. This is included in brackets following the site number and phase. This is followed by the feature and context numbers, e.g. Site 1 Phase 8B (66) F1 III 2. Some reports e.g. Small finds, Glass include only a selection of finds, a complete list in Site Phase order being available from the archive. Some categories of find are treated extensively commensurate with their value in our understanding of the Iron Age and Roman settlement e.g. The Peacock pavement, late Iron Age and Roman pottery and Celtic coins. All plans, site notes, archive material and finds are deposited with Leicestershire Museums, Arts and Records Service.

Geology and Topography

These sites are located on alluvial sand and gravel overlying keuper marl, typical of this area of Leicester. The survey of the natural ground level (Lucas, 1980-1) shows that, with the exception of Site 3, the area examined was at the top of the steep escarpment overlooking the River Soar to the west. The natural substratum contours show Sites 1, 5 and 7 at between 58m and 59m O.D. whilst Sites 2, 4, 6, and 8-12 lie between 57m and 58m O.D. *(ibid.* 4, Fig. 2). Although Site 3 lies between the two arms of the River Soar at 51m O.D. the present course of the river has changed and this may or may not have been the case during the Roman period (Buckley and Lucas, 1987, 52).

Summary

To highlight the critical evidence from these excavations the main results of the work can be summarised as follows.

1. Iron Age Settlement

Evidence of Iron Age occupation was present on Sites 1, 2, 4, 6, 8, 9 and 11. The earliest evidence, from Site 6, consisted of a possible circular building with associated pottery dating from the 1st century BC (p. 37). Gallo-Belgic imported pottery similar to that encountered in the Bath Lane area (Clamp, 1985, 41) was present on Sites 1-4, 8-9 and 11. This provides further evidence of an Iron Age settlement developing increasing contact with the Roman world in the last few years before the conquest (Clay, 1985).

2. Early Roman development

The post-conquest development may have had some military influence in the type and alignment of timber building used in the area. Pre-Flavian activity was present on Sites 1-4, 8, 9 and 11 with evidence of different alignments of timber buildings used during this time (see p. 46 Fig. 42). The later 1st century sees gradual Romanisation with piecemeal commercial activity (Sites 5, 6 p. 24 and 37). Extramural military activity may be present on Site 3 during this time perhaps in the form of a fortlet guarding the river crossing (p. 21). The 2nd century sees the establishment of a Romanised town proper with a street grid (Sites 2, 3, 5, 7 and 12 p. 47) and stone buildings including a town house or *mansio* (Site 1 p. 46).

3. Later Activity

Commercial activity into the 3rd century is present with shops being rebuilt (Sites 5 and 6 p. 35). The town house (Site 1) appears to have remained in use until the 4th century (p. 12) whilst elsewhere the streets appear to have been abandoned and cut by later features (Site 5 p. 36).

There is an apparent *lacuna* in this area between the 5th-10th centuries as is the case with other areas of Leicester at this time. Medieval and post-medieval activity in the form of pits and wells is present, reflecting the sites' locations, in some cases, to the rear of the medieval properties.

Site 1 Excavations beneath the Peacock pavement, 51-52 St Nicholas Street 1965 SK 5826 0446

Realignment of the road and redevelopment in the areas of St Nicholas Street and Thornton Lane in 1965 necessitated the removal of the preserved Roman mosaic floor known as the Peacock pavement (see below p. 48) from 51-52 St Nicholas Street to the then recently opened Jewry Wall Museum.

The removal of the floor allowed an examination of the deposits sealed below it to be undertaken, between December 1965 and February 1966, directed by Jean E Mellor (Mellor, 1968-9, 6; Acc. No. A653.1965). An area of 39 sq m was examined, divided into five sub-areas (lettered III, IIIA, V, VI, VII). Of these Area V was below the Peacock pavement whilst III and IIIA were below two adjacent tesselated pavements (see below p. 50). Area VI consisted of two small trenches immediately south of Area V while Area VII was a similar trench opened directly to the north of this area (see Figs. 2-4, 10-11). In contrast to the deposits below the Blackfriars pavement (Clay and Mellor, 1985) the information beneath the Peacock pavement was considerably more complicated with seven pre-pavement phases of activity being recognised.

Phase 1 (Fig. 2) Early -Late 1st century

The earliest evidence of activity on the site comes from a series of pits, post holes and gullies, in Areas III, IIIA, V and VI, cutting the underlying sand, gravel and keuper marl substrata. While their sequence of insertion is not clear they can be grouped as follows.

Phase 1A

Pit:	F77 (V 69-71, 117-8, 130, 135-45, 150-2, 161, 167, 235-8, 240)
Stake holes:	F147 (IIIA 90, 91); F148 (IIIA 92, 93); F149 (IIIA 94, 95)

Three stake holes, F147-F149, were located at the north end of Area IIIA, (all *c.* 0.10m in diameter by 0.20m deep) with fine light brown charcoal flecked sandy loam fills. In the north of Area V the lower layers of a large pit, F77 (1.60m in diameter) were located, the upper section having been disturbed by later activity. The fill of this pit consisted of various layers of red clay, sand, gravel and dark grey brown clay loams with heavy charcoal concentrations. A few sherds of pottery dating from the late Iron Age - early Roman periods were recovered.

Phase 1B

Pits:	F46 (F47) (III 51, 75, 128); F72 (V 50, 56-58, 60-63, 91-92, 231); F73 (F75) (V 49, 51-55, 59, 66-8, 76-81, 83, 113, 146-9, 153-160, 232); F76 (V 105-6)
Post holes:	F44 (III 68, 126); F45 (III 69, 127)
Stake holes:	F145 (VI 95, 96)
Channels:	F50 (IIIA 74, 81, 85); F136 (F140) (VI 27, 32-3, 37, 56-7, 93)
Gullies:	F138 (VI 31, 84); F139 (VI 47, 82)
Cobbled surface:	F54 (IIIA 75-7)

Further structural evidence was found in the form of two post holes (F44-5) and a stake hole, F145, in Areas III and VI. The post holes varied between 0.20 m diameter x 0.30 m deep (F44) and 0.45 m diameter x 0.60 m deep (F45) while the stake hole (F145) was 50mm in diameter. Again the fill of these features consisted of a fine light brown sandy loam. Cobbling, F54, in Area IIIA may be a remnant of a surface associated with this activity. Four pits can be assigned to this phase from Areas III, F46 (F47), and V, F72, F73 (F75), and F76. F46 was a shallow pit (0.25m deep with a minimum width of 1.50 m) containing a dark brown fine sandy loam fill. It may have formed the western extent of F72, a deeper (1.30m) feature containing various fills of clay loam, sand, gravel

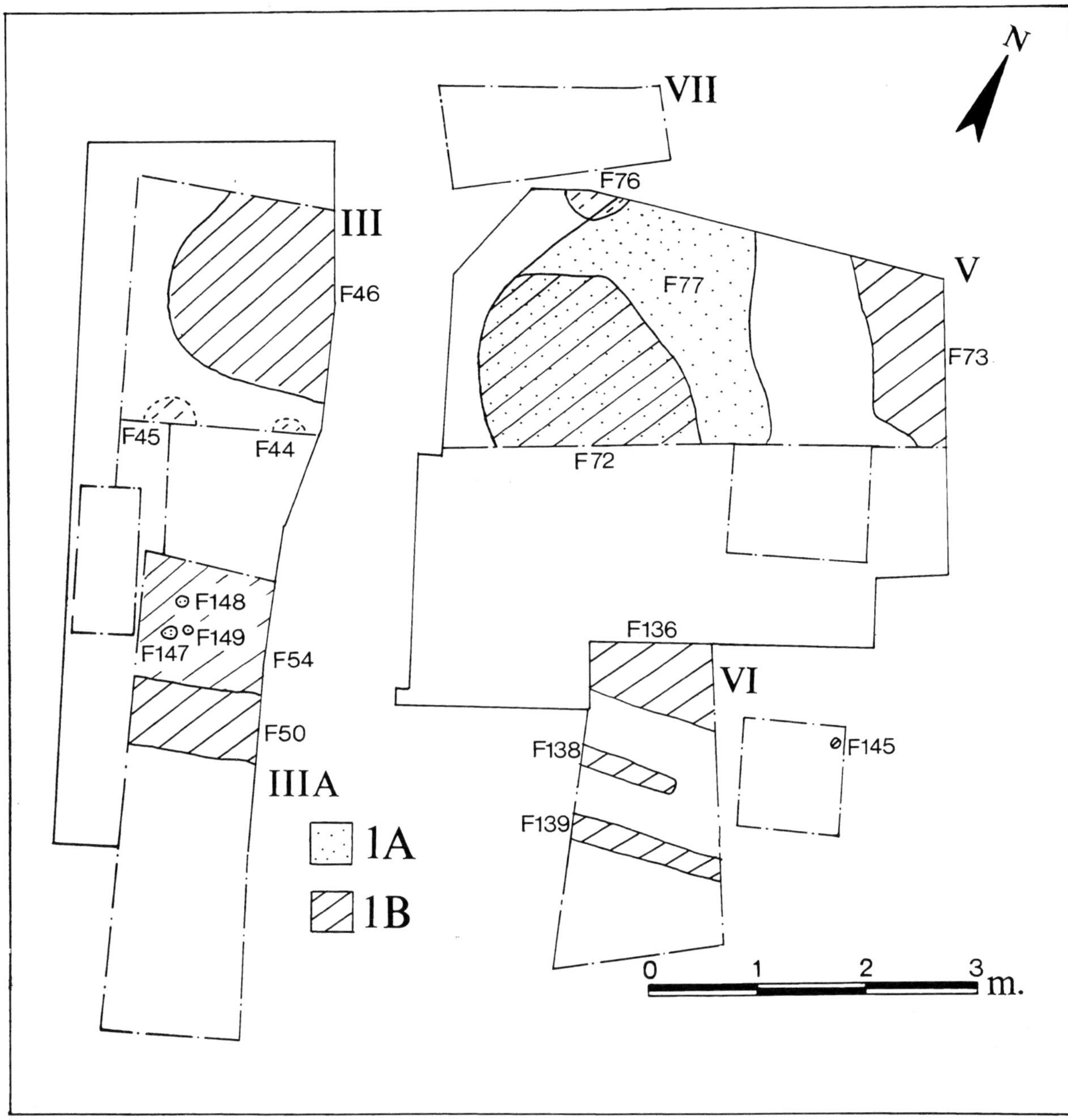

Fig. 2 Site 1, Phase 1

and much charcoal. One metre to the east of F72 part of a similar feature, F73, was located whilst 0.5m to the north evidence of a small pit, F76, (*c.* 0.8m diameter x 0.6m deep) was located in the north section. Fills of dark clay loam were present in these features. Pottery from these features suggested a pre-Flavian date for their use, F73 also including four brooch fragments (p. 139 Figs 73-4. 6, 20, 23 and 24), animal bone, iron and fired clay fragments. The fired clay included furnace lining or kiln bar material (see p. 156).

A channel (F50) 0.6m wide x 0.25m deep was located in Area IIIA on an east-west alignment. In Area VI, another possible channel or ditch F136/40 and two gullies F138 and F139 were also aligned east-west. The latter were *c.* 0.25m wide x 0.20m deep and all these features contained a similar fill of dark brown fine sandy loam.

Phase 1C

Make-up deposits:	F5I (IIIA 65-6); III 47,50; IIIA 70-1, 73, 88;V 65, 128-9, 131-2, 134, 162; VI 29, 30, 35, 49, 55; VII 14.

A period of levelling and make-up activity disturbing the tops of the Phase 1A and 1B features was evident from various layers covering the whole of the site. One discrete group of levelling layers could be identified in Area IIIA (F51). These consisted mainly of grey brown fine sandy loams, charcoal, keuper marl sand and gravel deposits. Material from Phase 1C layers included 1st century pottery, animal bone, a copper alloy penannular brooch (p.139, Fig. 74.19) and an iron nail.

Phase 2 (Fig. 3) Mid-Late 1st century

Phase 2A

Post hole:	F26 (III 63-4)
Stake holes:	F25 (III 65, 134); F27 (III 52-3, 66); F29-F43 (III 76-90, 105-119); F137 (VI 78-9)
Timber slot:	F160 (III 138-140)
Gully:	F146 (VII 18-22)

Make-up/occupation debris:III 45, VI 25-6, 28

Traces of a narrow timber slot, F160, were located between stake holes F29-F34. A narrow gully (F146) was located in Area VII on an east-west alignment partially disturbed by later activity. The

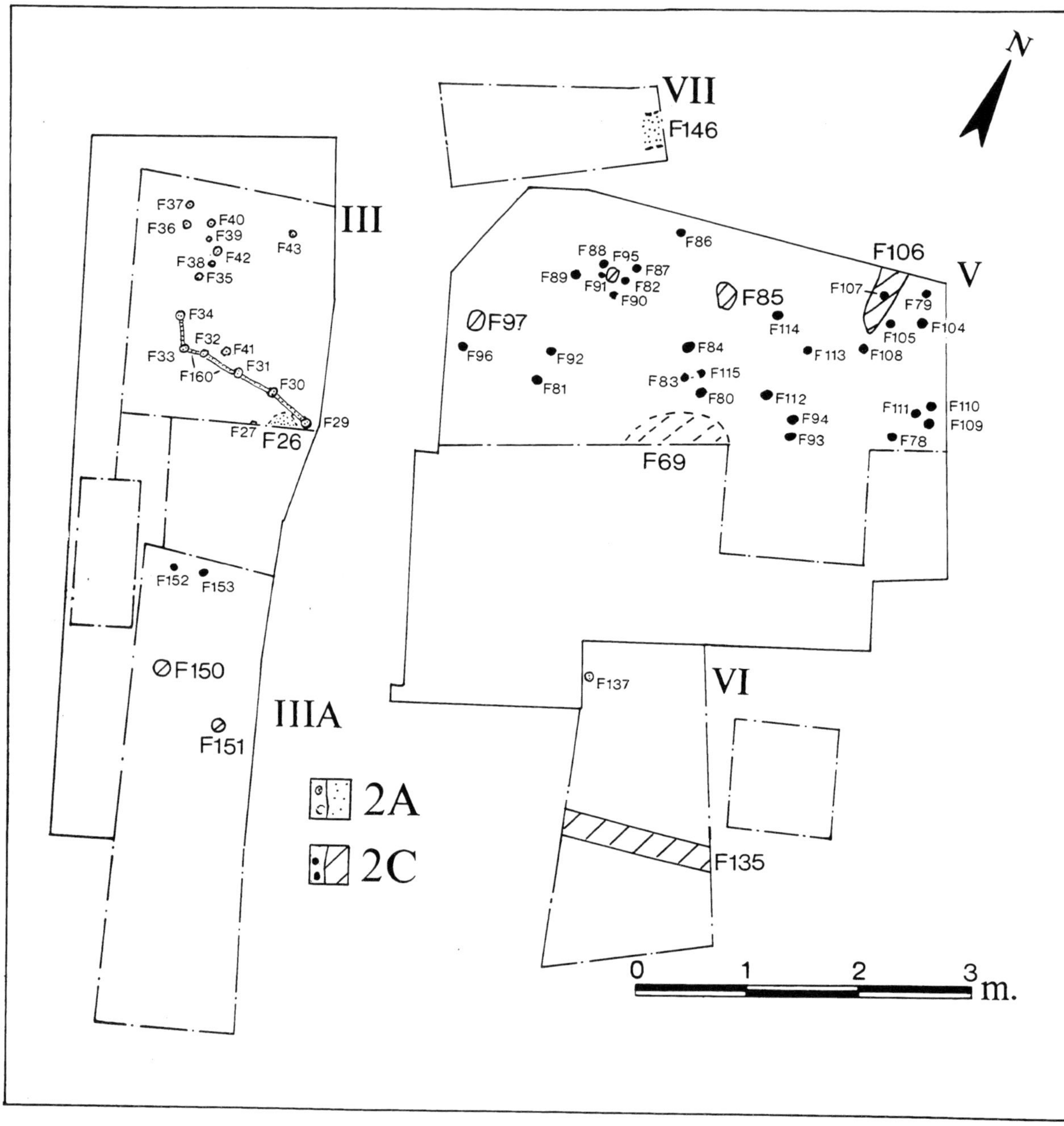

Fig. 3 Site 1, phase 2

fills of these features consisted of light brown fine sandy loams and charcoal. Sticky dark grey clay loams with heavy charcoal concentrations (III 45 and VI 28) and burnt clay, ash and charcoal deposits (VI 25, 26) may be associated with these structures.

Phase 2B

Make-up deposits:	III 46; IIIA 63, 67; V 47, 93-4
Cobbled surfaces:	F24 (III 59)

Make-up, levelling and possible cobbled surfaces were located in Areas III, IIIA and V in some cases sealing the Phase 2A structural features. These consisted of grey and orange sand, gravel, and compacted cobbling.

Phase 2C

Pit:	F69 (V 40-2, 46, 48, 228)
Post holes:	F85 (V 197-8); F95 (V 217-8): F97 (V 270-1)
Stake holes:	F78-84 (V 183-196); F86-94 (V 199-216) F96 (V 268-9) F104-5 (V 244-247) F107-15 (V 250-267)
Beam slot:	F106 (V 248-9)

Another group of post and stake holes denoted some further structural activity. Three post holes, F85, F97 (0.20m in diameter) F95 (0.15m diameter) and twenty eight stake holes, F78-84, F86-94, F96, F104-5, F107-115, *c.* 50mm in diameter were located in Area V. To the north of these part of a beam slot, F106, (0.30m wide x 0.20m deep) on a north east - south west alignment was examined which, although cutting F107, can be grouped in this phase.

All of these features contained a light brown fine sandy clay loam fill. A pit, F69, (0.50m in diameter) containing a clay loam, sand and charcoal fill in Area V, and a gully, F135, (0.25m wide x 0.10m deep), with a sand, gravel and silt fill in Area VI, may also be associated with this phase. Two post holes F150-1 (*c.* 0.20m x 0.15 deep) and two stake holes F152-3 (50mm diameter) were located in Area IIIA containing light brown fine sandy loam fills. A possible cobbled surface (III 43) with clay, ash and silt deposits (V 34, 44, VI 20, 36) may also be associated with this activity. 1st century pottery, copper alloy, iron and ash charcoal were recovered from F69.

Discussion of Phases 1 and 2

Little can be said about these phases within the limited area

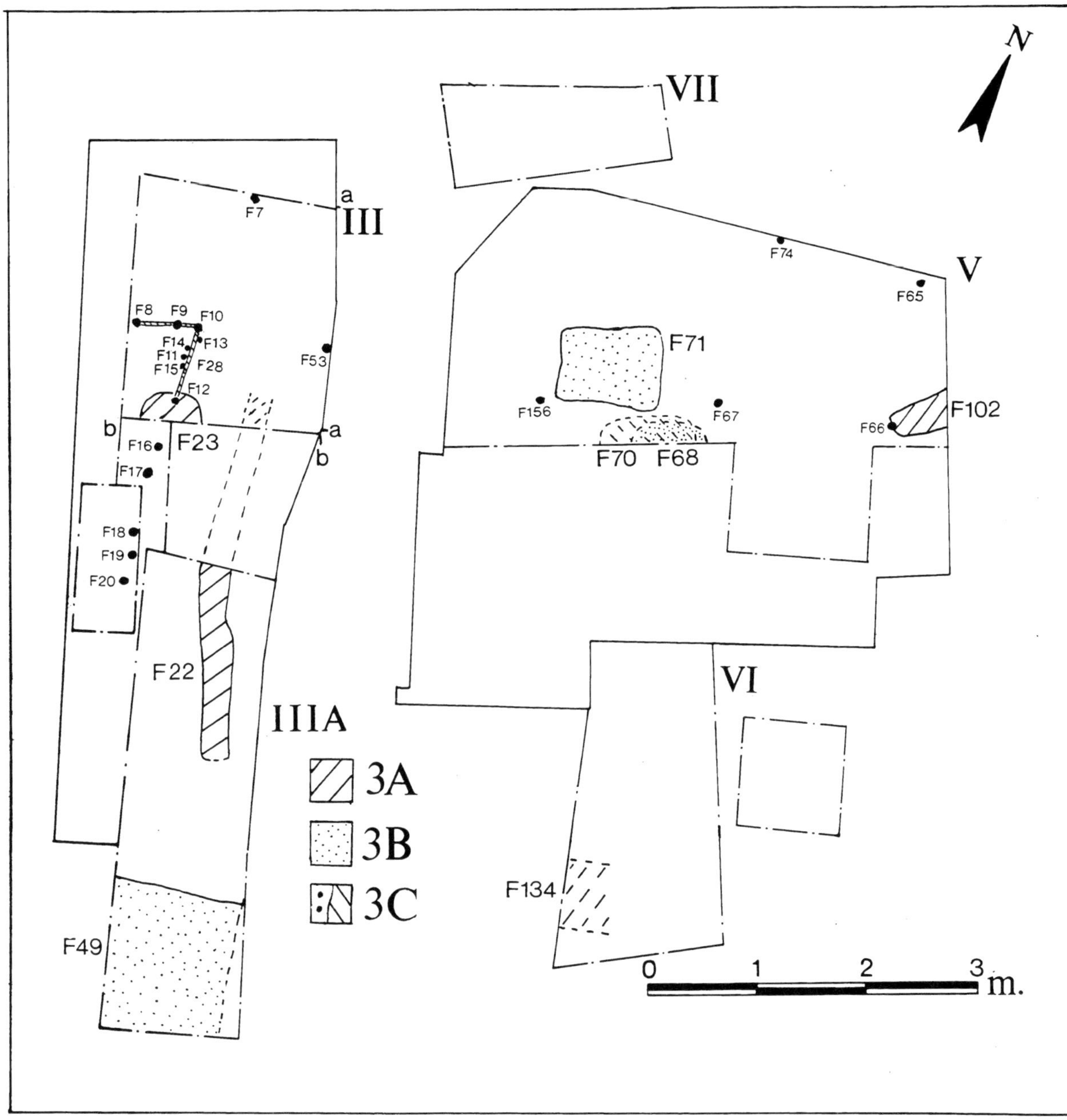

Fig. 4 Site 1, phase 3

examined. A general discussion of the late Iron Age-early Roman evidence from these sites is included below (p. 44). Activity in Phase 1A and 1B consisted of some large rubbish pits and a few isolated stake holes, gullies and channels. Industrial activity is suggested from fired clay fragments in F73. Phase 1C is a period of levelling and make-up activity disturbing and covering the Phase 1A and 1B features. Material from this phase suggests a pre-Flavian date. The pottery is predominantly in the local Iron Age tradition with some 'Gallo-Belgic' fine wares, Romano-British grey and white wares and some Claudio-Neronian samian. It is uncertain whether any of the activity is pre-conquest in date however.

Structures with more form to them can be seen in Phase 2A following the Phase 1C levelling activity. Here stake holes with narrow slots between them may suggest hurdled fences or walls for insubstantial buildings. Occupation deposits associated with these structures can be suggested (III 45, VI 28) and burnt clay, ash and charcoal layers (VI 25, 26) to the south of these structures may be evidence of their destruction. The activity appears to have been repeated in Phases 2B and 2C with further levelling and make-up preceding more stake and post hole structures.

A beam slot (F106) on a NE-SW alignment is the first evidence of more substantial buildings. A cobbled surface and occupation deposits can be associated with these structures. The few finds from this phase are similar to those from Phase 1 providing a general pre-Flavian date.

Phase 3 (Fig. 4) Late 1st-Early 2nd century

Phase 3A

Post hole:	F23 (III 55-6, 60-1)
Beam slot:	F22 (III 44, 67, IIIA 69); F102 35, 241)
Channel:	F134 (VI 50, 83)
Make-up deposits:	III 57-8, 62
Occupation debris(?):	IV 22

Various sand, clay and clay loam deposits in Areas III, IIIA and V may be associated with a beam slot, F22, post hole, F23, and two channels or slots, F102 and F134. The beam slot, F22, (*c.* 3.50m x 0.50m x 0.20m deep) was on a north-south alignment and contained a grey clay loam with charcoal. 0.25m west of this was a sand and gravel packed post hole setting, F23, (0.40m diameter x 0.50m deep) with a tapering post pipe (80mm - 50mm diameter x 0.45m deep). To the west of Area V a beam slot, F102 (0.30m wide x 0.25m deep) contained a grey clay loam fill while a channel to the west of Area VI, F134, had a grey/green compacted clay loam fill. A dark grey clay loam with heavy charcoal concentration in Area VI (22) and clay and loam deposits in Area III (57, 58, 62) can be associated with this phase of activity.

Phase 3B

Pits:	F68 (V 86-9, 227); F71 (V 39, 43, 230)
Ditch/pit:	F49 (IIIA 68, 72, 78-80, 84, 87)

Cutting the Phase 3A deposits in Area V was a very small pit, F68, (*c.* 1.0m wide x 0.50m deep) with a brown sandy loam and charcoal fill. At the south end of Area IIIA part of a ditch or pit, F49, was located. This contained deposits of red clay, sand, gravel and silt loams. A square cut pit, F71, (*c.* 1.0m x 0.8m x 0.5m deep) in Area V had fills of grey green clay loam, pebbles, charcoal and mortar. Material from these features suggested a late 1st century date including, in F71, a copper alloy weight (p. 147 Fig 76.60) and three unabraded and near complete pots which may indicate deposition soon after manufacture (V 39 - Fig. 51. 15-16, 19).

Phase 3C

Pit:	F70 (V 24-5, 45, 84-5, 229)
Stake holes:	F7 (III 72-3); F8-15 (III 32-9, 97-104); F16-20 (III 92-6, 120-4); F53 (III 130-1) F65-7 (V 177-82); F74 (V 166,233); F156 (V 272-3)
Timber slot:	F28 (III 40-9, 125)
Mortar surface:	F101 (V 17)
Cobbled surface:	F133 (VI 17-19); III 41; IIIA 58-61
Opus Signinum:	III 30, IIIA 57

Further activity, in the form of twenty stake holes, was evident from Areas III and V (F7-F20, F53, F65-67, F74, F156). These were similar to the Phase 2A structures, the stake holes varying between 50mm and 80mm in diameter and again having traces of narrow timber slots between the stake holes in Area III (F28). They contained fills of light brown fine sandy loams with oak, elm and ash charcoal. A pit, F70, (*c.* 0.80m diameter x 0.80m deep) in Area V cutting F68 may also be associated with this phase. Deposits of fine sandy loam, charcoal, mortar and several granite blocks (*c.* 0.15m wide) were found in this feature with late 1st-early 2nd century pottery, animal bone, copper alloy and oak charcoal present. Surfaces which may be associated with this activity included cobbling, (III 41, IIIA 58-61, F133), *opus signinum* (III 30, IIIA 57) and mortar (F101). Finds from F101 included copper alloy bowls (Fig. 75.42-3), inlay (Fig. 76.47), iron blade fragments, late 1st-early 2nd century pottery and fired clay.

Phase 4 (Fig. 10) Late 1st-Early 2nd century

Phase 4A

Pit:	F63 (F64) (V 11-2, 18-21, 36-7, 225)
Furnace/oven:	F60 (V 28-32, 169-76, 222)
Stake hole:	F103 (V 242-3)
Make-up:	III 54, 74; V 38; VII 8

Spreads of burnt clay and charcoal were examined in Areas III, V and VII. At the centre of Area V a small rectangular furnace or oven, F60 (0.60m x 0.50m wide) had been inserted. This had been constructed of stone and tile on three sides and included fills of fired clay, charcoal, ash and mortar. Material from this feature included pot, copper alloy, iron nails and a wall tile with graffito (see below p. 155). A stake hole, F103 (60mm in diameter) appeared to have been incorporated in the structure or had been used in the oven's construction. A pit, F63, was located immediately south of F60 cutting F68 (Phase 3B). This feature (*c.* 2.0m x 1.0m x 0.5m deep) contained red clay, gravel, limestone and dark brown clay loam deposits. Finds included copper alloy objects, a la Tene III brooch, (Fig. 73.12), an Iron Age coin (p .131), nails, late 1st-early 2nd century pottery, vessel glass, wall plaster, mortar, animal bone, oyster shells and one intrusive 12th century pot sherd. The impression of studded leather upholstery had also been preserved in V 21 (see below p. 150, Fig. 78.79)).

Phase 4B

Beam slot:	F155 (IIIA 105-6)
Cobbled surface:	F3 (III 29)
Make-up/ occupation debris:	IIIA 7, 55-6; V 13-16; VII 7

A beam slot, F155, (*c.* 0.25m x 0.10m deep) in Area IIIA and possible associated cobbled surfaces (F3 III 29, IIIA 7, 55) were examined. Also associated with this phase are loam and clay deposits with much charcoal and occupation debris in Area V (13-16) from which four iron nails were recovered, and a clay deposit in Area VII (7).

Discussion of Phases 3 and 4

A similar sequence of activity to that in Phase 2 appears to continue in Phase 3. Levelling and make-up layers were inserted prior to some structural activity indicated by a beam slot (F22) and post setting (F23). Use of this structure may be connected with two pits (F68, F71) and an occupation deposit (VI 22) (Phase 3A). Phase 3C sees the construction of more stake and post hole structures similar in form to those in Phase 2A. Much of the material from Phase 3 contrasts with the preceding phases in the very small proportion of pottery of Iron Age tradition in comparison to the Roman grey and white wares. A Flavian to early 2nd century date is suggested for this activity.

Phase 4 shows further evidence of site clearing followed by the insertion of new features including a small rectangular oven or kiln of unknown use incorporating stone and tile in its construction. A high firing temperature is suggested from partial fuel ash glazing on the oven lining (see below p. 156). Evidence of timber structures and occupation deposits again present. Large quantities of material were recovered from this phase, especially pit F63, and a date of *c.* 80 - 120 AD can be suggested. Both phases 3 and 4 indicate, in a small area, the evidence of Flavian expansion reflected elsewhere in Leicester (cf. Mellor, 1985; Clay and Mellor, 1985; Buckley and Lucas, 1987) and in other Roman towns (Wacher, 1975, 289-374). Timber appears to be the main structural component but *opus signinum* and wall plaster indicate increasing Romanisation in these buildings. This is also reflected in the wider variety and greater quantity of domestic refuse material present.

Phase 5 (Figs 5-7) Late 1st-Early 2nd century

Phase 5A Late 1st-Early 2nd century (*c.* 80-120)

Make-up:	III 24-8, 70, 132; IIIA 6, 25, 51-4

Various spreads of material were located in Areas III and IIIA consisting of clay, brown sandy clay loam, silt, turf, yellow sand and gravel. They varied between 20mm and 0.15m in thickness and contained finds of pottery, glass, copper alloy, iron, lead, mortar and bone.

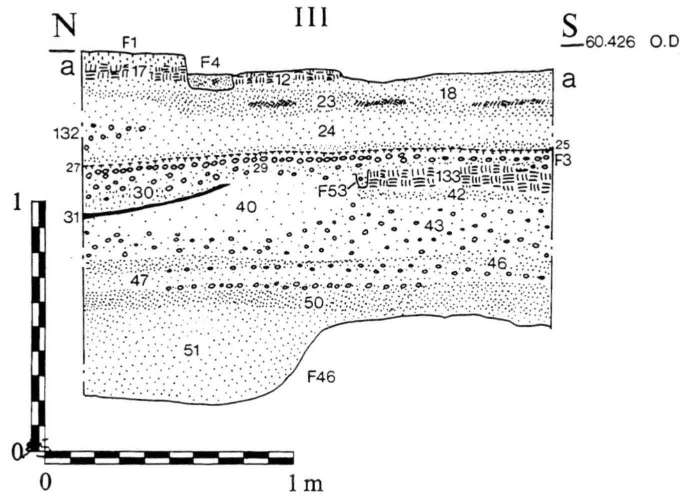

Fig. 5 Site 1 Section a-a Area III

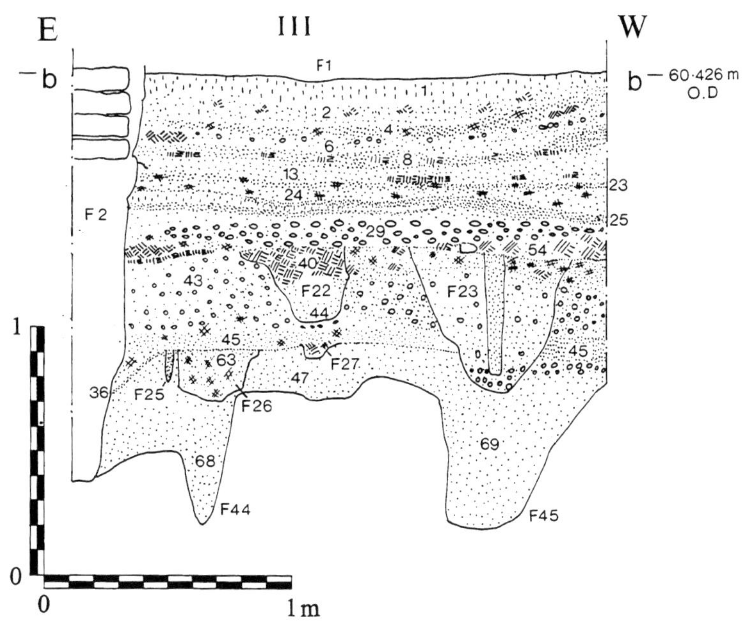

Fig. 6 Site 1 Section b-b Area III

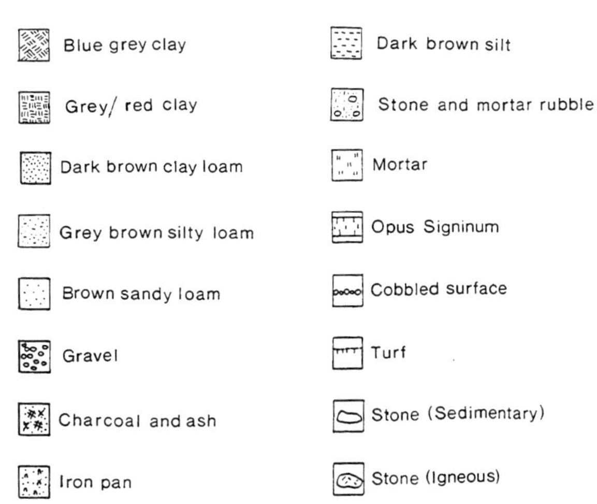

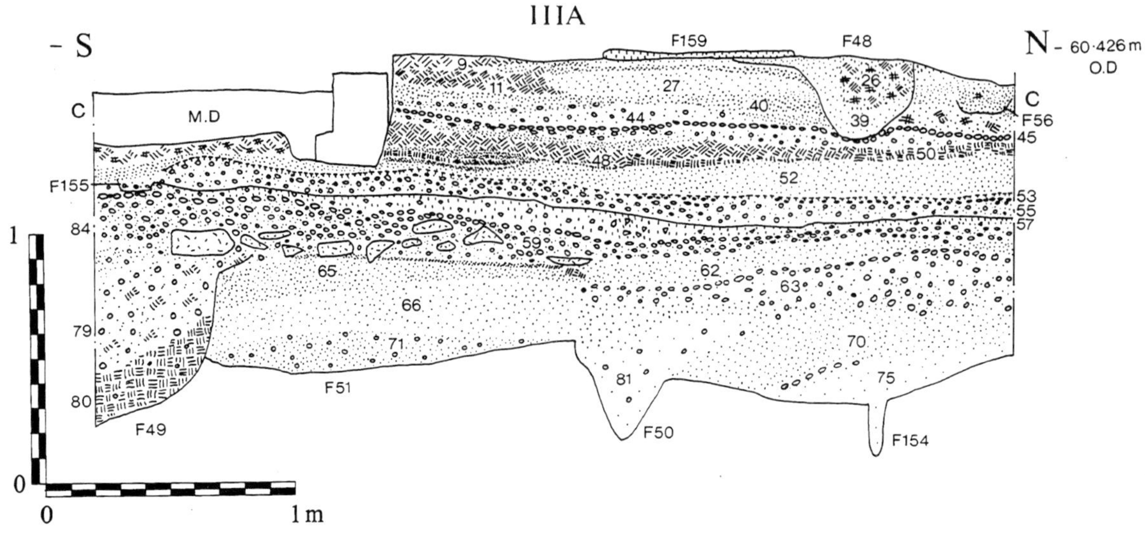

Fig. 7 Site 1 Section c-c Area IIIA

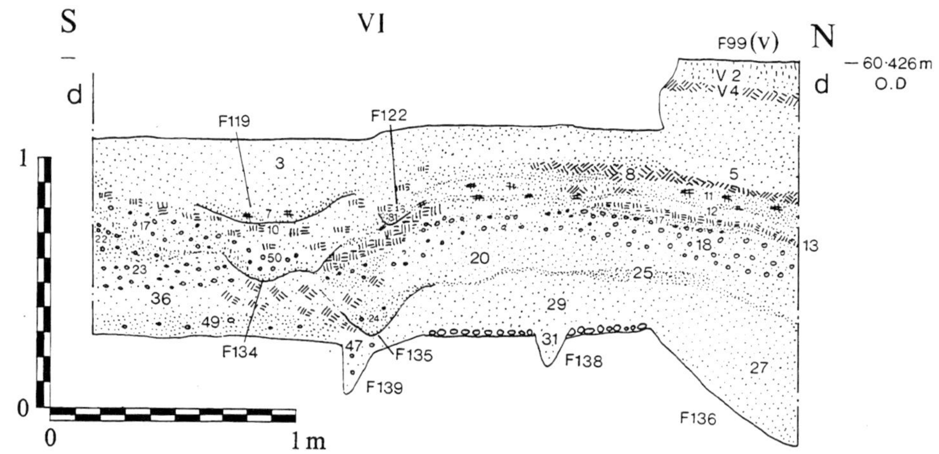

Fig. 8 Site 1 Section d-d Area IV

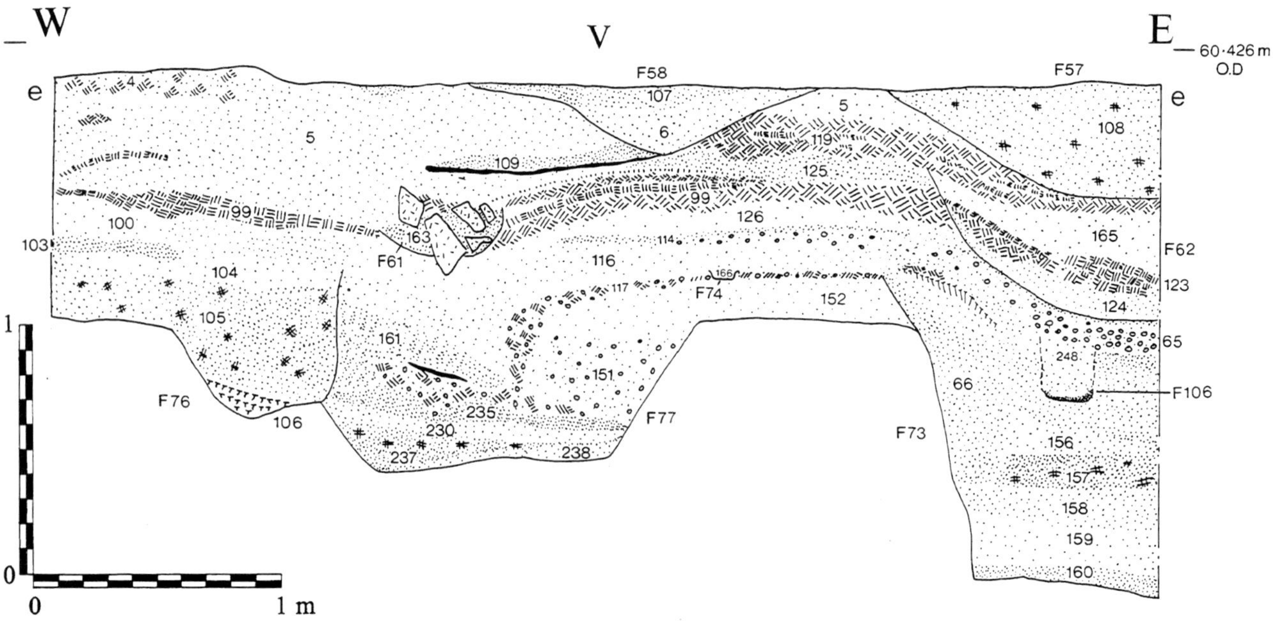

 Fig. 9 Site 1 Section e-e Area V

Phase 5B Late 1st-Early 2nd century (*c.* 80-120)

Make-up: III 19-23, IIIA 4-5, 20, 22-4, 46, 48-50; IIIC 6, 8; VI 15, 42, 85

Cobbled surfaces: IIIA 46; IIIC 2-5

Overlying the Phase 5A levels in Areas III and IIIA were similar deposits of yellow and grey sand, gravel, charcoal, light brown sandy loam and red clay. Yellow silt, brown sandy loam, charcoal and red/orange gravel in Area VI can also be assigned to this phase. Possible cobbled surfaces were present in Areas IIIA (46) and IIIC (2-5). A similar group of material to that in Phase 5A was recovered including furnace slag.

Phase 5C Early 2nd century (*c.* 110-130)

Make-up: III 12-15, 18 IIIA 3, 18-19, 21, 43-5, 47; V 102-4, 116; VI 13-4; VII 3-6, 21

Mortar surface(?): VI 94

Deposits of red clay, yellow and grey sand, brown sandy loam, orange sand, gravel and much charcoal were found in Areas III, IIIA, V, V1 and VII again containing similar material to Phases 5A and 5B. A possible mortar floor (VI 94) was also located.

Phase 6 Early-mid 2nd century

Phase 6A (Fig. 10) Early-mid 2nd century (*c.* 120-140)

Post hole: F123 (VI 52, 54, 87);

Stake holes: F120-1 (VI 58-9, 60-1); F122 (VI 46,81) F124-32 (VI 62-77, 97-8)

Gully: F56 (IIIA 36-38)

Make-up: III 8,10,16-7; IIIA 15-17; V 127; VI 11-2

Further deposits of brown fine sandy clay loam, yellow and red clay, ash and much charcoal were found in Areas III and IIIA overlying the Phase 5C levels to a depth of *c.* 0.15m. These contained some pot and glass fragments. Slight traces of structural activity were present in the form of a post hole (F123), eleven stake holes (F120-1; F124-F132) and a gully (F56) in Areas VI and IIIA. The post hole, F123, (0.30m diameter x 0.15m deep) contained a grey brown sandy loam fill with charcoal and mortar while the stake holes, (50mm in diameter) were filled with a dark brown fine sandy loam. Aligned east-west, the gully F56 (0.20m wide x 0.20m deep) contained a fill of light brown clay loam, mortar, charcoal and, at the east end, yellow clay.

Deposits of dark grey clay loam, charcoal, ash and mortar fragments were located in Areas IIIA and VI. A small pottery assemblage of *c.* 100-150 date, copper alloy and slag were recovered from this phase.

Phase 6B Early-mid 2nd century (*c.* 120-140)

Make-up deposits: III 5,7, IIIA 13-4, 40; V 33, 90, 100-1, 114-5, 126; VI 9,10

Cobbled surfaces: III 6; IIIA 29; IIIB 10,11

Deposits (*c.* 0.10m thick) of light brown fine sandy loam, red clay, grey blue clay, grey ash and brown silts were located in Areas III, IIIA, V and VI. Surfaces of cobbling were present in Areas III, IIIA and IIIB (III6, IIIA 29, IIIB 10, 11). Material from this phase included pottery (*c.* 100-150 date), copper alloy, iron, lead, glass, slag and wall plaster fragments.

Discussion of Phases 5 and 6

Phase 5 groups together a series of levelling and make-up deposits with no associated structures located within the area examined. This appears to have been formed from redeposited substrata, pit and occupation debris. Surfaces of cobbling and mortar may be present, much disturbed, in Phases 5B and 5C while trampled occupation debris may also be identified from Areas III (13, 23) and IIIA (5, 45). A large quantity and variety of material was recovered from these deposits perhaps suggesting spreads of rubbish and disturbed pit fills. Phases 5A and 5B can be dated to *c.* 80-120 whilst 5C may be slightly later, *c.* 110-130.

Phase 6 sees a continued build up of redeposited material together with some post and stake hole structures and a gully. Possible cobbled surfaces are again present in Phase 6B. A smaller quantity, though similar range, of material to Phase 5 suggests a date for Phase 6 activity of *c.* 120-140.

Phase 7 Early-Mid 2nd century (c. 140-150)

Phase 7A

Make-up/rubble: IIIA 35, IIIB 9, V 8-10, 97-99,112-3, 125

A series of clay, dark brown sandy loam, ash, mortar and wall plaster rubble spreads (*c.* 0.15 m thick) was located in Areas IIIA, IIIB, V and VI from which finds of pottery, copper alloy, iron and wall plaster were recovered.

Phase 7B (Fig. 10)

Pits: F62 (V 120-4,165,224); F118 (VI 51,53,88-9); F119 (VI 7,16,43, 45, 80)

Post hole: F61 (V 111,163,223)

A post hole and three pits were located in Areas V and VI; the post hole, F61, (*c.* 0.3m diameter x 0.25m deep), situated at the north end of Area V, contained fills of grey blue clay and mortar rubble. 1.50m south-east of F61 a pit, F62, (*c.* 1.0m x 0.45m deep) contained clay and dark grey brown clay loam. Part of a pit, F118, (*c.* 0.35m deep) was located at the north-east corner of Area VI containing a light brown sandy loam and charcoal fill. At the south end of Area VI another oval pit, F119 (*c.* 1.5m x 1.0m x 0.35m) was examined. Fills of wall plaster rubble, dark grey brown sticky clay loam, charcoal and limestone with some finds of pot, copper alloy, iron and a quern fragment were present.

Phase 7C

Make-up: III 3,4; IIIA 10-12,27-8,30; IIIB 5-8,12; V 5,96,109-10,119; VI 3-5,40-1

Overlying the Phases 6, 7A and 7B deposits in Areas III, IIIA, IIIB, V and VI, were various layers of clay, dark brown clay loam, charcoal, ash and yellow sand, varying between 20mm and 0.20m in thickness. Material from these layers included pottery, bone, copper alloy, iron, glass, tile, tesserae, wall plaster, furnace lining and oyster shells, most coming from V (5). This layer contained 63% by weight of all pottery from Phase 7 and nearly 10% by weight of the total late Iron Age - Roman pottery from the whole site (see below Table 2).

Phase 8 (Fig. 11) Mid 2nd-4th century

Phase 8A Mid 2nd century

Beam slots: F4 (III 9,71); F48 (IIIA 26,31-34,39,86, IIIB 3,4)

Post hole: F5 (III 11)

Two beam slots (F4, F48) on east-west alignments were located in Areas III and IIIA. F4 to the north (0.20m wide x 0.20m deep) had a dark brown fine clay loam fill with impressions of the oak beams surviving. At the east end a post hole, F5, (0.10m in diameter) was located, while 3.25m to the south another beam slot, F48, had been inserted. This was slightly larger, (0.35m x 0.25m deep) and contained orange/red sand, yellow clay, light brown fine clay loam, oak charcoal, mortar and wall plaster rubble. Finds of pottery, copper alloy, iron, glass and bone were recovered from these features.

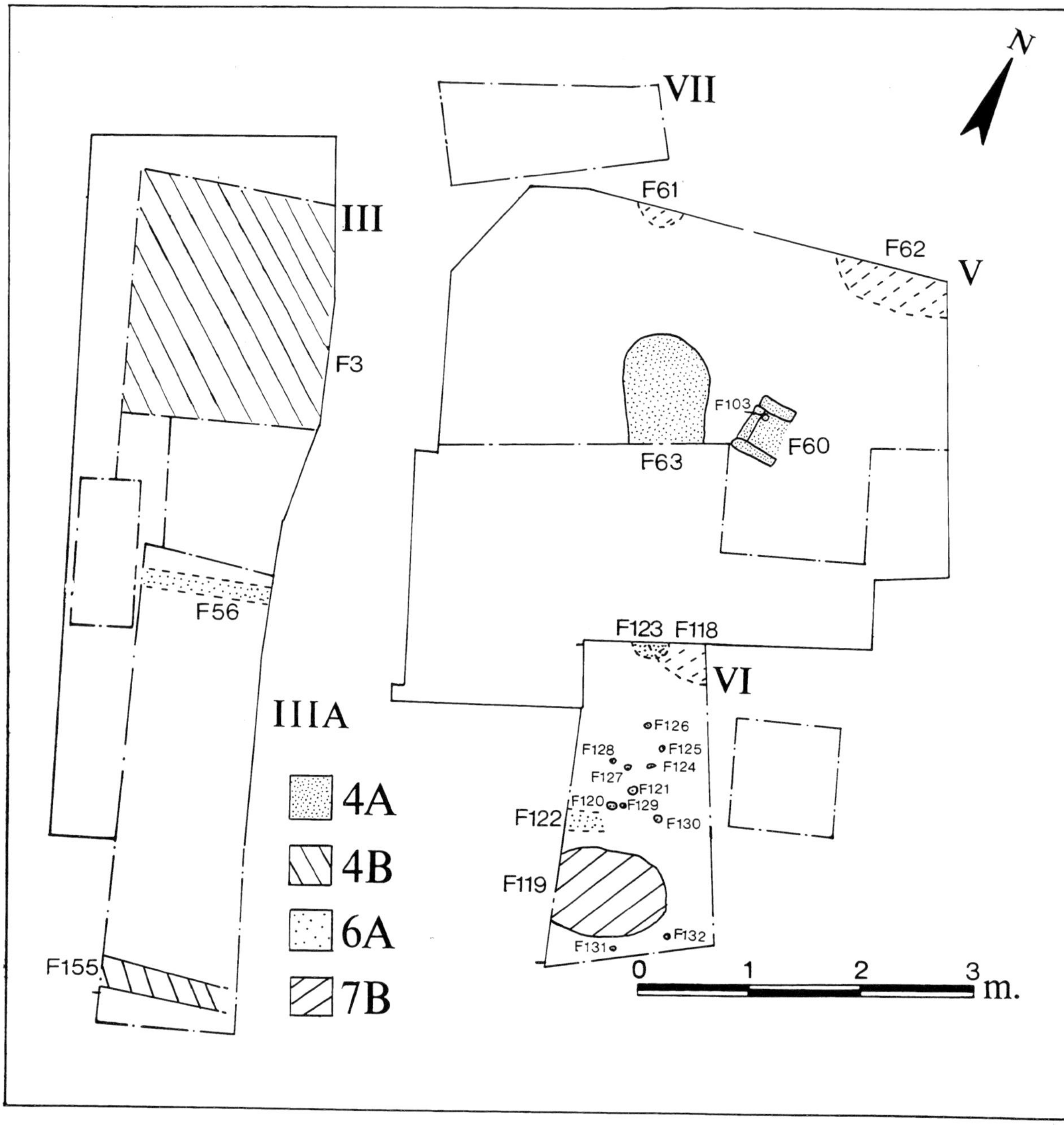

Fig. 10 Site 1, Phases 4, 6 and 7.

Phase 8B Mid 2nd century

Foundation trenches: F2 (III 91); F141 (VI 99); F142(VII 15,17,21)
Opus signinum floors: F1 (III 1,2,137, IIIB 1,2); F99 (V 2,4); F159 (IIIA 8,9)

The foundation trenches of three robbed stone walls were located in Areas III, VII and the eastern extension of VI (see Fig. 11). These consisted of a north-south aligned trench F2, (0.80m wide) abutting an east-west aligned trench, F142, (*c.* 0.75m wide x 0.75m deep). Foundation material in F142 consisted of packed sand and gravel with granite blocks 0.25-0.30m thick. 3.25m south of F142 another east-west aligned trench F141 (0.75m wide with a minimum depth (unbottomed) of 1.25m) was located in an extension east of Area VI. No trace of this feature was found in Area VI 0.25m to the west.

Opus signinum floors on a clay bedding were located in Areas III, F1, IIIA, F159 and V, F99 (all *c.* 0.10m thick).

Phase 8C Mid 2nd-4th century

Tessellated pavements: F98 (V 1); F157 (III 135-6); F158 (IIIA 107-8)

Overlying the *opus signinum* floors were three mosaic tessellated pavements (see below p. 48). They were secured to the *opus signinum* with lime mortar.

Phase 9 (Fig. 11) Medieval and Modern

Phase 9A *c.* 850-1100

Robber trenches: F2 (IIIA 1, V 22-3); F141 (VI38); F142 (VII 1)

Fills of loose fine sandy loams with much granite and sandstone rubble were found in the robber trenches F2, F141 and F142. Large concentrations of granite were found in F141 (VI 38). Finds from these deposits included medieval and Roman pottery and two bone pins.

Phase 9B *c.* 850-1100

Pits: F57 (V 108,219); F58 (V 6,107,220); F59 (V 7,221); F116 (VI 1,90); F117 (VI 2,91); F143 (VII 2,23)

Six pits were located in Areas V, VI and VII. At the north end of Area V a small shallow sloping pit, F58, (*c.* 1.30m in diameter x 0.30m deep) had a brown sandy loam fill. 0.30m to the east of this

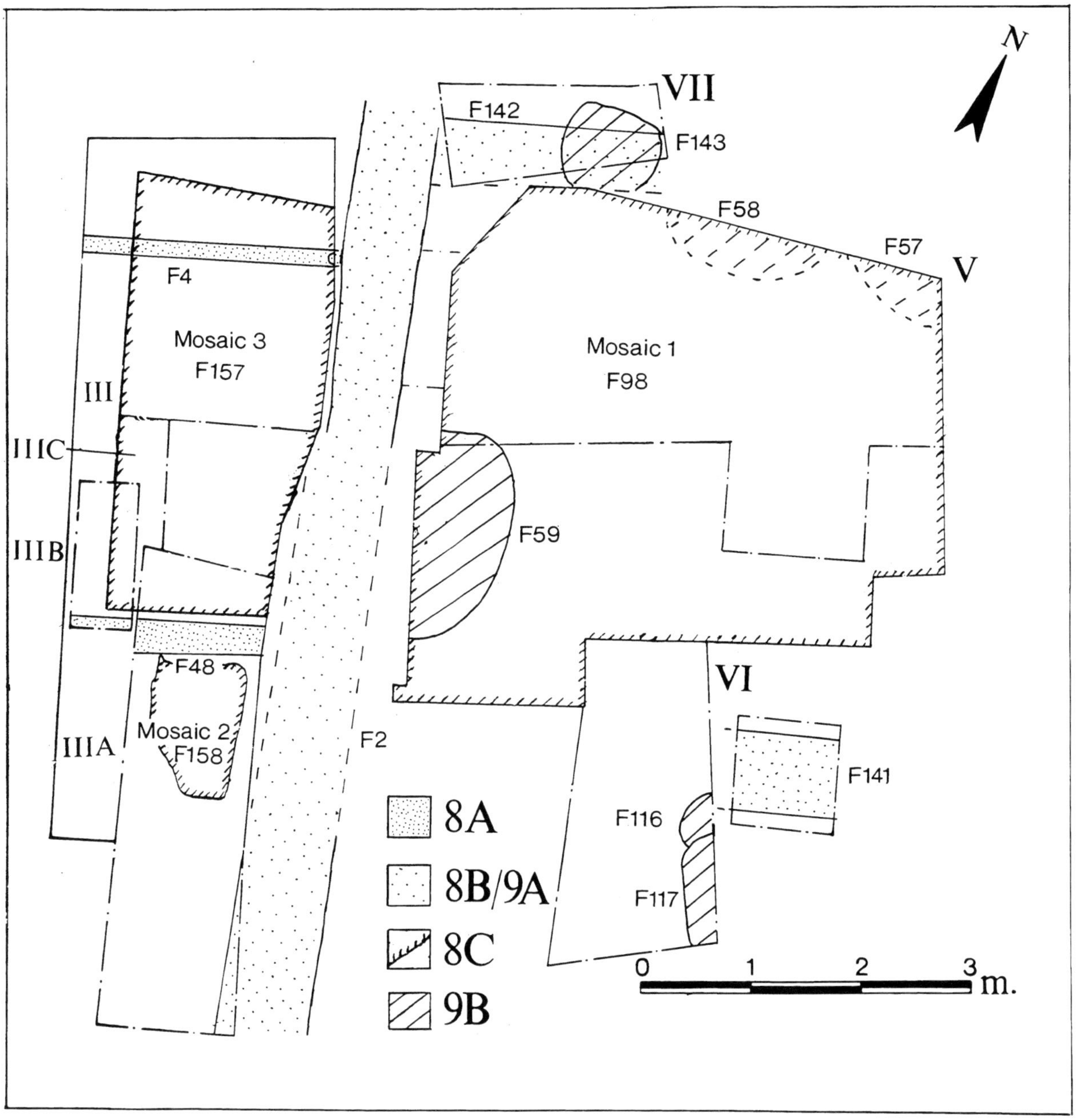

Fig. 11 Site 1, Phases 8 and 9.

feature another pit, F57, (minimum diameter 1.50m x 0.50m deep) contained a similar fill as did F59 (*c.* 2.0m x *c.* 1.0m) located to the west of Area V. A small pit F117 (estimated diameter 0.50m) was located in the SE corner of Area VI containing a brown sandy loam with a high charcoal concentration. Cutting this feature to the south part of an apparently rectangular pit F116 (minimum length 1.00m x minimum width 0.30m) with a similar fill was located. (Although F116 cuts F117, these two features are phased together.) F143 (*c.* 1.25m diameter) was located cutting F142 in Area VII. This contained a brown sandy loam fill with much sandstone and granite rubble. Material from this phase included 4th century Roman pottery, tile and medieval pottery.

Phase 9C 19th century

Make-up/rubble: IIIA 2; IIIC 1; V 3,95; VI 39;VII 19,20

Activity during the nineteenth century was evident from rubble and make-up deposits in Areas III, V, VI and VII. Residual medieval and Roman material was present including a 3rd century Roman coin (p. 134, 1).

Discussion of Phases 7, 8 and 9

Phase 7A consisted of similar spread deposits to those laid down in Phase 5 and again may be evidence of levelling and make-up prior to the insertion of the few Phase 7B features. Any further extent of this activity was impossible to deduce within the area examined.

More substantial make-up deposits were evident in Phase 7C probably in preparation for the construction of the Phase 8 building. Material from Phase 7 consisted of much redeposited pottery derived from Phases 3-6 indicative of levelling activities. A *terminus post quem* of AD 140 may be suggested for this phase.

The beam slots (F4, F48) in Phase 8A may be evidence of a timber structure immediately preceding the stone building (Phase 8B), or may possibly be foundations for partition walls within the main structure in view of the positions of mosaics F157 and F158. Only a small area of the stone building was examined. Deep (0.75m) foundation trenches for stone walls were encountered surrounding a room *c.*

7.5m square. This had first contained an opus signinum floor prior to the addition of a fine mosaic pavement, F98 (see below p. 48). A similar sequence occurred under the Blackfriars pavement (Clay and Mellor, 1985, 23). The mosaic pavement, F98, can be dated stylistically and from the samian tesserae used (see below p. 48) to *c.* 150. Two pavements (F157 and F158) were located in Areas III and IIIA which on stylistic grounds were probably added later, possibly in the 4th century (see p. 50).

Within such a small area examined the extent of this building is difficult to evaluate. However other mosaic pavements are recorded (Haverfield, 1918, 11a and 13c; Clarke, 1952, 41) immediately to the north and west of the site which suggests that it could have been an extensive building. The high quality mosaic flooring and the location of the building suggests that it was a town house for an important official or perhaps a *mansio*. The secondary mosaics (F157 and F158) suggest that the building had a long life with rebuilding perhaps late in the 4th century. This is supported by material found during the discovery of the pavements in 1898 (Tucker, 1899) which included 3rd-4th century pottery and coins. 4th century pottery was found in the Phase 9B medieval pits. Medieval pottery dated to *c.* 850-1100 provides a *terminus post quem* for the robbing of the walls of the building. Various pits (Phase 9B), some cutting the wall robbing, were inserted about the same time. No other evidence of medieval occupation is evident from the site although much medieval activity was recorded during excavations at St Nicholas Circle 100m to the east (Mellor and Pearce, forthcoming). A well was also noted when the pavement was first located. The next evidence of building is in the nineteenth century with various rubble deposits probably associated with the activity which revealed the Peacock pavement in 1898.

Site 2 Excavations in the south-west corner of St Nicholas Circle 1969 SK 5824 0434

Redevelopment at the western end of St Nicholas Circle for the construction of the 'Holiday Inn' in 1969 provided the opportunity for excavation in two areas. The northernmost area (SK 5822 0438) revealed evidence of a possible Romano-British temple (Mellor, forthcoming (b); Leicester Museums, 1969-70, 75; Wacher, 1975, 354, Fig. 79; Acc. No. A164.1969). Fifty metres south of this excavation three areas (I-III) were opened with the aim of locating the intersection of two roads within the Roman town, the alignments of which were indicated from earlier records (Goddard, 1870, 203; Clarke, 1952, 36; Leicester Museums 1959, 80). An area of *c.* 105 sq m was examined, the excavations being undertaken between May and August 1969, directed by Jean E Mellor for Leicester City Museums (Acc. No. A163.1969). Five phases of activity within the Roman period could be identified with a further phase of medieval pits cutting through the earlier levels. As a result of this latter activity much of the Roman evidence was disturbed and many relationships impossible to deduce. However evidence of 1st century-2nd century occupation and development could be examined.

Phase 1 (Fig. 12) Early-Mid 1st century

Various features cutting the substrata can be grouped in Phase 1 but their exact sequence is unclear. Phase 1A consists of features definitely cut by others in the Phase 1 group. Phase 1B includes the unrelated features and those cutting others while Phase 1C consists of the post and stake hole features which in some cases cut those grouped in both Phases 1A and 1B.

Phase 1A

Pits:	F20 (I 64-8, 86-7); F21 (I 69,130); F27 (I 94,136); F73 (III 48-50,92)
Gully/beam slot:	F28 (I 96,137)

The earliest features on the site consisted of a group of pits (F20, F21, F27) and a possible gully or slot (F28) in Area I with another pit (F73) in the south-east corner of Area III. The three pits in Area I are cut by Phase 1B features and their original dimensions are unclear. F21 (0.90m x 0.75m x 0.25m) contained a dark grey brown clay loam with charcoal and red clay. One metre north of this, F27 (*c.* 0.60m x 0.5m x 0.30m) contained a similar fill which included finds of early-mid 1st century pottery and animal bone. F20 immediately east of F27 (*c.* 1.0m x 0.50m x 0.30m deep) showed a succession of grey brown silty loam fills with lenses of charcoal. Tip lines were discernible to the west side and again contained mid 1st century pottery and animal bone. F73 in Area III (minimum width 1.0m x 0.30m deep) included fills of dark brown clay loam with iron pan and charcoal concentrations. In the north western corner of Area I a possible gully or beam slot (F28), cut by a later feature (F120) contained fills of charcoal, ash and dark brown clay loam with mid 1st century pottery, iron and animal bone present.

Phase 1B

Pits:	F15 (F10)(I 29,45,54,57-8,89-93, 107-8,110-2, 122); F17 (I 49-51, 53, 113, 127); F26 (I 78-9,82,135); F70 (III 32, 34-6, 89); F57 (II 103-6,154); F58 (II 108,155); F62 (II 129-30,159)
Channels:	F12 (I 39,43,48,60,83-5); F13 (I 41-2,95); F53 (I 189-90, 93-5,150); F54 (II 92,151); F72 (III 43-7,91)
Gully/pit:	F18 (I 59,128)
Hearth:	F87 (III 39,41)
Post hole:	F16 (I 46-7,126); F56 (II 104, 153)
Beam slots(?):	F52 (II 85,143); F91 (II 163-4)

Various pits, post holes, beam slots and channels can be grouped in this sub-phase. Four pits were located in Area I. The largest of these, F15 (2.5m x 2.0m x 0.75m), contained various fills of light brown fine sandy loam, ash, charcoal, yellow, red and grey clay, some possibly burnt, and brown silty loam. Finds included mid 1st century pottery, animal bone, slag, fired clay, and objects of bone, iron and glass. To the south east of F15 another pit F17 (1.2m x 0.4m) was recorded in the south section. This contained a dark grey green clay loam fill with finds of early-mid 1st century pottery, animal bone, copper alloy and fired clay. A post hole F16 (0.8m x 0.45m deep) immediately to the east of F15 consisted of an orange brown sandy loam filled post pit with brown silty loam and charcoal denoting the position of the post pipe. Early-mid 1st century pottery was present in this feature.

To the west of F15 a small irregular pit or gully feature, F18 (1.0m x 0.30m x 0.20m) was located, containing a fine light brown clay loam with some early-mid 1st century pottery present. Two channels were present in Area I. F12, aligned east-west (0.50m wide x 0.25m deep) cutting F28 in the north-west corner of the area, contained dark brown clay loam and sandy silt deposits with much charcoal again with mid 1st century pottery present. F13

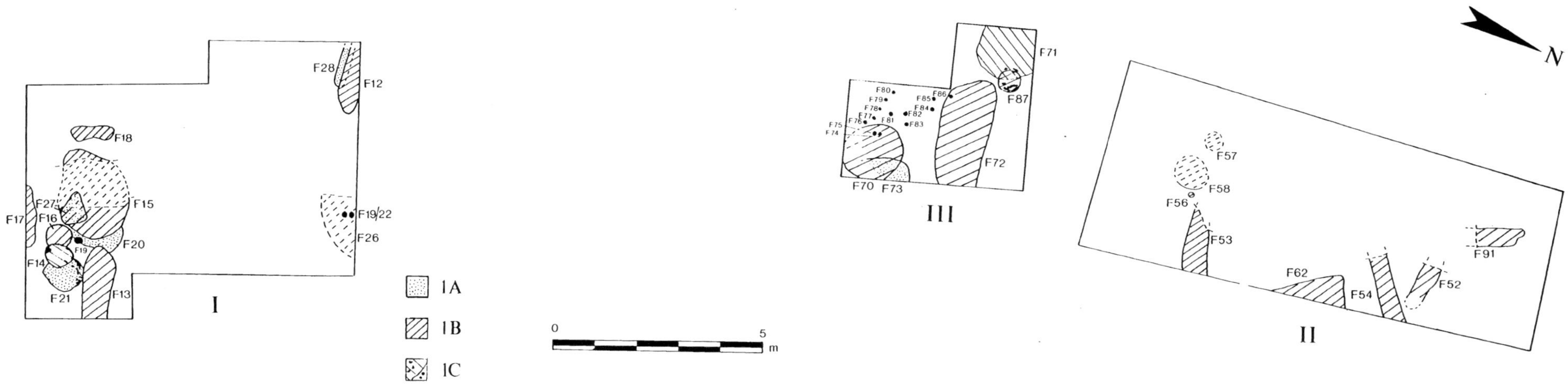

Fig 12 Site 2 Phase 1

Fig 13 Site 2 Phase 3

(0.60m wide x 0.25m deep) in the south east corner of the area cutting F20 and F21 contained similar material and finds to F12. Traces of another, bell-shaped, pit F26, (minimum width 1.80m x 0.80m deep) were present in the north end of Area I with fills of charcoal, ash, red clay and light brown fine sandy loam. Early-mid 1st century pottery was again present.

A pit F70 (1.5m diameter x 0.50m deep) with grey sandy silt and grey sand fills was located in Area III. One metre to the north a large channel feature F72 (minimum length 2.60m x 1.2m wide x 0.30m deep) contained dark brown fine silty clay with much charcoal over-lying dark grey green clayey silt. Immediately north-west of this feature was a small circular hearth F87 (0.60m diameter x 0.10m deep) containing charcoal and light brown fine sandy loam with a burnt clay lining. All of these features contained some early-mid 1st century pottery, with copper alloy fragments present in F70 and F72.

Three pits of varying size were located in Area II. In the eastern section part of a large square sided feature was encountered, F62 (minimum width 1.80m x 0.50m deep) containing a dark brown fine clay loam fill. Two smaller circular pits were situated 3m south-west of this. F57 (0.40m diameter x 0.30m deep) and F58 (0.90m diameter x 0.30m deep) contained fills of brown orange fine sandy loam and brown grey coarse sandy silt with pebbles, respectively.

A small post hole, F56 (0.15m x 0.20m deep) with a yellow clay fill was situated immediately east of F58. Two possible beam slots were also located in Area III, F52, and F91 (both *c.* 0.50m wide x 0.20m deep) containing light brown fine clay loam fills with a few sherds of early-mid 1st century pottery present in F52. Their alignments of north east - south west, and north west - south east respectively, may suggest that they formed part of the same building. Four metres south of these beam slots a channel, F53, (0.55m wide x 0.35m deep) on an east-west alignment contained brown orange fine silty loams, charcoal, grey orange clay loam and coarse orange silt with large quantities (45 sherds weighing 990g) of early-mid 1st century pottery. A second channel, F54, (0.60m x 0.50m) containing a dark brown fine clay loam was located, also on an east-west alignment 3.2m north of F53, cut in part by F92 (Phase 3) and F46 (Phase 5).

Phase 1C

Pit:	F71 (III 25,37-8,40,53-6,90)
Post holes:	F14 (I 44,124); F55 (II 103,152)
Stake holes:	F19 (I 62,129); F22 (I 74,131); F32 (I 103,141); F74-86 (III 57-82)

Two post holes, sixteen stake holes and a pit in Areas I, II and III can be assigned to this phase. F14 in Area I consisted of a large post hole (0.65m diameter x 0.50m deep) with a brown fine sandy loam and green marl fill which included finds of early-mid 1st century pottery, animal bone and a Hod Hill type brooch (p. 143 Fig. 74.15). Traces of a post hole much disturbed but apparently similar to F14 were found in Area II (F55). Three stake holes in Area I (F19, F22, F32) and thirteen in Area III (F74-F86) containing light brown fine sandy loams were located (all *c.* 0.15m diameter, with depths varying between 0.10m and 0.25m). A pit, F71, (*c.* 1.50m diameter x 0.45m deep) was revealed in Area III containing grey clay with iron pan staining, fine light brown silty clay, and rubble and fine light brown sandy loam fills. 1st century pottery including Flavian Samian and two 1st century brooches (p. 139 Fig 73. 4 and 10) were present in this feature.

Phase 2 Mid-late 1st century

Make-up:	I 34-6,40,52-3,56,61,63,70-3,75-6; II 71,84,86-7,111-2; III 24,26-30,33, 51-2

Various deposits of fine light brown sandy loam, clay and charcoal (I 36, II 71) were located overlying the Phase 1 features. These varied between 50mm and 0.20m in thickness, the largest build up being present in Area I where a sequence 0.40m thick was identifiable. Material from these deposits included mid-1st century pottery, an intrusive medieval sherd, animal bone, three copper alloy brooches, flint, tile, burnt daub and slag.

Phase 3 (Fig. 13) Late 1st-Early 2nd century

Pits:	F11 (I 30-1,37-8,123); F92(II 97-102,107)
Pits/post holes:	F67 (III 22,87); F68 (III 23,88)
Stake holes:	F29-30 (I 100-1,138-9); F33 (I 104, 142); F34 (I 106,143); F59-61 (II 122-4,156-8)
Channels:	F50 (II 81,147); F51 (II 78,88,148)
Gully:	F7 (I 10,119);
Robber Trench:	F49 (II 79,80,82,146)
Beam slots:	F23 (I 77,132); F24 (I 80,183)

Various features cutting the Phase 2 deposits were encountered in all three areas. Traces of two disturbed beam slots F23 and F24 were located in the northern section of Area I. They were on a north-south alignment and contained burnt clay with charcoal and red clay with orange brown sandy loam respectively. Two sherds of 1st-2nd century pottery were found in F24. Four stake holes F29-30, F33-34 (0.10m diameter x *c.* 0.10m deep) were present 5m south of the beam slots, again having orange brown sandy loam fills. To the west of these a gully F7 (minimum length 3.50m x 0.50m wide x 0.25m deep) was located containing a fine brown clay loam fill, with a sherd of a samian Drag 29 and animal bone present. One metre east of this feature, an oval pit had been inserted, F11 (1.75m x 0.70m x 0.20m deep), filled with dark brown fine clay loam with charcoal and ash and containing early-mid 1st century pottery, animal bone, a flint blade and an early 1st century copper alloy brooch (see p. 139. Fig 73.2).

Two pits or large post holes were located in Area III, F67 (0.90m diameter x 0.75m deep) and F68 (0.75m x 0.65m x 0.40m deep) containing dark brown fine clay loam, with many granite blocks in F67 perhaps serving as post packing. late 1st to early 2nd century pottery was present in both features. Three stake holes, F59-61, (*c.* 0.20m diameter x 0.10-0.20m deep) were located in the north end of Area II with fills of fine dark brown clay loam. A robbed foundation trench, F49 running parallel to two channels (F50, F51) on an east-west alignment was also present in the south of Area II. F49 (minimum length 1.70m x 0.50m x 0.15m deep) to the south had fills of grey-green sandy loam, grey brown coarse silt, charcoal and hard iron pan concentrations. F51 (minimum length 1.60m x 0.20m x 0.10m) to the north of F49 contained orange/yellow clay while F50 (minimum length 2.0m x 0.25m x 0.10m) was filled with an orange brown fine sandy loam. A rusticated grey ware jar waster or 'second', some two-thirds complete, was recovered from F49 (Fig. 54.65). Late 1st-early 2nd century pottery was present in all these features. A large pit F92 (*c.* 2.0m wide x 0.3m deep) was located in the east section of Area II having been disturbed by Phase 5 (F46) activity. Fills of brown silty loam with iron pan and charcoal concentrations, fine grey clay loam and orange, brown and grey silts were recorded while finds of early-mid 1st century pottery were present including sherds of the rare Cam.139 flagon (see below p. 64). It can be inferred that F92 was filled like F11, with material disinterred from phases 1 and 2 horizons. Copper alloy and stone objects, animal bone and a fragment of disturbed human bone were also found in this feature.

Discussion of Phases 1-3

Phases 1-3 at St Nicholas Circle show similar evidence of 1st century occupation to that encountered in other areas of Leicester (e.g. Kenyon, 1948; Hebditch and Mellor, 1973). Similar features and date ranges to Phases 1-3 at the Peacock pavement site can be suggested (see above p. 2). Most features consisted of rubbish pits, channels and gullies with some occasional structural evidence in the form of post holes, stake holes, beam slots and a wall trench. No plan of the structures can be suggested within the areas examined. The bell-shaped pit, F26 (Fig. 12) in Phase 1B may have previously served as a storage pit having a similar shape to Iron Age pits of this function (Cunliffe, 1978, 179). The gullies and channels suggest drainage and run-off facilities, the silt content in some of the features e.g. F72 indicating that they were holding water at some time. The Phase 3 channels in Area II, F50-1, show a sequence of renewal of drainage facilities continuing the gully position and alignment started by F53 in Phase 1B. The beam slots are only present in the form of fragmentary evidence. F52, F54 and F91 in Area II indicate a variety of alignment over a relatively short time. Depending on the buildings' functions, minimal Romanisation is perhaps suggested by this. These beam slot structures are usually a post-conquest phenomenon in British towns although pre-conquest examples are known (cf. Rodwell, 1979, 329). F49 appears to have been a foundation trench for a stone building which was robbed or not completed before the Phase 4 street metalling was inserted. The presence of slag and furnace lining suggests some industrial activity in the vicinity. Also of note is the pottery waster in F49 perhaps suggesting nearby pottery manufacture (cf. Mellor, 1975-6, 59).

Phase 4 (Fig. 14) 1st half of 2nd century onwards

Phase 4 consists of activity associated with the laying of metalled streets within the area examined. Re-metalling and the accumulation of road silts were evident but owing to later disturbances a clear sequence of re-metalling over the three areas examined was impossible to establish. Re-metalling therefore is grouped into two sub-phases whereas many different phases of road re-building may have taken place which at present cannot be extrapolated.

Phase 4A

Street metalling:	F1 (I 14-5,18,23, III 19-21)
Cobbled surface:	II 110
Ditch:	F8 (I 120)

A series of gravel spreads was located in Areas I, II and III overlying the Phase 3 features. The lower layers consisted of loosely packed orange pebbles, sand and gravel (I 18, III 20) *c.* 0.10m thick and included bone, pottery and tile fragments. Overlying these were solid packed pebble spreads (*c.* 0.15m thick) with compact even surfaces discernible (I 14, III 19, II 110).

Immediately east of these gravel spreads in Area I a ditch F8 (0.80m wide x 0.70m deep) on a north west-south east alignment had been inserted. This was not located in Areas II and III.

Phase 4B

Road silts:	F1 (I 11,13,17,20,22)
Ditch:	F8 (I 9,25-7)
Make-up:	II 55-7,59,61-2,65-7,69,73; 77, 83,109,118-9; III 17-8

Overlying the Phase 4A gravel spreads in Areas I, II and III were various deposits of sticky dark grey-brown silty clay, (up to 0.20m in thickness in Area II) sometimes mixed with red clay, loose gravel, pebbles, ash and charcoal. Finds included wall plaster, tile, iron, nails, glass, a coin, copper alloy, pottery (including one intrusive medieval sherd), animal bone, slag and oyster shells.

Infilling of the ditch F8 (Fig. 17) can be associated with this phase although part of this process may be contemporary with Phases 4C and 4D. Charcoal, grey-brown silty clay with iron pan and light brown fine sandy loam made up the fills of this feature which contained finds of tile, pottery, copper alloy, iron, glass and animal bone.

Phase 4C

Street metalling:	F1 (I 12,16,21,32; III 13-15)

Further orange gravel, pebble and yellow sand deposits were encountered in Areas I and III in part overlying the Phase 4A and 4B gravel spreads. Sometimes set in red clay (I 16) these varied between 10mm and 80mm in thickness and contained a 1st century coin, tile, pottery and animal bone fragments.

Phase 4D

Street metalling:	F1 (I 19,22; III 9,12)
Robber trench:	F3 (I 115)

Overlying the Phase 4C gravel deposits were other similar layers of orange-yellow gravels with yellow sand mixed with some dark brown silty clay material. Similar finds to those in the Phase 4A-C spreads were encountered.

Although not definitely of this phase or period the stone building evidenced by wall robbing, F3 (0.70m wide x 1.40m deep), in Area I is probably contemporary with the Phase 4 activity. The alignment of this wall was parallel with and adjacent to the ditch, F8 and gravel surfaces in Area I although no other structural evidence survived.

Phase 5 (Fig. 14) 4th century

Pit/quarry:	F46 (II 21-5,27-54,96,114-7, 120-1, 125-8,143)
Make-up:	II 17-20; III 5,8,10

Various spread deposits were located overlying the Phase 4 layers in Areas II and III. These consisted of brown-yellow fine sandy loam with grits at the north end of Area II, a thin deposit of yellow-green silty loam, dark grey green silty loam, clay and charcoal deposits (II 17-20). Yellow green silty loam with green clay, charcoal, red clay and limestone rubble was located in Area III (5, 8, 10). Finds of 2nd-4th century pottery (and one intrusive 11th-12th century sherd), tile, copper alloy, lead, stone tesserae and animal bone were found in these deposits.

A large pit or quarry F46 (Fig. 16) was located in the eastern section of Area II (*c.* 6.0m wide x 1.35m deep) cutting Phases 1-4 deposits. This contained a variety of different materials including grey green silty loam, charcoal, ash, orange sand and gravel, dark brown clay loam, with red, yellow and green clays. Finds from this feature included late 1st-early 2nd century pottery, tile, wall plaster, glass, copper alloy, iron, lead, slag, vitrified clay, animal bone and two 1st century coins.

Discussion of Phases 4 and 5

Observation of gravel spreads in Leicester has previously led to various identifications of Roman streets where the evidence has been very tenuous. The gravel spreads encountered at St Nicholas Circle were much disturbed by later activity and the relationship between them in the three areas is unclear. Two distinctive types of gravel make-up are evident from the site. Areas I and III do show evidence of substantial gravel and pebble construction with discernible surfaces, re-metalling and in Area I a roadside ditch (F8). Area II however has a thin gravel spread (110) with a large accumulation of silty clay material above it. While the level of the Area II gravel is comparable with the lowest levels of street metalling in the other areas there is no evidence of subsequent re-metalling. This may have

Figs 14 Site 2 Phases 4 and 5

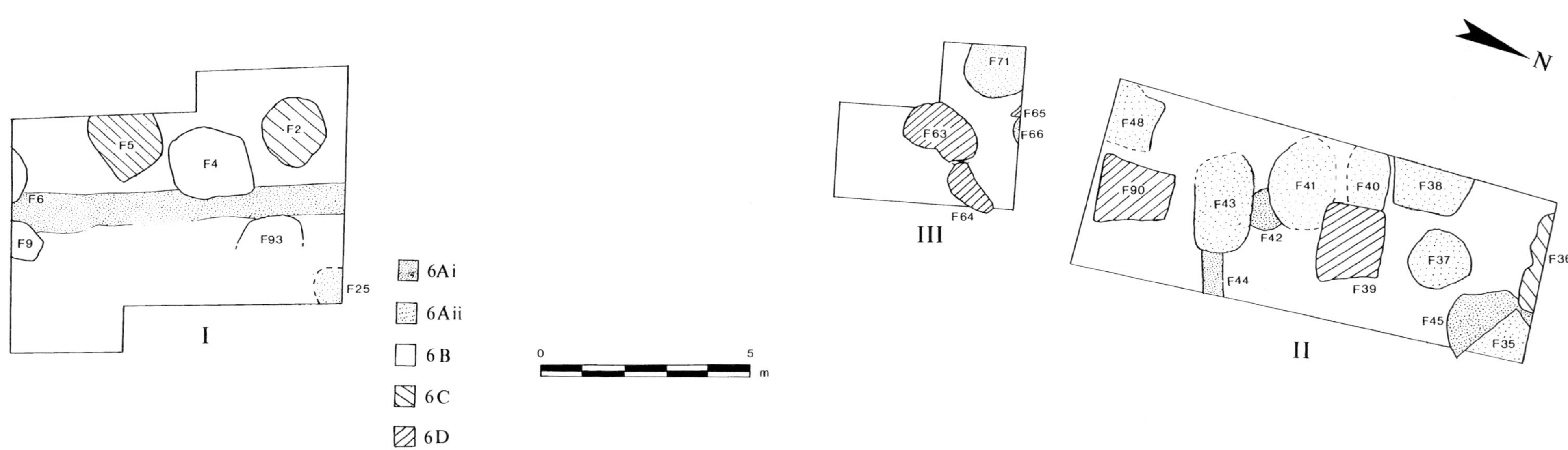

Figs 15 Site 2 Phase 6

been disturbed but it is perhaps more advisable to treat it as having a separate function rather than being a road. If it was part of the same road encountered in Area III it would be either on an irregular alignment to the known street grid or be *c.* 10m wide. A separate feature, perhaps a yard, which went out of use during the lifetime of the adjacent streets is perhaps a more feasible interpretation.

The metalling in Area I would appear to be part of one of the north-south aligned streets within the Roman street grid which may have previously been identified at Bath Lane (Clay and Mellor, 1985) and Ruding Street (Leicester Museums, 1960, 49).

The metalling in Area III aligns with the street on an east-west alignment previously identified running immediately south of the forum (cf. Hebditch and Mellor, 1973, Fig. 2). Re-metalling is evident on both areas. How many times this had taken place is difficult to estimate but three re-metallings may be evident in Area I (2, 12, 16). Five re-metallings were recorded at the Jewry Wall site, Leicester (Kenyon, 1948, 7) while recent evidence from London indicates re-metalling as many as twenty-five times in some areas. Even allowing for slippage the later re-metallings in Area I do appear to have outlived the use of the roadside ditch (see Fig. 17).

Material from the road metalling suggests a *terminus post quem* of *c.* 120-130 which is comparable with evidence from other sites where street metalling has been encountered (Hebditch and Mellor, 1973, 24). No finer refinement of dating for the various re-metallings is possible although a more general 2nd century date may be associated with the Phase 4D re-metalling. Material from the ditch (F8) also fits this date range.

The robber trench F3 may be indication of a stone building at the corner of the two streets although no further evidence of this structure survives.

In common with other areas of Leicester, evidence of later Roman activity is scarce. In Phase 5, mixed silty loam, clay, charcoal and rubble located in Areas II and III may be destruction deposits and some late Roman material is present. Late 3rd-4th century pottery is also present, residually in the Phase 6 medieval pits cutting the Roman layers.

The one feature which may be late or sub-Roman is the large pit or quarry F46 encountered in Area II. Although most of the material from this feature need be dated no later than *c.* 150, its location cutting the Phase 4 levels at the corner of a street intersection may perhaps suggest activity somewhat later, during the decline of the town's civic authority. Slag from this feature suggests iron smelting or forging activity with possible copper alloy smelting in the area although this may have been brought in during the Phase 4 road construction as hard core.

Phase 6 (Fig. 15)

Robbing of F3 (see above) and the insertion of a ditch, a hearth and twenty one pits during the medieval and post-medieval periods had disturbed much of the Roman levels. The medieval features can be separated into various sub-phases according to their morphology and material content. Phase 6A is sub-divided into i and ii based on the stratigraphy although these features are broadly contemporary.

Phase 6A i 11th-Early 13th century

Ditch:	F44 (II 13,141)
Robber trench:	F3 (I 4,24)
Pits:	F42 (II 11,139); F45 (II 26,142)

A 'v' shaped channel, F44, (0.65m wide x 0.55m deep) on a north east-south west alignment was located to the east of Area II cut to the west by F43. Two pits were also located in Area II, F42 (*c.* 1m diam x 0.5m deep), cut by F41 and F43, and F45 (*c.* 2.25m diam x 0.75m deep), to the north east cut by F35. These features contained dark brown clay loams with 11th-13th century pottery and animal bone. The robber trench F3 (see Phase 4D) had a fill of a light brown fine sandy loam with much rubble which included some 11th-13th century pottery.

Phase 6A ii 11th-Early 13th century

Pits:	F25 (I 81,134); F35 (II 2,132); F37 (II 4,134); F38 (II 5,9,10,135); F40(II 7,8,137-8); F43 (II 12,14,140); F48 (II 60,63-4,68, 72,145); F66 (III 11,86)

Seven pits were located in Area II and one (F25) in Area I varying between 1.50m and 2.00m in diameter and 0.30m and 0.55m in depth. These contained similar fills of dark brown clay loams with much ash and charcoal, F48 to the south of Area II also including red and yellow clay, pebble and dark grey silty loam. 11th-13th century pottery and animal bone were present in these features with copper alloy fragments in F40 and F48, the latter also including two Roman coins. A shallow pit F66 (*c.* 0.25m) could be identified in the north section of Area III containing a dark grey brown silty loam with much charcoal and with 11th-13th century pottery present.

Phase 6B Late 13th century

Pits:	F4 (I 5,116); F6 (I 8,118); F9 (I 28,121); F93 (I 144-5)

Four pits were located in Area I varying between 1.25m and 0.75m in diameter and 0.45m and 0.25m in depth. All contained dark grey brown clay loam with much charcoal and F4 included finds of 13th century pottery.

Phase 6C Late 15th-Early 16th century

Pits:	F2 (I 3,7,114); F5 (I 6,117); F36 (II 3,133)

Two circular pits F2 and F5 (1.80m diameter x 0.55m deep) were located in Area I which again contained a dark grey brown clay loam with much charcoal and gravel above a fine silty clay with iron pan staining. A silver penny of Edward III, (1356-61 see p. 138) and 14th-15th century pottery were recovered from F2 while a copper alloy stud was present in F5. Another pit F36 (1.25m wide x 0.50m deep) was located at the north end of Area II containing dark brown fine clay loam with finds of animal bone, 10th-16th century pottery, a 3rd century Roman coin and a copper alloy strap end.

Phase 6D 16th-17th century

Pits:	F39 (II 6,136); F63 (III 2,3,83); F64 (III 4,84); F90 (II 15,16,162)
Hearth:	F65 (III 6,7,85)

Two rectangular pits F39 (1.75m x 1.52m x 0.55m deep) and F90 (1.75m x 1.55m x 0.40m deep) were located in Area II containing dark brown grey fine loam fills with much charcoal and pebble and including medieval and post-medieval pottery with copper alloy and iron objects in F90 (see p. 150). Two further features were located in Area III; a pit F64 (1.30m x 0.60m x 0.35m deep) which although cutting F63, may be assigned to this phase and a possible hearth F65 in the north section cutting F66. F64 contained fills of dark grey clay loam with charcoal and brown silty

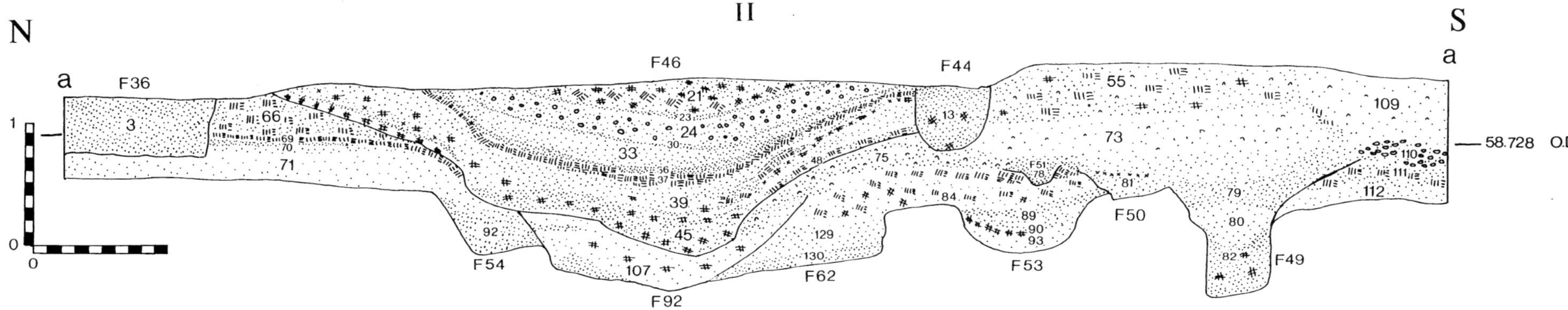

Fig. 16 Site 2 Section a-a Area II

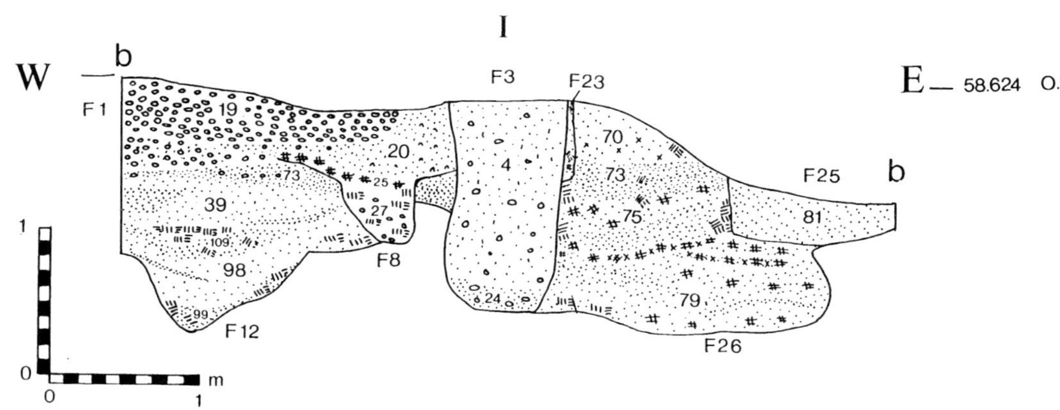

Figs 17 Site 2 Section b-b Arca !

loam with finds of medieval and post-medieval pottery. F65, only partially revealed,contained green clay, charcoal and showed evidence of burning.

Discussion of Phase 6

Medieval activity on the site consisted of wall robbing and pit digging which appears to have commenced no earlier than 1000. As is the case with many Leicester sites a *lacuna* appears in the archaeological record covering the late Roman and Saxon periods. The Phase 4D stone building was robbed and backfilled with material dated *c.* 1000-1250 which is comparable to other robbing phases in the city (see above p. 12 and e.g. Clay and Mellor, 1985 17). No structural evidence of medieval activity has survived and the pits encountered may indicate that the site is in the 'back yard' areas with buildings fronting onto the medieval streets to the north, south and west. A similar situation was encountered at the back of property boundaries which fronted onto the medieval Highcross Street (Mellor and Pearce, forthcoming). The Phase 6 pits contained material which suggests they were used for domestic refuse. Pottery from these features suggests that they were being inserted over a long period of time. The 1828 map of Leicester shows the area to have been residential with an inn, The Mitre and Keys built on the southern edge of the site. Further development in the late 19th century saw houses and shops constructed which remained until redevelopment in the late 1960s.

Site 3 Excavations at West Bridge 1967 SK5808 0433

The construction of a new traffic island in 1967 allowed an excavation to be undertaken with the aim of recovering some indication of how far the Roman town extended west. An area of *c.* 80 sq m was examined and divided into five areas with a smaller area (VI) *c.* 16 sq m, 10m to the north west being opened subsequently. This excavation was undertaken between July and September 1967 directed by Jean E Mellor for Leicester City Museums (Mellor 1968-9, 5, Acc. No. A568.1967 WB). Three main phases of Roman (Fig. 18) and two of medieval activity (Fig. 20) could be identified.

Phase 1 (Fig. 18) Early-Mid 1st century

Phase 1A

Ditch: F6 (I 26,48)
Gully: F27 (V 21,26)

Two features, a 'v' shaped ditch F6 (1.5m wide x 1.0m deep) on a north-south alignment and a gully F27 (*c.* 1.0m wide x 0.20m deep) on an east-west alignment are the earliest evidence of activity on the site. F6 was disturbed by modern foundations to the south and contained an orange-brown clay loam fill with charcoal flecking. F27, disturbed by Phase 3 activity, had a similar fill including 3 sherds of early-mid 1st century pottery.

Phase 1B

Make-up: I 23,27-8; II 13

At the north end of the site a series of thin (50mm-0.10m) orange, yellow and grey clay spreads was located overlying, in part, the fill of F6.

Phase 1C

Post holes: F43 (I 74-5); F44 (I 76-7)
Beam slot: F7 (I 30,49)

To the south of F6 a beam slot, F7 (0.25m wide x 0.15m deep) was located. Two post holes F43 and F44 (0.12m diameter x 50mm deep) were identified at the base of the slot. The slot was on a north-south alignment petering out to the north possibly having been disturbed by Phase 3 activity. The features contained a grey clay and charcoal fill with one sherd in each of early-mid 1st century pottery present.

Phase 2 (Figs. 18-19) Late 1st-Mid 2nd century

Phase 2A Late 1st century

Ditch: F3 (I 14,16,18,39,45; II 9-11; III 11-2; IV 14-16; VI 9,10,12)
Channel: F5 (I 21,47)

A ditch F3 (*c.* 2.50m wide x 1.60m deep)(Fig.19) was revealed running through the site on a north west - south east alignment. It had a steeply sloping south western face (60°) with a square cut channel at its base (0.25m wide x 0.30m deep), and a more gently sloping (35°) north eastern face. A 16m length was revealed in Areas I-IV while Area VI 10m to the north west confirmed its continued alignment. The initial filling of this feature consisted of a series of dark brown fine silts (0.35m thick) overlying in part blue-grey clay (0.30m thick) and contained some wooden stake fragments, a leather shoe with hobnails (see below p. 150 Fig. 78.78) and some late 1st-early 2nd century pottery.

Three metres to the east and on the same alignment as F3 a small channel F5 (0.45m x 0.20m deep) was located cutting the fill of F6. This again petered out to the north and contained a fine light brown clay loam fill.

Phase 2B Early-Mid 2nd century

Ditch backfilling: F3 (I 15,17,38; II15,17,22; III 9,10,20; IV 12-3,17 VI 8,11)

Subsequent filling of F3 owing to its different nature is separated into another sub-phase. Grey silty clay with pebble and iron pan staining, yellow, red and grey clay, red-orange sandy silt and grey clayey loam deposits were located overlying the Phase 2A silts in F3 and filling the upper parts of the ditch. Finds of late 1st-mid 2nd century pottery, lead and one fragment of human bone were recovered from these deposits.

Phase 3 (Fig. 18) 2nd-4th century

Phase 3A Mid-Late 2nd century

Road metalling: F1 (I 33, III 18; IV 2; V16; VI 5
Robber trench: F23 (V 22)
Channel: F25 (V 24)
Make-up: I 20,29,31-2,34-6; III 19;V 12,17-9

A robber trench F23 *c.* 1.0m wide was revealed on a north west-south east alignment in Area V.

Spreads of orange, green and grey clay with charcoal, closely packed pebbles, red gravel and green-grey silty clay deposits were located overlying some of the Phase 2B levels and underlying in part hard packed and closely grouped cobbles (F1). Mid-late 2nd century pottery, copper alloy, tile, plaster and slag were present in these spreads. A small channel F25 (0.30m wide x 0.20m deep) adjacent and parallel to F23 was also located.

Phase 3B Late 2nd-3rd century

Road metalling: F1 (I 4, I 11, III 6)

Further cobbling and gravel deposits were present overlying the Phase 3A spreads in Areas I and III with mid 2nd-3rd century pottery, copper alloy and slag present.

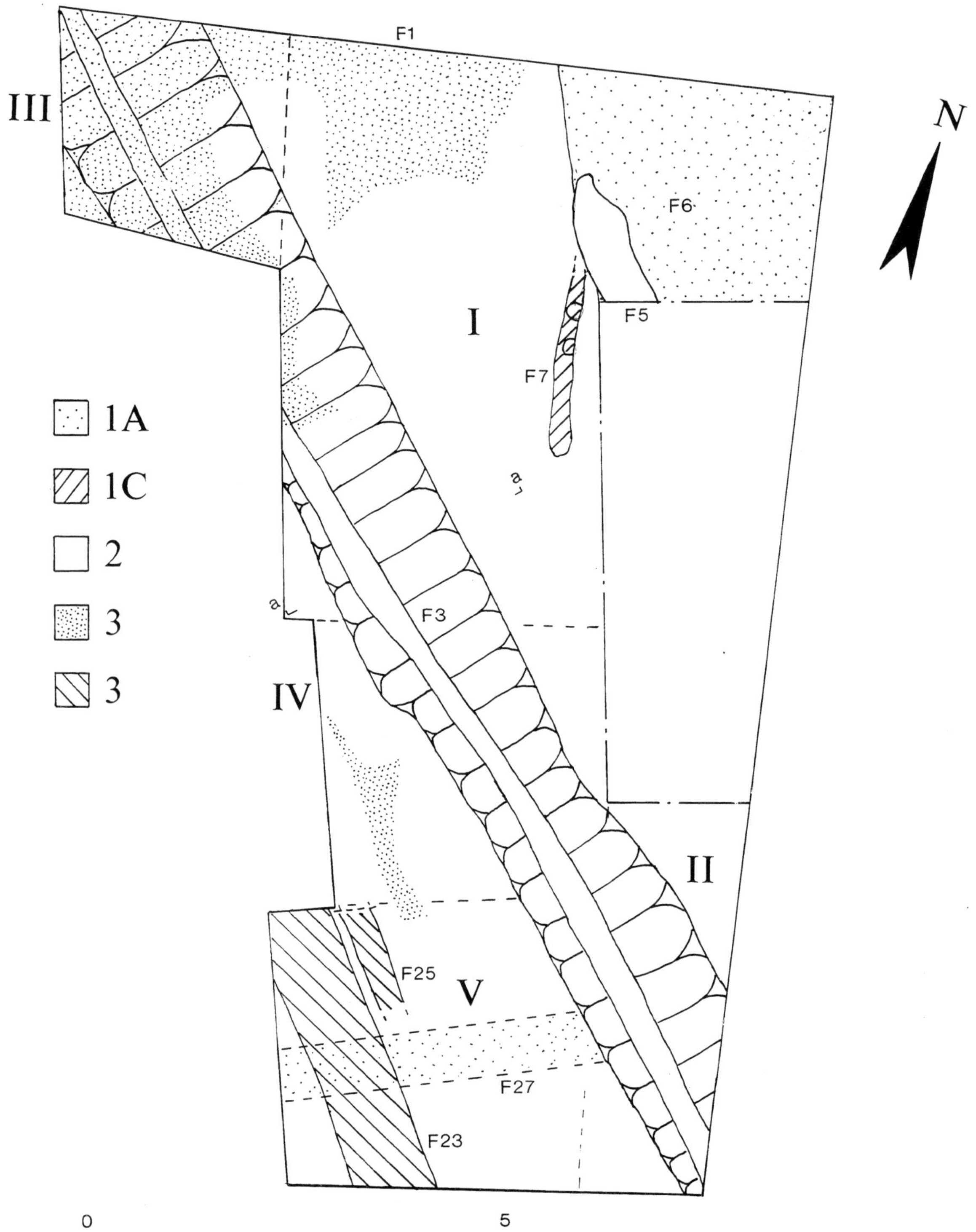

Fig. 18 Site 3, Phases 1-3

Phase 3C

Channel fill: F25 (V 7)
Road silts: F1 (III 8)
Make-up: I 12, II 4,5,12; IV 5; V 10-1,14-5

The fill of the channel, F25, consisted of a very dark grey clay silt with much charcoal and included 2nd-3rd or 4th century pottery and tile. Grey-brown clay with charcoal, yellow clay, silty clay and yellow sandy clay deposits overlying the cobbled areas (F1) were revealed containing 2nd-3rd century pottery, slag and tile. Further spreads of yellow silty clay and orange gravel were present overlying the Phase 2 levels and including 1st-3rd century pottery.

Phase 3D

Robber trench fill: F23 (V 4,9)

Yellow clay, fine light brown sandy loam, mortar, gravel, slate and limestone rubble made up the fill from the robber trench (F23).

The only material from this feature was three sherds of later 1st century pottery.

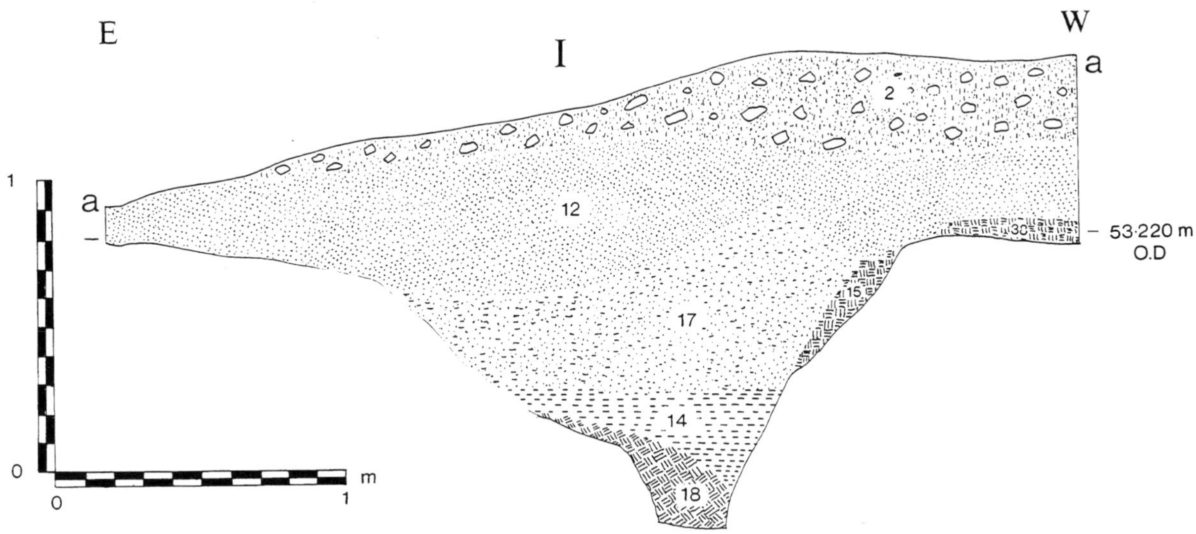

Fig 19 Site 3, Section a-a Ditch F3

Discussion of Phases 1-3

Phase 1 at this site shows some evidence of early-mid 1st century activity. Two channels in Phase 1A (F6, F27) may be evidence of pre-conquest activity, three sherds of early-mid 1st century pottery being present in F27. The overlying Phase 1B deposits possibly indicate levelling and clearance for the Phase 1C building, the only evidence for which is the beam slot (F7). The very little evidence from the fill of this feature (8 sherds) suggests an early-mid 1st century date including a sherd of post-conquest grey ware, this type of building method usually being associated with post-conquest activity (but see above p. 15). It is suggested that on the basis of alignment and position this feature is unlikely to be associated with and probably pre-dates the Phase 2 ditch.

The steeply sloping western side and the square cut cleaning channel in the Phase 2 ditch (F3) are characteristics of the *Fossa punica* or Punic ditch (Johnson, 1983, 47). Material from the primary silting of this feature, including several large pottery sherds with comparatively little abrasion (Fig. 55, 92-95, 97), suggests a late 1st to possibly early 2nd century date for its use. Even allowing for some intrusion of material owing to the nature of the soft water-logged deposits, a date in the fourth quarter of the 1st century can be postulated.

Within the small area examined the only other feature which may be associated with this ditch is a small channel, F5 on the same alignment. No traces of similar ditches or contemporary features were located during excavations of the Augustinian Friary site to the west. An explanation for its presence therefore is difficult and interpretations must be treated with caution. Punic ditches are often the outer defences of a fort's ditch sequence. The surviving width and depth of this feature suggests that it is small by fort defences standards (*ibid.* 48) but this may be explained by the high water table in this area so close to the river which may have prevented deeper digging. The main problem in relating this ditch to any large military establishment is the limited area available to the north east of the ditch which, from the latter's profile, is the area enclosed (cf. Clay and Mellor, 1985, 34). Much of this depends on changes in the river's course. Assuming that an eastern arm to the river was present in the Roman period (Buckley and Lucas 1987, 52) an area of *c.* 0.5 hectares only would be available to the north-east of the ditch. Perhaps an alternative to a fort can be suggested. A fortlet controlling the river crossing and the safety of traffic entering Leicester may be a possibility. Roadside fortlets are known from, for example, Appleby Dene, Northumberland (Hildyard, 1952) while control of river crossings with similar establishments is known from Cappuck, Borders Region (Richmond, 1953) and Bautrey, Nottinghamshire (St Joseph, 1953). These sites are usually square with rounded corners varying between 0.3 and 0.5 hectares in area defended by one or two ditches with a single rampart. A small fortlet 60m square would be possible within the area between the ditch and the eastern arm of the river (see Fig. 43).

A small military establishment of this nature would have been important in maintaining a presence in the post-Boudican climate. Its use in the Flavian period would have coincided with a time of increased military movement of consignments linked with northern fort building (Wilson, 1980, 33-7). Leicester's position on the Fosse Way may have been important during this period of expansion. The presence of lead seals attested to different military units found in Leicester, although conventionally dated to the 2nd-3rd centuries, supports its position as an important administrative centre (Clay, 1980, 317-20). While fortlets often replaced earlier, larger forts at for example, Caermote, Cumbria (Haverfield, 1903) and Cartlesham, Yorkshire (Richmond, 1925), any earlier military presence in Leicester is suspected but not proven (see below p. 46; Mellor, 1985, 34; Buckley and Lucas, 1987, 52). This ditch appears to have been deliberately backfilled in the early-mid 2nd century possibly to allow the construction of the Phase 3 stone building and laying of the gravel surfaces. Slag in Phases 3B & 3C was probably brought in with the gravel used in the road construction. Re-metalling evidence suggests that the latter may be part of a road system. A roadside ditch may be suggested from F25 which separates the gravel surface from the building (F23). Although this metalling and the building do not align with the known street grid within the town they may align with a west gate and known Roman settlements in the Anstey and Loughborough areas (Liddle, 1982, Fig. 20). A road in this direction might be expected perhaps continuing towards the settlement at Red Hill, Ratcliffe-on-Trent, 25km to the north-west. Alternatively however this metalled surface may be part of a yard area where a road approaching from the west might require open areas to facilitate control of the traffic approaching the west gate. Material from road silt above the re-metalled levels suggests use into the 4th century. No dating is possible for the robbing of the stone building, (F25), which may not have taken place, on the evidence of other robbing phases in the area, until the medieval period.

Phase 4 (Fig. 20) 13th century

Phase 4A 13th century

Beam slot: F4 (I 19,46)
Stake holes: F29 (I 55,64); F30-6 (I 56-70)

A beam slot, F4 (0.30m x 0.20m deep) cutting the Phase 3 deposits was located in the north-east area of the site on a north-south alignment. A dark brown fine sandy loam made up the fill of this feature which contained Potters Marston ware of *c.* 1100-1300 date. Associated with this slot were three post holes F32-F34 (0.20m in diameter x 0.15m deep) on a north-south alignment, 0.20m east of F4 and 0.15m apart. Three stake holes F29-F31 (0.10m in diameter x 0.15m deep and 0.25m apart) were located 0.20m south-east of the post hole group while two similar stake holes F35-6, on an east-west alignment were revealed 50mm to the west of F4 opposite F34. These features contained a fill similar to that in F4.

Phase 4B 13th century

Make-up: I 5,13,22,24-5; II 2,6,21; III 3

A series of deposits *c.* 0.20m thick was located in the north and south-east areas of the site. These consisted of dark brown fine clay loams, orange/red gravel, yellow, brown and red clay and grey brown silty clay with much charcoal. A 3rd century Roman coin, 12th-13th century pottery and iron fragments were recovered from these layers.

Phase 4C 13th century

Pits: F8 (I 37,50); F9 (II 3,18); F17 (III 7,22); F22 (IV 3,6,11,18); F28 (VI 6,28); F39 (I 9-10)

Six pits were located some of which cut the Phase 4B deposits. These consisted of F8 (1.60m wide x 0.45m deep) a square cut feature in the west section, F98 (1.15m diameter x 0.35m deep), a more circular pit in the south-east area, F17 partially located in the north-west corner of the site, F22 (*c.* 2.5m wide x 0.40m deep) in the west section, F39 (*c.* 2.0m wide x 0.45m deep) in the north section and F28 (1.5m x 0.35m deep) in Area VI. They all contained very similar dark brown fine clay loam fills with much charcoal and included 11th-early 13th century medieval pottery and a copper alloy needle (F8 I 37).

Phase 5 (Fig. 20) 13th-16th century

Phase 5A Late 13th-14th century

Pits: F2 (I 3,7,44); F10 (II 7,19); F11 (II 8,20); F16 (III 5,21); F24 (V 5,23); F26 (V 13,25); F41 (V 6,27); F42 (IV 4,7,9)

Further pits were located of varying sizes and depths. These consisted of F2 (2.90m x 2.50m x 0.55m deep), F10 (0.60m diameter x 0.25m deep), F11 (1.1m x 0.55m deep), F16 (2.45m x 1.35m x 0.85m deep), F24 (2.0m x 1.65m x 0.50m deep), F26 (*c.* 0.35m deep), F41 (0.75m diameter x 0.30m deep) and F42 (1.75m x 1.75m x 0.45m deep). Again these contained very similar dark brown fine clay loam fills with much charcoal and some gravel and clay deposits. Medieval pottery of 12th-early 14th century date, a stone spindle whorl (F2 I 3), a copper alloy buckle (F2 I 7), slag (F16 III 5) and animal bone were recovered from these features.

Disturbed human bone was also recovered from F16 (III 5).

Phase 5B 14th-15th century

Make-up: I 2, III 4; V 2,3

Spreads of sandstone, mortar, grey/brown fine sandy loam, gravel and silty grey clay with charcoal were located overlying the Phase 4 and 5A features varying between 0.10m and 0.25m in depth. Finds of 13th-15th century pottery, a wooden bowl fragment, tile and window glass were recovered.

Phase 5C 15th-16th century

Graves: F12-14 (I 40-2,51-3); F15 (VI 14-5); F18-21 (III 14-17,23-26)

Three groups of burials were found cutting the Phase 5B deposits. In the north-west area of the site four graves (F18-21) on east-west alignments were revealed also cutting the Phase 3 road surface. The graves (all *c.* 1.5m x 0.40m x 0.25m deep) contained dark brown fine sandy loam fills. Three metres to the south another group F12-13 was located having similar alignments, the graves being similar in size and fill. Another grave, F15, again of similar fill and dimensions was located in Area VI. These burials are published in Mellor and Pearce (1981) with osteological analysis by Ann Stirland (1981, 168). The codes used in that publication can be related to these features as follows: A=F12, B=F13, *C.*=F14, D=F15, E=F18, F=F19, G=F20, H=F21.

Discussion of Phases 4 and 5

There is no evidence for activity on this site between the abandonment of the Phase 3 road(?) probably in the early 4th century and the building of a timber structure in the early medieval period. The medieval activity can be divided into two, Phase 4 which probably occurred before the land became part of the precinct of the Augustinian Friary (Mellor and Pearce, 1981, 5, Fig. 1) and Phase 5 which covers the period of use by the Friary. The timber structure indicated by the beam slot, F4, post and stake holes is similar to that encountered during the Friary excavations (Phase 1) (*ibid.* 9) which was dated to the late 13th century. The function of these structures must remain in doubt; they seem to be relatively insubstantial. After this structure went out of use the area appears to have been used for garden or agricultural activity perhaps indicated by the Phase 4B deposits. Pits dug within the area are divided into different phases (4C and 5A) on the basis of the pottery found in them, the former dating to *c.* 11th-12th century, whilst the latter group of 12th-14th century date may have been used for domestic refuse from the Augustinian Friary. Some disturbance of earlier burials may be suggested by human bone fragments in F15. The spreads of building material (Phase 5B) are probably debris from the construction of the Friary's Phase 3 cloister area where similar material was

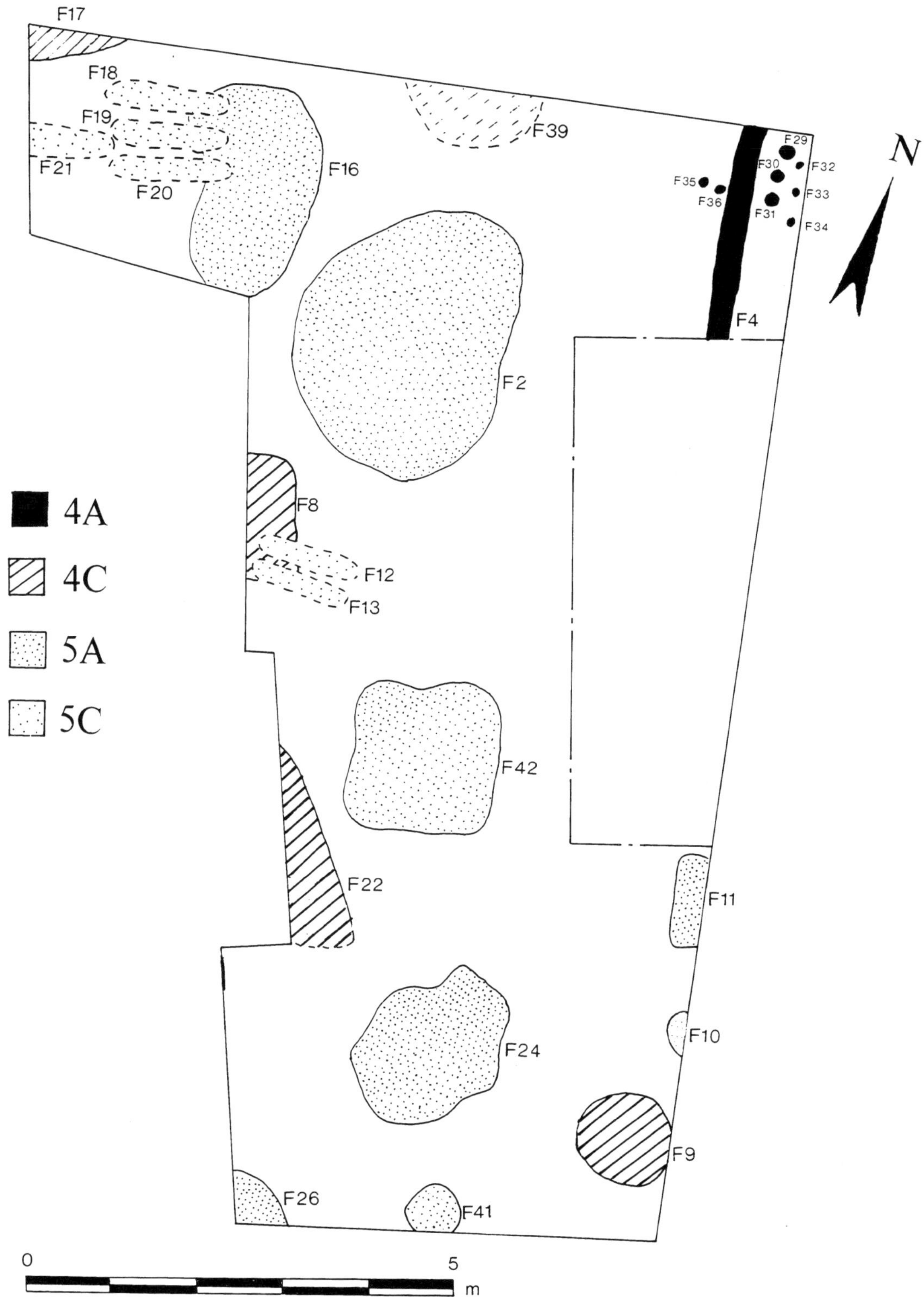

Fig. 20 Site 3, Phases 4 and 5

located (*ibid.* 17). Burials from the area (Phase 5C) are on osteological comparisons similar to the Friary Phase 7C burials of 15th-16th century date (Stirland, 1981, 168).

Phase 6 19th century

Make-up: I 1; II 1; II 16; III 1,2; IV 1; V 1; VI 1-4

Make-up deposits sealing the medieval features were located throughout the site. These are probably associated with early 19th century activity (*c.* 1830) connected with the construction of the Leicester and Swannington Railway. Animal bone, human bone, iron and pottery fragments were recovered from these deposits.

The later history of this site is discussed in Martin (1981, 3-4). It is now covered by a modern road complex.

Site 4 Excavations in Lower Redcross Street 1967 (Fig. 21) SK5826 0433

An excavation was undertaken to the south of Lower Redcross Street (now part of St. Nicholas Circle) by Jean E Mellor for Leicester City Museums between August and September 1967 (Mellor, 1968-9, 9; Acc. No. A568.1967 RC). Four areas were investigated covering *c.* 96 sq m in advance of road re-alignment development with the aims of further investigation within the Roman town and to examine part of the north precinct of Leicester Castle. Two phases of Roman activity were discerned which will be discussed here; the medieval phases will be discussed in the report on Leicester Castle (Buckley, forthcoming).

Phase 1 1st century

Phase 1A Early-Mid 1st century

Beam slots:	F8 (II 28,40), F9-11 (II 22-4,35-7) F19 (IV 11,28), F28 (V 15,39); F29 (V 21,40); F32 (II 41-2)
Post holes:	F12 (II 26,38) F13 (II 27,39) F30 (V 32,41); F35 (IV 36-7); F37-9 (III 21-6); F43 (II 43-4); F48 (II 54-5)
Stake hole:	F44 (II 45-6)
Pit:	F42 (V 13,46)
Channel:	F45 (V 9,10,45)

Shallow traces of several beam slots on east-west alignments were located in Areas II, IV and V. Two of these F8 (0.20m wide x 0.15m deep) and F32 (1.2m x 0.20m wide x 0.12m deep) in Area II contained traces of stake holes 0.10m in diameter at their east ends. Three similar features F9-11, 0.20m wide x 0.15m deep and 0.20m apart were located to the south of F8. Traces of three beam slots in Areas IV and V F19 (0.20m x 0.10m deep), F28 (2.8m minimum x 0.20m x 0.12m deep) and F29 (3.5m minimum x 0.20m x 0.15m deep) were on similar alignments to F9-11. Four post holes F48, F43 and F13 (0.20m diameter x 0.15m) in Area II and F35 (0.25m diameter x 0.12m deep) in Area IV are on the same alignment as beam slots F8 and F32 as is one stake hole, F44 (0.10m diameter x 0.10m deep) west of F43. All of these features contained a light brown fine sandy loam fill with charcoal flecking.

A pit F42 (*c.* 0.60m diameter x 0.30m deep), a post hole, F30 (0.30m diameter x 0.10m deep) and a north east - south west aligned channel F45 (0.65m wide x 0.30m deep) in Area V can also be assigned to this phase. They had similar fills to those above but with some clay silt present. Three post holes (F37-9) (all *c.* 0.20m diameter x 0.10m deep) containing light brown fine sandy loam fills were located in Area III. Where present (F9, F10, F12, F13, F28, F32, F42, F45) pottery from these features was of early-mid 1st century date.

Phase 1B Mid-late 1st century

Beam slots:	F27 (V 12,17,38); F49 (V 11,50)
Post holes:	F31 (V 33,42); F47 (V 47-8)
Channel:	F34 (IV 20-1, 35)

Two beam slots F27 (1.6m minimum x 0.30m wide x 0.15m) and F49 (1.35m x 0.30m x 0.15m) were located parallel to and cutting in part F29. Two post holes F47 (0.25m x 0.20m x 0.15m) and F31 (0.40m sq x 0.20m) continued this alignment to the east. A channel, F34 (1.7m minimum x 0.70m x 0.30m) on a north west - south east alignment was also located in Area IV. These features again contained light brown fine sandy loam fills with early-mid 1st century pottery present in F27, F31 and F49. A 1st century brooch (Fig. 73.3) was recovered from F27 and mid-late 1st century pottery from F34.

Phase 2 Late 1st century-early 2nd century

Post holes:	F20 (IV 12,29); F40 (IV 14-16, 43); F41 (V 44,49)
Channel:	F33 (IV 3,34)

Three post holes F20 (0.60m x 0.45m x 0.40m), F40 (0.50m x 0.45m x 0.42m) and F41 (0.75m x 0.45m x 0.40m) were located in Areas IV and V.

These contained fills of yellow sand and dark brown clay loam. A round-ended channel F33 (1.1m minimum x 0.60m x 0.30m) was located one metre east of F20 containing a dark brown sandy loam fill with much iron pan and charcoal. Material from F33 suggests a late 1st - early 2nd century date.

Discussion

Again evidence of early-mid 1st century activity was present on this site and rectangular timber buildings of probable early post-conquest date are suggested by the presence of beam slots and post holes. Some rebuilding was probably taking place (cf. F9-11) and this appears to have continued with the Phase 1B features F27 and F49 replacing F29 perhaps later in the 1st century AD. Phase 2 again includes evidence of a timber structure using substantial post holes. Although disturbed by medieval features to the west it can be seen to be on a different alignment from the earlier buildings but not yet corresponding with the known Roman street grid. (For a full discussion of the alignment of 1st century buildings in Roman Leicester see below p. 46).

The only evidence of later Roman activity comes from material found residually in the medieval and later features suggesting some activity up until the 4th century.

Site 5 Excavations in Redcross Street 1962-3 SK 5831 0439

Redevelopment in the area between Redcross Street, Thornton Lane and Harvey Lane necessitated excavation which was carried out by M H Hebditch for Leicester City Museums with the help of a grant from the Ministry of Works. An area of *c.* 40 sq m was examined separated into ten areas. Areas I - IX were excavated in the first season between June and December 1962 (Acc. No. A316.1962) whilst another area (X) was examined during August and September 1963 (Acc. No. A174.1963) to check the extent of some of the features encountered in 1962. The excavation revealed five main phases of occupation during the Roman period with some medieval activity (Phase 6).

Phase 1 1st-2nd century

Phase 1A (Fig.22) Late 1st century

Stake holes:	F80 (III 13-4); F81-3 (IV 33-8)
Gravel surface:	IV 25
Occupation debris:	IV 21-4, X 22

A gravel surface (IV 25) was located, overlying the substrata in Area IV, from which 1st century pottery, a Colchester brooch (p. 145 Fig. 74.21) and five iron nails were recovered. Associated with this surface were three stakeholes F81-F83 (0.10m diam,

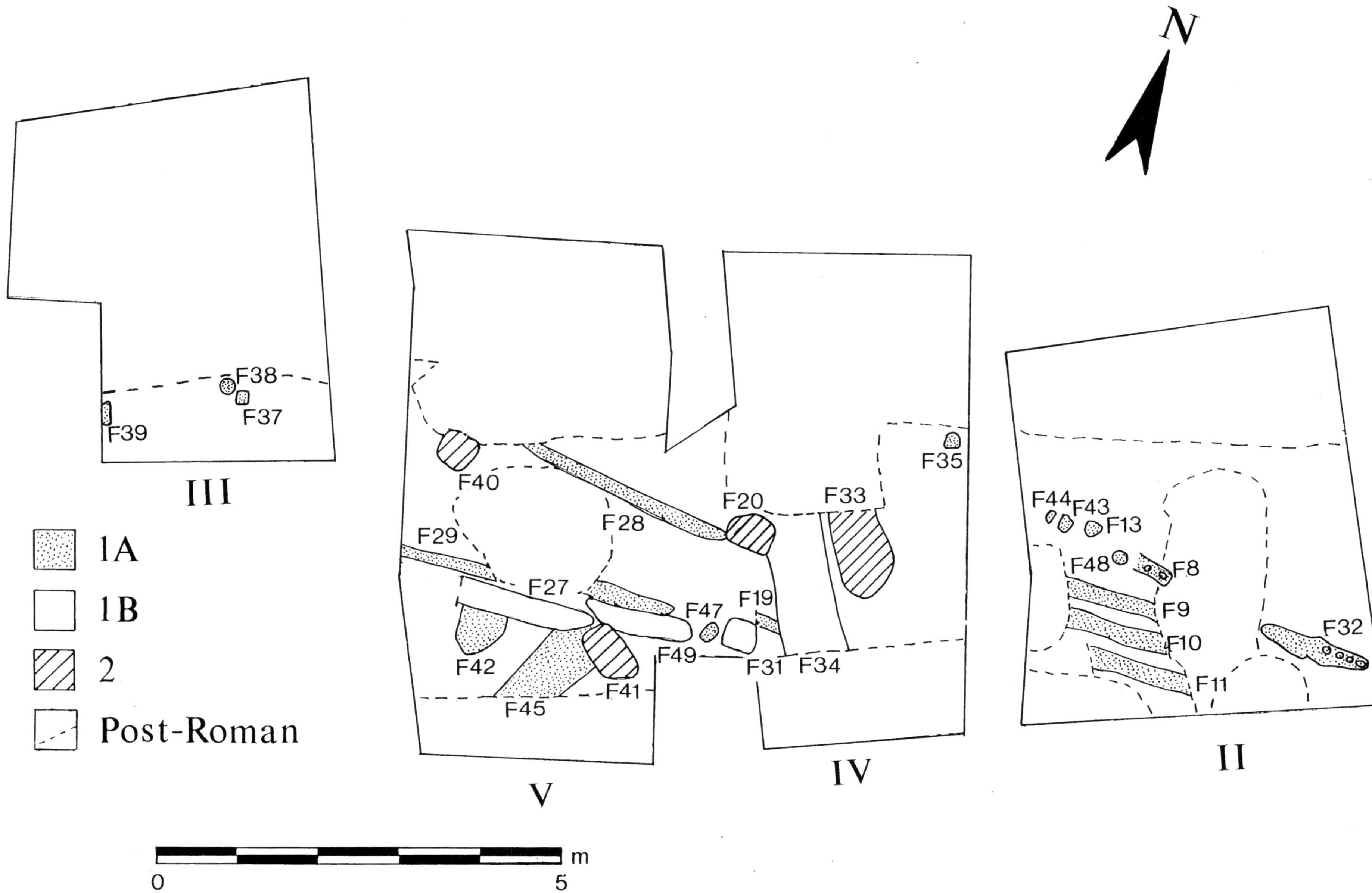

Fig. 21 Site 4, Phases 1 and 2

depths unrecorded). A similar stakehole in Area II, F80, can be included in this group. The gravel surface was overlain by 0.20m thick deposits of dark brown clay loam and silt with much charcoal. A loam layer in Area X (X 22) may be associated with these deposits. Finds of Neronian-Flavian pottery, an Iron Age silver coin (p. 131), copper alloy and iron objects were recovered from these layers.

Phase 1B Late 1st century

Gravel surfaces:	IV 20; VI 42
Make-up:	I 32; II 25; III 3,4; V 40; VII 17-9, 50; X 20-1

Another gravel surface, IV 20, was located overlying the Phase 1A deposits in Area IV. In Area VI a gravel layer, VI 42, may be associated with this surface. Further dark brown clay loam deposits were revealed in Areas I, II, III, V, VII and X. Green sand deposits in Area VII (VII 17,18,19) may also be grouped in this phase. Late 1st century pottery, a copper alloy pin and iron nails were recovered from these layers.

Phase 1C Late 1st century

Make-up:	I 25-7; II 22-31; III 2; IV 17,19,26; VI 40-1; VII 16

Deposits of green sand (I 27, II 29), red sand (II 28), grey sand (IV 19), red gravel (I 26, II 30), grey clay (I 25, III 2, IV 17,26) and grey brown sandy loam (II 22,31, VII 16) were located in Areas I-IV and VII. Pale grey silt (VI 41), ash and charcoal (VI 40) deposits were also present in Area VI. Material from these layers included late 1st century pottery, vessel glass, iron nails and copper alloy objects including a Trumpet brooch (p 145 Fig.74.24).

Phase 1D (Fig. 22) Late 1st century-Early 2nd century

Pits:	F43 (I 48,59); F48 (IV 49,50); F104 (X 40,44)

Three pits were located cutting the earlier Phase 1 deposits. F43 (*c.* 1.40m wide x 0.19m deep) containing a grey silty clay fill was located in the north section of Area I. In the north-east corner of Area IV F48, (*c.* 1.25 diam, depth not recorded) containing a brown sandy loam fill, was revealed while in Area X a shallow pit F104 (dimensions not recorded) was noted with a loose dark brown clay loam fill. No finds are recorded from F43 and F48 whilst a bone toggle (p. 147 Fig. 77.64) and late 1st-early 2nd century pottery were recovered from F104. The latter included highly vitrified sherds suggesting proximity to some industrial activity.

Discussion of Phase 1

The earliest activity recorded from the site is the gravel surface located in Area IV (IV 25). The remains of this are too insubstantial to suggest its function but it may have formed part of a yard. Some form of timber structure may be associated with this surface by the four stakeholes (F80-83). The deposits overlying the surface (IV 21-3) may be interpreted as occupation debris, material from which suggests a Neronian-Flavian date for its accumulation. A gravel surface of similar appearance and date was located in Site 1 Phase 1B (see p 2). A second phase of gravel surface may be indicated by IV 20 (Phase 1B). Some make-up activity can be suggested from Phases 1B and 1C within a general late 1st century context. These were later cut by Phase 1D pits. Although much domestic and possibly industrial debris was present in Phases 1B-1D no associated buildings were located.

Phase 2 2nd century

Phase 2A (Fig. 22) Early 2nd century

Beam slots:	F15 (IV 29,41); F59-61 (IV 42-4,54-6); F50 (IV 56)
Stake holes:	F46 (II 24,48); F57-8 (VII 56-7,68-9) F68-71 (I 53-8); F72-9 (II 43-47); F94 (II 66-7)
Post holes:	F46 (II 24,48); F51 (VI 32,48)
Pits:	F35-6 (V 26-7; 46-7); F37 (VII 37,66); F39 (VIII 2,3,38-43); F40 (VII 44,67); F41 (VI 2-4, 25-7); F42 (V 28,41); F95 (IV 16,18,53)

Traces of four linear features, probably beam slots, were located in Area IV cutting the Phase 1 deposits. F15 was aligned roughly north-south (3.0m long x 0.10m wide x 0.6m deep) whilst at right angles to it, three similar features F59-F61 were faintly discernible varying between 0.60m (F59,F61) and 1.50m (F60) in length. 0.45m to the east of F60, F50 (0.6m long) may be a continuation of the same feature. These features contained a fine light brown sandy loam fill with a sherd of late 1st-early 2nd century grey ware present in F15. A group of one post hole F46 and twelve stake holes F68-79, was revealed in Areas I and II (*c.* 0.10m - 0.12m in diameter and 0.15m - 0.30m in depth). Two similar stake holes F57 and F58 located in the south section of Area VII and a single post hole F51 (*c.* 0.20m diam x 0.20m deep) revealed in the west section of Area VI may have been part of the same phase of activity. The fills of these features, where recorded, were light brown fine sandy loams. Eight possible pits can also be assigned to this phase. One of these F95 (*c.* 0.55m wide x 0.30m deep) was present in the south east corner of Area IV having been cut by the Phase 4A wall F6. Late 1st-early 2nd century pottery was recovered from the fill of dark brown clay loam with much iron pan and charcoal. In Area V two pits were located: F35 (dimensions not recorded) was situated central to the area whilst F42, a straight-sided, flat bottomed feature (*c.* 1.0m x 1.0m deep) was in the east section. Both F35 and F42 contained sandy loam fills with late 1st-early 2nd century pottery whilst one fragment of window glass was recovered from F35. In the south east corner of Area V another pit F36 (*c.* 2.25m min width x 0.50m deep) was recorded. This may be part of the same feature as F41 (*c.* 2.50m wide x 0.50m deep) in the south west corner of Area VI. F41 contained fills of red gravel, dark grey brown clay loam, charcoal, green sand and dark grey organic silt. The type of fill in F36 is not recorded. Both features contained similar groups of artefacts, late 1st-early 2nd century pottery, copper alloy, vessel glass and five iron nails being recovered from F36 whilst a large assemblage of early 2nd century pottery, a copper alloy lock ward (p. 147 Fig. 75.40) and vessel glass were found in F41. A similar situation occurs with two pits F39 and F40 to the north of Area VII perhaps being part of the same feature, their relationship obscured by a baulk and Phase 4A wall (F90). F39 (dimensions not recorded) contained green silt, grey brown clay loam and sandy red gravel fills with large quantities of early 2nd century pottery and some vessel glass. F40 (dimensions and fill not recorded) contained late 1st-early 2nd century pottery, copper alloy and iron fragments. To the south of F39/F40 in Area VII another pit F37 (dimensions and fill not recorded) was located having been cut by Phase 4A walls (F21 and F90). Late 1st-early 2nd century pottery was recovered from this feature.

Phase 2B Early-mid 2nd century

Make-up:	I 24,40,47; II 11; IV 15,27; V 15-6; VI 11,39; VII 13-5,22; X 19

Deposits, 0.20m thick, of grey brown sandy loam (V 15, VI 11, VII 14), red sand and gravel (IV 27, VI 39, VII 15) and lightbrown

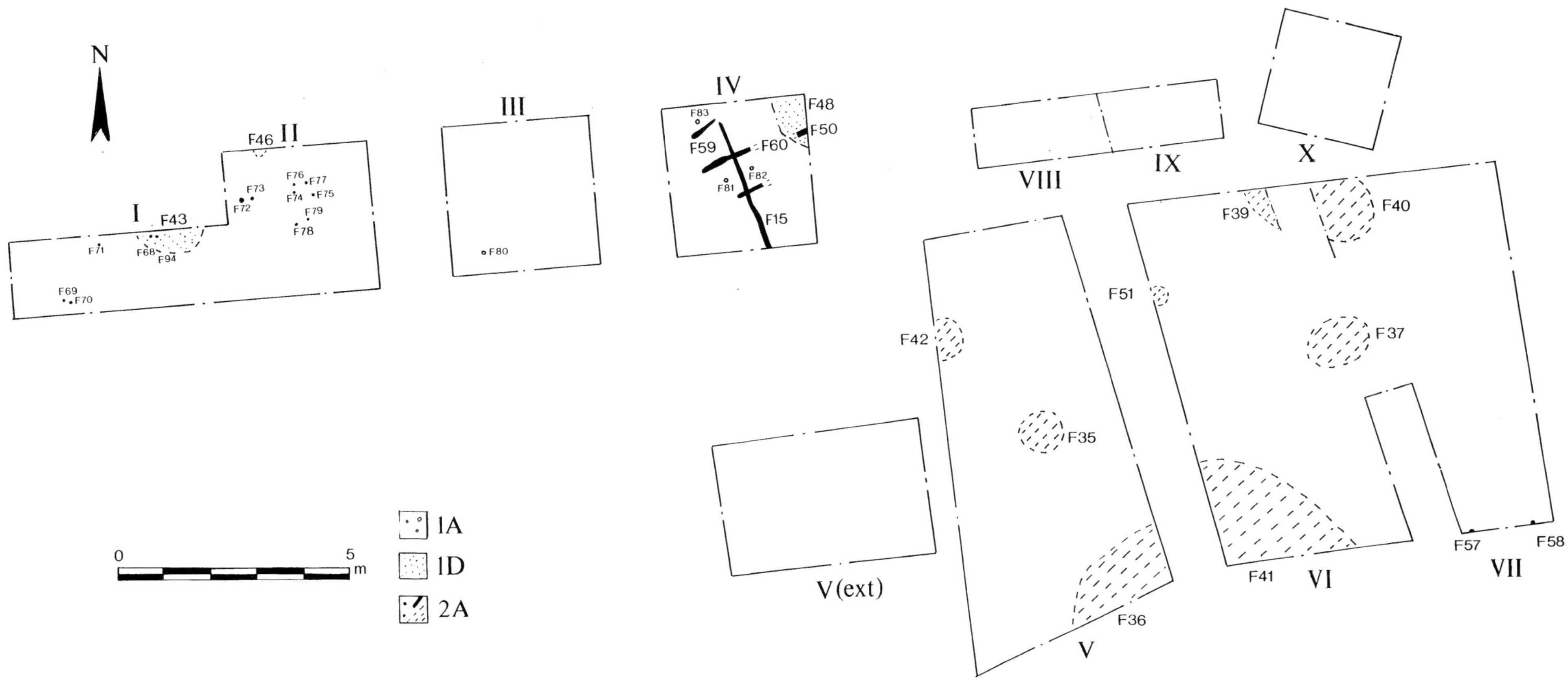

Fig. 22 Site 5, Phases 1 and 2

sandy clay (I 40, II 11) containing 1st-early 2nd century pottery, vessel glass, copper alloy fragments and an iron nail were revealed. Dark brown fine clay loam deposits with much charcoal and ash (I 47, IV 15, VII 22, X 19) were also present partially overlying the other Phase 2B layers. Early-mid 2nd century pottery was present.

Phase 2C Early-mid 2nd century

Make-up: IV 10-1,13-4; V 8,14; VI 9,10,30-1; VII 10,21,25-9; IX 6-10; X 6,7,9,10, 35-6

Similar deposits sealing those in Phase 2B were encountered. Red sand and gravel (IV 13,14, VII 21, X 10), red clay (X 35) and sandy rubble (IX 7,9, X 9) were again partially sealed by dark brown fine clay loam deposits with much charcoal (IV 10,11, V 8,14, VI 31, VII 10,25-29, IX 8,10, X 6,7,36). Much 1st-mid 2nd century pottery was recovered together with vessel glass, window glass, bone objects (p. 147 Figs 77.65 and 78.72), a glass melon bead, a copper alloy Polden Hill type brooch (p. 145 Fig. 74.22), a copper alloy object, lead sheet and iron fragments.

Discussion of Phase 2

The beam slots located in Area IV probably formed part of a rectangular timber building erected late in the 1st or early in the 2nd century. From their size and position they may have formed joists for a timber floor (see also Site 6 Phase 7B below p. 40). The group of stake holes located in Areas I and II forms no coherent pattern and may have been inserted over a long period of time.

Various pits can be associated with this phase. Of note amongst these are F39 and F41 which contained large quantities of material including samian ware vessels in unabraded condition and several broken and worn mortaria (see pp. 64, 68). It is possible that pottery was being sold or redistributed from the Phase 2A building. Material recovered from F39 and F41 suggests that these pits were sealed by *c.* 130/140.

Two phases (2B and 2C) of redeposited sediments were located sealing the Phase 2A timber building features. Phases of levelling and make-up activity following the destruction of the timber building may be suggested from these deposits. The dark brown fine clay loam layers with charcoal may be occupation debris associated with these activities. No associated building phases can be related to this phase which can be dated to the first half of the 2nd century.

Phase 3 (Fig. 23) 2nd-3rd century

Phase 3A Early-mid 2nd century

Street metalling: F64 (I 20,22-3; II 7,9,10,18,23,26; III 11-2)
Pits: F49 (IV 8,46); F56 (VII 51-4,71); F105 (X 42,45); F106 (X 11,13,16-8,52)
Shallow scoop: F66 (VII 65,70)
Make-up: IV 9; VI 7,8; VII 9

Layers of red sand and gravel amounting in thickness to *c.* 0.5m were located in Areas I, II, III (F64). Possible surfaces of hard packed pebbles may be discerned (I 20, II 7, III 11). An area of *c.* 8 sq.m. was exposed indicating a surface *c.* 4.0m wide (east-west).

Two features in the east section of Area VII can be assigned to this phase. F56 a large square cut feature (2.20m diam x 1.10m deep), disturbed by later wall foundations (F21 Phase 4A), contained fills of charcoal, red gravel, sandy loam and silt whilst F66 a shallow feature (0.30m wide x 0.15m deep) 0.30m to the south of F56 contained a red gravel fill. Two pits were also noted in Area X. F105 (0.50m diam x 0.15m deep) contained burnt bone and charcoal with traces of a wood or wattle lining whilst F106 (dimensions not recorded) had a yellow sand and charcoal fill. Copper alloy, iron and lead fragments were recovered from this layer. Another pit F49 in the section of Area IV contained late 1st-early 2nd century pottery.

Pale grey sand deposits *c.* 0.15m thick were located in Areas IV, VI and VII and can be grouped with this phase of activity. 1st-2nd century pottery, copper alloy, iron and lead fragments were recovered from these deposits.

Phase 3B Mid 2nd century-Early 3rd century

Beam slots: F13 (I 33-7,60); F16 (I 38,61); F38 (VI 24,52); F45 (I 49,62); F47 (IV 12,45); F84 (IV 39,40); F85 (V 50-1, VIII 11-2); F86 (VIII 13-14); F87 (V 54-5); F88 (VI 59,60); F89 (VII 80-1); F103 (X 33-4,37,43); F108 (X 38,54)
Wall fillets: F99 (V 60); F100 (V 61)
Oven/furnace: F96 (VI 75-6); F97 (VI 77-8)
Stoke pit(?): F55 (VI 43,50)
Pit: F52 (VI 33-5,49)
Make-up: I 19,46: V 13;
Floor levels: IV 7; V 6; VI 29; IX 5,11

Two north-south aligned beam slots were located in Area I. F13 (0.40m wide x 0.25m deep) was situated 0.30m east of and parallel to the Phase 3A gravel surface and had been cut by the Phase 4A wall (F44) along the same alignment. The straight sided feature contained grey clay loam with rock packing along both sides and showed traces of post holes within the fill. 2nd century pottery was recovered from this fill. 2.5m to the west, a second beam slot, F45 (0.35m wide, depth not recorded) was discernible in the north section along the same alignment as F13. Only faint traces of the grey brown sandy loam in this feature remained as it had been cut by a medieval pit (F63). An east-west aligned beam slot F16 (dimensions and location not recorded) containing two iron nails was noted as joining F13. Associated floors may be represented by clay deposits with a thin mortar spread 0.10m thick, (I 19; I 46). Two north-south aligned walls were located in Areas V, VII and VIII (F85, F89) joining three east-west aligned walls (F86, F87, F88). These consisted of timber beam slots (0.20m wide x 0.20m deep) with a daub wall surviving to a height of 0.40m in places. Traces of other beam slots which may be connected with these were found in Areas IV (F47, F84), VI (F38) and X (F103, F108). Late 1st-2nd century pottery was found in F38 and F47 which also contained a copper alloy ring while mid 2nd-early 3rd century pottery and iron nails were present in F103. In Area V an *opus signinum* floor layer, V 6 (*c.* 0.15 thick) with rubble foundations was located. Plaster fillets ($^1/_4$ round) F99 (30mm radius) marked the junction between the daub walls, F85 and F87, and the *opus signinum* surface (see Pl.2). A square fillet, F100, (30mm sq.) formed the angle between F85 and the surface south of F87. This had been chamfered off at an angle part of the way along F85. Other possible floor levels were located consisting of a green clay layer VI 29, (0.15m thick), a thin mortar spread, IV 7, and *opus signinum* with rubble foundation (IX 5,11). 2nd century pottery, a copper alloy fragment and iron nails were present in these layers.

Wall plaster fragments had survived adhering to the clay walls F85 and F87. These indicated that the walls north of F87 and west of F85 had firstly been painted red before another layer of wall plaster was added which was painted green. The walls to the south of F87 and west of F85 showed one phase of red painted wall plaster.

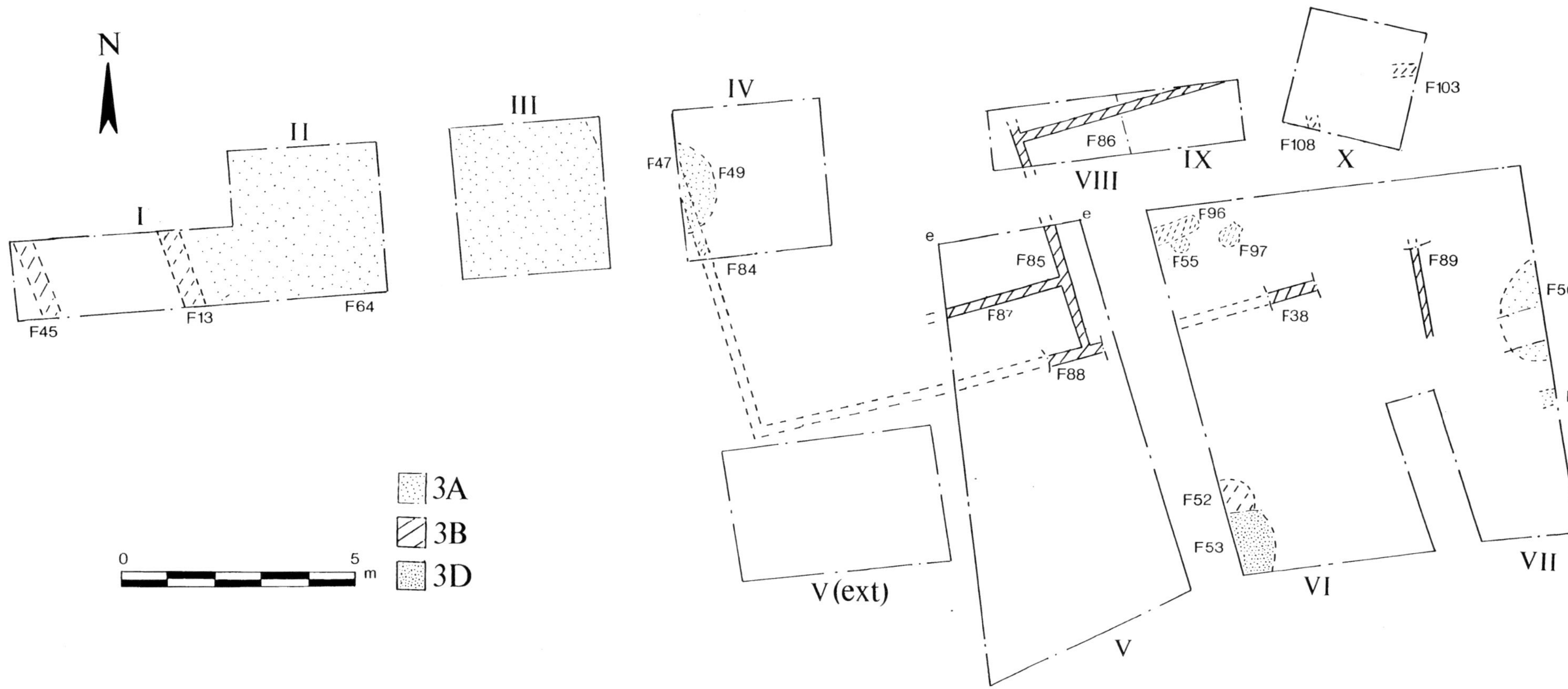

Fig 23 Site 5 Phase 3

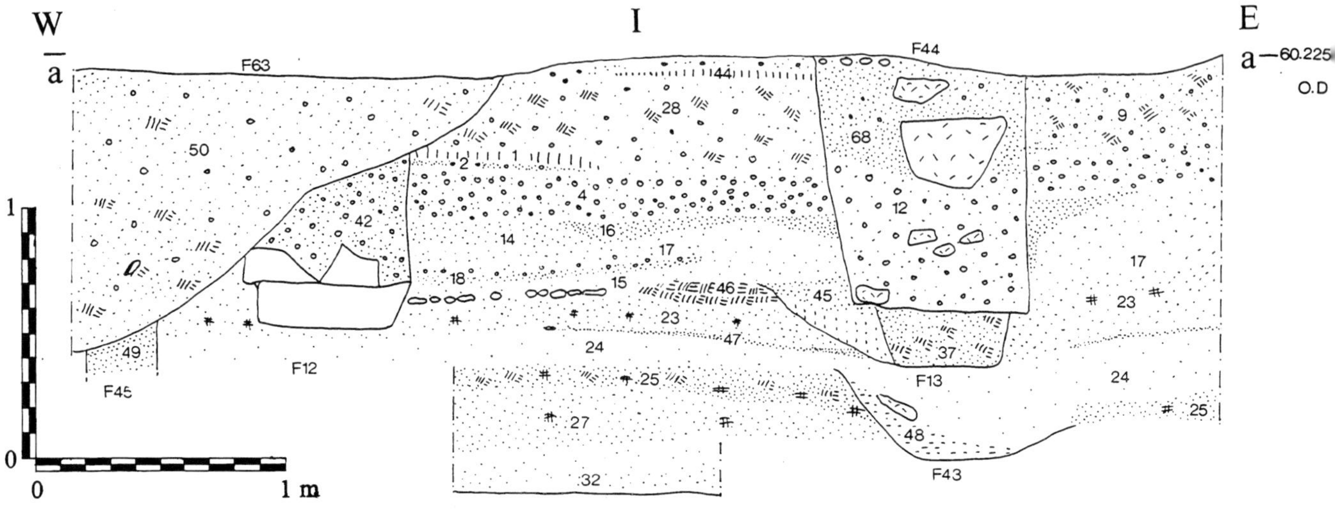

Fig. 24 Site 5, Section a-a Area I

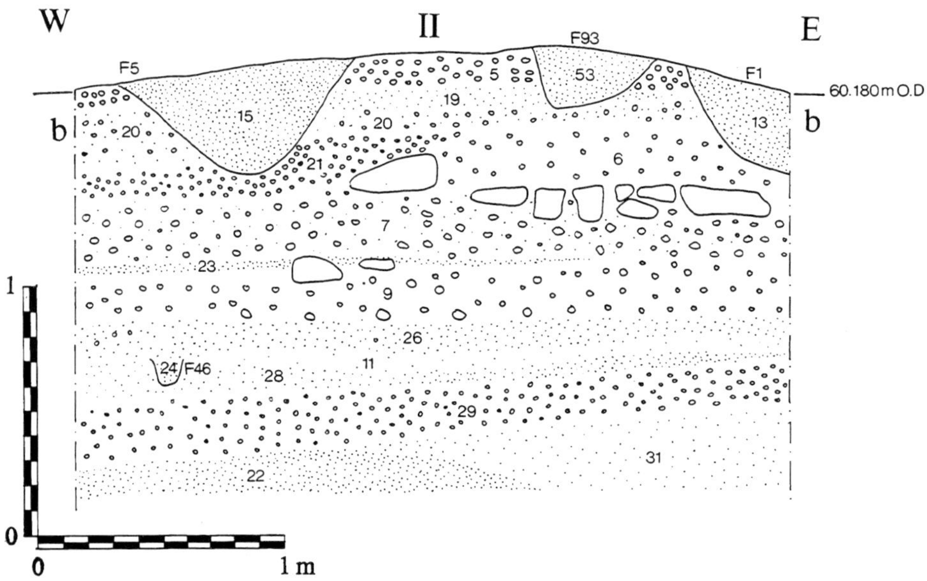

Fig. 25 Site 5, Section b-b Area II

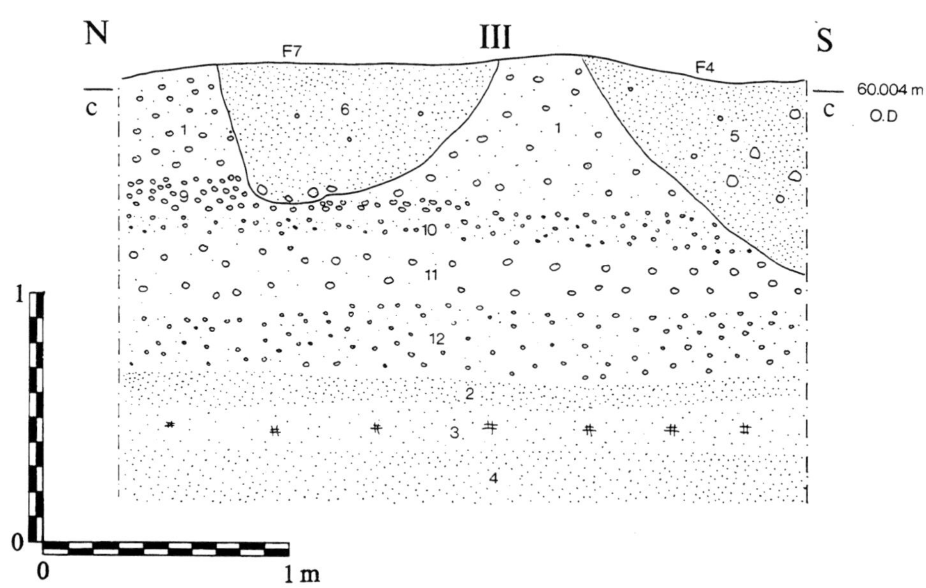

Fig. 26 Site 5, Section c-c Area III

Four other features may be associated with this phase. Two ovens or furnaces were located in Area VI. F96 (0.3m wide x 0.30m deep) containing brown sandy loam with a charcoal lining was situated to the north east of the area whilst a similar feature F97 (dimensions not recorded) to the west of F96 contained a similar fill. A shallow feature F55 (dimensions not recorded) may be connected with F96 perhaps serving as a stoke pit. To the south another small pit F52 (*c.* 1.0m diam x 0.30m deep) was located to the south-west of Area V containing sandy loam and red clay fills.

Make-up deposits of sandy loam were located in Areas I and V with a disc brooch (p. 145 Fig. 74.27) present in the latter area.

Phase 3C Late 2nd-Early 3rd century

Street metalling:	F64 (I 9-11; II 6,16,21,27; III 9,10)
Make-up:	I 13-16,21,41,45; IV 3-6; V 2-5, 9-12; VI 6,28; VII 23-4 48-9,55 X 1-5

Further red/orange sand and gravel spreads (*c.* 0.20m thick) were located in Areas I-III overlying the Phase 3A deposits. Surfaces may be present represented by I 9, II 6 and III 9. Sandstone street foundations were present in Area II. Other deposits adjacent to F64 and between F13 and F45 were revealed in Area I consisting of red gravel and green sand with 1st-2nd century pottery and vessel glass. Layers 0.15m thick of grey/green sand, grey silt and red clay with charcoal and mortar fragments were located in Area IV containing 1st-2nd century pottery and vessel glass. Similar material including some sandy debris was also present in Areas V and VI with 2nd-early 3rd century pottery, vessel glass, wall plaster, a 1st century coin, a copper alloy Colchester brooch, (p. 145 Fig. 74.20), a copper alloy ring, iron nails and a bone counter. Various green clay, brown sandy loam and grey sand layers were present in Area VII containing 2nd century pottery whilst grey yellow and red sand, rubble and charcoal were located in Area X containing 2nd century pottery.

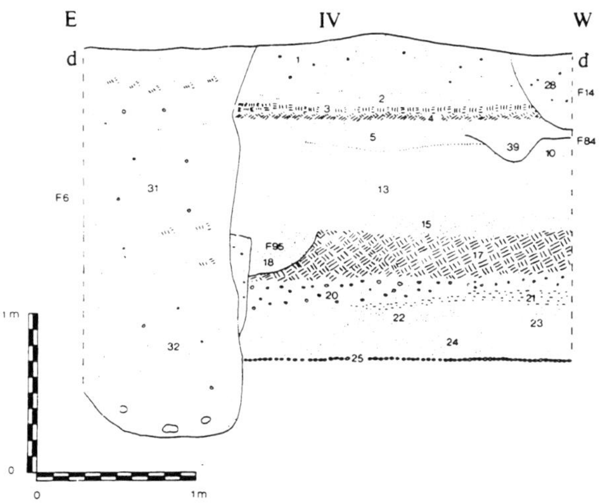

Fig. 27 Site 5, Section d-d Area IV

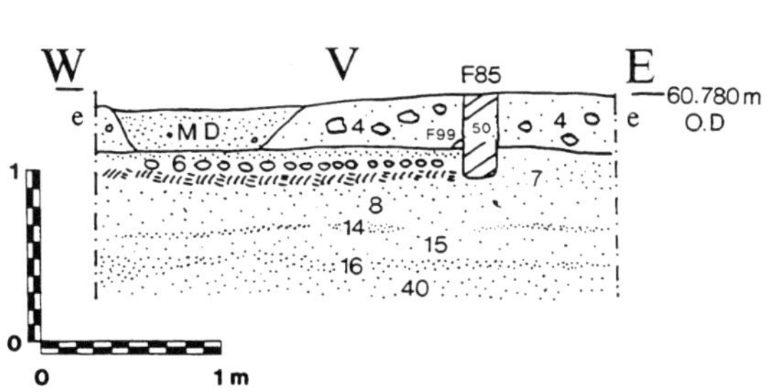

Fig. 28 Site 5, Section e-e Area V

Phase 3D Late 2nd-Early 3rd century

Street metalling:	F64 (I 7,39; II 5,19,20; III 1)
Pit:	F53 (VI 36-8)
Make-up:	I 17-8; VII 7,8

Further gravel surfaces were located in Areas I - III (F64). Adjacent to these in Area I were other red/orange sand and gravel layers (I 17,18). Green clay layers *c.* 10mm thick were located in Area VII containing late 2nd - early 3rd century pottery and some vessel glass. A pit F53 (*c.* 0.6m diam x 0.25m deep) cutting F52 in Area VI with a grey sand and clay fill can also be assigned to this phase.

Discussion of Phase 3

Street metalling is evident from the gravel surfaces revealed in Areas I - III. These are part of a north-south aligned street *c.* 4.0m wide. Its construction is similar to that encountered on Sites 2 and 3 with successive gravel deposits and large pebbles used as foundation. Two phases of re-metalling (Phases 3C and 3D) can be discerned overlying the earlier road surfaces. The street appears to have been constructed in the first half of the 2nd century which coincides with the other evidence from streets found in Leicester (see above p. 15 Site 2 Phase 4). The re-metalling appears to have taken place in the 2nd or early in the 3rd century. Phase 3A also shows evidence of the area being used for rubbish pits and some make up layers perhaps in preparation for the Phase 3B building.

Two timber buildings (Phase 3B) indicated by beam slots, floor levels and partially surviving clay walls were revealed to the east and west of the street. Later distur-

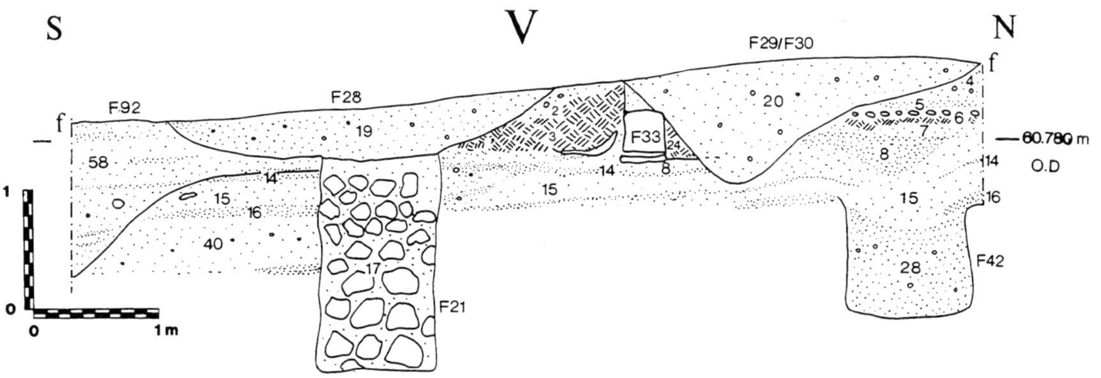

Fig. 29 Site 5, Section f-f Area V

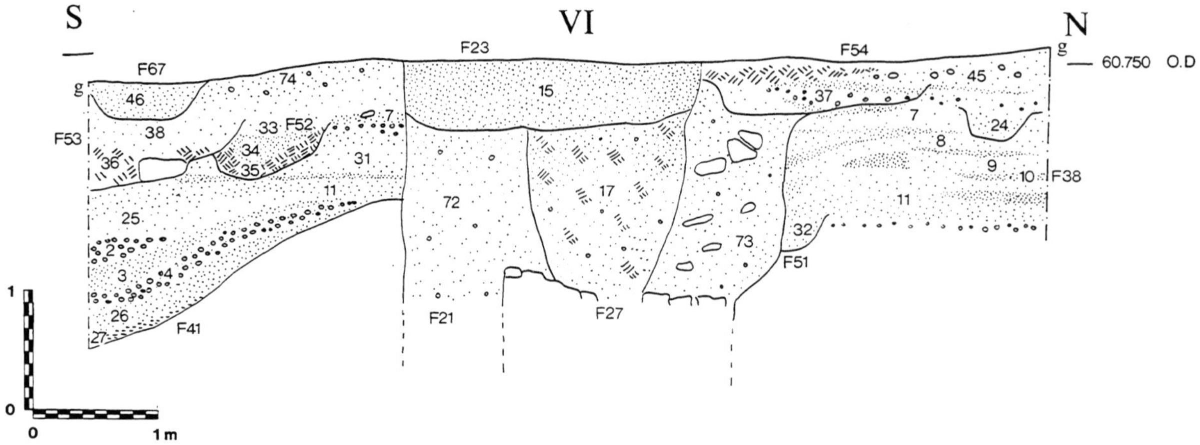

Fig. 30 Site 5, Section g-g Area VI

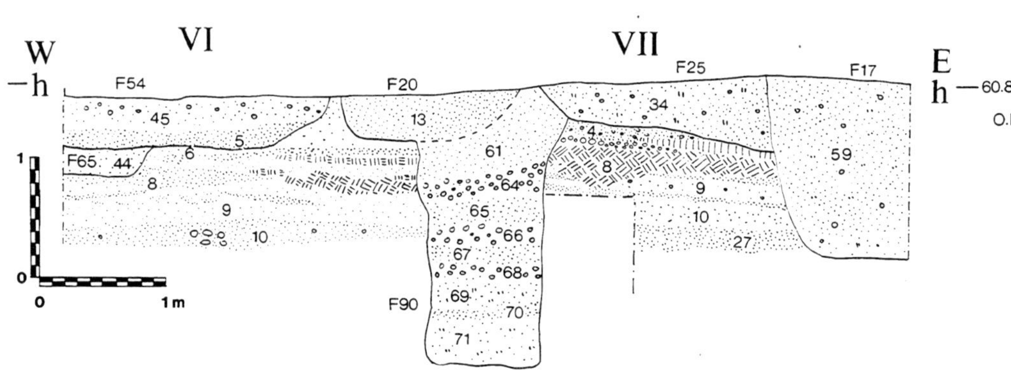

Fig. 31 Site 5, Section h-h Area VI and VII

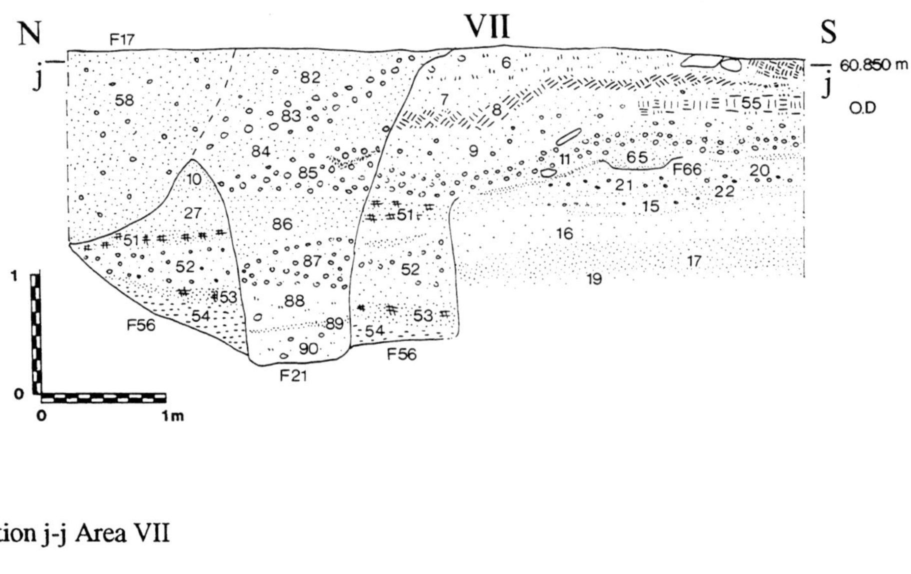

Fig. 32 Site 5, Section j-j Area VII

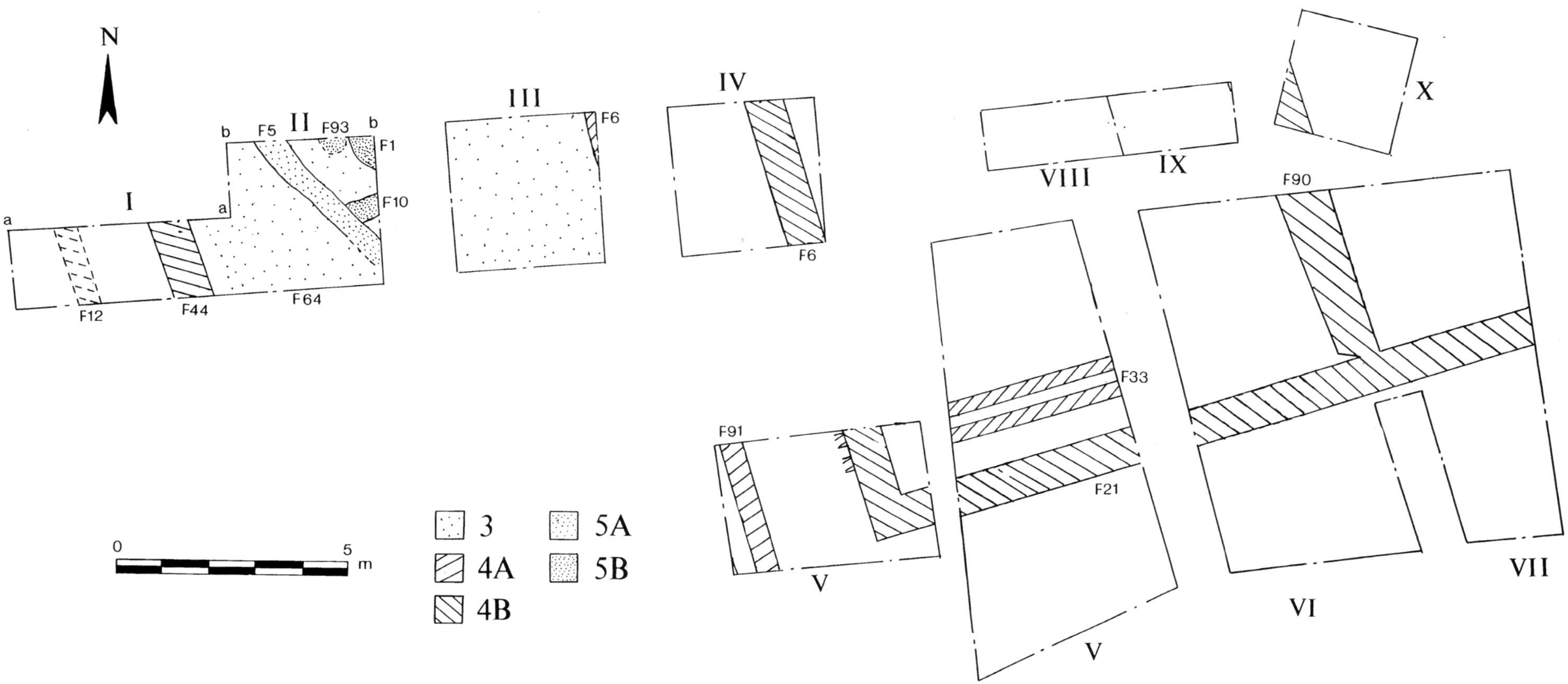

Fig. 33 Site 5, Phases 4 and 5

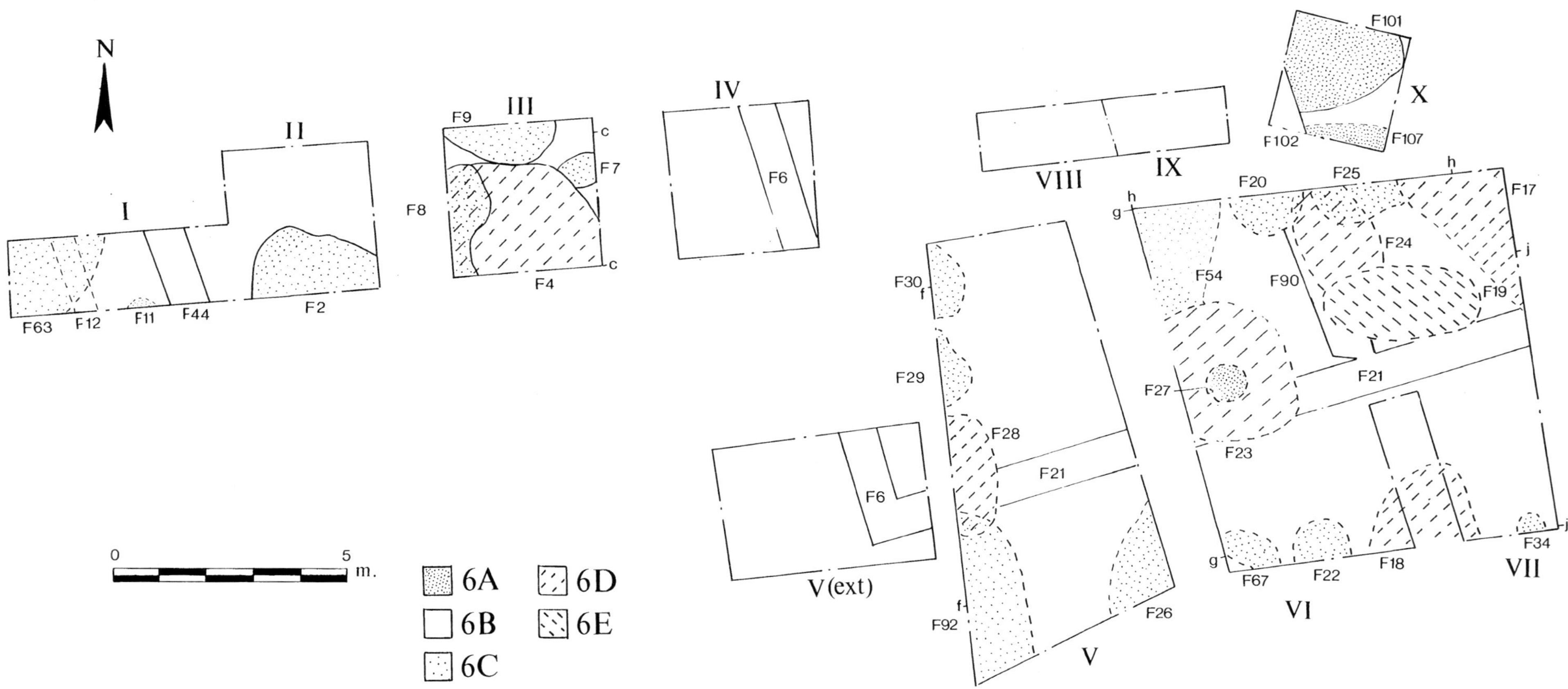

Fig. 34 Site 5, Phase 6

bances had destroyed much of the westernmost building which included two parallel beam slots (F13 and F45) 2.8m apart aligned with the north-south street. More evidence however survived for the building to the east. Beam slots with surviving heights of clay wall indicated a timber building running east-west away from the street with a minimum length of 12.5m. The wall to the east, F89, was on a slightly different alignment and may have been part of another building or a different phase of rebuilding. Three different rooms could be discerned at the front of the building divided by clay walls with painted wall plaster and mouldings between the wall and floors.

Floor levels to the south of F88 suggest that the building extended further in that direction and another wall may have been destroyed by the Phase 4A stone wall F21. Other rooms to the rear of the building included one 4.5m wide which contained two ovens or furnaces (F96, F97). Again an eastern wall to this room may have been destroyed by a Phase 4A wall (F90). The layout of this building suggests that it may have been a shop fronting on to the street with a workshop at the rear. Slags from the furnaces (F96, F97) indicate that copper working may be one of the processes undertaken in the workshop. Similar arrangements with shops fronting on to streets with workshops to the rear are well known from various Roman towns including London, Colchester and St. Albans (Perring, 1987, 150). The position of this building adjacent to a street approaching the forum would be a desirable location for a shop. A *terminus post quem* of the mid 2nd century can be suggested for the construction of this building. The Phase 3C and 3D deposits in Areas IV - VII and X may be occupation debris and traces of later floor levels (e.g. VII 7, 8). Material from these deposits suggests use of the building through the 2nd and possibly into the early 3rd century.

Phase 4 Late 2nd-3rd century

Phase 4A (Fig. 33) Late 2nd-Early 3rd century

Drains: F33 (V 24-5,42); F91 (III 19,20; V 56-7)

Two stone lined drains were located in Areas III and V. Immediately to the east of and parallel with the street F64, a channel F91 (0.25m wide x 0.20m deep) was lined by stone walls (0.25m wide) and contained a green clay fill. This was located in Areas III and V (ext.). Running at right angles to F91, a similar feature F33 was revealed in Area V containing a green clay and grey silt fill with 2nd century pottery present. The relationship between F91 and F33 and any continuation of F33 to the west had been destroyed by later disturbances.

Phase 4B (Fig. 33) Early 3rd century

Robber trenches: F6 (IV 48); F12 (I 63); F21 (V 38); F44 (I 69); F90 (VI 62); F102 (X 46)

Make-up/Floors: I 1-5; II 1-4; VII 6; IX 2,3

Six robbed wall foundation trenches were located in Areas I, IV-VII. Two of these F12 and F44 were from north-south aligned walls parallel to the western edge of the street F64. F44 immediately west of the street consisted of a square cut trench (0.85m wide x 1.0m deep) whilst 1.25m to the west was a similar feature F12 (0.70m wide x 1.10m deep). Mortar floors (I 1, II 1) overlying rubble foundation (I 2,4,5; II 4,5) can be associated with these features.

Two metres to the east of the street another north-south aligned robber trench F6 (1.2m wide x 2.3m deep) was located in Areas IV and V ext. This turned at right angles to form another robber trench, F21 (1.10m wide x 1.30m deep) running east-west through Areas V-VII. 10m to the east of F6 a robber trench on a north-south alignment, F90 (1.0m x 2.15m deep) was located in Area VI. A continuation of this feature to the north can be suggested from F102 in Area X. Part of the foundation trench to F90 survived indicating that it abutted F21 at right angles. An *opus signinum* floor (VII 6, IX 2, X 23) overlying a rubble floor foundation (IX 3) may be associated with F21 and F90. 2nd-early 3rd century pottery was present in IX 3.

Phase 4C Early 3rd century

Floor levels: I 28,44; II 12

Make-up(?): VII 4,5,46-7

New mortar floor levels with rubble foundations overlying the Phase 4B levels in Area I and II were located (I 44,28, II 12). 2nd-mid 3rd century pottery was recovered from the rubble foundations (I 28, II 12). Clay and sand deposits in Area VII (4,5,46,47) were located overlying the *opus signinum* floor. Large quantities of 2nd-early 3rd century pottery were recovered from these levels.

Discussion of Phase 4

Two stone-lined drains were inserted (Phase 4A) to the east of the street late in the 2nd or early in the 3rd centuries. From their positions F91 may have had the function of a roadside ditch and was inserted during the continued use of the Phase 3B shop and workshop. F33 however cuts the Phase 3B floor levels and therefore was inserted after the building or at least the southern part of the structure had gone out of use.

The Phase 3B building was eventually replaced by a building with stone foundations along the same alignment. This building was a minimum 7.25m long by 5.0m wide with a north-south wall, F90, which although inserted later than F6 and F21 was perhaps still part of the building's initial construction phase. To the west of the street another stone building was evident again replacing the previous timber structure. The relationship of the two walls F12 and F44 in this building is unclear; if contemporary they may have formed a corridor. Both buildings showed evidence of new floors being inserted with *opus signinum* floors initially present in the eastern building. Wall plaster in the robber trenches of these buildings suggests its presence on the walls of the building - no evidence of tessellated pavements was discovered however. This may suggest that the buildings were once again used as shops along the same lines as the 3B timber structures, and not the more palatial town houses found in Site 1 and in the Bath Lane area (Clay and Mellor, 1985, 35). Material from the floor foundations of these buildings can be dated to the mid 2nd-mid 3rd century and construction within the first half of the 3rd century can be suggested.

Phase 5 (Fig. 33) 4th century or later

Phase 5A 4th-5th century (?)

Pits: F1 (II 13,49); F93 (II 53-4)

Channel: F10 (II 17,51)

Destruction debris(?): IX 1,12-3; X 41

Dark earth (?): X 31

Three features were located cutting the street metalling (F64) in

Area II (Pl. 3). Two shallow pits, F1 (0.45m diam x 0.30m deep) and F93 (0.60m x 0.25m deep) were located to the north of the area, containing dark grey brown silty clay loam. A channel F10 (0.80m wide x 0.50m deep) on a south west-north east alignment with a similar fill was revealed to the east of the area. 3rd-4th century pottery was recovered from this feature. Spreads of red and yellow sandy rubble with mortar fragments were located in Areas IX and X. A possible "dark earth" deposit was also recorded from Area X (31).

Phase 5B 4th-5th century (?)

Channel: F5 (II 15,50)

A channel on a north west-south east alignment was located in Area II cutting the street metalling and the fill of channel F10. Late 3rd-4th century pottery and one fragment of window glass were recovered from its dark grey brown clay loam fill.

Discussion of Phase 5

Phase 5 activity on the site can be suggested as taking place in a late Roman or sub-Roman context. Rubble deposits in Areas IV, IX and X may be evidence of the Phase 4B stone building falling into disrepair and eventually out of use. The channels and pits cutting the road metalling at an angle to the street grid suggest that the town street plan was no longer being adhered to at least in this area. The "dark earth" deposit in Area X may be similar to others found in Leicester and other towns, e.g. St. Albans, London and Canterbury, which can be dated to late Roman or sub-Roman phases (e.g. Frere, 1966, 93; Macphail, 1981, 309). Material from this phase can be dated to the 3rd-4th century although this may be residual. Early Saxon pottery was recovered from Phase 6A (IV 1) and a medieval pit (Phase 6C, F25) (see p. 115) suggesting some nearby activity during this period. A similar situation with 4th and 5th century activity cutting into the Roman street levels is known from Canterbury (Frere, 1966, 93).

Phase 6 (Fig. 34) 11th-16th century

Phase 6A 11th-12th century

Well: F27 (VI 16-23, 53)
Pits: F101 (X 47-51); F107 (X 29,30,53)
Make-up: IV 1,2

A stone lined well, F27, (0.95m diam x 6.32m deep) was located in Area VI. Fills of rubble, clay and dark brown silty loam were located with organic silt towards the base of the feature. 10th-11th century pottery, Roman pottery, a vessel glass fragment and a copper alloy object were recovered from this feature. Two pits can also be assigned to this phase from Area X both having been cut by the later Phase 6B wall robbing (F102 X 32). Both F101 (*c.* 2.5m diam x 2.25m deep) and F107 (dimensions not recorded) had fills of black soil and sandy debris. Spreads of sandy rubble (IV 1,2) containing 10th-12th century pottery can be assigned to this phase of activity.

Phase 6B 12th-Early 13th century

Robber trench fill: F6 (IV 30-2); F12 (I 30-1, 42); F21 (V 17, VII 45,82-90); F44 (I 12,68); F90 (VI 61,64-71, IX 4); F24 (VI 73); F102 (X 32)

Robbing of the Phase 4B stone walls and foundations was evident. The top 0.90m of F27 had also been robbed at about the same time. Fills of light grey sandy clay, charcoal, mortar, gravel and rubble were found in the robbed out features. Finds of 12th-early 13th century pottery, Roman pottery, five Roman coins, vessel glass, iron fragments (including 38 nails), wall plaster and lead sheet were recovered from these fills. Fragments of human bone (see p. 155) were also recovered from F21 (V 17).

Phase 6C 13th century

Pits: F2 (II 14,52); F7 (III 6,17); F8 (III 7,15); F9 (III 8,16); F11 (I 29,65); F14 (IV 28,47); F20 (VI 13,54); F22 (VI 14,55); F25 (VII 34,74); F26 (V 18,43); F29 (V 20,44); F30 (V 21,23,45); F32 (VII 35,76); F34 (VII 36,72); F54 (VI 1, 5, 37, 45, 63); F63 (I 50,64); F67 (VI 46,57)

Seventeen pits were located varying in diameter from 0.55m (F67) to *c.* 3.0m (F92) and in depth between 0.25m (F54) and 1.40m (F2). The fills, where recorded, consisted of dark grey brown loose sandy loam with much charcoal, yellow sandy rubble, gravel and clay.

Finds of medieval, Saxon and Roman pottery, ten Roman coins, bone pins, vessel glass, iron and copper alloy fragments were recovered from these fills.

Phase 6D 15th-16th century

Pits: F4 (III 5,18); F17 (VII 30,58-62,79); F18 (VII 31,75); F23 (VI 15,56); F24 (VII 33,63-4,78); F28 (V 19,48)

Six pits, some cutting the Phase 6C features, were located. These varied in diameter from 1.25m (F23) to 2.75m (F28) and in depth between 0.30m (F23) and 0.8m (F4). Fills of dark brown clay loam and yellow sandy rubble were revealed in these features. Medieval and Roman pottery, five Roman coins, vessel glass, window glass, two knife blades, an iron fragment, a copper alloy trumpet brooch, a box mount and a spatula were recovered from these features.

Phase 6E 15th-16th century

Pit: F19 (VII 32,77)

A pit F19 (*c.* 1.6m x 1.2m wide) cutting F24 in Area VII was revealed containing a brown sandy loam fill.

Discussion of Phase 6

As is the case with other sites in this area, many medieval rubbish pits were revealed cutting the Roman deposits. These appear to have been inserted from the 12th-16th centuries. Robbing of the stone foundations from the Roman buildings appears to have taken place in the 12th-13th centuries as is the case for other robbing phases in the town. The human bone in F21 is probably derived from an earlier period (cf. Clay, 1985, 30). The stone lined well which can be dated to the same period went out of use perhaps two centuries later, being robbed and cut by a later medieval pit (F23). Again no medieval structures were located in this site and a 'back-yard' area can be suggested similar to that encountered in Site 2.

Unphased

Make-up: V 7, 29-37; VIII 1-10

Area V extension (to the west of V) and Area VIII were excavated rapidly in spits to ascertain wall junctions. Make-up deposits were encountered but were not described in detail. These deposits may correspond to Phases 2 and 3 in general terms but cannot be phased with any certainty. Late 1st-3rd century pottery, six Roman coins, copper alloy and iron fragments were recovered from these levels.

Site 6 Excavations at 51 Thornton Lane 1963 SK 5828 0443

Excavations were undertaken at 51, Thornton Lane, Leicester (Acc. No. A305.1963) directed by M H Hebditch for Leicester City Museums, between August and October 1963 in advance of further redevelopment. An area 6.3m x 3.35m was examined between Thornton Lane and St. Nicholas Street. Within this small area eight phases of activity could be identified. Some contamination was apparent so date ranges are tentative.

Phase 1 (Fig. 35) Late 1st century BC-Mid 1st century AD

Phase 1A Late 1st century BC

Channel: F53 (174-5)

A channel F53, (0.6m wide x 0.25m deep) with a butt end to the south-east was located cutting the natural substratum and containing a light grey sandy loam.

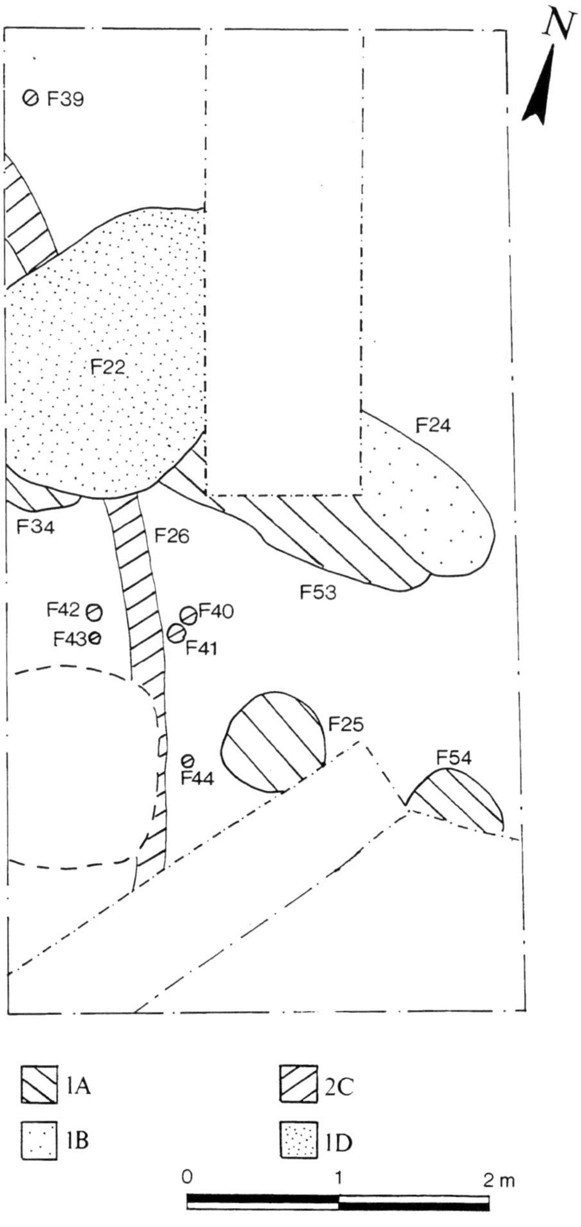

Fig. 35 Site 6, Phase1

Phase 1B Late 1st century BC

Channel recut: F24 (108-9)

Post holes: F25 (110-1); F34 (127-9); F54 (179-80)

F53 had been recut 0.15m to the north. The fill of this recut F24 (0.6m wide x 0.20m deep) consisted of much charcoal, pebbles and light grey sandy loam with several large sherds of Iron Age pottery and an intrusive glass fragment present. Post holes F25 (0.6m diam x 0.45m deep) F34 and F54 (both *c.* 0.30m diam x 0.45m deep), located to the south of F24 may be associated with this phase. F25 contained a grey sandy loam fill with large stones and red clay perhaps used as packing, while F34 and F54 also contained grey sandy loams.

Phase 1C Early 1st century AD

Wall slot: F26 (112-3)

Stake holes: F39-44 (130-5, 181-6)

A slot, F26 (0.25m wide x 0.3m deep) was located 0.4m west of F25. This contained a dark brown grey clay loam fill. A similar fill was found in six stake holes, F39-F44 (0.15m diam) which may be associated with F26.

Phase 1D Early-Mid 1st century AD

Pits: F21 (98-9); F22 (100-5)

A pit, F22 (2.25m x 2.0m x 0.65 deep) was located to the west of the site cutting F24, F26 and F34. The dark brown grey clay loam, sandy silt, red marl and charcoal fill held Iron Age pottery and a little intrusive 2nd century and medieval pottery, fragments of fired clay, copper alloy and vessel glass. Another pit, F21 was also noted (dimensions and fill not recorded). Both pits included fragments of Cam. 113 butt beakers (Fig. 65. 242-3), and early-mid 1st century pottery including single sherds of grey ware (Fig. 65. 244-5).

Discussion of Phase 1

The features in Phase 1A-1C may tentatively be interpreted as evidence for Iron Age round buildings. The channel and re-cut (F53, F24) from its shape and pottery present is possibly the butt end of an eaves drip trench while post holes F25 and F54 may have formed part of the wall structure for the building. Pottery is very often found in abundance at the terminals of eaves drip channels (cf. Clay, 1992).

A later phase can be suggested by the timber slot, F26, which may have served either as a wall slot or palisade trench. The stake holes F39-F44 may indicate repairs. As only a small area was exposed interpretations must be tentative, however the features are consistent with different phases of an Iron Age round building and are the only evidence of this type of Iron Age structure so far located in Leicester. The pottery recovered from F24 is difficult to date (see below p. 72). No imported fine wares were present as located elsewhere (see p. 69; Clay and Mellor, 1985, 30) and a late 1st century BC date or earlier may be suggested. The pottery is in the Ancaster-Breedon tradition and shows some similarities with that excavated at the Iron Age settlement at Enderby 5km (3.2 miles) to the south west (Clay, 1984-5; Clay, 1992). F22, cutting the house features, includes later Iron Age and Roman material and may date from the first half of the 1st century AD.

Phase 2 1st-Early 2nd century

Phase 2A Mid 1st century

Cobbled surface: 45,200

Occupation debris(?): 44

Overlying the Phase 1 features was a cobbled surface one course thick (45,200). Above this was a spread of dark brown fine clay loam with much charcoal (44). Early-mid 1st century pottery was recovered from this phase.

Phase 2B Late 1st century

Make-up: 42-3, 59-61

Various deposits of sand, gravel, and red clay were located (*c.* 0.20m thick) overlying the Phase 2A surface. A similar deposit to 44 above, of dark brown clay loam and charcoal was located overlying the sand, gravel and red clay layers. Mid-late 1st century pottery, iron, lead and fired clay fragments were recovered from these deposits with some later Roman and medieval intrusions.

Phase 2C Late 1st-Early 2nd century

Make-up: 37,41,58

Further deposits of sand and gravel with clay loam and charcoal layers overlying them were located. Late 1st-early 2nd century pottery (with some later Roman and medieval intrusions) was present in these deposits.

Phase 2D (Fig. 36) Late 1st - Early 2nd century

Wall foundation: F23 (106-7)

Traces of the corner of a building with stone footings were revealed to the west of the site. This feature (*c.* 1.25m wide) aligned north west-south east, turned at right angles to the north and consisted of one to three courses of irregular granite blocks (*c.* 0.25m - 0.35m long and 0.10 - 0.25m wide). Some late 1st - early 2nd century pottery was recovered from this feature.

Phase 3 Late 1st- Early 2nd century

Phase 3A Late 1st - Early 2nd century

Make-up: 28-36, 38-40

Deposits of yellow sand and gravel, light brown fine sandy loam and grey, red and yellow clay, *c.* 0.35m thick overlying the Phase 2 levels were located. A thin layer of grey clay loam with iron pan (31) was also revealed. Late 1st-early 2nd century pottery, iron fragments, vessel glass and intrusive later 2nd century and medieval pottery were recovered from this phase.

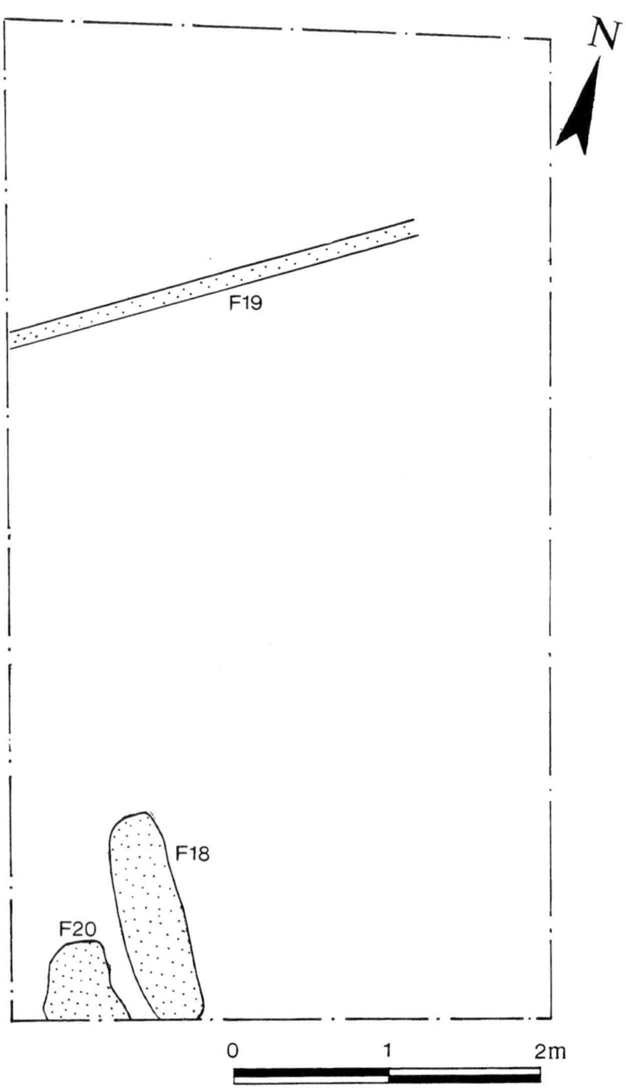

Fig. 36 Site 6, Phase 2D

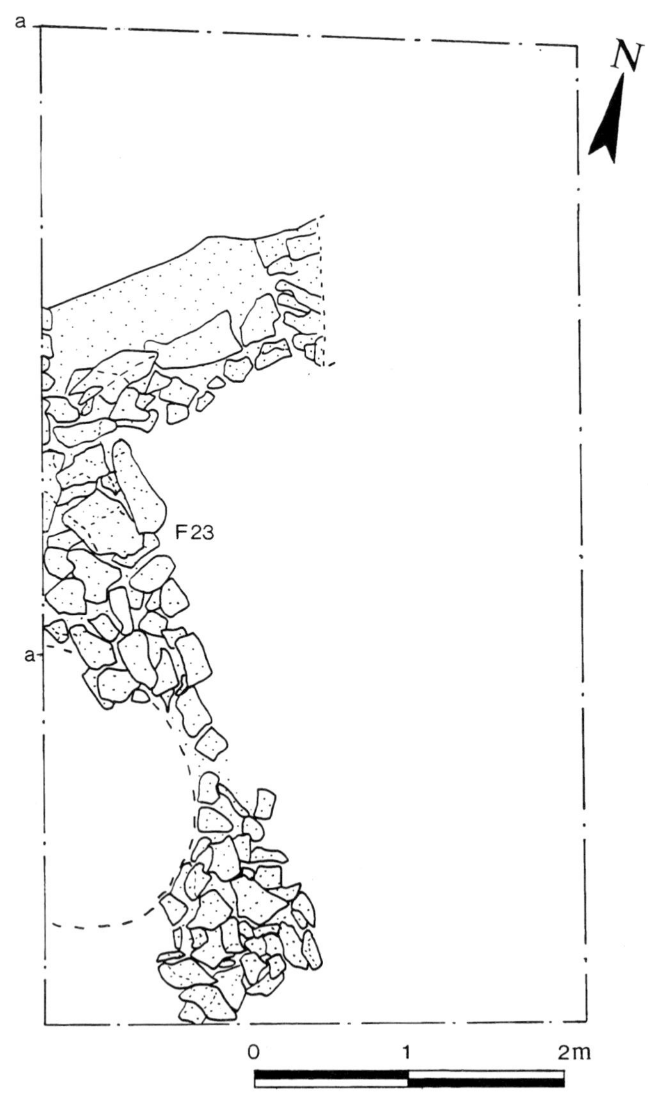

Fig. 37 Site 6, Phase 3B

Phase 3B (Fig. 37) Late 1st-Early 2nd century

Daub wall: F19 (94-5)
Hearth: F18 (92-3)
Pit: F20 (96-7)

A daub wall, F19, was located on the same east-west alignment as the north wall of F23. This consisted of a straight sided feature 0.15m wide x 0.35m deep having a blue grey core with yellow clay (*c.* 20mm thick) adhering to either side. Lattice scoring was evident on the blue grey clay to form a key for the yellow clay surface. Stake holes for wattle posts and traces of hurdling could be discerned in the grey blue clay. The feature may have been supported on a timber beam which has since rotted away.

To the south of the site a long narrow hearth F18 (0.85m x 0.30m x 0.27m deep) was located. This showed evidence of burning with reddened clay sides and contained much charcoal with some sandy loam. 0.25m to the east of this feature a pit F20 (0.50m wide) was located in the south section containing a fine sandy loam fill.

Discussion of Phases 2 and 3

Phases 2 and 3 show evidence of various levelling and make-up activities with occupation debris and two phases of building. The Phase 2A cobbled surface overlying the Phase 1 features is similar to other surfaces found in Leicester of an early post-conquest date (see above p. 2; Hebditch and Mellor, 1973, 81). Following two phases of levelling and make-up deposits a building with stone footings was inserted. The footings may have served as support for a timber wall of late 1st century date. Further make-up deposits in Phase 3A overlay these footings before another timber building (F19) on the same alignment as F23 was inserted. Evidence of a wattle and daub wall was recovered from this feature (94). A hearth F18 and a pit F20 may be associated with this building. Within the small area examined little can be said about the function of these buildings. A date in the late 1st or early 2nd century can be suggested for these activities.

Phase 4 Early-Mid 2nd century

Phase 4A Early-Mid 2nd century

Make-up: 25-7, 57

Deposits of grey and yellow clay, brown sandy loam and sandy rubble (0.90m thick) were located sealing the Phase 3B features. Late 1st-mid 2nd century pottery and fragments of vessel glass, copper alloy and iron were recovered from these deposits.

Phase 4B (Fig. 38) Early-Mid 2nd century

Pit: F13 (82-3)

Cutting the Phase 4A deposits to the south an oval pit F13, orientated north-south (*c.* 0.90m x 0.70m x 0.70m deep) was located containing sand, dark brown clay loam with iron pan, charcoal and gravel fills. Finds of late 1st-early 2nd century pottery, intrusive medieval pottery, iron, window glass, vessel glass and a glass counter were recovered from this feature.

Phase 4C Early-Mid 2nd century

Floor levels: 21-4
Make-up: 52-6, 176-7
Occupation debris(?): 51

Deposits of dark brown clay loam, yellow sand with mortar patches and orange clay were located. Dark grey silty loam with much charcoal (23,51) can be associated with these deposits which contained late 1st-mid 2nd century pottery and fragments of a head-stud brooch (p. 141 Fig 73.8), a glass bowl, a melon bead and bone working waste.

Phase 4D (Fig. 38) Early-Mid 2nd century

Pit: F17 (90-1)

A pit, F17 (dimensions not recorded) was noted cutting the Phase 4C deposits. This contained a light brown fine sandy loam with iron pan patches.

Phase 5 2nd-Early 3rd century

Phase 5A Early-Mid 2nd century

Occupation debris: 19
Make-up: 20,50

A dark brown silty clay loam deposit was located overlying grey clay and yellow sand layers (0.15m thick). Two sherds of 1st-2nd century pottery, a copper alloy spoon fragment and a square bottle sherd were recovered from these deposits.

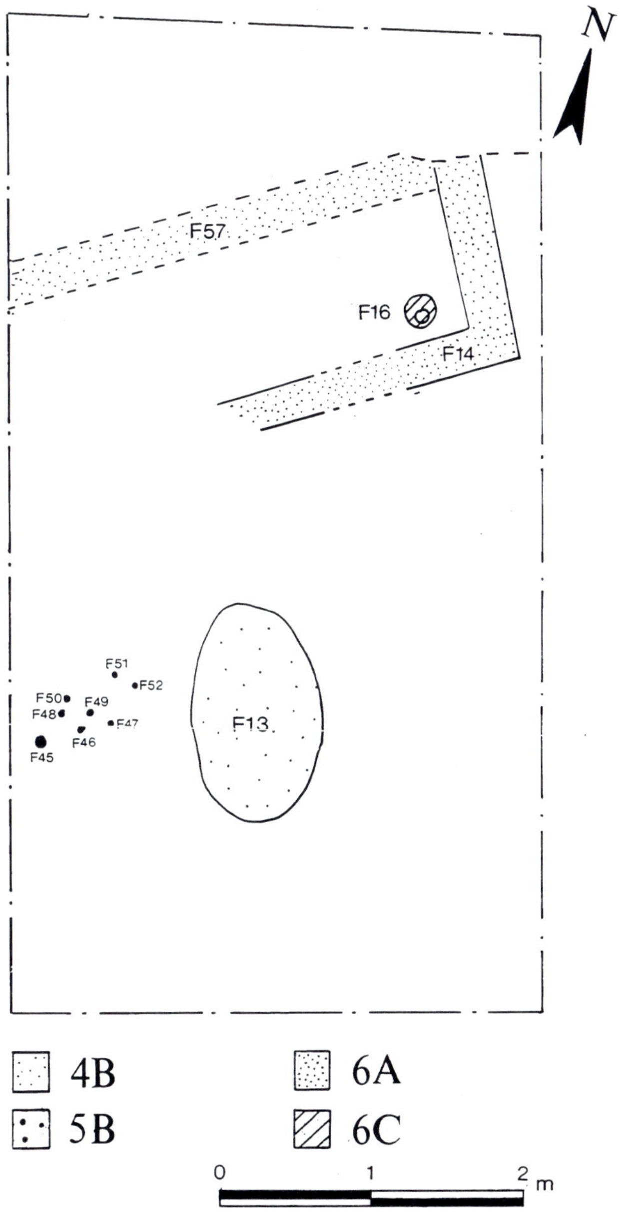

Fig. 38 Site 6, Phases 4-6

Phase 5B (Fig. 38) Early-Mid 2nd century
Stake holes: F45-52 (166-173, 188, 195)
Eight stake holes varying between 40mm (F51) and 70mm (F52) in diameter and 60mm (F51) to 0.10m (F52) in depth were located cutting the Phase 5A deposits. These contained a light brown fine sandy loam fill.

Phase 5C Mid 2nd-Early 3rd century
Occupation debris: 17
Make-up: 18,178
A grey silt deposit (17) with much iron pan was located overlying yellow sand layers 0.10m thick. These contained mid 2nd-early 3rd century pottery, window glass, a knee brooch (p. 143 Fig. 74.17), a bone pin and a bone counter.

Discussion of Phases 4 and 5

A sequence of different activities was discernible in these phases. These included the redeposition of material for possible floor levels in Phase 4C (21,54), pits being inserted in Phase 4B and 4D and the accumulation of apparent occupation debris in Phases 4C (51), 5A (19) and 5C (17). The only structural activity located was the group of stake holes in Phase 5B although no pattern to these was discernible. Material recovered from these phases suggests activity within the 2nd-early 3rd centuries.

Phase 6 (Fig. 38) Early 3rd century

Phase 6A Early 3rd century
Post setting: F16 (88-9)
A post setting F16 (0.20m in diam 0.17m deep) with a post pipe (0.11m in diam x 0.17m deep) was located to the east of the site. The post pipe contained a grey fine sandy loam with a tile and granite packing.

Phase 6B Early 3rd century
Pit: F15 (86,97)
Make-up: 15-6
Overlying F16 was a yellow sandy clay deposit 0.10m thick containing one sherd of vessel glass. A pit F15 (fill and dimensions not recorded) was noted in the north section of the site. A dark grey silty loam (15) was also located overlying F16 containing mid 2nd-early 3rd century pottery, iron, fragments of a square bottle and fired clay.

Phase 6C Early 3rd century
Beam slots: F14 (84-5); F57 (201-2)
A beam slot F14 (0.32m wide x 0.15m deep) cutting the Phase 6B deposit was located on an east-west alignment. To the east of the site this feature turned through 90° to continue north-south. Fragments of lead and a copper alloy spoon were recovered from the fill of F14. Another beam slot, F57, 1.0m north of F14 was located in the west section.

Phase 7 Early 3rd-4th century

Phase 7A Early 3rd century
Make-up: 9-14
Deposits 0.20m thick of sand and gravel, clay and grey silt were located, covering most of the site, containing 1st-early 3rd century pottery, iron and lead fragments and vessel glass.

Phase 7B (Fig. 39) Early 3rd century
Beam slots: F11 (78-9); F27-F33 (48-9,116-22)
Stake holes: F35-F38 (123-6,196-9)
A beam slot, F11, (0.40m wide x 0.20m deep) on an east-west alignment was located to the north of the site. This contained a grey sandy loam from which one sherd of vessel glass was recovered, with, at its eastern extent, a large stone 0.40m square. Along the southern edge of F11 the remains of plaster fillets (1.3m long) were located. Seven narrow timber slots, F27-31 (0.35m long x 0.12m wide x 0.10m deep) were located on a north-south alignment 0.70m apart at right angles to F11. Two narrow slots F32 and F33 (0.10m wide x 0.10m deep) were located between F29 and F30, 0.28m apart and parallel with F11.

The slots contained grey sandy loam with much iron pan and some voids (48). Six sherds of late 2nd century pottery, vessel glass, and twenty one nails were recovered from this fill.

Four stake holes F35-F38 (0.10m diam x 0.15m deep) were located running parallel to F11. These were situated 1.45m south of F11 and 0.50m apart and contained a light grey brown sandy loam fill.

Phase 7C Early 3rd century
Cobbled surface: 6
Foundations: 7,8
A cobbled surface with pebble and red clay foundations was found overlying the timber slots and stake holes to the south of F11. A very little 2nd century pottery, iron nails and a mid 2nd century coin were recovered from this phase.

Phase 7D (Fig. 39) Early 3rd century
Robber trench: F12 (81)
Floor level(?): 46
Make-up: 5
Occupation debris(?): 47
A robber trench on an east-west alignment to the north and at a 30° angle to F11 was located. Deposits of sandy loam, mortar patches and grey silt loam may be associated with this phase.

Phase 7E 4th Century
Make-up: 1-4
Further deposits of sandy loam and clay were overlain by a silt deposit with much iron pan. Pottery of 2nd-3rd or 4th century date, vessel glass, iron and copper alloy fragments were present in these levels.

Discussion of Phases 6 and 7

Some building activity was evident in Phases 6A and 6C. This consisted of one post hole and two beam slots respectively. Other activity included the insertion of a pit and the accumulation of occupation debris in Phase 6B. Clearer evidence of building activity was present in Phase 7. Following levelling and make-up (Phase 7A) a timber walled building was erected including a timber floor. This was supported on floor joists which were indicated by slots F27-F33 (Pl. 5). The timber floor had later been replaced by a cobbled surface with clay and pebble foundations (Phase 7C). A similar building with evidence of floor joists was found on Site 5 Phase 2A (see p. 26). A stone building on a slightly different alignment appears to have superseded this structure (Phase 7D F12). Patches of mortar (46) may be part of a floor associated with this building. Possible occupation debris (47) was located overlying this. Similar material was present (1,2) overlying a clay deposit which again may have served as a floor (Phase 7E).

Building activity in Phases 6 and 7 appears to have taken place within the first half of the 3rd century with occupation debris in Phase 7E suggesting use into the 4th century. Again within the small area examined the buildings' functions are unclear.

Phase 8 11th-16th century

Phase 8A (Fig. 40) 11th-13th century

Pits: F6 (68-9); F10 (76-7)
Robber trench fill: F12 (80)

Two pits were located to the centre (F6) and to the east (F10) of the site (dimensions not recorded). These contained a "black soil" with early medieval pottery.

The robbing of the Phase 7D stone building may also be associated with this phase. Loose black soil and rubble with some early medieval pottery, an iron blade and a stone moulding are recorded from this feature.

Phase 8B (Fig. 40) 16th century

Pit: F2 (64-5)

A large pit F2, cutting F6 (minimum length 2.50m x 1.30m) was located to the west of the site. The depth and fill of this feature are not recorded although an iron knife blade was recovered.

Phase 8C 16th century

Pit: F9 (74-5,161,164)

A straight sided pit (minimum length 2.25m x 1.50m) was located to the south of the site cutting F2 and F6 and cut by F3, F7 and F8. The depth and fill of this feature are not recorded.

Phase 8D (Fig. 40) 16th century

Wells: F3 (66-7,114,151-60); F8 (72-3,115, 136-50)

A well, F8 (minimum diameter *c.* 2.5m) was located in the south-west corner of the site cutting F2 and F9 and cut by F7. This contained a light brown clay, red clay, yellow sand and grey silt fill with a dark stain around the edges perhaps indicating the presence of a wood lining. Another well, F3 (minimum diameter *c.* 2.5m) was located to the east of the site. This again showed traces of a

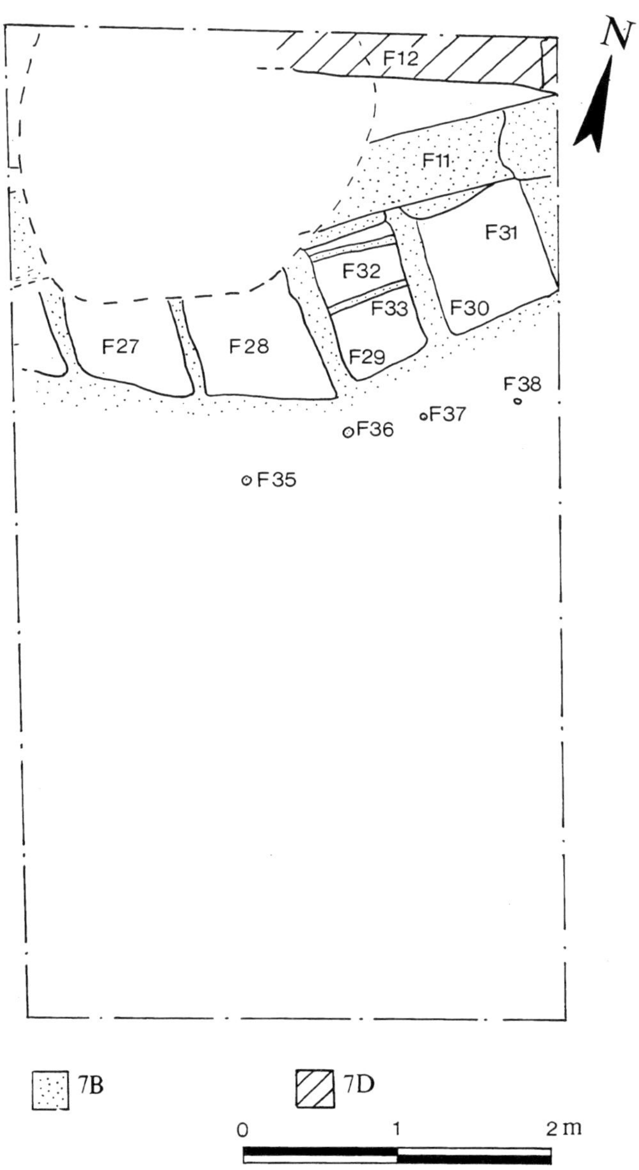

Fig. 39 Site 6, Phase 7

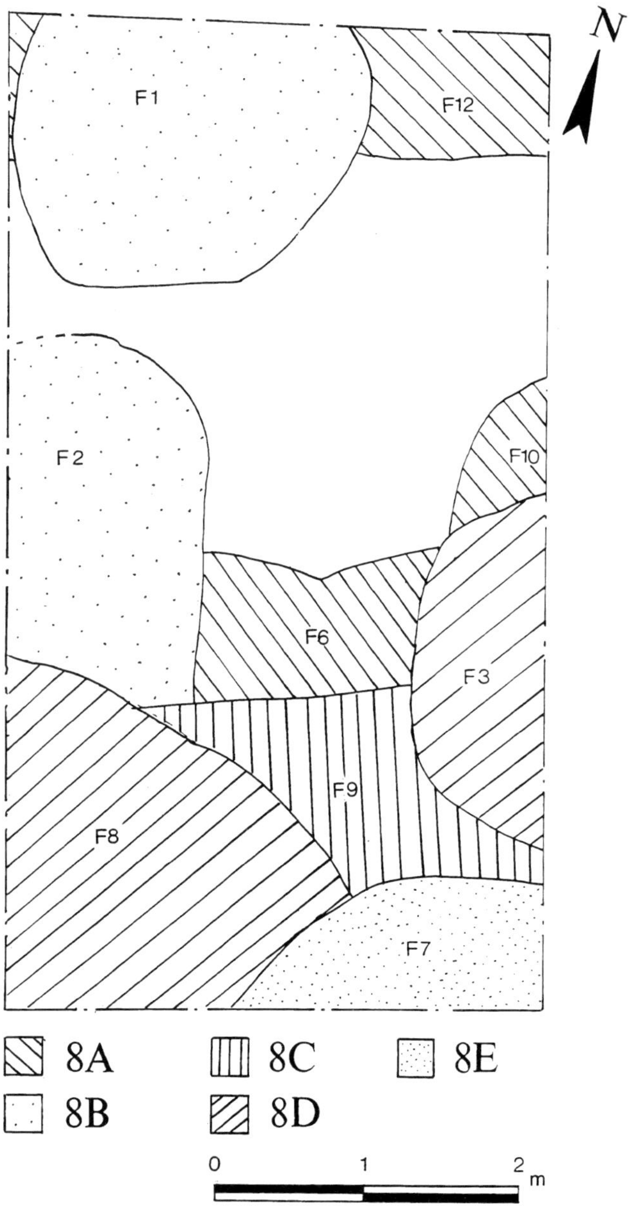

Fig. 40 Site 6, Phases 8

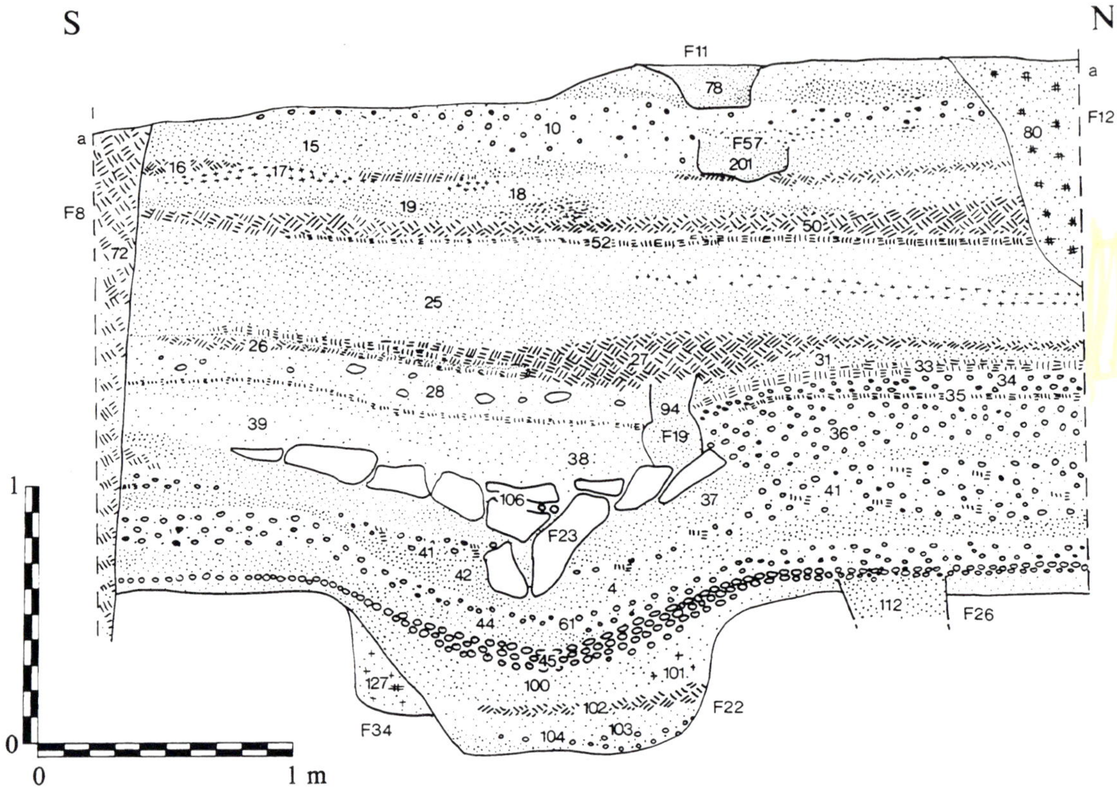

Fig. 41 Site 6 Section a-a

wood lining *c.* 50mm thick surrounding a fill of light brown clay. Late medieval pottery, iron and copper alloy fragments were recovered from these features which were not completely excavated.

Phase 8E (Fig. 40) 16th century

Pits: F1 (62-3); F7 (70-1); 187

To the south-east of the site a pit (F7) cutting F8 and F9 was located (fill and dimensions not recorded). To the north-west a circular pit F1 (2.3m x 1.6m x 1.0m deep) contained a dark grey clay loam fill with much charcoal. (Context 187 contains material from F7 and F8 excavated as one feature). Medieval pottery and iron fragments were recovered from these features.

Discussion of Phase 8

Again pits are the dominant feature of the medieval-post medieval periods in this area. Of interest however are the two wood lined wells contrasting with the stone lined well found on Site 5. Material from these features suggests a date of *c.* 1000-1250 for Phase 8A and *c.* 1500-1600 for Phases 8B-8E.

Site 7 Excavations at 28 Thornton Lane 1963 SK 5836 0443

Two areas were opened at 28 Thornton Lane by M H Hebditch for Leicester City Museums in advance of building development between August and September 1963 (Acc. No. A306.1963). The areas were both 3m x 2.6m, 1.3m apart on a north-south alignment.

Phase 1

Cobbled surface: 6

A cobbled surface was located in Area 1.

Phase 2

Walls: F2 (8); F3 (9)

Pit: F4 (10)

Two stone walls *c.* 0.7m wide were located resting on the Phase 1 cobbled surface. F2 was aligned east-west with F3 forming a turn north-south located in the east section. The walls were constructed of granite and limestone with no evidence of mortaring. To the south of Area 1 a pit (F4) was located cutting the cobbled surface.

Phase 3

Wall: F1 (7)

Cobbled surface: 3

Make-up: 4,5

Deposits of brown and red clay were located in Area 1. Overlying these was a later east-west aligned wall *c.* 0.75m wide with an offset, located to the north of F2 and F3. This was constructed of irregular granite blocks up to 0.25m square. The offset to the south side only was one course deep. A cobbled surface (2) located also in Area II may be associated with this wall.

Phase 4

Make-up: 1,2

Floor: 11

Later activity included the laying of a brick and stone floor (11) with associated clay and loam deposits (1,2).

Discussion

The cobbled surface (6) located on this site is the east-west aligned street previously located on Site 2 and south of the forum (p. 15; Hebditch and Mellor, 1973, Fig. 2). No further evidence of Roman activity was located and the street was not excavated. Medieval activity was evident from the walls and pit encountered in Phases 2 and 3. The insubstantial nature of the walls F2 and F3 may mean they were not used for a building but may have formed a property boundary.

Site 8 Watching Brief at Castle Street 1970 (Townhouses) SK 5826 0428

In June 1970 a watching brief was conducted during the construction of new town houses on the west side of Castle Street by Elizabeth Blank for Leicester City Museums (McWhirr, 1971-2, 63; Acc. No. A124.1970). Nine trenches (I-IX) 6m x 1m and 4.6m apart were observed on E-W alignments whilst two (X and XI) (2m x 1m and 3m x 2m) were opened to the north of those trenches. Within the constraints imposed by a limited watching brief a sequence of four main phases of activity could be discerned. The medieval phases and material will be considered in Buckley, forthcoming.

Phase 1

Phase 1A

Make-up: 25

The earliest evidence of activity on this site was a disturbed substratum horizon of fine sandy loam.

Phase 1B

Stake holes: F4-F7 (21-4,60-3)
Pits: F3 (26-33,59); F11 (43,67); F12 (44,68)

Four stake holes F4-F7 (*c.* 15mm diameter x 25mm deep) were observed in Trench II on an east-west alignment having fills of light brown fine sandy loam. A pit, F3, (*c.* 1.5m wide with a surviving depth of 0.6m) can also be associated with this phase. The dark brown fine sandy loam, charcoal and pebble fills in this feature contained a little 1st century pottery. Two other pits were noted in Trench IX, F11 and F12 (both *c.* 1.5m wide x 0.60m deep) with grey clay fills.

Phase 2

Make-up: 15,34-5,40-2

Light brown fine sandy loam with some charcoal, grey clay, sand and gravel deposits were located overlying the Phase 1 features in Trenches II and IX.

Phase 3

Phase 3A

Pits: F2 (12-4,16-20,58); F13 (70,75)

A pit, F2, (1.5m diameter x 1.6m deep) was located in Trench II cutting F3 and containing fills of grey clay, charcoal, sand and gravel. Another pit, F13, observed in Area VI can be assigned to this phase.

Phase 3B

Pit/ditch: F8 (4-11,47-8,64)

Part of a large pit or ditch F8 (minimum width 3.2m x 1.0m deep) was located in Area II cutting F2 and F3. This contained orange sand, grey clay, charcoal, pebble and mortar rubble with some 1st-2nd century pottery present.

Phase 3C

Ditch: F9 (45,49-57,65)

A ditch, F9 (*c.* 4m wide x 1.75m deep) was located in Areas IX, X and XI on a north-south alignment with a turn to the east at its southern extent. This contained fills of orange gravel, sand, grey clay and charcoal. Material dating from the 1st-4th century was recovered from this feature, including a quern fragment (p. 150 Fig. 78.77).

Phase 4

Phase 4A

Make-up: 3,69,71,73-4

Deposits of orange sand and grey sandy loam were located in Trenches II, VI, VII and VIII containing Roman and medieval pottery including one sherd of Cistercian ware.

Phase 4B

Cobbled surfaces: F1 (2)

Sand and gravel deposits (0.40m thick) with cobbled surfaces were located in Trenches II, VI, VII and VIII, overlying the Phase 4A deposits.

Phase 4C

Oven: F10 (36-9,66)

A stone lined oven was located in Trench IX containing deposits of clay, charcoal and ash.

Discussion

Within the limitations of the area examined little can be said about this site. Mid-late 1st century activity is again suggested from the Phase 1 features. Further levelling in Phase 2 probably took place early in the 2nd century whilst the Phase 3 pits can also be loosely associated with 2nd century activity. The large ditch, (Phase 3C F9) contains 1st-4th century pottery but may be a post-Roman feature. Phase 4 shows evidence of medieval activity including a cobbled road on a north-south alignment which, from the evidence of the sherd of Cistercian ware, may have been laid after 1450. The position of this road suggests it may be the medieval street known as the Hollow, and not as previously reported, a Roman street (McWhirr, 1971-2, 63). The oven, F10, of unknown use may be evidence of late medieval or early post-medieval activity.

Site 9 Watching Brief at Everards Brewery, Castle Street 1966 SK 5833 0426

A watching brief was undertaken during reconstruction work at Everards Brewery, Castle Street in January 1966 by J A Danniel for Leicester City Museums (Acc. No. A622.1966). A 2.6m deep section was exposed and examined. This showed evidence of pits, cutting the natural clay substratum, which contained early-mid 1st century material including a Claudian copy coin. Other pits contained 2nd century material with, of note, a copper alloy miniature axe and Triton's Trumpet shell. Medieval activity was represented by further pits and a large ditch (*c.* 5m deep x 4m wide) on an east-west alignment. At the north end of this feature its fill included a solid mortared foundation (2.6m long x 1.0 wide and 2.6m deep). From this limited information some early-mid 1st century activity is again suggested. The presence of a miniature axe may be evidence of a temple or shrine in the area (see below p. 147) whereas the medieval activity may be associated with Leicester Castle (see Buckley, forthcoming)).

Site 10 Watching Brief at St Nicholas Circle 1971 SK 5833 0435

During the building work for a new petrol station, on the south side of St Nicholas Circle, in September 1971 a watching brief was undertaken by Jean E Mellor for Leicester City Museums (Acc. Nos. A471.1971, A476.1971). In examining a trench, 23m x 5.6m, evidence of street metalling and road silts was encountered on a north-south alignment. Below this, grey silt overlying the natural substratum contained 1st century pottery. A sherd of Nottingham ware face jug was also present in a pit cutting the Roman deposits.

The road metalling encountered during this work probably represents the north-south aligned street also encountered on Site 5.

Site 11 Excavations in Newarke Houses Gardens 1939 SK 5833 0413

A re-examination was undertaken of the records and material from the trial excavations in Newarke Houses gardens conducted by Mr F Cottrill in 1939 (Acc. Nos. 20.1939; 253.1951; Clarke 1952, 25). This suggests that the earlier ditch (*c.* 2.6m wide x 1.0m deep) on a north west-south east alignment disturbed by the medieval castle ditch, contained some pottery of late Iron Age date (*ibid.* Fig. 4 and Fig. 6.1). Parallel and to the south of this ditch were four stake holes (*c.* 15mm in diameter) which were probably contemporary. Much residual Roman material was also recovered.

Although, in view of the later disturbances, this evidence is inconclusive it does suggest pre-Roman activity 200m to the south of that so far encountered in Leicester (see Fig. 1).

The size of the ditch may suggest it had some demarcatory function, perhaps in part defensive. If this interpretation is correct it is the only evidence for any pre-Roman perimeter ditch so far discovered in Leicester and may be part of a southern boundary to the late Iron Age settlement.

Site 12 Excavations at Applegate Street, 1964 SK 5837 0435

A small scale excavation was undertaken at Applegate Street (Acc. No. A366.1964) in 1964 directed by M H Hebditch and M D Card. The records of this work are incomplete but indicate a stone lined drain and several phases of road metalling cut by later medieval pits. Roman and medieval pottery, bone, glass, copper alloy objects and a Roman coin were recovered from this excavation. The road metalling formed part of the east-west road encountered on Site 2 (Phase 4A F1).

Discussion

In assessing the importance of these sites it must be remembered that most can only provide a limited indication of the nature of the occupation owing to the restricted areas examined. In view of this it is proposed to isolate various elements found on these sites which may be of significance within the development of Iron Age and Roman Leicester rather than comparing the sites' chronological development. It is not proposed to duplicate previous assessments of Leicester's early development (eg Clay and Mellor, 1985; Mellor, 1985) but to offer amplification or alternatives where this may be possible.

1. Timber Buildings (and associated features)

Structural elements were encountered in isolated and fragmentary form with no complete plan of a building being recovered. Different types of building however could be identified.

The earliest structure located in these excavations is a putative Iron Age round house partially exposed in Site 6 (Phase 1A above p. 37). This is the only evidence for a possible Iron Age circular building so far identified in Leicester and the material associated with it may suggest occupation from the 1st century BC.

Other evidence of possible Iron Age occupation includes pits and gullies from Sites 1, 2, 4, 6, 9 and 11 with a range of material similar to that encountered in the Bath Lane area (Clay and Mellor, 1985) including two Corieltauvian coins (see below p. 131). One of the pits from Site 2 (Phase 1B, F26) may, from its shape, have been originally used as a storage pit (see also Clay and Mellor, 1985, 18 Fig. 15, F28 and F29).

From an examination of the Iron Age pottery recovered from Leicester, three possible groups may be discerned (see below p. 72). The earliest of these consists of the material from Site 6 Phases 1A and 1B which comprises native wares of Ancaster-Breedon tradition with a starting date within the 1st century BC (or possibly earlier). A second group, consisting of native wares with a few "Gallo-Belgic" imports including Site 6 Phase 1D, Site 11 and pit 8 from the Jewry Wall Site (Kenyon, 1948; Jarvis, 1986), may be dated to the late 1st century BC - early 1st century AD. Material from the last few decades before the conquest until *c.* AD 70 makes up the third group. This includes more types of "Gallo-Belgic" import with some early Roman wares and is represented on Sites 1-4, 8-9 and on the Bath Lane group of sites (Clamp, 1985). In addition 20% of the brooches recovered from these sites (below p. 139) are of pre-conquest date. This appears to confirm that a settlement at Leicester (*c.* 10 ha in area) originating in the 1st century BC was developing contacts with the Roman world by the last few decades before the Roman conquest (Clay, 1985). Imported Iron Age pottery (Jarvis, 1986, Clamp, 1985, 41) and possible evidence of coin manufacture (Clay, 1985, 30) is consistent with Leicester being an important tribal centre. (*ibid.* 31).

The next phase of timber buildings consists of isolated linear beam slots of pre-Flavian date located on Sites 1, 2, 3 and 4. Although some pre-conquest examples exist in

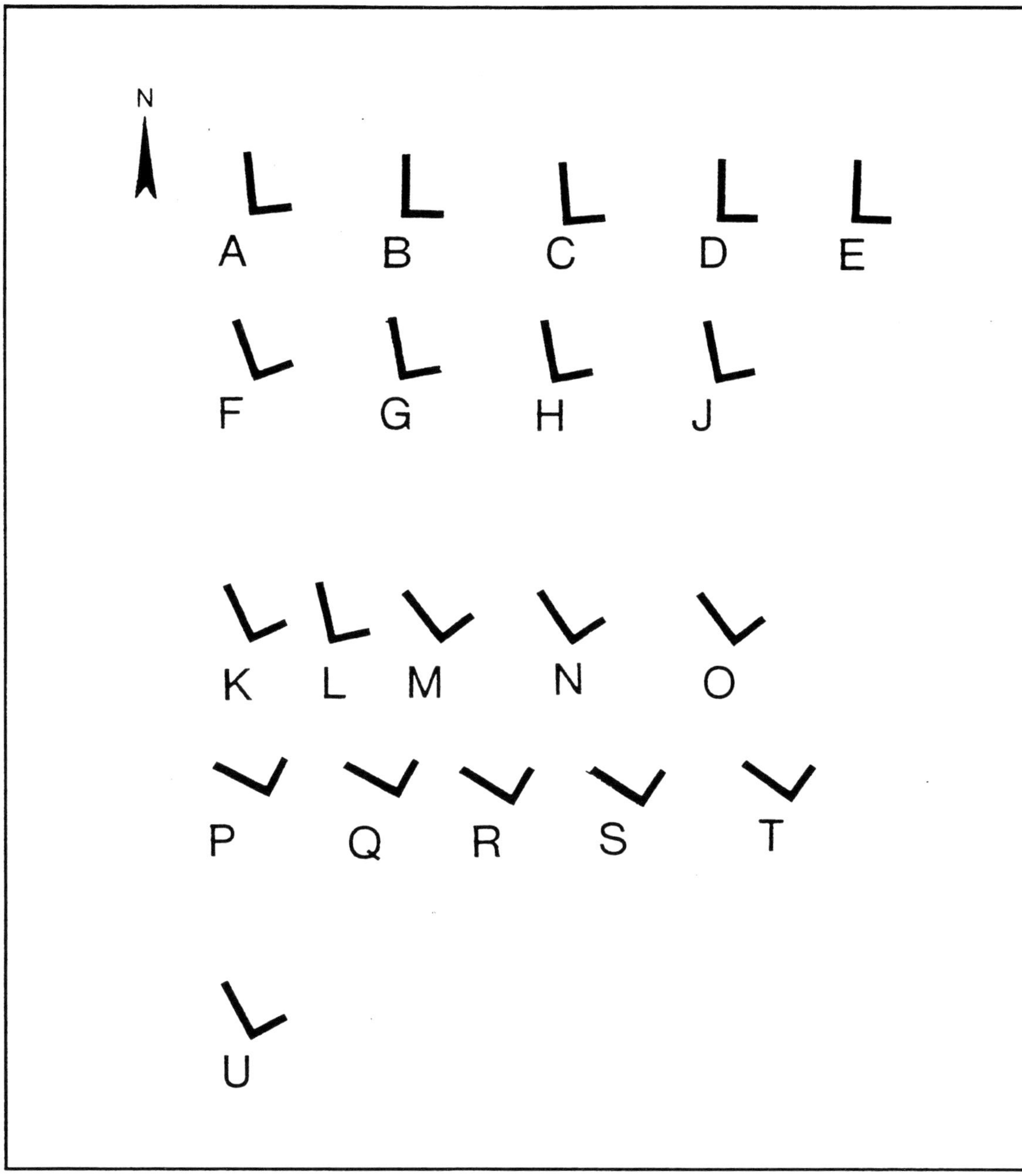

Fig 42 Alignments of 1st century AD timber buildings in Leicester

1.	Pre-Flavian		
A	Site 1	Phase 1B	F138 And F139
B	Site 2	Phase 1B	F52
C	Site 4	Phase 1A and 1B	F9-11, F27, F29, F49, F31
D	Site 4	Phase 1A	F8, F28, F32
E	Site 4	Phase 3B	62 (Clay & Mellor, 1985, 6)
F	Site 2	Phase 1B	F54, F91
G	Site 3	Phase 1C	F7
H	Bath Lane		
	Site 1	Phase 3D	31, 37 (Clay & Mellor, 1985, 6)
J	Jewry Wall		
	Site	Building SEI (Kenyon, 1948,11)	
2.	Flavian		
K	Site 1	Phase 2C	F135, F106
L	Site 1	Phase 3A	F22
M	Site 1	Phase 3A	F102
N	Site 5	Phase 2	F13, F59-61
O	Site 6	Phase 2D+3B	F19, F23
P	Site 2	Phase 2	F23, F24
Q	Site 4	Phase 2	F20, F40, F41'
R	Bath Lane		
	Site 1	Phase 3E	27, 46 (Clay & Mellor, 1985,6)
S	Bath Lane		
	Site 2	Phase 4A	F11,F56, F58 (Clay & Mellor, 1985,19)
T	Jewry Wall		
	Site	Building SEII (Kenyon, 1948,11)	
3.	2nd century- 4th century		
U	Street Grid		

the south east (Rodwell, 1979, 32) this method of construction has been traditionally regarded as an introduction by the Roman army. However identifying military elements in early domestic styles of building is probably not possible (Perring, 1987, 149). Pre-Flavian activity also includes cobbled surfaces located on Sites 1, 5 and 6 and noted elsewhere in Leicester (Hebditch and Mellor, 1973, 7). One approach in trying to understand the development of these timber buildings in Leicester is by examining their alignments (Fig. 42. A-K). Two different alignments within the pre-Flavian period appear to have been used (A-E and F-J) perhaps suggesting different phases of construction. While acknowledging the paucity of information available these building phases may indicate a uniformity of alignment over a wide area (*c.* 20 ha) along the east bank of the Soar within the central area of the later Roman town. This uniformity has more in common, perhaps, with buildings within a fort than with a native settlement or vicus. Leicester has long been considered a possible location for a fort, possibly for Legio XIV during the Plautian campaigns (Webster, 1980, 125-7; Mellor, 1985). A fort might be expected to be situated close to an existing tribal centre thereby maintaining control by utilising the existing social structure (Millett, 1984). It is feasible that these timber structures of the early post-conquest period were part of such an establishment although the lack of other structural and artefactual evidence from Leicester precludes any definite conclusions.

Stronger evidence of activity with a military connection is present on Site 3 (F3) and the possibility of a fortlet commanding the river crossing to the west of the town is outlined above (p. 21). Further work in the area is required to test this theory.

Timber buildings are also present on Sites 1, 2, 4, 5 and 6 dating from the Flavian period and reflecting the growth of the town at this time. The alignments of these buildings differ from those of the pre-Flavian period. This might suggest that neither the plan nor the buildings of the pre-Flavian occupation, be they military or civilian, were utilised in the early development of the town as has been suggested for other Roman towns for example Colchester, Lincoln, Gloucester, Exeter or Wroxeter (Crummy, 1982). Three phases of development might be suggested from the building alignments datable to the Flavian period. This might suggest a relatively slow development (Walthew, 1974, 194) with different building phases still not adhering to a strict town plan. Although increased Romanisation is evident from the artefactual evidence (e.g. wall plaster and use of *opus signinum*) there does not appear to have been a coherent response to Agricola's encouragement to develop a Romanised town (Tacitus 21). Whether Leicester had been formally created the *civitas* capital at this time might, from the evidence so far recovered, be doubtful. There is no evidence of public buildings before the end of the 1st century although timber phases such as those identified at Silchester (Frere, 1984 (a), 311 Fig. 31) may not have been recognised within the small areas examined. The more typical form of building appears to be a shop with work areas for example Sites 1 (F60) and 6 (F18).

The next major building phase occurs *c.* 125-150 following the establishment of the street grid and concurrent with the provision of public buildings. Timber buildings of this period are present on Sites 1 and 5, the latter showing the clearest evidence as to function from any of the buildings recorded on these sites. Here a shop fronting onto a north-south aligned street with a workshop containing hearths to the rear was located. This street led north towards the forum and it would be safe to suggest that this was within the commercial heart of the town. Evidence of an extension to the rear of this building was apparent (Site 5 Phase 3B F89). This is a regular occurrence due to the limited space along the fronts (Wacher, 1975, 64). Residential quarters were usually in the upper storeys with the business area below (*ibid.* 63). New floors were added to this building later in the 2nd century which continued in use until replaced by a stone building in the first half of the 3rd century. Similar sequences with shops being rebuilt in stone on a piecemeal basis are known from other towns, for example Cirencester (*ibid.*). Evidence from Site 6 Phase 7B suggests that timber buildings were being constructed as late as the 3rd century.

2. *Stone Buildings*

The walls of the stone buildings from these sites had been robbed and consequently the date of these structures was uncertain. Although described as stone buildings it should be remembered that stone foundations often had timber superstructures. Stone footings for a timber structure are evident from Site 6 (Phase 2D F23). The earliest stone foundations however are from Site 2 (Phase 3 F49) of late 1st - early 2nd century date. Although this building adhered to the street grid it appears to have been robbed early in its life as the robbing was sealed by later road metalling phases.

The most complete evidence for a stone building is from Site 1 where a substantial building was constructed *c.* 140-160 with a high quality mosaic pavement perhaps added slightly later (see p. 11). Although only part of this building was exposed its extent is suggested by adjacent tessellated pavements recorded earlier. Both the Peacock and Blackfriars pavements (Smith, 1985, 38) are amongst the finest mosaic floors known in Britain and might reflect the importance and wealth of the respective owners. Together with the courtyard house from Blue Boar Lane (Wacher, 1975, 348) these buildings were probably town houses although the possibility of one or two of them serving as *mansios* should not be overlooked. The mid 2nd century emergence of these substantial town houses is a phenomenon noted elsewhere. They may have developed from villas with this movement into towns perhaps reflecting a need for security or the increased prestige of town life at this time (Walthew, 1975, 196). Of note is the apparent long life of the Site 1 building with mosaics added perhaps late in the 4th century (p. 50). Evidence for other stone build-

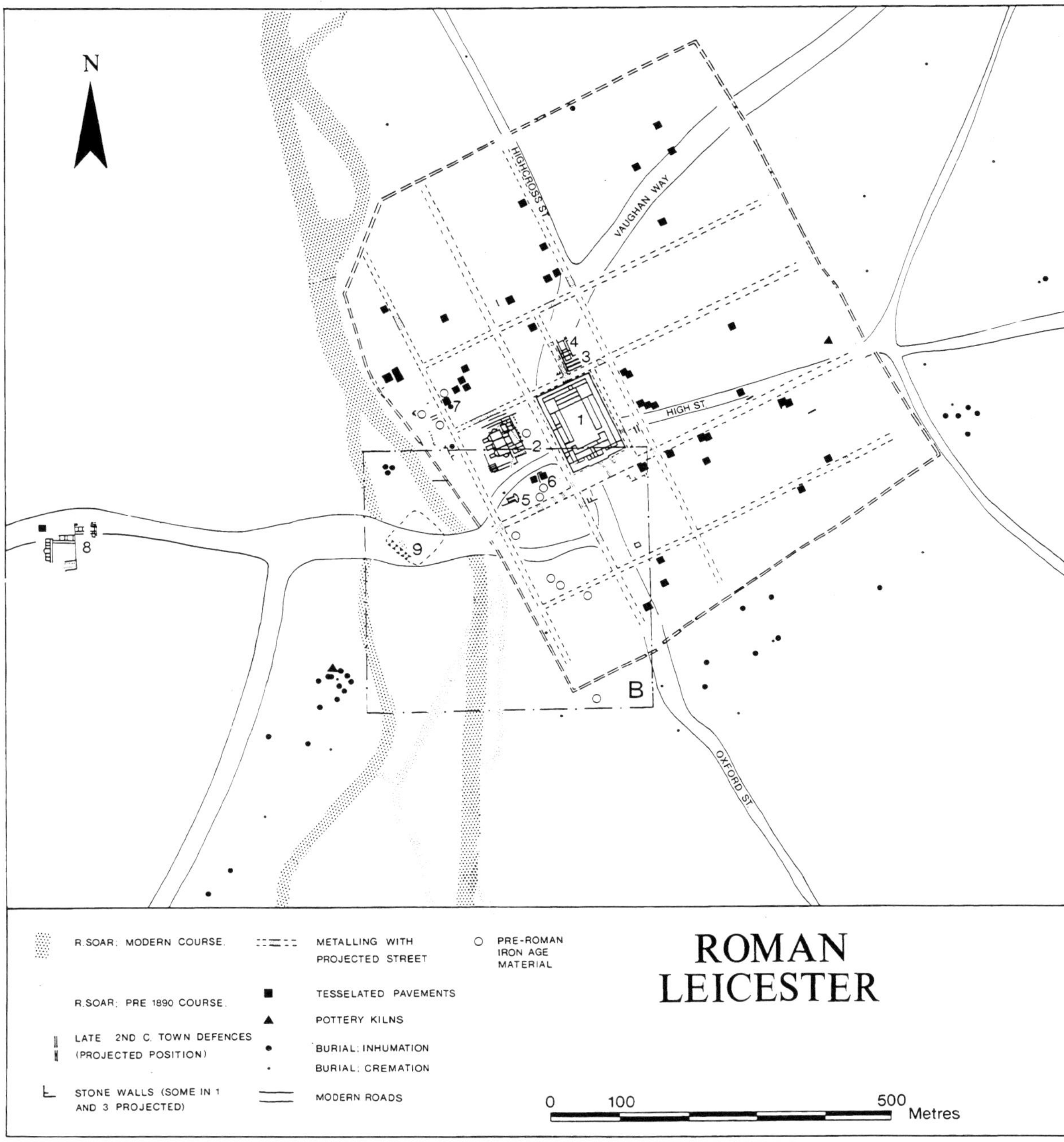

Fig. 43 Roman Leicester showing area of sites discussed (B Fig. 1). 1 Forum; 2 Jewry Wall Baths; 3 Macellum; 4 Blue Boar Lane Town House; 5 Temple (Mithraeum?); 6 Site 1; 7 Blackfriars Mosaic; 8 Norfolk Street Villa; 9 Site 3.

ings is present on Sites 2, 3, 5 and 6. The building in Site 3 was located to the west of the street metalling adjacent to the west gate. Extra-mural buildings along approach roads are known from other towns (Esmonde-Cleary, 1985, 74) and a similarly positioned building has been located to the west of the road approaching the north gate of Leicester (Buckley and Lucas, 1987, 49). On Site 5 the stone building replaced the timber shop early in the 3rd century although the building probably retained the same function. A similar situation could be identified on Site 6 where the early 3rd century timber building was replaced later in the century with one of stone.

3. The Street Grid

Evidence of metalled streets was encountered on Sites 2, 3, 5, 7 and 12. Material recovered from these features and associated roadside ditches (Sites 2, 3 and 5) suggests use from the first quarter of the 2nd century. Material sealed below the earliest metalling (Site 2) can be dated to the early 2nd century perhaps as late as 120. Construction of the street grid within the same phase of building as the public buildings might be suggested. No evidence of earlier roads was located and the function of the supposed early street metalling at the Jewry Wall site (Kenyon, 1948, 10) might be questioned. The first half of the 2nd century sees the imposition of a street grid, construction of public buildings and increasing use of stone reflecting a rapid increase in Romanisation perhaps following the town's official appointment as a *civitas* capital.

All the streets show considerable evidence of re-metalling, later surfaces indicating a rise in the street level of, in places, 0.5m. This rising street level is noted from many Roman towns necessitating the insertion of new floors to prevent a sharp drop from street to floor level. Make-up deposits pre-dating the street grid are also noted from all these sites and this may have been an attempt to create level raised surfaces on which to place the timber buildings to facilitate drainage. Terracing may have been necessary to counteract the slope west towards the river which may have affected Sites 2, 4, 9 and 10 (Lucas, 1980-1, 6; Clay and Mellor, 1985, 29). Possible roadside ditches were located on Sites 2, 3 and 5, the latter constructed with a stone lining. Material from the extra-mural ditch in Site 3 (F25) indicates its use into the 4th century. Site 5 shows evidence of the eventual abandonment of the street system at least in that area. Here channels and pits were located cut into the final road surface perhaps indicating sub-Roman activity. Material from these features suggests that this was taking place as early as the 4th century although rebuilding within the Site 1 town house was being undertaken at about the same time. Evidence from other areas of the town may also indicate the end of civic control in the town late in the 4th century. By this time the forum, basilica and market hall had been damaged by fire and not rebuilt (Wacher, 1975, 357). The "dark earth" deposits often found in sub-Roman contexts in various towns, for example Verulamium, Canterbury and London (Frere, 1966, 63; Macphail, 1981) may have been present in Site 5 and are known from the south-eastern area of the forum (Mellor, forthcoming (a)).

Synthesis

These excavations have provided further evidence for the development of an urban settlement at Leicester. Its origins appear to date from the mid 1st century BC as an Iron Age settlement. This was to develop in importance in the last few decades before the Roman Conquest with increasing trading contacts with the continent perhaps via the south-east. The status of the late Iron Age settlement remains unclear but a tribal centre of some importance might be inferred. Any military presence immediately after the conquest remains elusive, however a fortlet guarding the river crossing to the west is a possibility. The late 1st century sees gradual Romanisation with piecemeal commercial activity. By the mid 2nd century the town had a street grid, stone built public buildings and palatial town houses. Commercial activity of 3rd century date is present while the town house or *mansio* was still in use in the 4th century. Other areas show decline in the 4th century with street metalling being dug into (Site 5). No evidence of 5th-10th century activity is present in this area and the medieval and post-medieval activity is almost exclusively restricted to pits located to the rear of properties.

The Peacock Pavement and associated Mosaics David J Smith

Discovery

Three mosaics were unearthed in July 1898 when shops were being rebuilt on the site of the former no. 51-52 St Nicholas Street (Site 1) (Page, 1907, 187, 188, 205, 206, Pl. 1). Leicester City Corporation acquired the site in 1911 and the mosaics were then made available for inspection *in situ* until their removal to the Jewry Wall Museum in 1965. The largest, the 'Peacock' mosaic, is now on exhibition. This is described below as Mosaic 1 (F98). The other two, which remain in store, are described as Mosaics 2 (F158) and 3 (F157).

Dating

The removal was followed by the excavations reported above (p. 2-12) and by examination and conservation, resulting in the discovery of important evidence affording a *terminus post quem* for all three mosaics. In particular, examination by Mr B R Hartley of the underside of Mosaic 1, while the mosaic was inverted in the Museum for consolidation, revealed that many of the red 'tesserae' were actually fragments of samian ware (cf. Hartley, 1979). Most proved to be from straight-sided vessels of Dragendorff forms 18/31 or 31, 18/31R and 33, of the Hadrianic or early Antonine period. Some twenty-five preserved traces of moulded decoration. Mr Hartley concluded: 'The *terminus post quem* for the Peacock pavement should, therefore, be placed at AD 140/145, and as the bulk of the datable pottery is certainly rather earlier than this, it seems likely that the date is not much later. Even if fragments had been selected for the excellence of their glaze, some later Antonine pieces might have been expected if the mosaic were much later.'

The mosaic overlay 'beds' of *opus signinum* on clay packing which may have been earlier floors (p. 10). Beneath these were deposits of make-up containing pottery dating from the late 1st century to *c.* 140 (p. 11).

Mosaics 2 and 3 lay in separate rooms adjacent to that paved by Mosaic 1 and at a slightly higher level (Figs. 6, 8 & 9). Both also overlay what appeared to be earlier floors of *opus signinum* sealing pottery again not later than *c.* 140 (p. 11). As will be seen, however, a considerably later date can be suggested for these.

Mosaic 1: The Peacock Mosaic (F98)

Description. Pl. 6

This mosaic was originally 5.59m (18ft 4in) square; and despite losses the clearly symmetrical design can be described as if still intact. Briefly, it comprised a square of 2.11m containing nine octagonal panels, all formed by a continuous simple guilloche inter-braided at angles, resulting in four poised-square compartments diagonally about the central panel and twelve triangular compartments around the periphery. Surrounding the square was a band of white 30mm wide and then (now preserved on only two adjacent sides) a band of 'cornice' pattern (cf. Smith, 1975, *passim*) between two grey/blue bands having a total width of 353mm. There was the usual plain surround of red (tile) tesserae (averaging *c.* 20mm cubed) but the exact size of the room paved by this mosaic is unknown.

Within the plain surround the tesserae average *c.* 18mm cubed. The colours employed are black, dark blue, light blue, blue/grey, brown, light grey, red, yellow, and white (the background). The black are of limestone from Ticknall in Derbyshire. The dark and light blue, in the eyes of the peacock's tail, are of opaque glass (*smalti*). The blue/grey and light grey are of lias limestone, the red of tile as well as of samian ware, the yellow again of opaque glass, and the white of local lias limestone and of carboniferous limestone from Derbyshire. The brown are said to be of ironstone from eastern Leicestershire.

In the central panel was depicted a peacock, frontally, with tail outspread. Unfortunately only the tail and left foot remain. The bird was surrounded by a circle of round-tongued double guilloche.

The panels 'above' and 'below' each contained an octagonal linear pattern in blue/grey comprising a central square and, contiguously on each side, an elongated hexagon subdivided into two pairs of lozenges with a poised square between the pairs. The central square contained a 'squared' pseudo-floral motif composed principally of four hearts arranged diagonally with their points tangent to a central circlet. The poised squares on either side of the pattern contained a poised solid square bearing a poised knot and the other two a poised floret with four ogival petals. The lozenges each contained a small solid lozenge.

In the panels on the other two sides of the central panel a floral motif was inscribed in a circle of simple guilloche. This in turn was surrounded by two concentric linear circles framing a pattern of superimposed thorns. The floral motif - 'the Leicester flower' (Smith, 1975, 282-3) - comprised a central circlet, four ogival petals, each with a median white spine tapering from the circlet to the tip of the petal and coloured red on one side of the spine and brown on the other, and alternating with the petals, four pointed excrescences.

In the four corner panels another floral motif was inscribed in a circle of simple guilloche which in turn was surrounded by a linear circle and then a circle of wave-pattern. The floral motif comprised a central dot in a circlet from which radiated eight petals, rounded to the tip, with a surrounding frill of eight pointed excrescences alternating with eight rounded excrescences. The four poised squares diagonally about the central panel each contained, in a poised linear square, a poised 'squared rosette' (here of four heart-shaped petals) with the addition of four pointed excrescences to adapt its circular shape to fill the square (cf. Smith, 1975, 274-5).

A solid blue/grey triangle was inscribed in the white triangles in the corners and on two opposite sides of the design and a pattern of three tangent solid blue/grey triangles was inscribed in those on the other two sides.

A double filet of white tesserae separated the design from the surrounding border of 'cornice' pattern between two blue/grey bands. The pattern comprised a band of almost tangent horizontal open ovals, quasi-tangent to the bands above and below and linked by a small V and inverted V respectively tangent to the band above and to that below, all in blue/grey. The outline of the ovals was thickened on either side to form an almost circular internal white ground for the motif that each enclosed. The motifs, in a repeating series of three, were an ivy leaf, a bulbous 'tulip', and an ivy leaf with curled tip. Each stood on a short stem springing from the bottom of the oval. All petals and leaves were 'shaded' in transverse bands of different colours and the guilloche was similarly shaded but longitudinally.

Commentary

Designs forming nine octagonal panels, 3 x 3, are characteristic of a 'western tradition' in Romano-British mosaics during the period *c.* 150-200 (Smith, 1975, 281-5; *ibid.*, 1984a, 362-3; *ibid.* 1984b). Generally, all the panels, or all except the central panel, contain a floral motif, and the same or similar floral motifs are found in more than one mosaic. Figured panels are exceptional, but apart from the figured central panel here this mosaic is typical of the 'western tradition'. Another typical and also more or less contemporary example, the mosaic of *c.* 140/150 from the Blackfriars site in Leicester, has recently been described and discussed and its parallels elsewhere have been noted (Smith, 1985). There are, however, differences between these two mosaics both in standard of execution and decorative repertory.

In execution the Peacock mosaic is generally less elaborate and its 'cornice' pattern in particular is notably inferior. On the other hand, the two flowers with eight rounded petals in the Peacock mosaic are more elaborate than their four counterparts in the Blackfriars pavement which have no surrounding frill. The two 'Leicester' flowers in the Peacock mosaic are paralleled more or less closely by those in the Blackfriars pavement, but the intricate shield-patterns of the latter are absent from the Peacock mosaic while the lozenge-patterned octagons of this pavement are absent from the other. Like the shield-patterns, however, the lozenge-patterned octagons originated in mosaics of the Italian black-and-white tradition. Their earliest known appearance in Britain is in a mosaic of *c.* 75/80 at Fishbourne (Cunliffe, 1971, I, 85, Pl. lxxvi; cf. Smith, 1975, 270) and, with variations, they are widely found in Britain and elsewhere from the 2nd century onward. Another feature of the Peacock mosaic, but not of the Blackfriars pavement is the employment of the 'squared rosette'. Like the 'cornice' pattern this is a distinctive and distinctively British motif of the Antonine period (Smith, 1975, 274-5). The geometric repertory of this mosaic is therefore instructive, but the most interesting motif is undoubtedly the frontal peacock with outspread tail which forms its centrepiece. This is as yet the only instance in Britain of this motif, the distribution of which is essentially Mediterranean, and must be one of its earliest known representations in Roman mosaics - if not the earliest - in a history extending from the 2nd century AD to the mid-6th (Dunbabin, 1978, 166-9; cf. Levi, 1947, 130, 322-3). The bird was sacred to Juno, and so could symbolize the season of Summer over which Juno presided; but it was also associated with Dionysus and, its outspread tail suggesting the star-studded heaven, long enjoyed popularity in both pagan and Christian funerary art. Furthermore, it is clear, from its association with evidently talismanic motifs, such as victorious racehorses (Ennaifer, 1983, 836-8, Fig. 28; cf. Dunbabin, 1978, 168-9, Pl. 92), that the image of the peacock came to be one of the many such lucky symbols. At the same time, however, its value simply as a colourful and possibly expensive decorative feature, not necessarily symbolic, perhaps cannot be excluded from consideration. As with all symbolic or potentially symbolic motifs any assessment of significance must take account of context; and it may be that here, in an obviously important domestic room, the image of a peacock with outspread tail was chosen at least as much for its decorative appeal as for any other reason.

All things considered, this mosaic is almost certainly datable to *c.* 150 and attributable to the workshop which produced the Blackfriars pavement; but the less meticulous standards suggest that it is the later of the two.

Mosaic 2: (F158)

Description and Commentary (Pl. 7)
Mosaic 2 originally survived as a fragment 1.82 x 1.67m (Leic Mus leaflet) but is now reduced to 1.40 x 1.17m. It was formed of red (tile) and grey (limestone) tesserae of differing sizes, apparently reused and irregularly laid, and preserved part of a rectangular grey panel with a *semis* of poised crosslets of five white (limestone) tesserae (cf. Balmelle, 1985, Pl. 108 d), of very irregular size and form, spaced *c.* 110mm apart in rows *c.* 140mm apart. This pattern is so far unparalleled in Britain but the standard of execution and the coloured background both suggest a date probably in the later 4th century (cf. Johnson, 1979-80, 5). Patching was almost certainly necessitated by poor construction rather than by long use.

Mosaic 3: (F157)

Description and commentary (Pl. 8)
Mosaic 3 originally survived as a fragmentary pavement *c.* 4.56 x 2.28m. Three sections are now preserved. It bore a form of chessboard pattern in grey and white, in the basic oblong units of which the foot of a black L equivalent to three squares abutts against the foot of a reversed white L, and a white square and a black square occupy the space between their verticals, the colours counterchanged. This unit was repeated contiguously in ten rows, each of ten units, those in alternate rows reversed. There had been an approximately central panel, but of this there remained only part of the grey linear border two tesserae wide surrounded by a dotted simple filet (row of alternating grey and white tesserae: Balmelle, 1985, Pl. 1b). Surrounding the entire pattern was first a contiguous bichrome dotted simple filet, then contiguously a black band 150mm wide, and then contiguously a white band 65mm wide. At one end a narrow panel of black tesserae contiguous with the white band, 1.025m long but 210mm less than the width of the mosaic, was bounded on its other long side by a white band 65mm wide. The tesserae, of limestone, averaged 14mm cubed except in the narrow black panel where they were smaller, and the mosaic had a plain surround of tesserae averaging 20mm cubed.

This particular elaboration of the simple chessboard-pattern had been developed in the Italian black-and-white tradition as early as the 2nd century AD (cf. Balmelle, 1985, Pl. 117c: example from Rome) but is as yet unparalleled in Britain. It may be observed, however, that a different elaboration in a panel at Verulamium, assigned to *c.* 300, was also surrounded contiguously first by a dotted simple filet, then by a black band, and then by a white band (Wheeler and Wheeler, 1936, 108, 148, Pl. xlviii, B). It is possible that Mosaic 3 was laid at the same time as the Peacock mosaic but its standard of execution suggests a later date. Though probably not as late as Mosaic 2 it could certainly date from the 4th century (cf. Johnson, 1979-80, 4). Again, patching suggests long use.

The Iron Age and Roman Pottery
Richard Pollard

Introduction

The sites in this report produced material mainly of the 1st and 2nd centuries AD. The late Iron Age pottery in particular is well represented, and should be looked at in conjunction with that from Jewry Wall (Kenyon, 1948; Jarvis, 1986) and Bath Lane (Clamp, 1985). The first century of Roman rule, up to the death of Hadrian or thereabouts, is the period to which the great bulk of Romano-British vessels can be dated. There are few large, closely datable groups, but amongst these is a group of pits with interesting samian and mortaria assemblages (Site 5, F35-37, 39-42), and an early Roman feature with a fine collection of early to mid 1st century AD vessels and an Italian flagon in an amphora fabric (Site 2, F92). These groups, along with a handful of others, have been subjected to detailed form-fabric analysis using EVEs as the measure of quantification of vessel types. Detailed statistics of the occurrence of wares by site and phase, in tabular form, are included in the archive; selected aspects are published herein.

Methodology and Abbreviations

The pottery is quantified by sherd count and weight. In addition, selected groups are quantified by EVEs, using rims, by fabric and form. The general principles adhered to in defining and describing fabrics are discussed elsewhere (Pollard, forthcoming (a)). The following abbreviations are used.

Inclusions

Frequency (% of field covered by type of inclusion)

Sp	Sparse	(up to 9%)
Mo	Moderate	(10-19%)
Fr	Frequent	(20-49%)
Ab	Abundant	(50%+)

('field' = area of fracture examined; % are visual estimates using comparison chart)

Size of grain (quoted as a range, not an average)

VF	Very fine:	up to 0.1mm
F	Fine:	0.1 to 0.25mm
M	Medium:	0.25 to 0.5mm
C	Coarse:	0.5 to 1mm
VC	Very coarse:	larger than 1mm, quoting the largest size measured

Shape of grain (as Orton, 1977a)

R	Rounded
SA	Sub-angular
A	Angular

Sorting (in size) of grains (as Orton, 1977a)

i/a	ill-assorted
w/s	well sorted

Wares

C	Colour-coated ware
PR	Pompeian Red ware (Peacock, 1977b)
LG	Lead glazed ware
TR	Terra Rubra
TN	Terra Nigra
MW	Micaceous ware; Central Gaulish 1st century (Tyers, 1981)
MD	Mica dusted ware
MO	Mortarium fabric
AM	Amphora fabric
WW	White ware
WS	White slip ware
OW	Oxidised ware
GW	Grey ware
BB	Black-burnished ware
DS	Derbyshire ware
CG	Calcite gritted ware
GT	Grog tempered ware
MG	Mixed gritted ware
SW	Sandy ware
MC	Miscellaneous coarse ware

TS, SG, CG, EG, LaG, MV, Lz: South, Central, East Gaulish, La Graufesenque, Les Martres-de-Veyre, Lezoux (for samian ware).

The wares and fabrics identified in this report are described elsewhere (MacRobert, 1987, forthcoming; Pollard, forthcoming (a)), with a few exceptions, newly defined, presented herein. (Summary descriptions of the former appear below, pp 112-114).

Additions to the Fabric Type Series

Lead glazed ware 4

Fabric. Hard, with hard or very hard glazed surfaces, and fine fracture (finely irregular x 20). Wheel thrown. Grey (N6) throughout or dark grey (N4) with yellowish-red (5YR 5/6) margins, or (dark) brown (7.5YR 4/2) with yellowish-red (5YR 4/6) margins, or dusky red (2.5YR 3/2) merging into margins of very dark grey (2.5YR 3/1) and dark reddish-brown (2.5YR 3/4) respectively int and ext. A very dark grey 'skin' covers the under-glaze surface where the margin is yellowish-red or dark reddish-brown. A crazed lead glaze covers both surfaces, pitted in LG4A, of even texture in LG4B. The glaze is generally dark olive grey (5Y 3/2) to olive (5Y 3/4 to 5Y 5/4), although the interior of a beaker from Norfolk Street is olive yellow (2.5Y 6/6) and thick. Fr-Ab, VF(-F), sometimes Sp M-C, quartz inclusions are characteristic, although black iron ore (Sp-Mo, VF-F) can occur.

Forms. A footring base from Site 2 (F46; .200) may be from a closed form: the glaze appears thinner and less lustrous int. Parallels include examples from Arthur's 'South-East English' group (1978, Fig. 8.2, eg. nos. 1.2, 5.2-3) and 'Little Chester' group (*ibid.*, Fig. 8.13, eg. nos. 2.1, 7.1). This base is in the grey version of LG4A; a body sherd in an identical fabric came from St. Nicholas Circle (Pollard, forthcoming (b)) and may be from a Drag 30 or 'vertical-sided beaker' (Arthur, 1978, Figs. 8.2 and 8.3, Type 5, and Figs. 8.13 Type 4.1 and 8.14 Type 8.1-2).

Source. Uncertain. The sherds with yellowish red margins in LG4A are very similar in fabric other than colour, and virtually identical in glaze. They bear white barbotine under-glaze decoration that is typical of the 'South-East English' group, for which Staines is a possible production site (Arthur, 1978, 298-308). They include a Drag 30 from Great Holme Street (Pollard, forthcoming (f); Arthur, 1978, Fig. 8.3 Type 5(.12)) and bowl(?) sherds with 'hairpin' decoration from Site 12. The even-glazed sherd (LG4B) from Norfolk Street is also paralleled in this group (Pollard forthcoming (e), no. 230; Arthur, 1978, Fig. 8.2 Type 2.1-2). Grey fabrics appear to be commonplace in this group. An LG4A hemispherical bowl with very dark grey/dusky red/very dark grey sandwich (MacRobert, 1983, Fabric 47 and Fig. 26.202) is very similar to a Little Chester vessel (Arthur, 1978 Fig. 8.14 Type 12.1).

Table 1

The stratified pottery from Sites 1-6, summarised from the full archival report prepared by Richard Pollard. Samian stamps were identified by Brenda Dickinson. Geoff Dannell prepared dating lists of the samian for Sites 1-4, and Richard Pollard for Sites 5 and 6. Those wares most significant for dating purposes are shown in bold. Intrusive Roman sherds are shown in square brackets. See p 51 for ware abbreviations, and pp. 112-114 for summary fabric descriptions. "Trans" embraces GT5-6, MC1, MG3-4; rc indicates colour-coats with rough cast clay pellet decoration.

Site 1 Phase	Wares present	Sherd count	Weight (g.)	Date of pottery
1	**TSSG**, **C21**, **TN**, **TR**, AM1, AM8, AM16, **WW**, **WS1**, OW, **GW**, CG1, MC2-3, **Trans**	466	9,406	Early 1st c AD-(early) Flavian
2	**TSSG**, **TN**, **MO15**, AM9A, AM18, WW, **WS1**, OW, **GW**, CG1, MC2-3, **Trans**	118	2,627	"
3	**TSSG**, **C3(CG?)**, TN, MD, **MO7**, AM9A, AM13, AM18, AM19, AM25, WW3NG, **WW5**, WW, WS, OW, **GW**, CG1, MC2-3	223	6,259	Late 1st-early 2nd c
4	**TSSG**, **C14**, MD, **MO7**, **MO12**, AM4, AM7, AM9A, AM13, AM23, **WW5**, WW, WS4, WS, OW, **GW4/7**, GW, CG1, MC2-3, Trans,	715	10,968	"
5	TSSG, **TSMV**, **TSCG**, **C2CG**, **C3rc**, PR6, MD, [MO4], **MO7**, AM7, AM9A, AM12, AM19, **WW5**, WW, WS, OW, GW, **BB1**, CG1, MC2-3, Trans	511	7,758	Late 1st-early 2nd *c.* (5A-5B); *c.* 110-130 or 1/2 2nd c (5C)
6	TSSG, **C3rc**, MO7, AM9A, WW, OW, GW, **BB1**, CG1	67	668	*c.* 120-140 or 1/2 2nd c
7	TSSG, **TSMV**, **C11rc**, MD, **MO4**, MO7, AM9A, AM18, **WW5**, WW, WS, OW, GW, **BB1**, CG1, MC2-3	532	7,381	Late 1st-early 2nd c (7A-7B); 1/2 2nd c (7C)
Site 2				
1	**TSSG**, [TS CG], **TN**, **TR**, [MO12], [MO18], AM2, AM25, **WW3NG**, **WW**, [WW], **WS1**, WS11, OW, **GW**, [GW] [BB1], CG1, MC2-3, **Trans**	842	16,564	Early 1st c AD-(early) Flavian
2	**TSSG**, **TN**, AM7, AM9A, AM25, **WW3NG**, WW, **WS1**, **WS4**, WS11, OW, **GW**, CG1, MC2-3, **Trans**	358	5,932	Pre-Flavian to Vespasianic
3	TSSG, **TSMV**, TN, TR, MD, AM12, AM25, WW3NG, WW, WS1, WS11, WS, OW, **GW4/7**, GW, CG1, MC2-3, Trans	424	9,553	Early-mid 1st c AD (F11, ?F24, F92); Late 1st-early 2nd c (?F7, F49-51, F67-8)
4	TSSG, **TSCG**, [C3], **C3rc**, **C11rc**, [C13], TN, TR, MD, **MO7**, **MO12**, AM7, AM9A, AM12, AM19, WW3NG, **WW1**, **WW5**, WW, **WS4**, WS, OW, **GW4/7**, **GW11**, **GW12**, GW, **BB1**, CG1, **CG3B**, MC2-3, Trans	1170	21,194	Early-mid 1st c AD (I 16-7); Late 1st-1/2 2nd c (rest)
5	TSSG, TSMV, **C2NV/LR**, **C3rc**, **C17**, C19, **LG4A**, MD, **MO7**, **MO12**, **MO18**, AM9A, AM11, AM12, AM19, **WW1**, WW, WS, OW, **GW4/7**, **GW11**, GW, **BB1**, CG1, MC2-3, Trans	727	10,035	Late 1st-1/2 2nd c (F46); 2/2 2nd-4th c (make-ups)
Site 3				
1	**TR**, **WW3NG**, **WS1**, **OW**, **GW**, CG1, MC2-3	13	43	Early-mid 1st c AD
2A	**TSSG**, MD, **MO7**, **MO9**, **WW5**, WW, OW, GW, CG1	100	2,630	Late 1st-early 2nd c
2B	TSSG, **TSMV**, **MO12**, **WW5**, WW, WS, OW, GW, **BB1**, CG1, MC2-3	119	2,395	Late 1st-mid 2nd c
2A+2B	CG1 (Fig. 56.110)	39	3,900	1st-early 2nd c
3	TSSG, TSMV, **TSCG**, **C2**, **C2NV/LR**, **C2NV**, **C3**, TN, **MO4**, **MO6**, MO15, MO18, AM3, AM9A, AM28, WW3NG, WW5, WW, WS1, WS, OW, GW, **BB1**, CG1, **CG3B**, MC2-3, Trans	280	5,438	Mid 2nd to 3rd c (or to 4th c)
Site 4				
1	**TSSG**, **TN**, **GW**, CG1, MC2-3, **Trans**	123	2,208	Early-mid 1st cAD, except F34 (Phase 1B): Mid-late 1st c AD

Phase	Wares present	Sherd count	Weight (g.)	Date of pottery
2	**TSSG**, **WW5**, WW, **WS**; OW, **GW**, CG1, MC2-3, **Trans**	85	1,139	Late 1st-early 2nd c

Site 5

Phase	Wares present	EVEs	Date of pottery
1	**TSSG**, TN, MD, **MO7**, WW, WS, OW, GW, CG1, MC2-3	8.27	Mid 1st c AD-early 2nd c
2	TSSG, TS Lezoux (1st c), **TSMV**, **TSCG**, TS(EG?), **C2LR**, **C2rc**, **C3rc**, **C17rc**, **C2NV**, **C12**, C14, TN, MD, **MO7**, **MO8**, **MO10**, **MO12**, MO15, **MO18**, **MO19**, **MO22**, AM3, AM7, AM9A, AM12, AM18, AM19, AM23, **WW1**, **WW5**, WW, **WS4**, WS, OW, **GW1**, **GW4/7**, **GW11**, GW, **BB1**, CG1, MC2-3	101.47	1/2 2nd c
3A-B	TSSG, TSMV, **TSCG**, **C3rc**, **C11**, MD, **MO4**, MO7, MO8, MO10, MO12, AM4, AM9A, AM12, WW5, WW, **OW**, GW4/7, **GW**, **BB1**, CG1, MC2-3	25.32	Mid 2nd-early 3rd c
3C-D	TSSG, TSMV, **TSCG**, **C2(LR?)rc**, **C2NV/LR**, **C2NV**, **C3rc**, LG1, MD, [MO1], **MO4**, MO8, MO12, MO15, MO18, AM7, AM9A, AM9B, AM12, WW5, WW, WS, **OW**, GW4/7, GW11, **GW**, BB1, CG1, **CG3B**, MC2-3	36.89	"
4	TSSG, TSMV, **TSCG**, **TSEG**, **C2NV/LR**, MD, **MO4**, MO12, MO18, MO19, **MO24**, AM7, AM8, AM9B, WW, WS4, WS, **OW**, GW4/7, **GW**, **BB1**, **BB2**, CG1	16.43	"
5	**C2NV**, C3NV, **C17NV**, **GW**, CG1B	0.76	4th c

Site 6

Phase	Wares present	Sherd count	Weight (g.)	Date of pottery
1B(F24)	**CG1**, **GT7**, **SW1**, **MC4-5**	16	4,512	Late 1st c BC
(1A, 1C)		0	0	-
1D	[TSCG], [TS(EG?)], **WW3NG**, **GW**, [BB1], CG1, MC2-3	570	17,928	Early-mid 1st c AD
2A	CG1, MC2-3	17	576	"
2B	**TSSG**, [TSCG], [C2NV], [C13], **TN**, TR, [MO2], **MO8**, AM7, AM9A, [AM23], AM25, **WW3NG**, **WW5**, WW, WS, OW, GW11, **GW**, [GW], CG1, MC2-3, **Trans**	126	3,241	Mid-late 1st c
2C-D	**TSSG**, [TSCG], [TS(EG?)], [C5], [C13Ox], C14, TN, [MO4], MO8, AM7, AM9A, [AM9B], AM12, **WW5**, WW, OW, [OW], GW, [GW], [BB1], CG1, [CG1B], MC2-3	187	5,822	Mid 1st-early 2nd c
3	**TSSG**, [C12], C14, [MO4], MO8, AM7, AM9A, AM12, AM30, WW, **GW4/7**, GW, CG1, Trans	75	1,708	Late 1st-early 2nd c
4	TSSG, **TSMV**, TS(CG?), **C2(LR?)rc**, C14, C18, **LG5**, TN, MD, MO8, **MO12**, **MO14**, **MO18**, AM7, AM9A, AM12, AM19, WW5, WW, WS, OW, **GW1**, GW4/7, GW11, GW, **BB1**, CG1, MC2-3	425	7,993	Late 1st-mid 2nd c
5	**TSCG**, **TS(EG?)**, TN, WW5, WW, **OW**, GW, **BB1**, CG1, MC2-3	41	381	Mid 2nd-early 3rd c
6	TSCG, **C2NV/LR**, WW, **OW**, **GW**, **BB1**	29	290	"
7A-D	TSSG, **TSCG**, C2, WW1, WW3NG, WW, WS, **OW**, **GW1**, GW, **BB1**, CG1, MC2-3	85	1,305	"
7E	**TSCG**, **TSEG**, **C2(NV/LR?)**, **C2NV**, **C17NV**, MD, AM12, **AM23**, WW2(NV?), WW, **OW**, GW, **BB1**, CG1	48	864	2nd to 3rd or 4th c

Table 2 Iron Age and Roman Pottery: Assemblage size by site

Site	1	2	3	4	6	8	9	10	11a	11b
Sherd Count	2728	3770	721	742	1925	585	228	39	16	82
Weight(grams)	47161	69022	16623	12782	48920	13519	11814	414	1029	3371

Note: Site 11a = A253.1951; Site 11b = A20.1939

Date. Probably late Flavian to early Hadrianic (cf Arthur, 1978, 295).

Lead glazed ware 5

Fabric. Hard, with very hard glazed surfaces and irregular fracture. Wheel thrown. Dark grey (N4) with a crazed and pitted olive to dark olive (5Y) glaze very similar to LG4A. Characterised by Ab F-M i/a SA quartz (Site 6, 453).

Forms. Unknown.

Source. Uncertain. Brassington (1971, 64) describes a group of vessels from Margidunum as having a 'granular grey fabric with thick dark green glaze' (*ibid.*, Fig. 11. 276-9, 282-2), and has noted that lead glazed wares in the Midlands exhibit considerable variation in fabric (*ibid.*, 62).

Date. As LG4; typesherd from Site 6, phase 4C (I 22).

Other Lead glazed wares from Leicester

The earliest are Central Gaulish wares, of which the 'buff' variant has been recorded (MacRobert, 1983, Fabric 106; 1987, 66, LG2; LG1 is reserved for Greene's (1979) Fabric A). LG3 is a fine, grey fabric, sometimes with oxidised margins and unglazed int, found on Elbow Lane (MacRobert, 1989) and Great Holme Street (Pollard, forthcoming (f)) in beaker forms. LG6 has a white slip overall under the glaze, and barbotine(?) over the slip, resembling examples from Mancetter in decoration (O'Neil, 1928, Pl. xxv.21) and Wall in the presence of the slip (Arthur, 1978, Fig. 8.15 No. 17); a beaker identical to these two parallels was recovered from Great Holme Street, with a mottled yellow/pale yellow/olive (5Y) glaze overall.

Colour-coat 19

Fabric. Finely irregular, hard to very hard, smooth (slipped) surfaces. Reduced core, oxidised margins, and reddish slips feature. Fabric inclusions vary from 'fine' to 'coarse' sandy, with quartz, white mica and iron ore. Wheel thrown.

Forms and decoration. Base sherd, flat (dish?) from Site 2. Bowl and ?platter from Site 5 and St. Nicholas Street respectively, with painted decoration.

Source. Probably Swanpool (M Darling, pers. comm). The pottery from the Swanpool kilns has been discussed recently, from which it would seem that these vessels represent the first evidence for penetration by the Swanpool potters as far as Leicester (Darling 1977, 35).

Date. 4th century, on stylistic grounds (*ibid.*, 1).

Illustrations. 207, 301.

Colour-coat 21

Fabric. Finely irregular, smooth, hard, wheel thrown. Light brown to pink (7.5YR 6/4-7/4) with partial light grey core and int margin (10YR 7/1), and light red (2.5YR 6/6) mottled (variable thickness) overall slip. Inclusions: Sp VF-C, R, SA(?) i/a quartz; Sp-Mo (-Fr on surfaces) VF-F white mica; Sp VF-F 'gold' mica; Sp VF-VC (3mm) R, A, SA(?) i/a red iron ore.

Form. Platter, cf Drag 18.

Source. Uncertain. The fabric is 'indistinguishable from Lincoln fabric 6' and the form 'would equate reasonably well with (Darling forthcoming) Fig. 25.2, no. 6 from a Hadrianic level at (Lincoln) East Gate with much residual pottery' (M Darling, pers comm). A Lincoln source appears a distinct possibility.

Date. Pre-Flavian, from context.

Illustration. 1.

Mica dusted ware 1C

Fabric. Finely irregular, hard, smooth, within the range of WW3. Mica coating on int and upper face of rim and flange of bowl. Similar to MD1A and 1B. Wheel thrown and knife trimmed.

Form. Flanged rim bowl, cf Marsh, 1978 Type 34.

Source. Uncertain, possibly Midlands.

Date. Flavian-Trajanic from context and form.

Illustration. 16.

White ware 9

Fabric. Soft to hard, harsh (abraded) fabric with fine fracture, wheel thrown. Black to grey core (N2 to N6) with pinkish grey margins and surfaces (7.5YR 6/2 to 7/2). Inclusions: Mo-Fr M-C (median C), R, fewer SA, w/s quartz; Sp (VF) F-C, SA, A i/s red and black iron ore; Sp-Mo (Ab on surfaces) VF-F white mica; Sp (Mo on surfaces) VF-F 'gold' mica; Sp C-VC (2mm), SA, R, calcite.

Form. Unknown

Source. Unknown

Date. Flavian-Trajanic from context (Site 3, F3, II10; residual in Site 3 II 4, II 5).

White slip ware 11

Fabric. Finely irregular, soft, smooth ext, rough int, wheel thrown. Reduced core, yellowish red margins (5YR), pale brown int surface (10YR 6/3). Ext surface bears thick, matt pink slip (7.5YR 8/4). Falls within the MG2 and SW2 ranges with the addition of a slip, which can lend the fabric an appearance deceptively like a Romano-British ware (eg WS2, WS4). The mixed range of inclusions which can comprise some or all of quartz, calcite, grog and ?iron ore, is characteristic. A 'white' slip may also have been applied to the beaker, no. 63, in fabric GT2.

Forms and decoration. Closed forms, possibly including fine scored butt beakers and flagons.

Source. Uncertain, probably East Midlands.

Date. Derived presumably from North Gaulish WW3 beakers of Tiberian to Neronian date, a closer date cannot be elucidated.

Illustration. 63(?).

Grey ware 11

'Highgate Wood type' fine grey ware, described elsewhere (Clamp, 1985, 47). Date: very late 1st to early or mid 2nd century in Leicester. Illustrations: Clamp, 1985, Fig. 34.107-108; nos. 85, 269, 270.

Grey ware 12

Fabric. Soft to hard, fine, smooth wheel thrown ware, burnished ext. Reduced, usually very dark grey to black surfaces, sometimes a reduced 'sandwich' in fracture. To the unaided eye devoid of inclusions except sometimes Sp calcite and/or Sp-Fr white mica on surfaces. Fabric falls within GW2 range; decoration differentiates GW12.

Forms and decoration. Forms in Leicester include bowls and beakers. Rouletting in combination with stamped or incised motifs, or in unusual patterns such as the zigzag (no. 306), arrowhead and vertical zone (Pollard, forthcoming (a), no. 73), and lozenge (Clamp, 1985 Fig. 34.130). Stamps include blocks (no. 84), circles (Todd, 1973 Fig. 29.45), and rosettes (no. 307). Incised motifs in combination with stamps (no. 84) are included, but alone or in combination with bands of rouletting (eg nos. 32, 98) these motifs are deemed to fall outside the GW12 category, as is zonal rouletting on its own (eg no. 130). 'London type ware' and 'London ware' can include GW12 (eg Perrin, 1980; Marsh and Tyers, 1976; Monaghan, 1983).

Source. The existence of an East Midlands-Nene Valley style of stamp-impressed and scored grey ware has been touched on by several authors (eg Woods, 1972, 35-36; Rodwell, 1978, 271 and no. 118; Howe, *et al* 1980, 10.14; Perrin, 1980), but no comprehensive survey of the evidence has been published to date. A wide range of styles is exhibited by the material from the Commandant's House at Margidunum (Oswald, 1948a, eg Pl. xi, 6,9; Pl. xiii, 8; Pl. xvi. 7,8). Production sites cannot be positively attested. Some East Anglian imports may also occur in this fabric; see also GW13 and no. 118 (Pollard, forthcoming (e)).

Date. Within the Flavian-Hadrianic period, not later than the second quarter of the 2nd century.

Illustrations. 84, 312, 313.

Miscellaneous coarse wares 2, 3

'Umbrella' fabric codes for Late Iron Age to early Roman native wares, used where clearly residual and when it is sufficient simply to determine the quantity of the 'native' element in an assemblage, without distinguishing individual fabrics. CG1 is often extracted, as mid and late Romano-British wares can appear very much like the early CG1A without diagnostic traits.

MC2:	'coarse':	GT1, 3; MG1; SW3; CG1, 2A, 3A
MC3:	'fine':	GT2, 4; MG2; SW2

SW1, MC4-5, GT7

See pp. 72-4 for discussion (Late Iron Age wares).

Table 3 Iron Age and Roman Pottery: Cumulative frequency statistics by phase

Site	1		2		3		4		6		5
	WEIGHT	SHERD COUNT	WEIGHT	SHERD COUNT	WEIGHT	SHERD COUNT	WEIGHT	SHERD COUNT	WEIGHT	SHERD COUNT	EVE
Phases 1	20.0	17.1	24.0	22.3	0.3	1.8	16.3	15.4	45.9	38.3	2.8
1 - 2	25.5	21.4	32.6	31.8	53.9	37.6	27.8	30.2	64.4	54.5	37.0
1 - 3	38.8	29.6	46.4	43.1	86.7	76.4	37.2	41.0	67.9	58.4	58.0
1 - 4	62.1	55.8	77.1	74.1	92.4	87.2	43.8	44.6	84.2	80.5	63.5
1 - 5	78.5	74.6	91.7	93.4	96.3	93.1	84.5	85.0	85.0	82.6	66.0
1 - 6	79.9	77.0	99.8	99.7	98.1	97.4	99.6	99.5	85.6	84.1	72.9
1 - 7	95.6	96.5							90.0	91.1	
1 - 8	96.7	97.8							97.3	97.2	
1 - 9	99.5	99.7									
all + u/p	100	100	100	100	100	100	100	100	100	100	100

Phases above lines are Iron Age and Roman, below lines includes post-Roman.
u/p = unphased.

The Illustrated Decorated Samian *Geoffrey B. Dannell (Figs. 44-47)*

Site 1

Phase 1B

1. Drag 29, SG. The rouletted central moulding, and the light paste and slip are consistent with an early date. The earliest piece from sites examined by GBD (Sites 1-4, 8). Rivetted. *c.* AD 30-45. (954) F72: V 50.

Phase 3B

2. Drag 37, SG. The small leaf wreath was used by many Flavian potters, including Bassus & Coelus, and Calvus. *c.* AD 70-85.(950) F71: V 39.
3. Drag 37, SG. Double-bordered ovolo with thin, bent tongue, slightly canted to left, ending in small three-pronged claw. It is similar to, but smaller than, that used by Memor, and its cleanliness suggests that it is an original design. Two examples exist from London (Museum of London Box 36). *c.* AD 70-85? (950) F71: V 39.

Phase 3C

4. Drag 37, SG. The medallion, without central rosette, appears from Burghöfe, cf Ulbert 1959, Taf. 40.9, with a free style design. *c.* AD 80-100? (902 + 944) F63: V 21; + F70: V 24; phases 4A, 3C.
5. Drag 37, SG. Ovolo as no. 19 below. The leaf is probably the one from Knorr 1919, Textbild 36. *c.* AD 75-90. (940) F101: V 17.
6. Drag 37, SG. Mercator ovolo(?), cf no. 19 below. *c.* AD 75-90. (963) F133: VI 17.

Phase 4A

7. Drag 37, SG. Stamped by Mercator in the mould, cf Hermet 1934, Pl. cxix. 1 for a bowl from a very similar mould with the less often used tuft. The figures are a dog, O.1925, and a hare, O.2074. *c.* AD 75-90. (947) F60: V 32.
8. Drag 37, SG. Style of M. Crestio. The geese and double-bifid tendril binding occur in his work, and that of Mercator. The hare, O.2055, is recorded on a stamped Drag 37 of M. Crestio from Leicester. *c.* AD 70-90. (902) F63: V 21.
9. Drag 37, SG. Ovolo as no. 19 below. This is in the panel style of Mercator, with the same leaf as no. 19 below, and a lion, O.1394 type. *c.* AD 75-90. (911 + 902) III 27, + F63: V 21; phases 5A, 4A.
10. Drag 37, SG. Possibly the same bowl as no. 9; the figure appears to be a bestiarius. *c.* AD 75-90. (896 + 902) F63: V 19 + V 21.
11. Drag 37, SG. Double-bordered ovolo, with slight rounding of the outer border to the left, while it is more perpendicular to the right. The tongue is central, with a trident tip turned to the right. A Drag 37 with a similar ovolo and stag, O.1738, comes from London (Museum of London), there with a gladiator, O.1020. The reduced dogs, O.1932, used by Iucundus, Modestus, and Rufinus, confirm this piece as belonging to a workshop making Drag 29 as well. *c.* AD 70-85. (938 + 939 + 896) F64: V 11; + V 13; + F60: V 19; phases 4A, 4B, 4A.
12. Drag 37, SG. A similar vessel to no. 19 below; the style is not well shown by Knorr (1919). The small leaf from there is joined by a narrow lozenge-shaped one, and a basal wreath made from a palm leaf, cf *ibid.* Taf. 57.25. The bird is ibid. Taf. 57.23. The putto, O.436, is on a Drag 30 with the group ovolo from Rottweil, cf Knorr 1912, Taf. xvi.2. *c.* AD 75-90. (902 + 965) F63: V 21; + F142: VII 1; phases 4A, 9A.
13. Drag 29, SG. Similar design to those of Coto, cf Knorr 1919, Taf. 27. *c.* AD 65-80. (902) F63: V 21. See also no. 4 for Phase 4A, F63.

Phase 4B

14. Drag 37, SG. Perhaps a blurred version of the Crucuro ovolo, cf Hermet 1934, Pl. lxxxiv. 3. *c.* AD 75-90. (939) V 13. See also no. 11.

Phase 5A

15. Drag 37, SG. Free style scene, probably by Germanus; his lioness, O.1544. *c.* AD 65-80. (909) III 25.
16. Drag 37, SG. Similar to an ovolo from Ribchester (publication forthcoming; information kindly sent by Mrs. F. Wild), and cf Hermet, 1934, Pl. lxxxii. 7, by C.I. Sa(binus?). *c.* AD 70-85? (909) III 25.
17. Drag 37, SG. Mercator style; his leaf, cf no. 12, and bird, cf Knorr 1919 Taf. 57.24. *c.* AD 75-90. (922) IIIA 25.
18. Drag 37, SG. Segmented leaf above basal wreath of compound leaves. Flavian. (925) IIIA 52. See also no. 9.

Phase 5B

19. Drag 37, SG. Style of Mercator. His ovolo, shared with M. Crestio, cf Knorr 1919, Textbild 36. It often shows an assymetry, with the core shifted to the left. His dog, O.1925 type, cf Hermet 1934 Pl. cxix. 1, and bird, cf ibid. Pl. lxxxi. 7, with a different ovolo. For other details cf Knorr 1919, Taf. 57: grass tuft 13, bud 14, binding 16, column 20, bird 23. The basal wreath is made from the segmental leaf, cf no. 12. Also large palmate leaf. Rivetted, one rivet still surviving. *c.* AD 75-90. (907) III 23.
20. Drag 37, SG. Ovolo shared by M. Crestio and Crucuro, cf Knorr 1919, Textbild 5. *c.* AD 70-90. (907) III 23.
21. Drag 37, SG. Double-bordered ovolo with defective outer border, straight tongue and trident tip. A similar one is known from London (Museum of London 11950G) on a Drag 30. *c.* AD 75-90? (921) IIIA 24.

Phase 5C

22. Drag 37, SG. Feet to left of satyr? The trilobed motif from the St. Andrew's Cross was widely used, cf Knorr 1919, Textbild 12. The small leaf is on Drag 37 in the style of Mercator (Museum of London). The basal wreath is also common, but more often associated with makers of Drag 29, cf *ibid.* Textbild 6. *c.* AD 75-90. (924) IIIA 47.

Phase 7C

23. Drag 37, SG. Legs of stag, probably O.1709. *c.* AD 80-100? (936) V 5.
24. Drag 37, SG. The large bud is found on stamped work of Iucundus ii, cf Knorr 1919, Taf. 43E. *c.* AD 70-90. (936) V 5.
25. Drag 37, SG. Ovolo used by M. Crestio and Crucuro, cf Knorr 1919, Textbild 5. *c.* AD 70-90. (936) V 5.
26. Drag 37, SG. Much reduced hare, presumably a copy; perhaps O.2078 type. The upright striated rod was used by M. Crestio (Museum of London). *c.* AD 70-90. (936) V 5.
27. Drag 37, SG. Mercator ovolo; the majority of the details are shown by Knorr (1919, Taf. 57). *c.* AD 80-95. (936) V 5.
28. Drag 37, SG. Deep double-bordered ovolo with straight tongue ending in a trident tip, slightly to left. Perhaps by Criciro. The overlapping wreath is probably a bud rather than a leaf, cf Knorr 1919, Taf. 10. *c.* AD 75-90. (936) V 5.
29. Drag 30, SG. The details on this piece have not been found in a search for parallels. *c.* AD 60-80. (936) V 5.

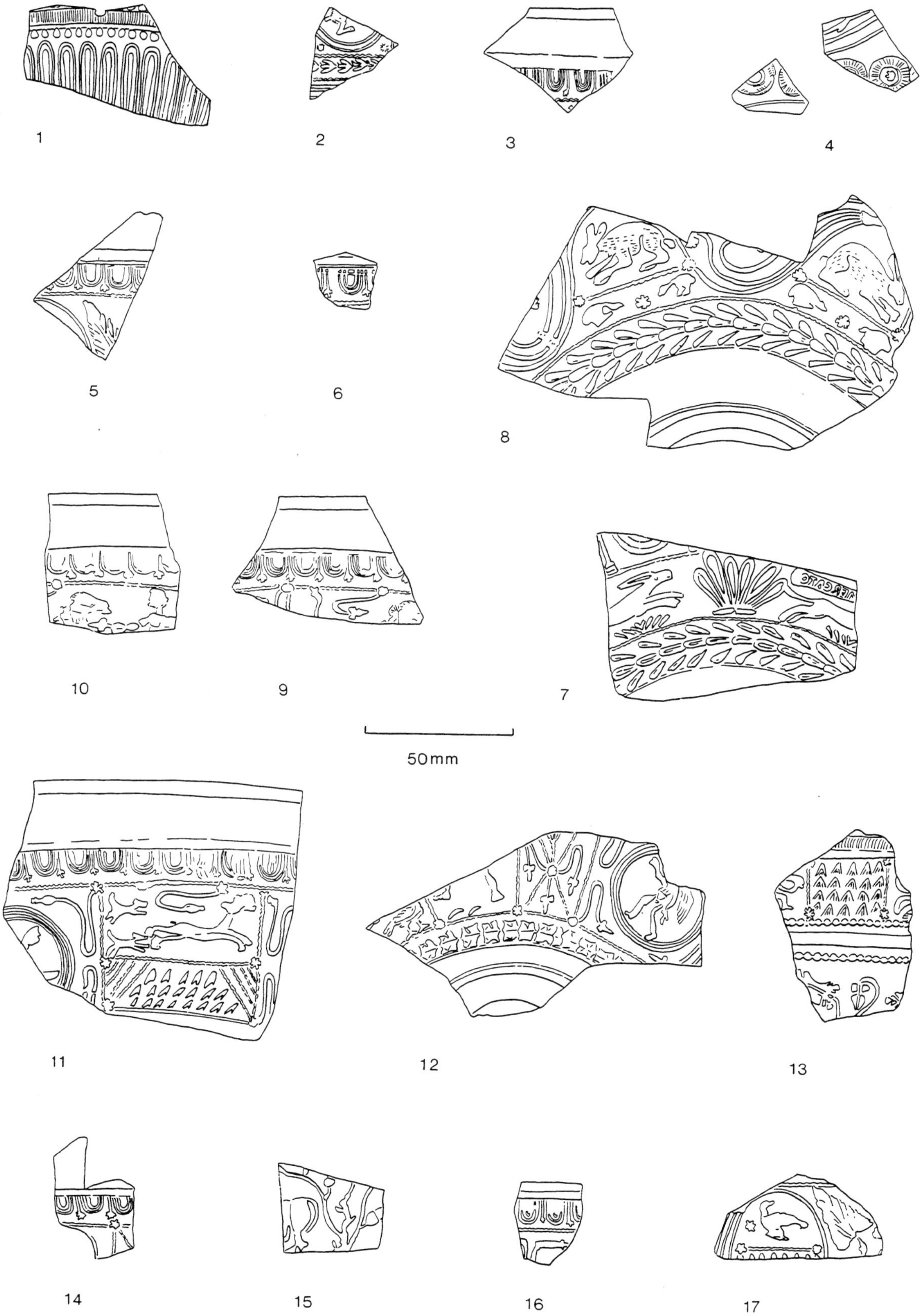

Fig 44 Decorated Samian Ware Site 1 (1-17) Scale 1:2

30. Drag 37, SG. M. Crestio ovolo; the boar, O.1670 type, and pendant are on bowls with the ovolo from London (Museum of London 6532L and 4403G). The lanceolate leaf is on signed work from Richborough, cf Simpson 1968, Pl. lxxxi. 21. Note the beaded borders. *c.* AD 70-90. (960) VI 5

Phase 9A

See no. 12

Site 2

Phase 3

31. Drag 37, Les Martres-de-Veyre. Igocatus style; his figures, D.493 and 643, and vase, Rogers' T9. *c.* AD 100-120. (1379) F67: III 22.
32. Drag 37, SG. Both Crucuro and Mercator could have produced this piece, cf Knorr 1919, Taf. 29.12 and 57.11 for the frond; the hound is O.1925. *c.* AD 75-90. (1379) F67: III 22.

Phase 4B, F8

33. Drag 29, SG. The upper zone is similar to one used by Sabinus, cf Knorr 1919, Taf. 69B; the birds are O.2247 and 2288 types. The lower zone medallions contain a satyr butting a ram, O.727, used on a vessel in the style of Mommo, cf Oswald 1948b, Pl.xii.1, and the same firm used the frond in the St. Andrew's Cross motif, cf Knorr 1919, Taf. 59.11. The damaged medallion has a bird, O.2295, which is more usual on Neronian vessels. The birds and frond were also used by Meddilus, cf *ibid.* Taf. 54, and the St. Andrew's Cross motif is similar to one with a Severus ovolo from London. *c.* AD 70-85. (1318 + 1323 + 1325 + 1322) F8: I 9 + I 25 + I 27; + F3: I 24; phases 4B, 6A.
34. Drag 37, SG. By Frontinus; both ovolo and doe O.1775 are on a mould of Drag 30 with his tab stamp from La Graufesenque, and the head alone on another signed one, cf Hermet 1934 Pl. xxvii. 55. There is a connection here with Germanus, who also used the doe, but the trees in their free style designs differ. Rivetted. *c.* AD 70-85? (1374) II 118.
35. Drag 37, SG. This ovolo is known from Camelon, Catterick, Chichester and Verulamium, cf B. R. Hartley 1972, D.73. It also occurs on the temple site at Leicester in the same insula as Site 2 here, Jewry Wall Museum accession A164.1969.2031 (Pollard forthcoming (b)) *c.* AD 75-95? (1374) II 118.
36. Drag 37, SG. Probably the Mercator ovolo. *c.* AD 75-90. (1374) II 118.
37. Drag 37, SG. This is similar to the smaller Calvus ovolo, but more closely packed, and the rosette tongue is set higher. *c.* AD 70-85. (1374) II 118.
38. Drag 37, SG. The basal wreath was used by a long list of Flavian potters, cf Knorr 1952 Taf. 49, but the short striated rods indicate a maker of Drag 29. *c.* AD 70-85. (1362 + 1375) II 67 + II 119.

Phase 5, F46

39. Drag 37, SG. This is the larger ovolo used by Calvus, cf Knorr 1942, and also used by Mercator. The hound is O.1994, often used by Mercator. *c.* AD 75-90. (1336) II 27.
40. Drag 37, SG. Large, truncated, triple-bordered ovolo with tongue to left, probably ending in a hollow circle, cf Hermet 1934, Pl. xxxv. 31. *c.* AD 80-95? (1342 + 1345) II 40 + II 43.
41. Drag 37, SG. Burnt, but probably later Flavian. The bifid leaf is sometimes used as a wreath, cf Knorr 1912, Taf. 23.4 and 8. The birds are reduced copies. The legs to the right may be of a Pan. *c.* AD 85-100? (1345) II 43.

Phase 6A

See no. 33 above

Phase 6C

42. Drag 37, Lezoux. Acanthus leaf, Rogers' K10. *c.* AD 125-140. (1332) F36: II 3.

Site 3

Phase 2A, F3

43. Drag 37, SG. An individual double-bordered ovolo with central tongue, ending in a rosette which overlaps the left-hand border. None of the details are sufficiently diagnostic to help ascription. Flavian. (716) I 18.
44. Drag 37, SG. Double-bordered ovolo with tongue to right, ending in fine claw? This is not the one used by Memor or Mommo; the outer border is too rounded and is slightly higher to the left, giving an altogether different profile. It is not dissimilar to that used by C.V. Albanus. The stag is an O.1738 type. Flavian. (719) III 12.

Phase 2B, F3

45. Drag 37, SG. Single-bordered ovolo with tongue to left ending in 'lanceolate' swelling? Flavian. (717) III 9.
46. Drag 37, SG. Large leaf used by Calvus and Mercator, cf Knorr 1952, X. *c.* AD 70-85. (718) III 10.

Phase 3C, F1

47. Drag 37, CG. The ovolo is unclear; the figure appears to be a putto. Hadrianic. (732) III 8.
48. Drag 37, CG. Rogers' ovolo B206. Antonine. (732) III 8.

Phase 5B

49. Drag 37, CG. Rogers' ovolo B22, probably by Acaunissa. *c.* AD 125-150. (737) V 3.

Site 4

Medieval levels

50. Drag 30, SG. Calvus style. His ovolo, which occurs on a signed version of the spouted Drag 37 from Fishbourne, cf Dannell 1971, Fig. 130.49, found at La Graufesenque (information from Alain Vernhet; the bowl also has a tab stamp of Patricius). The ovolo was also used by Mercator (Museum of London 5481G). The palmate leaf occurs with this ovolo at London (*ibid.* 11751G), and has links with Sabinus, cf Stanfield 1937, Fig. 11.92. *c.* AD 65-80 (415 + 417) F2: II 12; + (chip from rim) IV 1; phases 3B, 6.
51. Drag 37, SG. Very reduced copy of bear, O.1614, which, with the wreath, was used by Iucundus ii (Museum of London). *c.* AD 70-85. (422) F22: IV 19.
52. Drag 37, CG. Venus, D.185, with leaf, Rogers' H99, probably by Cinnamus. *c.* AD 150-170. (425) F26: V 8.

Site 8

Phase 3A

53. Drag 37, CG. Cinnamus ovolo 3, Rogers' B143. To the right, a pygmy with sword. The sherd is heavily burnt. *c.* AD 145-165. (133) F13: VI 70.

Phase 4A

54. Drag 37, SG. Mercator ovolo, cf Knorr 1919, Taf. 57. *c.* AD 75-90. (134) VII 71.

Phase 4C

55. Drag 37, CG. Probably from the Quintilianus group; they used the rosette, Rogers' C21, and the seated figure, D.527.

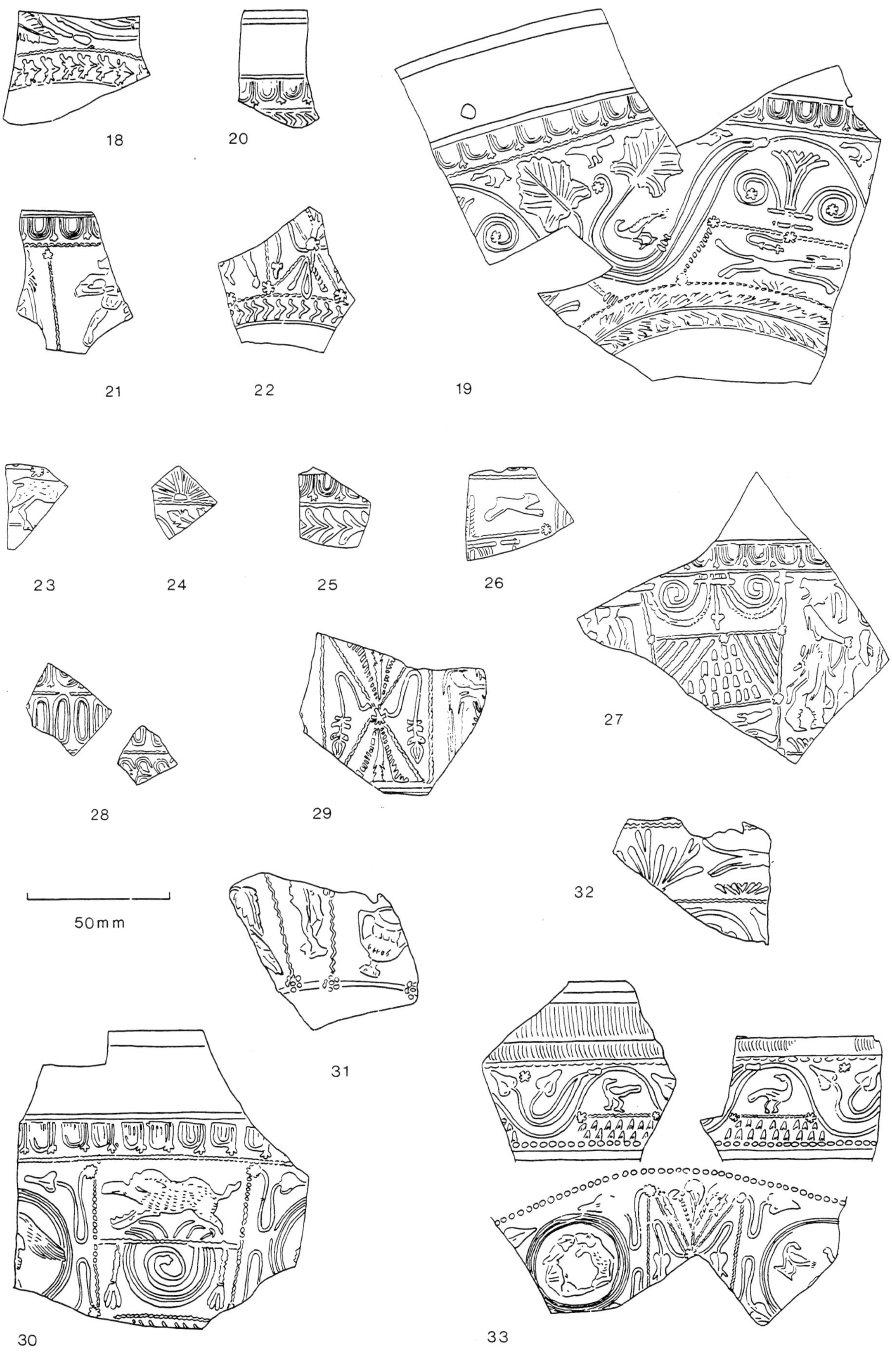

Fig 45 Decorated Samian Ware Site 1 (18-30); Site 2 (31-33) Scale 1:2

The gladiator is the one used by Paterclus: note the right foot, which is different from Oswald's types. *c.* AD 125-145. (136) F10: IX 36.

Unstratified

56. Drag 30, Les Martres-de-Veyre. Donnaucus style, cf S & S 1958, Pl. xlvi.545. *c.* AD 100-120. (132) IV.

Samian stamps from key phases. Edited by Richard Pollard from reports by Brenda M. Dickinson.

A full catalogue of all stamps is in the archive. Stamps from Site 5, phase 2A, are detailed owing to the unusual nature of the group (nos. 35-56, and no. 90, also referred to in Dickinson's discussion). The numbers used in the full catalogue are retained, hence the gaps in the selective list published here. Numbers in brackets are site accession numbers, at end of entry except for nos. 30-56 and 90, where they appear after pottery of origin.

Site 1

Phases 1, 2 ,6, 7 : no stamps

Phase 3A

1. IIIA 62. Niger ii, Drag 29, La G^{a}. *c.* 50-70 (891)
2. F71: V 39 + (ph 4A) F60: V 31. Crestus, Drag 18, La G^{b}. *c.* 65-90 (898 + 897)
3. F71: V 39. Severus i, Drag 18R, La G^{b}. *c.* 70-90 (900)
4. F71: V 39. Murranus, Drag 27g, La G^{b}. *c.* 50-65 (901)

Phase 4A (see also 2)

5. F60: V 32. Billicuro, Drag 18, La G^{b}. *c.* 70-90 (899)
6. F63: V 19. Illiterate, Drag 15/17 or 18, SG. Neronian-Flavian (896)
7. F63: V 21. Patricius i, Drag 18, La G^{b}. *c.* 65-90. Graffito under base (Fig. 49.G2 p. 72) (902)

Phase 5A

8. IIIA 54. Crestus, Drag 15/17 or 18, La G^{b}. *c.* 85-100 (890)

Phase 5B

9. III 21. Fragment, Drag 27, SG. Flavian-Trajanic (889)
10. IIIC 6. Castus i, Drag 27g, La G^{a}. *c.* 50-65 (893)

Site 2

Phases 1-4 : no stamps

Phase 5, F46

14. II 38. Fragment, Drag 15/17R or 18R, SG. Flavian or Flavian-Trajanic (1309)
15. II 45. C. Silvius Patricius, Drag 15/17 or 18, La G^{b}. *c.* 70-90 (1311)
16. II 45. Mon- (illiterate?), Drag 18, La G^{c}. *c.* 70-85 (1310)
17. II 45. Sextus-Canus or Sextius Can-, Drag 27(?), La G^{b}. *c.* 80-110 (1312)
18. II 46. Roppus ii, Drag 15/17R or 18R, MV^{b}. *c.* 100-120 (1313)

Site 3

Phase 1 : no stamps

Phase 2A

23. F3: II 10. Severus i, Drag 18, La G^{b}. *c.* 70-90 (714)

Phase 3C

24. F1: III 8. Fragment, Drag 18/31, CG. Hadrianic or early Antonine (715)
25. II 5. Calvus i, Drag 15/17, La G^{a}. *c.* 70-90 (712)
26. II 5. Paterclus ii, Drag 18/31, MV^{b}, Lz^{b}. *c.* 110-125 (713)

Site 4

Phases 1, 2 : no stamps

Site 5

Phases 1, 5 : no stamps

Site 5

Phase 2A

30. Calvus i, 5t, Drag 27g (burnt), OFCΛLVI, La G^{b}. (1) F39: VII 2.The site record for this stamp includes Caerleon, Chester and York. *c.* AD 70-95.
31. Censor i, 3g', Drag 27, OF•CE<N>, La G^{b}. (2) F39: VII 2. Stamps from this broken die are noted only on Drag 27, but the full die (OF•CEN) was used on dishes and a few bowls of Drag 29. This is almost certainly a stamp of Censor i, though the C is more like a G. *c.* AD 75-100.
32. Censor i, 8a, Drag 15/17R, CENSSORFEC, retrograde, La G^{b}. (3) F39: VII 3.There is little internal dating for this stamp but, like nos. 31 and 64, it will fall within the range *c.* AD 70-100.

33-34. Cosius Iucundus, 1a', Drag 18 (2), OFCO•IV<C>, La G^{a}. (4 + 5) F41: VI 26 + VI 27; (6) F36: V 27.A stamp from the complete version of the die (1a) occurs at Newstead, which should mean that the broken die was in use *c.* AD 85-110.

35. Cotio, 1a', Drag 33a, ƆOϒIO:C, La G^{a}. (7) F39: VII 2.This is from a modified die, on which the T has been recut so that it looks like a C. There is no site dating for either version, but the forms and fabrics suggest a range *c.* AD 80-110.
36. Frontinus, 28a, Drag 27g, FRONTI, retrograde, La G^{b}. (8) F36: V 27. Frontinus's decorated ware is probably not much earlier than *c.* AD 80, but he may have been making plain forms before that. This particular stamp occurs at Chester and Rottweil. *c.* AD 75-100.
37. Germanus i, 13c', Drag 18, [<GER>MA]NIOF, La G^{a}. (9) F41: VI 26.Stamps from this die occur at Burghöfe and there are two possibly from the pottery store there, destroyed in AD 69. There is also one from Wilderspool, however, which will be Domitianic. *c.* AD 65-90.
38. Gaius Iulius, 2a, Drag 18R, OFGΛI•IVL, La G^{a}. (10 + 11) F39: VII 2 +VII 3.The fabric and coarse rouletting of this dish suggest a Flavian-Trajanic date. Other examples of the stamp occur at Caerleon and Heidelburg-Neuenheim. *c.* AD 80-110.

39-42. Memor, 3a', Drag 27g (4), ΛEMORISΛ (4), La G^{a}. (12) F39: VII 3; (13, 14, 15) F41: VI 27. This stamp comes from a die which originally gave MEMORISM, but most of the examples noted by B. M. Dickinson and B. R. Hartley were stamped after the die had been reduced at both ends, through wear or fracture. A stamp from the full die occurs at Newstead and the reduced version is known from Butzbach and Walton-le-Dale. *c.* AD 80-100.

43. Mercator i, 11a, Drag 27g, MERC, La G^{b}. (16) F39: VII 43.There is no site dating for this stamp, but Mercator worked in the Flavian-Trajanic period, as the style of his decorated ware shows. *c.* AD 80-110.
44. Mommo, 9j, Drag 27g, [OF]MOM, La G^{b}. (17)

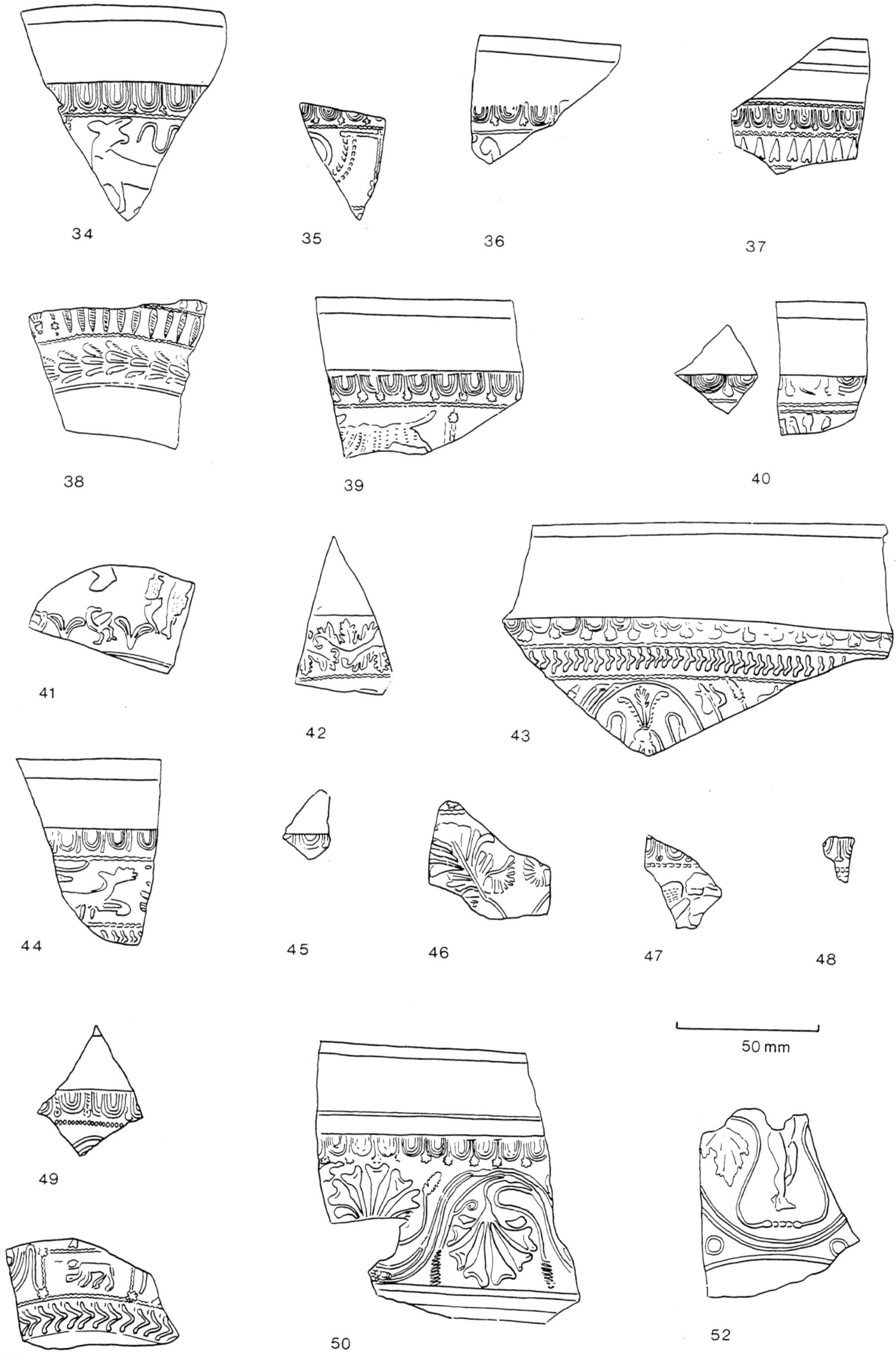

Fig 46 Decorated Samian Ware Site 2 (34-42); Site 3 (43-49); Site 4 (50-52). Scale 1:2

F40: VII 44. Mommo worked in both the Neronian and early-Flavian periods, though the bulk of his output is probably after AD 70. His wares occur in the Boudican burning at Colchester and in the Pompeii Hoard of AD 79. This particular stamp appears on plain ware at Castleford and on Drag 29 at Arles. *c.* AD 65-85.

45. Niger ii, 3b''', Drag 27g,)FNGII, La G^{a}. (18 + 19) F41: VI 26 + VI 27.This comes from a die which was modified four times, starting as OFNGRI and ending as FNGIII . There is no dating evidence for the final version, but this stamp, from the third modification, occurs on the pre-Flavian Drag 24, while there are a few stamps from earlier versions of the die at Flavian foundations. 3b''' probably falls within the range *c.* AD 60-75.

46-47. Paterclus ii, 17a; Drag 18, 18/31; PATERCLO (20 + 21) F39: VII 2 + VII 3; (22) F39: VII 43. This potter worked at both Les Martres-de-Veyre and Lezoux, though the fabrics associated with this die suggest that it was used only at Les Martres. Other stamps from dies used there occur in the London Second Fire groups and on a Trajanic Drag 15/17. A stamp from Die 17a at Binchester should be pre-Hadrianic. *c.* AD 100-125.

48-50. Pudens, 6a, Drag 27g (3), OFPVDE, La G^{b}. (23) F39: VII 3; (24 + 25) F41: VI 26 + VI 27; (26) F41: VI 27. Pudens occasionally made pre-Flavian forms, but the bulk of his output is Flavian. This particular stamp occurs at Carlisle and the Nijmegen fortress, while others come from Emerkingen (before AD 75), Chester and Ilkley. A few examples of Drag 29 are known. *c.* AD 70-85.

51. Rufus iii, 4a, Drag 27, OFRVF, La G^{b}. (27) F35: V 26.There is no evidence that this stamp was used in the pre-Flavian period, though Rufus probably began work in the 60s. Examples of 4a occur at Newstead and the main site at Corbridge. *c.* AD 70-95.

52. Sabinus iii, 16b, Drag 27g, OFSΛB, La G^{b}. (28) F41: VI 27. Sabinus iii worked in both the Neronian and early-Flavian periods and his range is *c.* AD 55-85. This cup is Flavian. *c.* AD 70-85.

53. Virilis i, 6a, Drag 18R, OF•VIRIL I (29 + 30) F41: VI 26 + VI 27.This occurs in a Flavian-Trajanic group at La Graufesenque and at the Saalburg, but it is also noted on Drag 29. *c.* AD 75-110.

54. Virilis i, 6c, Drag 18, OFVIRILI, La G^{b}. (31 + 32) F41: VI 26 + VI 27. A stamp noted from the Saalburg (3), Watercrook and the main site at Corbridge (2). It is not likely to be earlier than *c.* AD 85, therefore. *c.* AD 85-110.

55. MIIИ on Drag 15/17 or 18 etc., SG. (33) F39: VII 2. Possibly a stamp of a potter in Nem- or Men-, but more probably illiterate. Flavian or Flavian-Trajanic.

56. COS...VI on Drag 27, SG. (34) F36: V 27. Probably a stamp of Cosius Iucundus or L. Cosius Virilis. Flavian-Trajanic.

Phase 2B

57. VI 11. Vitalis ii, Drag 27, La G^{b}. *c.* 70-95 (35)

Phase 2C

58. IV 14. Mercator ii, Drag 18/31, Lz^{b}. *c.* 125-150 (36)
59. VI 9. Illegible, Drag 27g, SG. Flavian or Flavian-Trajanic (37)
60. VI 31. Nequres, Drag 27g, La G^{b}. *c.* 60-85 (38)

Phase 3A

61. VI 7. Ave vale, Drag 29, La G^{c}. *c.* 70-85 (39)
62. F49: IV 8. Logirnus, Drag 15/17 or 18, La G^{a}. *c.* 70-90 (51)
63. VI 7. Illiterate, Drag 27, SG. Flavian or Flavian-Trajanic (40)
64. VII 9. Censor i, Drag 15/17R or 18R, La G^{b}. *c.* 80-100 (41)
65. VII 9. Tasgillus ii, Drag 18/31R, MV^{a}. *c.* 100-125 (42)

Phase 3B

66. V 13. Pontus, Drag 27, La G^{b}. *c.* 70-95 (44)
67. V 13. Illiterate, Drag 27, SG. Flavian or Flavian-Trajanic (45)
68. F38: VI 24. Logirnus, Drag 15/17 or 18, La G^{a}. *c.* 75-90 (46)
69. VI 29. Certus ii, Drag 33, Lz^{b}. Early to Mid-Antonine. (47)

Phase 3C

70. V 12 + (unphased) V 31. Verecundus ii, Drag 27g, La G^{c}. *c.* 70-100 (43 + 63)
71. VI 28. Fragment, Drag 38, CG. Mid- to late Antonine (48)
72. VII 24. Fragment, Drag 27g, SG. Flavian-Trajanic (49)
73. X 3. Vitalis ii, Drag 18, La G^{b}. *c.* 70-95 (69)
74. X 5. Murranus, Drag 18, La G^{b}. *c.* 60-75 (70)
75. X 5. Rufus iii, Drag 18, La G^{b}. *c.* 65-90 (71)
76. X 5. Vitalis ii, Drag 18, La G^{a}. *c.* 80-100 (72)
77. X 5. Illiterate, Drag 27g, SG. Flavian or Flavian-Trajanic (73)

Phase 3D

78. F64 : I 39. Gongius, Drag 33, Lz^{b}. *c.* 140-165 (50)

Phase 4B

79. I 4. Banoluccus, Drag 18/31, Lz^{c}. *c.* 140-170 (52)

Phase 4C

80. I 28. Aventinus ii, Drag 18/31 or 31, Lz^{a}. *c.* 150-180 (53)
81. VII 47. Illiterate(?), Drag 15/17 or 18 etc., SG. Flavian or Flavian-Trajanic (see no. 55 above) (54)

Area 5, unphased

90. Calvus i, 5ff, Drag 15/17R, OFCALVI, La G^{a}. (64 + 65 + 66) V 32 + 33 + 34. This stamp was used mainly on rouletted dishes, though there are a few examples on bowls of Drag 29, with decoration typical of the period *c.* AD 70-85. The site record includes Carlisle, Camelon and Newstead. *c.* AD 70-90.

Site 6

Phases 1, 3, 5, 6 : no stamps

Phase 2B

114. I 42. Cotto ii, Drag 29, La G^{a}. *c.* 70-85 (424)

Phase 4A

115. I 25. Severus i, Drag 33a, La G^{b}. *c.* 85-105 (423)

Phase 7A

116. I 10 + (ph 8E) F1 : I 62. Aeturnus, Drag 31, Lz^{a}. *c.* 155-185 (422 + 425)
117. I 4. Divicatus, Drag 33, Lz^{b}. *c.* 140-160 (421)

Conventions

Each entry gives: excavation report catalogue number, potter's name (i, ii, etc., where homonyms are involved), die number (nos. 30-56, 90), form of vessel, reading of stamp (nos. 30-56, 90), pottery of origin, discussion (nos. 30-56, 90), date.

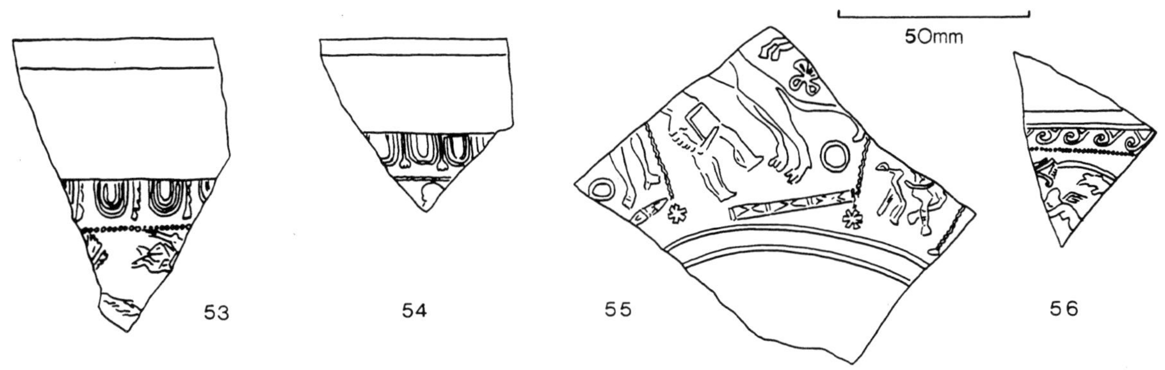

Fig. 47 Decorated Samian Ware Site 8 (53-56) Scale 1:2

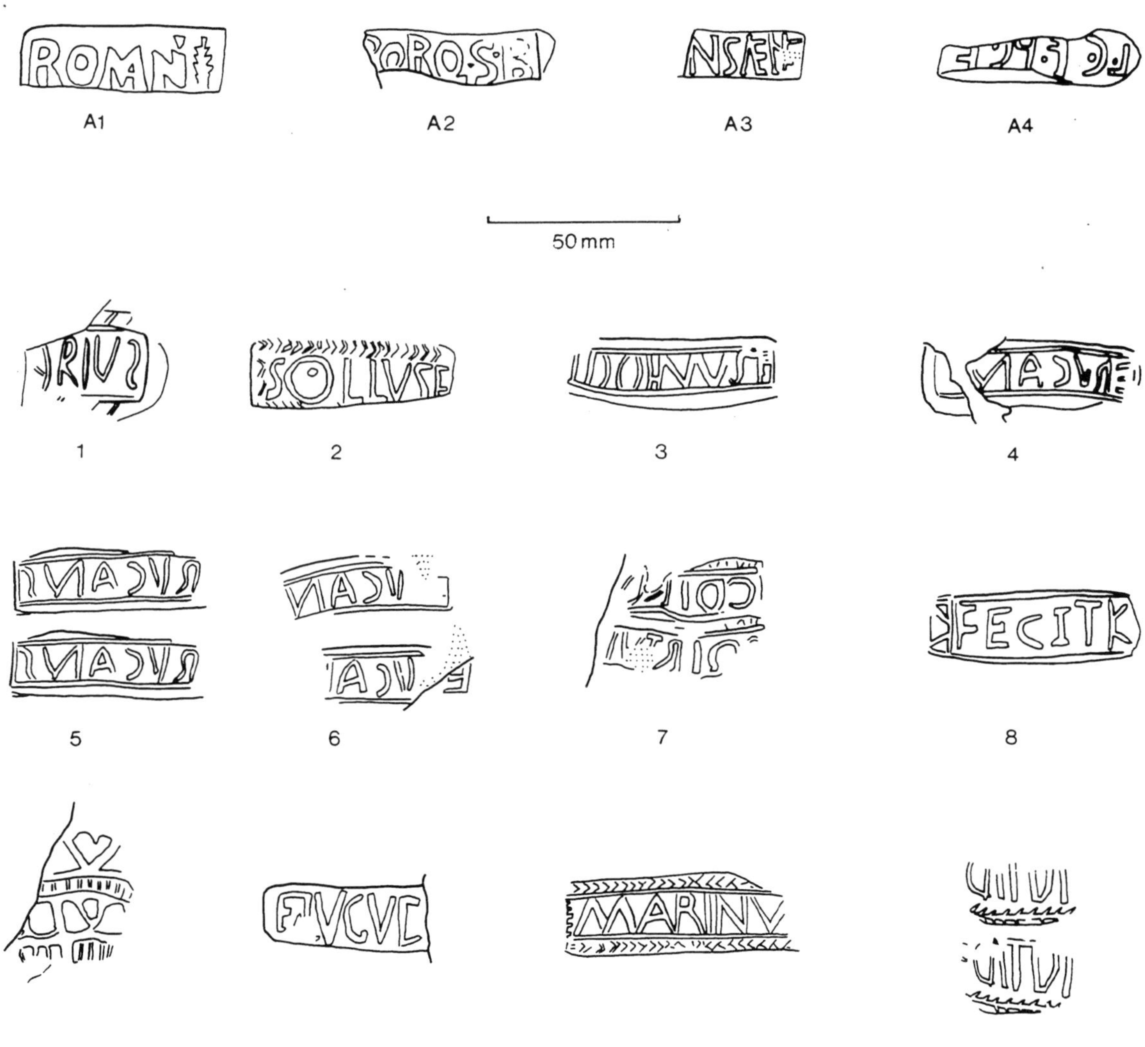

Fig. 48 Amphora Stamps (A1-A4); Mortarium Stamps (1-12) Scale 1:2

(a), (b), (c) in superscript indicate:

(a) A stamp attested at the pottery in question.

(b) Not attested at the pottery in question, but other stamps of the potter known from there.

(c) Assigned to the pottery on the evidence of form, fabric, distribution etc.

Underlined letters are ligatured.

Letters in [ ] brackets restore the readings of broken dies.

Letters in ( ) brackets do not register on the stamps in question.

Discussion of the stamped samian from Site 5, phase 2A. Brenda M Dickinson

Among the stamped samian from Site 5 were some substantially complete cups and dishes by nine different potters, eight working at La Graufesenque, the other at Les Martres-de-Veyre. As these vessels occurred in three separate features, all thought to have been filled in a single operation, the question of whether they may have come from a shop or store arises.

All the vessels have unworn, or very slightly worn, footrings. Some also have inside their bases the remains of the rings of grit which separated pots in the kilns, but wore off rapidly when they were used. Some of the stamps appear more than once and in more than one feature. The potters involved are Censor i (nos. 31-32), Cosius Iucundus (nos. 33-34), Gaius Iulius (no. 38) Memor (nos. 39-42), Niger ii (no. 45), Pudens (nos. 48-50), Rufus iii (no. 51), Sabinus iii (no. 52), and Virilis i (nos. 53-54), all South Gaulish, and the Central Gaulish Paterclus ii (nos. 46-47). A dish with a stamp of Calvus i (no. 90) belongs to none of the relevant features, but is approximately half-complete, with an unworn footring.

In addition, there are several less-complete vessels in the filling, mostly without surviving footrings, though one with an illiterate stamp (no. 56) has an unworn footring. Almost all of the more-or-less complete vessels are Flavian or early-Trajanic, but the cup stamped by Niger (half-complete) might be thought to be earlier. However, it is stamped with a very devolved version of a die which began in the 60s, and it could itself have been produced in the 70s. The two Central Gaulish dishes could be early-Trajanic, but might be as late as the 120s.

It would not be totally impossible for the more complete vessels, unused when discarded, to have reached the site together or over a relatively short time, in the 80s, apart from the dishes stamped by Paterclus, and the cup by Niger.

On the evidence of the samian, the filling of the features in question, if it really does represent a single operation, cannot have taken place before *c.* AD 100 at the earliest. The latest potter present, Paterclus ii, was certainly working at Lezoux after AD 125, having moved from Les Martres-de-Veyre, and is most unlikely to have started work in the 1st century.

The presence of so much unused pottery is in itself unusual, unless we are dealing with a shop or store. If so, most of the discarded stock seems to have remained unsold for a remarkably long time.

The Amphorae

Stamps on Amphorae from Site 5. Cesar Carreras and David F Williams (Fig. 48)

All stamps are on Dressel 20 handles in fabric AM9A.

A1. ROMANI
CIL 3130. Bonsor (1931) 93. Callender (1965) 1541. Remesal Rodriguez (1977) 224.
Produced at Las Delicias in Flavian period.
ST. RO<u>MA</u> <u>NI</u> (palm_N)
Dating: Fishbourne AD 43-75
Augst AD 30-90
Cala Culip Vespasian
Typology Flavian-Trajanic
Other examples: Chester, Fishbourne, London, Sea Mills, Campfield, Cirencester and Hengisbury Head.
(392) VI 10, Phase 2C

A2. PORQSH
New stamp
ST. (P?)OR(Q?)(.)S(.)(H?)
No dating
(394) VII 9, Phase 3A

A3. HISPANISAENI
CIL 2916. Callendar 1559. Ponsich (1979), 43, 79. Remesal Rodriguez (1977) 131.
Produced at Huerta del Nicasio in Flavian period.
ST. .]<u>NI</u> S <u>AE</u>N
Dating: Avenches AD 50-100
Elchenville Flavian
Augst AD 90-130
Other examples: Caersws, York, Cirencester, Sea Mills and London.
(398) VII 48, Phase 3C

A4. LCFFC
CIL 2746a. Callender 823. Remesal Rodriguez (1989) 4.
Produced at Cerro de los Pessebres
ST. LC(.)F(.)FC
No dating
(399) VII u/s, residual in a medieval feature (M. Hebditch site notes).
R.J. Pollard reads the stamp as L(.)C(.)F(.)FC(.)E, equating with Callender 823 (b), and Fig. 8.31.

Additions to the Fabric Type Series

Amphora Fabric 25.

Two variations on the fabric described elsewhere (MacRobert, 1987, 66) occur here. The first comprises a pair of light grey (10YR 6/1-7/2) bodysherds from Site 6, 41 + 42, of uncertain form. The second comprises the flagon, Camulodunum 139 (no. 57).

Cam 139 is in a reddish brown fabric (2.5YR 5/4) with very pale brown ext slip (10YR) and light reddish brown (5YR) int surface. This is the Campanian amphora fabric (Peacock, 1971, 164, Fabric 2; Williams, 1987, 80-1 and Fig. 42.46; Williams and Peacock, 1979, Fig. 34.6). The one-handled flagon may date to *c.* AD 1-80, or more narrowly to AD 20-60, and is apparently rare in Britain (cf Hawkes and Hull, 1947, 243-244). I am grateful to A. P. Fitzpatrick for comment on this vessel.

Amphora Fabric 28

A soft (abraded), fine-fractured fabric with a harsh feel from the presence of Mo F-C R, SA i/a quartz inclusions (cf the less sandy AM15 - Pollard, forthcoming (a)). Other inclusions: calcite, Sp-Mo C-VC (3mm) A, SA and platey, i/a; red iron ore, Sp, F-VC (5mm), R, A, i/a; Fr VF white mica. A grey (N5) fabric with red-

Table 4: The Amphorae: Fabric quantification by Site

	Sherd Count										Weight (grams)										Types (sites in brackets)
Site	1	2	3	4	5	6	8	9	11	Totals	1	2	3	4	5	6	8	9	11	Totals	
Fabric																					
1.	1									1	2									2	
2.		1								1		20								20	
3.			1		1					2			17		30					47	Dr 2-4?(5)
4.	1				1					2	88				45					133	
5.			2				1			3			57				19			76	Dr 2-4?(8)
6.					1					1					10					10	stopper (5)
7.	4	7	1		19	53				84	439	554	20		1312	1154				3477	London 555(2); Cam 186C(5) Cam 186?(5,6): Dr 21/22?(5) stopper (5,6)
8.	3			2	1					6	69			17	6					92	stopper (5)
9A.	20	38	3	3	36	31	2	1		134	3132	5242	679	309	6531	2142	282	1400		19717	Dr 20(all);Dr 14(5); Haltern 70(5); cylindrical(2)
9B.	2	1		2	2	2			1	10	317	127		108	722	237			473	1984	Dr 20(1,2,4,5,6,11)
10.		1			1					1					42					42	Rhodian?(5)
11.		1			1					2		125			120					245	
12.	6	21		1	89	17				134	122	837		18	3376	801				5154	Pelichet 47(2,5,6); Dr 2-4? (2,5); stopper (1,2,5)
13.	2									2	88									88	
16.	1									1	69									69	
18.	5				3					8	74				216					290	Cam 189(1); 'carrot' handle(5)
19.	5	3			5	1				14	100	72			162	5				339	Fishbourne 148.3(1,5); British Bi(1)
23.	4	1			1	2				8	175	10			50	18				253	Cam 189?(1, 5); Verulamium 1918? (2. 6); Kingsholm 117? (5)
25.		66								66		1622								1622	Cam 139 (2)
25.	1					2				3	110				31					141	misc
28.			2							2			50							50	
29.					1					1					41					41	Pelichet 47? (5)
30.						1				1						6				6	
Totals	55	140	9	8	162	109	3	1	1	488	4782	8609	823	452	12663	4394	301	1400	473	33898	

dish yellow (5YR) margins and int surface, and very pale brown to yellow (10YR 7/4-7/6) ext surface. Wheel thrown, possibly with a wiped ext. Type unknown, presumed to be an amphora. Site 3, I 31, phase 3A.

Amphora Fabric 29

A hard, finely irregular smooth wheel thrown fabric, very pale brown (10YR 8/4). Inclusions: quartz and unidentified rock fragments (including feldspars?): Ab i/a VF-C, A; ironstone(?) Sp, M-C aggregates. Possibly Pelichet 47/Gauloise series. Site 5, VII 45 (F21) phase 6B, residual.

Amphora Fabric 30

A hard, finely irregular, smooth, light red to reddish yellow (2.5YR to 5YR 6/6) fabric. Characterised by C-VC mica plates highly visible on surface, and high calcite content in fracture; cf AM3 (Pollard, forthcoming (a)), with more visible calcite, and more Fr C-VC mica. Inclusions: calcite, Ab w/s VF-F, Sp M, SA; 'gold' and 'white' micas, each Mo, i/a, VF-VC (2mm) with median *c.* 0.5-1.0mm, total Fr; red iron ore, Sp, i/a, F-C, A; quartz Sp M-C, Mo(?) VF, i/a, A; black rock fragments or mineral, Sp, F-C, A. Type unknown, presumed to be amphora. Site 6, I 28, phase 3A.

Discussion (Table 4)

A total of 488 sherds, weighing 33.898 kg, was recovered, being present on all sites with analysed assemblages except Site 10. Three fabrics predominate: AM7, AM9A, and AM12, with the types occurring most frequently in each being respectively Camulodunum 186 (Beltran I/IIA, Peacock and Williams 1986 Classes 17-18), Dressel 20 (*ibid.* Class 25), and Pelichet 47 (*ibid.* Class 27; formerly classified as Dressel 30: Peacock, 1978). Minimum vessel numbers have not been calculated (cf Sealey, 1985), although any future synthesis of the amphorae from Leicester could adopt this method of calculation. These three types are generally the most common in horizons of Flavian and later date. Dressel 2-4 may occur in four fabrics here; AM3, AM5, AM9A, and AM12 (cf Pollard, forthcoming (a)). Pelichet 47 would appear to have eclipsed this type as the major amphora carrying wine into Britain by the 2nd century, and is overall probably the second most common amphora in Britain, conceding primacy to the olive oil amphora Dressel 20. Imports of both appear to have peaked during the 2nd century (Peacock, 1978; Williams and Peacock, 1983), with a more restricted trade down to the mid 3rd century. Dressel 20s of late 2nd century+ date generally occur in the more compact, reddish AM9B, with its salt-whitened surface contrasting more emphatically with the undersurface than on the grey-buff AM9A.

Several less familiar types are present. These include Haltern 70 (Peacock and Williams, 1986, Class 15) (nos. 171, 206) and its alleged offspring London 555 (a rough cast sherd, cf Green, 1981 Fig. 19.13) (Sealey, 1985); Fishbourne 148.3 (Cunliffe 1971; Timby 1985a; Pollard, forthcoming (a)) (no. 170) (see report below by Williams); the Rhodian type (Peacock and Williams, 1986, Class 9; Timby 1985a; Peacock, 1977a; Sealey, 1985) (no. 213); several sherds of rilled 'carrot' vessels including a Camulodunum 189 rim (Peacock and Williams, 1986, Class 12) (no. 13), a base possibly of the same form or of Kingsholm 117 (Timby 1985a; Sealey, 1985; Peacock and Williams, 1986, Class 66) (no. 169), and sherds possibly of Verulamium 1918 or 1919 (Wilson, 1984; Pollard, forthcoming (a)); and an unclassified type (no. 183). A sherd of British Bi from Site 1 (unstratified: III A 1 (.971); idenfication confirmed by R. Tomber, *pers comm;* Peacock and Williams, 1986, Class 43) is a very unusual record for Eastern England. The fabric, AM19, is a variant on the usual for this type. In addition, Site 2 produced one flagon, Camulodunum 139, in AM25: this comprises 4.9% by weight (13.6% by sherd count) of the total collection of amphora fabrics. Stoppers occur in fabrics AM6, 7, 8 and 12.

A Note on the Petrology of examples of Amphora type Fishbourne 148.3 from Leicester David F. Williams

Three rims of this type were submitted to the author for analysis. All are from sites around the forum.

1) A302.1971.1978 (Pollard forthcoming (a), no. 169)
2) A295.1973.1854
3) A421.1965 (Todd 1973, Fig. 28.18)

The above are three amphora rim-sherds of an unusual type previously published from Period I levels at Fishbourne (Cunliffe, 1971, Fig. 100, Type 148.3). The rim of this form is quite distinctive, and can perhaps be best described as having a small bead-rim sitting on top of a larger one. All three sherds are in a hard, rough sandy fabric, light to darkish buff outside surface colour (7.5YR 8/6 to 7/4), with a reddish-brown core. Small samples were detached from each of the Leicester sherds for thin sectioning and study under the petrological microscope. This showed a similar range of non-plastic inclusions and texture in the fabric of all three rims. The principal components are frequent grains of subangular quartz up to 1.20mm in size, though the majority are of a smaller size-grade than this, flecks of mica, limestone and a little foraminifera. The closeness in fabric of all three sherds suggests a common area of origin, but this is difficult to predict given the fairly common range of inclusions, apart from pointing to a sedimentary environment. Other examples of this particular amphora type have been encountered by the writer from York, Dorchester and Colchester as well as Fishbourne itself. All have a similar fabric to the Leicester sherds.

The Mortaria

Stamped Mortaria Kay Hartley (Fig. 48)

Site 3

1 MO4. The broken stamp is from one of the eight dies of Sarrius, with the last letter reversed. This die does not appear on his latest work; his activity may be dated to *c.* AD 135-165/170, and took place in at least two potteries, at Rossington Bridge, Doncaster (Hartley, 1986, 148-149), and Mancetter-Hartshill. 'White' fabrics were confined to the latter, which supplied Sarrius' Midlands customers. This particular vessel was so heavily overfired or burnt before fracture that it is extremely hard and pale grey throughout; the surface is almost vitrified. Profile: Fig. 55.111.(608) II 4, phase 3C.

Site 5

2 MO7. The broken stamp is from the most commonly used die of Sollus. More than a hundred mortaria of his are known, including four from Brockley Hill where he may have worked and four from Scotland. The rim-forms made by him are consistently early in type, and a date within the period AD 60-100 is reasonably certain. Profile: Fig. 59.149.(224) F41: VI 25, phase 2A.

3 MO10. A worn vessel with a stamp of Doinus. Evidence for his workshop has been found at Brockley Hill, and more than a hundred mortaria of his are known from sites throughout Britain, including three from Flavian sites in Scotland. Activity within the period AD 70-120 is certain, and it is probable that the die used for this example belonged to the early part of his career, AD 70-100. Further discussion may be found in K.F. Hartley 1972, 375 and Fig. 145.19-20. The fabric is at the coarser end of the MO10 range; it is by no means the finest version of Verulamium region fabric. Profile: Fig. 59.150.(234+236) F41: VI 25; + F39, VII 43, phase 2A.

4 MO12. A retrograde stamp of Erucanus; the vessel was slightly burnt before fracture. Only one die-type is known for Erucanus, giving retrograde stamps with ER and NV ligatured. Mortaria of his have been noted (up to mid 1987) from the following sites: Bainbridge, Doncaster, Kirkby Thore, Leicester (up to 11), Manduessedum, Melandra Castle, Northwich (2), Ribchester (2), Templeborough, Tripontium, Vindolanda, Wall, Wilderspool (2), and Wroxeter. The fabric used (of which that of nos. 5 and 6 below is a slightly less sandy variant) and the distribution show that Erucanus worked in the Midlands. A single surface find from the pottery production area at Manduessedum (Mancetter) cannot be taken as proof of manufacture there but the distribution is a typical one for these potteries, especially the very high number at Leicester which was the nearest large market. The fabric also fits with production there before *c.* AD 130-140. The Bainbridge stamp is from a Flavian-Trajanic deposit outside the east gate, dated AD 80-125. The rim-profiles of the three vessels from Redcross Street (Fig. 59.151-153 below) are unlikely to be later than AD 110 and might be as early as AD 80, but a few of his

mortaria have profiles which would best fit a date in the early 2nd century. A date of AD 80-120 must cover the period of his activity with the proviso that some of his work is almost certain to be 1st century. Profile: Fig. 59.151.(239) F39: VII 38, phase 2A.

5 MO18. More than one-third of the rim of a vessel generally similar, but not identical, to no. 6, with two stamps from the same die impressed close together. The surfaces are in a better condition than no. 6, though worn nonetheless, but there is some discolouration. Profile: Fig. 59.152. (250+252) F39: VII 2 + VII 3, phase 2A.

6 MO18. Fifteen joining fragments comprising *c.* 90% of a vessel which has been subjected to unusually heavy wear. The upper surface is exfoliated and all surfaces have suffered varying degrees of discolouration. The two stamps impressed close together to the right of the spout are, unusually, not complemented by impressions on the opposite side. Profile: Fig. 59.153. (251+253) F39: VII 2 + VII 3, phase 2A.

7 MO22. Two retrograde stamps from the single die of Coertutinus areimpressed close together on this vessel fragment; they read COIRTV'I' . None of his stamps show more than a single upright stroke between the O and R but the spacing suggests that E is intended. Neither spelling of this celtic name is otherwise recorded. His mortaria have now been noted from Alcester (Warks: 3), Baginton, Coleshill (Warks), Holditch (Staffs), Leicester (up to 9), Manduessedum (2), Margidunum, Tripontium (2) and Wilderspool (2). As with Erucanus, all the evidence from distribution points to production in the Mancetter-Hartshill potteries, but the rim-profiles suggest a slightly later date, within the period AD 90-130 (from Leicester, cf Hartley 1973a Fig. 24.4, and a vessel from the Shakespeare's Head site, Pollard, forthcoming (d)). Coertutinus's work is unusual in that he used two widely differing clays, one producing the normal cream mortaria, while the other, an iron-rich clay, produced hard red fabrics similar to this example. Four mortaria with his stamp are known in this fabric, all of them from Leicester; unstamped fragments from at least three other such mortaria, which could well be his, are also recorded from Leicester (e.g. Fig. 55.91 below). Although the potters of the Mancetter-Hartshill industry very rarely produced mortaria from such clays, they were available and were freely used for making other kinds of vessel. Profile: Fig. 59.154. (258) F39: VII 2, phase 2A.

8 MO7. A rim fragment with a 'fecit' counterstamp. The letters on the namestamp always associated with this counterstamp are not clearly delineated but the name intended is evidently Martinus or Marinus (cf K.F. Hartley, 1972, 373 and Fig. 145.27). Fourteen mortaria with either name- or counterstamp surviving have been recorded, from sites throughout England. The mortaria are typical of products of the potteries in the Verulamium region, and the rim-profiles point to a date *c.* AD 70-110. Profile: Fig. 60.172.(228) VII 25, phase 2C.

9 MO12. A broken stamp of Vitalis IV, whose kilns have been excavated at Hartshill. Excluding mortaria from the kilnsite, up to forty-eight vessels have been recorded with stamps from the same die; these include six from Leicester (e.g. Pollard, forthcoming (a), no. 204 in fabric MO18, and a vessel from Silver Street, Pollard forthcoming (*c.*), in MO14) and one from Scotland, at Newstead. The rim-profiles used by Vitalis, his association with other potters at Hartshill, and the single stamp from Scotland indicate activity within the period AD 110-145. This example is not one of his latest products. Profile: Fig. 60.173. (238). VII 9, phase 3A.

10 MO7. A worn mortarium with discoloured surface. The stamp, which reads F.LVGVDV when complete, is a counterstamp of Albinus, who appears to have worked in the Verulamium region *c.* AD 60-90. Some fifteen of his mortaria are known from Leicester, with an overall distribution throughout Roman Britain (cf K.F. Hartley, 1972, 371-2 and Fig. 145.2-11; Hartley 1984, 281-2, nos. 55-61; Hartley, 1987, 79 and Fig. 35.60). Profile: Fig. 61.185. (25). V 7, phase 3A.

11 MO7. The stamp is from one of the many dies of Marinus. More than a hundred of his mortaria are known from occupation sites in Roman Britain including three or four from Newstead, Scotland. His workshop was at Brockley Hill where fifteen of his stamps have been found. The Newstead vessels should be earlier than AD 105, and a stamp from Richborough is from a pit filled *c.* AD 90 (Bushe-Fox, 1949, 251, 17(B)(i)). This evidence, plus the range of rim-forms made by him point to the period *c.* AD 80-120 for his work. Profile: Fig. 63.214.(219) V 36, unphased.

Site 9

12 MO4. There are two potter's stamps, impressed close together. No other examples of this stamp are known but it is so distinctive that identification will certainly be possible when further examples are found. The rim profile (Fig. 67.295) points to a date within the period AD 140-180.(12).

Site 11 (A20.1939)

13 MO7. (not illustrated). Fragmentary namestamp.]IM[(?), letters with serif, herringbone border. The rim profile (Fig. 68.302) points to a date within the Neronian-Flavian period (cf. Wilson 1972 and 1984 no. 95). (Report by R. J. Pollard) (10) I 3.

Additions to the Fabric Type Series

Mortarium Fabric 22

Fabric. Hard, smooth, fine (finely irregular x20), wheel thrown. Inclusions: Mo F-C, Fr(?) subvisible-VF, SA, A, R, i/a quartz; Sp F-VC (2mm), SA i/a black and red iron ore; Sp VF white mica; Sp white (?)calcite, VF-VC (3mm), R, SA. Mo trituration grit of flint (up to 7mm), quartz and black ironstone. Light red (2.5YR) core, reddish yellow (5YR 6/6) margins, and a very pale brown to yellow (10YR 8/3-8/6) overall slip. The fabric falls within the range of WS2, resembling MO11 (late Swanpool ware: Pollard forthcoming, (a)) except for the trituration grit.
Discussion and illustrations. See no. 7 above.

Mortarium Fabric 24

Fabric. Hard to very hard, smooth, fine to finely irregular fracture, wheel thrown. Inclusions: Fr VF-M, Sp-Mo C, SA, R, i/a translucent and opaque quartz; Sp VF-C, A, i/a red iron ore. Ab trituration grit of M-C, SA, A, R, quartz, with Sp iron ore as in fabric, and Sp, C, 'gold' mica, packed closely overall on the interior; there are some slight indications of fine concentric scoring. Kay Hartley comments: huge mortaria of this general type, in this fabric, with this kind of trituration and with a corrugated exterior were imported from the Rhineland in the second half of the 2nd century and probably in the first half of the 3rd century. They are widely but thinly dispersed and generally similar ones have been noted from Carlisle (publication forthcoming), Colchester (Hull, 1963, Fig. 5.8), Exeter (Bidwell, 1979, Fig. 69.244), Greta Bridge, Southwark (Hammerson and Murray, 1978, 366, Fig. 163.1230), and York. They may have had a specialised use in bakehouses or workshops.
Illust. 198. Roughly one-quarter of a very similar vessel in the same fabric was recovered in one piece associated with pottery of

Table 5: The Mortaria: Fabric quantification by Site

	Sherd count										Weight (grams)									
Site	1	2	3	4	5	6	8	9	11	Totals	1	2	3	4	5	6	8	9	11	Totals
Fabric																				
1. Oxfordshire				1	2					3				10	146					156
2. "		1	1	2		1				5		29	9	53		44				135
3. "			5		2		7						48		55					103
4. Midlands/Mancetter-Hartshill	2		4	3	14	12		8	2	45	62		323	189	1525	881		913	121	4014
6. Lower Nene Valley			1	1						2			7	130						137
7. Verulamium region	23	8	9	1	49	1			2	93	1672	498	550	156	7234	140			559	10809
8. North Gaul					12	24				36					1067	1327				2394
9. " (?)			1		1					2			17		35					52
10. Verulamium region (?)					4					4					958					958
12 .Midlands/Mancetter-Hartshill	1	8	1		6	3				19	54	875	345		517	314				2105
14. Midlands					1	2				3					1135	187				1322
15. North Gaul/South-east Britain	2		1		5					8	195		65		1174					1434
17. South-west Britain (?)			2							2			62							62
18. Midlands/Mancetter-Hartshill		2	9	1	33	1	1			47		137	113	74	4592	336	218			5470
19. " "		1			3					4		15			1670					1685
22. Midlands		2			1					3		160			125					285
24. Rhineland					1					1					680					680
Totals	28	22	34	9	134	44	1	8	4	284	1983	1714	1529	512	20913	3229	218	913	680	31801

the late 2nd to mid 3rd century from the Norfolk Street villa (Pollard, forthcoming (e)), which lay within sight of Roman Leicester.

Discussion (Table 5)

The dominant position held by three fabrics, MO4, MO7 and MO18, reflects general trends in Leicester. The Verulamium region was the major exporter of mortaria to the city from *c.* AD 60-100, with an overall date range within *c.* AD 50-140. The development and expansion of Midlands potteries, notably at Mancetter-Hartshill, from *c.* AD 80 through the reign of Trajan, eroded the former region's market share in both the Midlands and the north (Hartley, 1973b). Evidence is accumulating that fabrics with a mixed trituration grit suite featuring *c.* 30% or more quartz (MO12, MO13(?), MO14, MO18) were produced in far greater abundance than those with grog grit (MO4, MO19) from the time of the inception of the Midlands industries in the days of Erucanus up to the early Antonine period. This is apparent both at Leicester (cf Pollard, forthcoming (a)), and, for example, at Doncaster (Hartley, 1986, Fabric 11). The fine 'pipeclay' fabric MO4 was used virtually to the exclusion of all others by the potters of Mancetter-Hartshill after this time.

These trends in mortarium production and trade are important for dating 2nd century assemblages. The mortaria from phases 3-8 on Site 1 include, by weight, 83.5% of MO7, 3% of MO12 and 3.5% of MO4. Those from phase 4 and F46 on Site 2 (the pottery from which levels covers the period *c.* AD 60-150) include 64.1% of MO12, 24.6% of MO7 and 11.3% of MO18. It is of equal significance that on Site 2, where over 75% of pottery by weight had been deposited by the end of phase 4 (*c.* AD 150), MO4 is entirely absent. The group of pits from phase 2A on Site 5 (F35-37, 39-42) held a mortarium assemblage which tells a similar story for the very late 1st to early 2nd century. The EVEs statistics are not directly comparable with weights statistics (cf Orton, 1975), but studies of Leicester assemblages have demonstrated that the general picture obtained from the two quantification methods can be remarkably similar (cf Pollard forthcoming (a)). Here, MO18 comprises 66.3%, MO7 + the finer variant MO10 20%, and MO12 5.9%. The remainder is made up of MO22 (4.7%) and the Gallo-Belgic MO8 (3.1%), both fabrics having a *terminus ante quem c.* AD 150.

There are other points of interest in the collection from these sites. Two sites (1 and 3) included wall-sided mortaria in MO15, of Claudian date (cf Hartley, 1981, 196), both in assemblages in which 'native' Late Iron Age to Neronian wares predominate. The former, though the sole sherd in its context (VI 36) is in phase 2; the latter is associated with Gallo-Belgic fine wares (4.7% by weight), 'native' fine and coarse wares (44.9%), calcite gritted wares (37.1%), the early white slip ware flagons (see below p 71) (2.6%) and single sherds of an unidentified white ware and a Romano-British grey ware (totalling 0.5% by weight). It can be seen therefore that mortaria were amongst the earliest Roman imports to be acquired by the population of the nascent city. The earliest deposits at Jewry Wall to contain this form (Kenyon's Mortarium Type A) were provided by the excavator with a *terminus ante quem* of *c.* AD 75-80 (Kenyon 1948, 42).

The phase 2A pits from Site 5 provide vital evidence for the dating of the beginnings of the Midlands (Mancetter-Hartshill?) mortarium industry. The three vessels bearing the stamp of Erucanus, to which may be added a fourth, heavily worn, unstamped fragment from nearby (V 30, in MO12), and the vessel with the Coertutinus stamp, were associated with a group of virtually mint condition samian vessels almost all of which are Flavian or Trajanic (p 64). It seems likely, in order to account for the relative conditions of mortaria and samian, that the former must be amongst the earliest products not merely of this industry but of these specific potters.

The 'Coertutinus' fabric and the Rhineland import have been discussed above. A third fabric of particular interest is MO17, represented by a vessel from Site 3. Unhappily, it is found in a medieval level, but is thought to be a 2nd century import from the south-west or Midlands (Pollard, forthcoming (a)). It is of a form with a beaded rim and probably hooked flange, perhaps resembling Fig. 55.94 here.

The Gallo-Belgic and Related Wares

The term "Gallo-Belgic" was coined by G. Chenet in the 1920s (Hawkes and Hull, 1947, 202-4). Research by British scholars in recent years has been conducted by Valery Rigby and Jane Timby, and it has been recognised that some types were made in Central Gaul rather than in the province of Gallia Belgica (e.g. the platters Cam 1 and Cam 4), whilst the butt beaker Cam 113, for which a British source was favoured by Hawkes and Hull (*ibid.* 238-9), is now thought to have been made in northern Gaul (Rigby, 1989, 137). Production of terra nigra may also have occurred in Germania Inferior, at Cologne (*ibid.* 126), and in Britain, at Camulodunum (Rigby, 1986, 226).

Several major reports on "Gallo-Belgic" wares by Rigby appeared in the 1980s with form type series developed for site assemblages (Rigby, 1981a, 1986, 1989). Cross-referencing between these series is limited, with the Camulodunum series used as a common reference point in view of its entrenched usage. Fabric classification is consistent, based on a modified version of the Hawkes and Hull model (1947, 204). Subdivision is restricted to variants of terra rubra and to the differentiation of micaceous - formerly and erronously referred to as "mica-dusted" (Rigby, 1981a) - TN from the remainder. Attempts at sub-dividing the non-micaceous TN (*ibid.*, 159) have been dropped (Rigby, 1989, 121). Dates for "Gallo-Belgic" forms are best sought in the Baldock (Rigby, 1986, 230-1) and King Harry Lane (Rigby, 1989) reports. The latter contains a detailed discussion of the typology of Cam 113 (pp 136-41). Timby's research (1982, 1987) may be published in a revised form in the 1990s.

The study of Leicester's assemblages gathered momentum in the 1980s with a re-evaluation of the Jewry Wall site material by Jarvis with advice from Rigby (Jarvis, 1986), publication of a diverse assemblage by Clamp (1985) including two stamps on TN (Rigby, 1985), and thin sectioning programmes by Timby (1982) and by Ian Freestone for the British Museum, the last of white and cream slipped wares.

Form and Fabric attributions in the following catalogue are by the writer.

Terra Nigra

Site 1

Platter, Cam 1, micaceous TN, Central Gaulish (Fig. 50.2), with graffito (Fig. 49.G1; p.70). *c.* 10 BC-AD 25. (217). F47, III 51, phase 1B.

Platter, Cam 5. Date range within *c.* 15 BC-AD 65 in TN (223). F73, V 59, phase 1B. Second example, identification uncertain. (219). III 70, phase 1C.

Platter, Cam 8. *c.* 20-65. (221). F28, III 49, residual in phase 3C.

Platter, Cam 13. Three examples from King Harry Lane are given dates which span the period 1-60, whilst the "hybrid" Cam 12/13 is dated 25-50 (Rigby 1989, 123; 1986, 230 respectively). (220). F54, IIIA 77, phase 1B.

Platter, Cam 16. *c.* 40-85. (222). F73, V 49, phase 1B.

Platter sherds. Bases from two contexts. (218). F49, IIIA 68, phase 3B. A second vessel with a marked "kick" : (224). VI 28, phase 2A.

Site 2

Platter, Cam 5. Residual, or long lived vessel. (235). F1, I 17, phase 4B.

Platter, possibly Cam 7 or 8. Base with small footring and offset at wall/base angle. Early variants of Cam 7 were made from the beginnings of the industry, *c.* 15 BC-AD 15 (Baldock form 8 : Rigby 1986, 230), whilst Cam 7/8 and Cam 8 forms cover AD 20-60, and Baldock 9 (= Cam 7) AD 1-25. (236). residual in F42, II 11, phase 6A.

Platter, Cam12. *c.* 1-25. (237-239). Residual in F92, II 97 + II 102, phase 3, contemporary in F55, II 103, phase 1C. One vessel.

Platter, Cam 14. *c.* 40-60. (240). F71, III 25, phase 1C.

Platter, flat base with slight footring; rouletted internally (241). Probably residual, or a survival, in III 33, phase 2.

Site 3

Platter rim, Cam 13 or 14. (596). Residual in V 18, phase 3A.

Platter, large vessel, small footring. (594). Residual in F1, I 11, phase 3B.

Cup, Cam 56C, or biconical beaker. Cam 56C is *c.* 20-60, whilst the beaker is a Neronian to early Flavian development, in 'eggshell' ware at least (Greene 1979, 120; Ward 1981, 54). This example is in 'normal' TN, with walls *c.* 4mm thick. (595). F1, I 11, phase 3B.

Platter, micaceous TN, Central Gaulish. Tall footring, probably Cam 1. (213). Residual in V 27, medieval level.

Site 4

Platter base, small footring. (212). Residual in F24, V 3.

Carinated bowl(?). Fig. 57.114, cf Ward 1981, no. VII 1. Fabric contains Mo VF (Sp F) quartz, Sp F iron ore (red and black), Sp A F-M white unidentified inclusions. Pinkish grey core (7.5 YR 6/3), grey to black margins (N5-N2), black polished surfaces. TN carinated bowls in Britain appear to be predominantly Neronian-Flavian (Greene 1979, 111). (262). F28, V 15, phase 1A.

Site 5

Platter, Cam 5. (755). VII 14, phase 2B.

Platter, Cam 12. (376). III 4, phase 1B.

Site 6

Platter Cam 5. (92). I, unstratified.

Platter, Cam 13. (96). I 42, phase 2B.

Platter, sherds. Bases from two vessels, the former with rouletting internally. Both residual (95). I 37, phase 2C; (94). I 22, phase 4C.

Vessel type unknown. (93). Residual in I 19, phase 5A.

Site 10

Platter. (21). Unstratified.

Site 11 (A253.1951)

Platter, Cam 8. (10)

Terra Rubra

Site 1

Platter, Cam 5(?), TR1, burnt. TR1 is thought to have been readi-

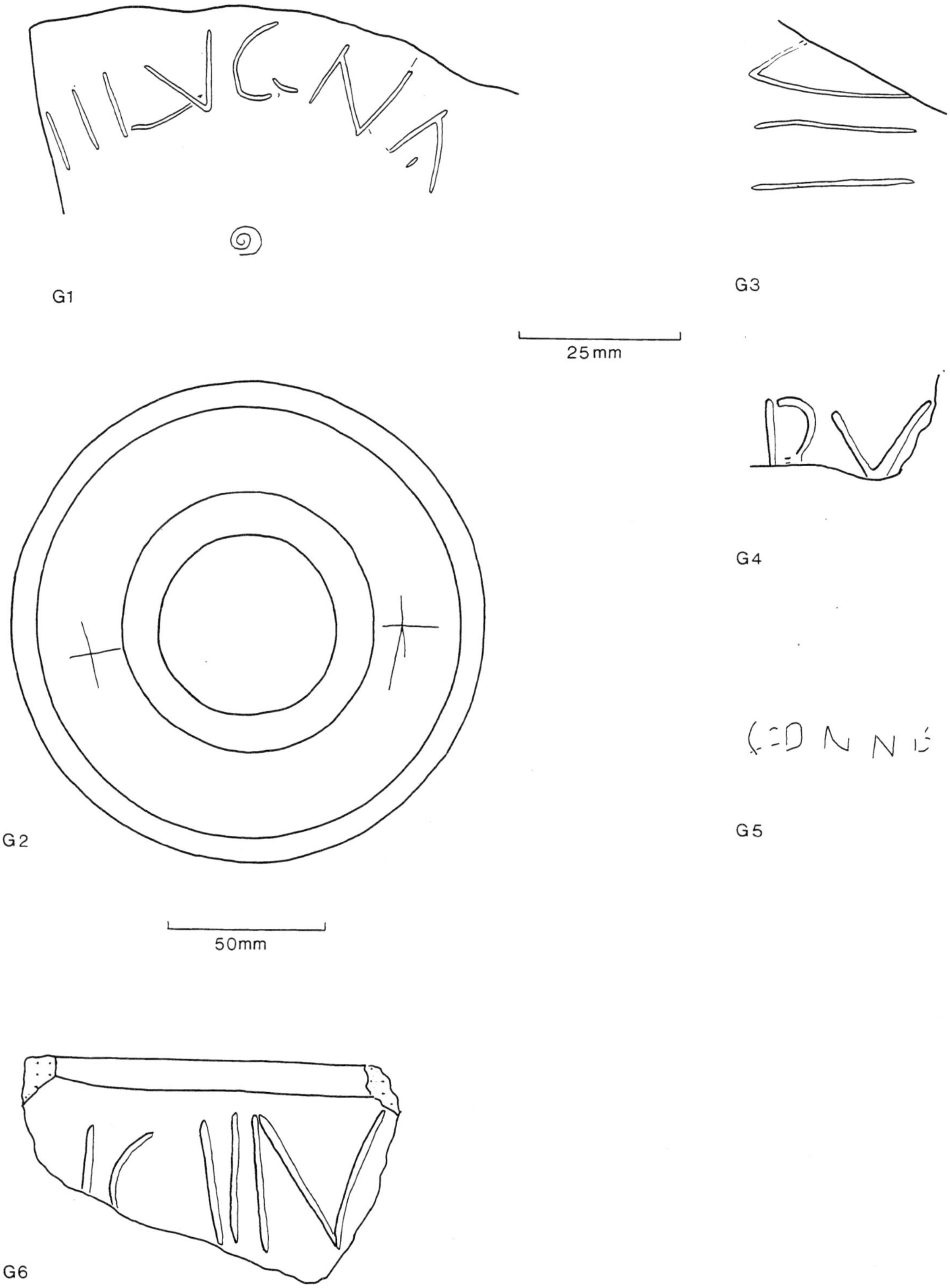

Fig 49 Roman pottery graffiti Site 1 (G1-G2); Site 5 (G3-G4); Site 9 (G5). Wall tile inscription Site 1 (G6) Scale 1:1 except G2 and G6 1:2.

ly available in Britain from the thirties AD, when only TR1C was made of the TR1 variants (Rigby, 1981a, 164). Rigby's reports are difficult to interpret: at Baldock Cam 5 is subdivided into Baldock 14A and 14B, of which only 14A is present in TR1C. The use of a nought in Tables 10-11 appears to indicate that the form was made in the ware, but the form-ware combination does not occur at Baldock. The date ranges cited are 15 BC-AD 5 for form 14A, and 1-55 for 14B (all fabrics) (Rigby, 1986, 230). Cam 5 at King Harry Lane is not subdivided, but is equated with KHL "GB form 6" and Oberaden 88 (Loeschke, 1942). Here it is stated that the form was "standardised before 10 BC in TR1, out of production by AD 40, in TR2 and TN, by AD 65" (Rigby, 1989, 123). TR1C as a ware is dated *c.* 15 BC-AD 65 or *c.* 1-60 (*ibid.* 1986, 223; 1989, 126). (225). F73, V 55, phase 1B.

Cup, Cam 56(A?), TR2. The form is equated with Baldock 16; Cam 56A (Baldock 16A) is there dated *c.* 1-40, and Cam 56C (Baldock 16B) *c.* 20-60. TR2 was produced *c.* 1-65, but mainly *c.* 20-65 (Rigby, 1986, 1989). (226). F73, V 59, phase 1B.

Site 2

Platters in TR1A. Two vessels represented by base sherds. TR1A is dated to *c.* 15 BC-AD 25 (*ibid.*). (232) F20, I 86, phase 1A; (231) residual in F1, II 55, phase 4B.

Beaker base, form uncertain, TR3 polished on exterior. Convex wall seemingly recurving to a sharply angled flat-bottomed base, suggesting a butt or girth beaker, perhaps Cam 112, which is dated *c.* 1-50 (Rigby, 1986, 231). The fabric is finely irregular in fracture, and "pale" TR3 in colour - pink (7.5YR 7/4) with reddish yellow (5YR 6/7) surfaces. Partly burnt. (233 + 234). Residual in F92, II 98 + II 102, phase 3.

Site 3

Platter in TR1C, small footring and marked basal "kick". (597). F27, V 21, phase 1A.

Beaker in Oxidised ware 1. This fabric may include TR, and the rouletted sherd would conform to TR3A (Rigby, 1981a, 159). The straight band of rouletting has wide, sub-ovoid impressions, in a single row. (636). F1, I 11, phase 3B.

Site 6

Platter in TR?2, very abraded, with footring (100). I 42, phase 2B.

Beaker in TR1A. Probably a tall, cylindrical vessel with low carination, King Harry Lane form GB21 (Rigby, 1989, 122 and 132; Rigby, pers comm). Fig. 66.261. It is associated with "other Gaulish imports of late Augustan date" at KHL. (97,98) I 42, I 60, phase 2B.

Cup, campanulate lower body, in TR1C (99). I 42, phase 2B.

Micaceous jars (MW)

The publication of a group of mica dusted jars from Skeleton Green (Partridge, 1981, 99-103) focussed attention on the importation of a range of wares from Central Gaul in the first half of the first century AD. The jars broadly equate with Cam 102/262 (KHL CJ1). The British Museum has undertaken a research programme on a range of petrologically related wares embracing these jars, micaceous TR, and cream slipped flagons (Rigby and Freestone, 1986). Positive identification of the jars has yet to be made at Leicester, but pending petrological analysis the writer is confident that one sherd from Bath Lane/Welles Street (Clay and Mellor, 1985, Site 6) is from the shoulder of such a jar; it is definitely mica dusted. A sherd from Blackfriars (*ibid.*, Site 2) "is of the same fabric type" as the group discussed by Rigby and Freestone (Freestone, in correspondence, 1988). Its smooth exterior lacks either "dusting" or slip, but it is a body sherd, and thus below the zone that was given a micaceous coating (the rim and upper shoulder). The cream slips have poor adhesion. No clear examples of micaceous jars have been recognised from the sites that are the subject of this volume.

"Cream slipped" flagons (WS1)

Several vessels have been thin sectioned as part of the British Museum programme mentioned above. So far only one sherd, from Bath Lane (Clay and Mellor, 1985, Site 1), has been placed in the Central Gaulish group (Clamp, 1985, Fig. 33.80, is a handle from the same context, and on visual inspection in the same ware). This is the sherd referred to by Rigby and Freestone (1986, 11, erroneously attributed to the Blackfriars site), and again by Rigby (1989, 120). The KHL report states that the Leicester example falls outside the norm for form details and fabric of the ware (*ibid.*). Definitive reports on the other Leicester vessels analysed have yet to appear at the time of writing, but the comparatively weak definition of rim detail, and early results from thin sectioning, suggest that they may fall in the group of "silty wares" discussed in the King Harry Lane report (Rigby, 1989, 192-7; Freestone, 1989, 264-5), for which source(s) have yet to be identified (Freestone, in correspondence, 1989, doubts the conclusions of Freestone and Rigby 1988 on this point). Rigby and Timby (pers comms, 1985) have both felt these vessels to be later than the Central Gaulish imports. The "collared flagons" mentioned by Rigby (1989, 195) are Fig. 53.58-9 below. Similar vessels in "silty ware" are also known from Ashton, Northants. Production in the Hertfordshire/Northamptonshire-Buckinghamshire area seems a plausible hypothesis, on the evidence currently available, for the Leicester collared flagons (see also Kenyon, 1948, Flagon Type A.15). Ring neck vessels also occur in Leicester, but it is not certain that these belong to the same group (Fig. 53.50, Pollard forthcoming (a), no. 123): they do not feature in the King Harry Lane "Silty Wares" range. A mid first century AD date for the British "collared" flagons seems most likely.

White wares (WW3)

Butt beakers (Cam 113, Skeleton Green type 40).

Early claims for a south east English source (Hawkes and Hull 1947, 238-9; Clamp 1985, 41) have largely been denied by recent research. Extensive discussion of their typology has been published (Rigby, 1981a, 162, 173; 1989, 136-141) and it is now considered that "most, if not all, were imported from Gaul", with the majority "likely to have been made to the north west" of the Marne-Vesle valley. The general source area of "northern Gaul" is favoured (Rigby, 1989, 137).

A detailed form classification following the KHL model of the Leicester material has yet to be attempted. Two of the nine rims recovered from the sites published herein appear to conform to the earlier type prevalent at Skelton Green, with the remainder of the generally heavier-lipped type common at Camulodunum, which was produced up to *c.* 60 (Rigby, 1981a). Production of the general form had begun by 10 BC (Rigby, 1986, 232). A near complete vessel from Blackfriars is of KHL 4C3 (Clamp, 1985, Fig.

31.2 and Pl. 8).

Body and base sherds may be confused with pentice moulded beakers imported to eastern England from northern Gaul, where they were made from the 1st to 3rd centuries AD (Gillam 42; Richardson and Tyers, 1984; Pollard, 1987 Type VIII G.1(1) and no. 357), and with Midlands rouletted beakers and jars of a later 1st and (?)early 2nd century date (e.g. Pollard, forthcoming (a), no.35).

"Skeleton Green" rims: Site 2, F11, I 30, phase 3 (359). Site 8, VI 69, phase 4A (30).

"Camulodunum" rims : Site 2, F11, I 31, phase 3 (360); F71, III 56, phase 1C + III 33, phase 2 (389, 391); F92, II 102, phase 3 (382). Site 5, IV 22, phase 1A (438). Site 6, F21, I 98, phase 1D (Fig. 65.242) (168); F22, I 104, phase 1D (Fig. 65.243) (169). Site 11, I 18 (A20. 1939.11). Body sherds only were found on Sites 1 and 3.

Other white wares

No other Continental imports have been identified from these sites. Body sherds could easily lie unrecognised amongst the general "white ware" assemblage. For example from Site 1 F49, IIIA 68 and IIIA 72, phase 3B (345-6); and Site 8, IX 57, phase 3C (31). No example of Cam 114 was found, but the form is known elsewhere in Leicester (Clamp, 1985, Fig. 31.3).

Discussion

It is clear that Leicester benefitted from the importation of a wide range of Gaulish pottery from the late Augustan period onwards. The assemblage may appear impoverished by the standards of sites in Hertfordshire and Essex, but occurences of types rare in Britain overall, such as the GB21 beaker here, and a poppyhead beaker in TR3 "probably from the Epernay region of France and thought to be unique in Britain" from Blackfriars (Clamp, 1985, 41 : Site 2, A12.1977.218, from F28, 4, phase 1), demonstrate its quality. Leicester lay on the northern fringe of the distribution of TN and TR, and there is little if any evidence to suggest redistribution by whatever means of "Gallo-Belgic and related wares" from Leicester to hinterland communities (Timby, 1987). Research by Willis (in prep) may clarify this situation.

Graffiti on Roman Pottery - Richard Pollard, with contributions by Mark Hassall (Fig. 49)

Site 1

G1 Micaceous terra nigra (Fig. 50.2). Graffito incised after firing on base ext. Mark Hassall writes ":]IILVGNA, probably for V]ELVGNA, the double stroke at the beginning is, as usual, for E, and Velugnus (the masculine equivalent) is the only name to be listed in the reverse index of Mocsy (1983). There is one example from Worms, an inscription set up by a certain Amandus Velugni f(ilius) - son of Velugnus - who came from Deva, Chester (CIL XIII 6221). Technically, Velugnus has the form of a cognomen. The corresponding nomen, Velugnius, is also attested on an inscription from Bastogne (CIL XIII 3632)". (217) F47: III 51, phase 1B

G2 South Gaulish samian, Drag 18, stamped by Patricius i of La Graufesenque (Dickinson no. 7 above). Two crosses, incised after firing on underside of base on opposite sides of footring. (902) F63: V 21, phase 4A

Site 5

G3 AM12. Smooth exterior wall suggests Dressel 2-4 rather than the commonly lightly rilled Pelichet 47. Graffito incised after firing on body ext. Mark Hassall writes: "it reads]VII, vii, '7'. This numeral is found fairly commonly as a graffito on amphorae and is possibly an indication of capacity; probably complete at the beginning" (409) V 35, unphased.

G4 CG1A. Ledge rim jar (Fig. 63.223). Graffito incised after firing on body ext, truncated by breakage of vessel. Mark Hassall writes: "graffito perhaps reads P X[..., p(ondo) x..., '10 pounds (or more)'". (844) V 29, unphased.

Site 9

G5 OW2. Flagon(?), bodysherd, burnished ext (Fig. 67.285). Graffito incised, after firing, on body ext; legend probably complete. Mark Hassall writes: "I read it as CONNE, for which two conceivable interpretations may be forwarded: for CORNE(LIVS); or for CONN(A)E, 'property of Conna', which seems possible as a name although it is apparently unattested". (16) Unstratified.

G6 Wall tile; see p.155.

Pottery of the Later Iron Age and of the Iron Age/Roman Transition in Leicester

Introduction

Fine wares of "Belgic" style, in the sense used by Thompson (1982), have long been recognised in Leicester, along with contemporary jars, storage jars and imports, thanks to the publication of the report on the excavations at Jewry Wall (Kenyon 1948, in particular 124-135). The earliest material from that site has been re-examined (Jarvis, 1986), and the corpus extended by the assemblages from a group of sites immediately to the north (Clamp, 1985). The sites covered by the present report also revealed large quantities of pottery of what may be called the "Belgic" pottery phase. Moreover, Site 6 has provided a unique group of vessels whose characteristics recall the pottery of Iron Age sites such as Breedon and Enderby (Wacher, 1964; Cunliffe, 1978; Elsdon, 1992). The publication of this group enables the ceramic sequence in Leicester to be pushed back beyond the "Belgic" phase, in all likelihood into the 1st century BC, at a time when imports of pottery from the Roman world had yet to penetrate the interior of eastern Britain.

The Pottery from Site 6 Phase 1B F24 (Fig. 64.230-241)

The group comprises sherds of at least nine vessels, comprising four or five forms in five fabric groups. Aside from the lower body of a combed jar in calcite gritted ware (CG1A: no. 241), there are no fabric links with the mainstream wares of the "Belgic" phase, and the very simple jar forms do not encourage the perception of direct links in vessel types between this group and the later phase. The absence of obvious intrusive sherds is a remarkable feature of this group; it is also worth noting that the fabrics (CG1A apart), occur with only the greatest rarity in "Belgic" and later phases on sites so far examined in Leicester.

The fabrics may be defined as follows:

Sandy ware 1 (SW1).
Quartz: Mo-Fr (no. 237) or Ab (nos. 238, 239), SA, i/a, F-C, Sp VC in coarser fabric. Red ironstone: Sp, A, C. Combusted vegetable matter (straw?): Sp or absent, VC. Surfaces can be wiped or burnished, giving a smooth finish tending to soapy in finer sherds. Hard, with finely irregular to irregular fracture. This fabric falls under the "umbrella" fabrics SW3, SW4 (Pollard, forthcoming (a)); considerations of typology and context determine assignment to SW1.

Grog tempered ware 7 (GT7).
A hard, soapy, hackly-fractured fabric. Mo ?grog, C-VC (5mm), SA, i/a. White calcium carbonate, Sp, C. SA. Sp combusted vegetable matter. The 'grog' could comprise clay lumps resulting from imperfect preparation of the potting clay rather than temper.

Miscellaneous coarse ware 4 (MC4).
A hard, soapy, hackly fabric, distinguished by numerous inclusions of rock fragments and feldspar. The rock fragments may include diorite (cf. the medieval Potters Marston Ware: Sawday, 1989, 1991), numerous intrusions of which occur to the west of Leicester (Ford, 1972, 32-35). Rock fragments: Mo, C-VC (5mm, occasionally 10mm), A, i/a, coarse grained. Feldspar: white, pink opaque, translucent, Mo, C-VC (2mm), A, i/a. Quartz: Mo, M-C, SA, i/a. Combusted vegetable matter (straw?): Sp, VC. Soft green 'pellets', unidentified, occur in one vessel (no. 234): Sp, C, R, w/s. Fabric coarseness does not appear to be determined simply by size: the coarsest vessel (no. 234) would appear to be smaller than one of the finer ones (no. 230). Surfaces are wiped, but not burnished.

Miscellaneous coarse ware 5 (MC5).
A finer version of MC4, with Sp rock fragments, feldspar, and quartz, in a fine matrix. The fabric is paralleled by MG1, which has "Belgic" stylistic affinities, but considerations of form and decoration suggest a distinct ware. The two vessels (nos. 235, 236) are amongst the smallest from F24.

Calcite gritted ware 1A (CG1A).
A hard, soapy, irregular, hackly and often laminar fabric. Late Iron Age and early Roman vessels are probably mostly coil built, wheel throwing apparently being introduced in the 2nd century, if not by the end of the 1st century AD. Calcite : Fr-Ab, up to 3mm visually, mostly white and platey, but sometimes Sp VC (5mm and larger) SA light grey also, probably limestone. The platey inclusions are probably fossil marine shell. Quartz, generally Sp or absent, but localised scatters of Mo-Fr can occur, i/a and of variable shape, generally VF-C. White mica : Sp VF-F. Black and red iron ore : Sp. Flint : absent or Sp. Combusted vegetable matter, including cereal husks : absent or Sp. Colour variable, but early vessels often exhibit 'flashing off' effect of firing, giving red (2.5YR) to reddish brown surfaces and margins. Ext. and int. surfaces are visually similar, with a range from pink, reddish yellow and various browns and greys. Cores are visually differentiated, with light grey to black common. Clays of the Jurassic System suitable for the manufacture of calcite gritted wares stretch to as far west as the eastern periphery of modern Leicester.

The one vessel (no. 241) is likely to be an early example of the ware, on account of its patchy colouration and oblique combing. Later vessels, of the Roman and possibly late pre-conquest periods, tend to be fired to a more even colour (eg Fig. 63.223), although this is not a universal trait.

Discussion

These fabrics are all hand made, probably coiled, and exhibit firing characteristics indicative of bonfires. The vessels are generally reduced, with patches of 'buff' and 'red' on the surfaces. A colour sandwich can occur.

Decoration is confined to burnishing, which is finest on the lid, and generally deep 'combing' with a toothed tool or possibly in some instances a stiff bunch of twigs (eg no. 230).

The basic jar form has a simple lip sometimes with a slight ledge (no. 231), defined by a weak offset on the 'shoulder'. Two sizes are apparent (nos. 230 and 231 on the one hand, and nos. 236 and 237 on the other), the dimensions of which are sufficiently distinct as to suggest the perception of two types of vessel by potter and user. The form brings to mind a vessel from Jewry Wall (Kenyon, 1948 Fig. 35.2), and more generally the in-turned simple lip jar (eg Fig. 66.258-260 here).

There could be a link here between "pre-Belgic" and "Belgic" phases involving an inherited tradition on which the fine wares of the latter were imposed, but this cannot be taken as proven even within the terms of typological studies.

The second jar form has an out-turned lip, and appears to lack the offset (no. 238). Typological links with vessels in later contexts can be made (eg. Fig. 56.109), but again the form is fundamentally simple.

The calcite gritted ware vessel may belong to a plain rim (cf. nos. 258, 259, and Clamp, 1985 Fig. 31.23), bead rim (*ibid.*, Fig. 32.24) or everted (Fig. 67.280 here) form.

The lid is of domed shape, a form favoured by the producers of "Belgic" style pottery (eg Thompson, 1982, type L5), but not unique to them.

The offset-shoulder jar occurs in SW1, MC4, and MC5, the out-turned lip jar and lid in SW1, whilst GT7 comprises a jar shoulder (no. 240).

SW1 has been encountered sporadically alongside "Belgic" pottery on Sites 1 and 2 in early levels, and also occurs at Blackfriars (Bath Lane Site 2, Clamp, 1985 Fig. 32.39, re-classified).

On balance, these occurrences are likely to be residual. The MC4-MC5 group, and GT7, are previously unrecognised in Leicester, though the 1st century BC pottery from Enderby (Elsdon, 1992) includes a fabric not dissimilar to MC4, with 'gold' mica clearly visible on the abraded surfaces. Dioritic rocks outcrop around Enderby. The offset-shoulder jar, tending to have a lower shoulder, is a feature of Enderby pottery, and also of the 'Breedon-Ancaster' style (Cunliffe, 1978 Fig. A:13). The decoration of the latter is similar to the Site 6 group, and to bead rim and plain rim vessels from the Jewry Wall site (Kenyon, 1948 Figs. 34.21, 35.2). The 'notched' rims of Breedon vessels (Cunliffe, 1978 Fig. A:13 nos. 1,2) recall the Blackfriars vessel in SW1, and also a CG1A 'ledge rim' jar from Site 2 (Fig. 52.34).

The dating of the F24 group is elusive. Cunliffe envisaged a 'bowl continuum' stretching across the Midlands from the Leicestershire Trent to the Berkshire Thames (*ibid.* Fig. 3:9), characterised by 'scored wares, continuing the techniques of the Breedon-Ancaster style' (*ibid.* 50), and dated to the 2nd to 1st centuries BC. The presence of the calcite gritted 'combed' jar provides a link with the "Belgic" phase; this ware is absent from the Iron Age site at

Enderby. However, the absence of Imperial Roman and "Belgic" fine wares is remarkable, even given that the assemblage is not large (166 sherds, of which only 2 are in CG1A). Augustan-Tiberian imports have been encountered elsewhere in Leicester, but the settlement seems to have missed out on the trade in Italian wine carried in Dressel 1 amphorae up to around 10 BC (Sealey, 1985, 25). F24 must have been sealed by the thirties AD, for at such a late date Gallo-Belgic and related fine wares are to be anticipated (cf Kenyon's dating of "Belgic" ware in Leicester: 1948, 124-125). Augustan vessels are by no means common in Leicester, and could easily have evaded incorporation into a single feature. The earliest date for Leicester's "Belgic" native wares has not been established. The common assumption that they can be dated by association with imported fine wares is not proven, and indeed at Silchester the former appear to anticipate their imported 'Gallo-Belgic' counterparts (Timby, 1985b). If this were the case in the East Midlands, F24 could be pushed back into the 1st century BC.

The "Belgic" pottery phase

Pottery of "Belgic" style was found in abundance on several of the sites covered in the present report, notably Sites 1,2,4 and 6. The stratified, phase 1 assemblages from the first two sites, along with F92 (Site 2, phase 3), and F21 and 22 (Site 6, phase 1D), were subjected to detailed analysis of forms, using EVEs (rims) to quantify their presence (Table 6). The Bath Lane fabric type series (Clamp, 1985) has been revised to take greater account of temper/inclusions, in order to test the hypothesis that fabric was in part determined by form. The size of the sample thus studied is: weight, 53.451 kg: sherds, 2302; EVEs 24.63.

The dating evidence for these contexts includes imported fine pottery (summarised below, pp. 75-6), and other pottery, a brooch and vessel glass. The upper end of the date range of this pottery phase is more securely established than the lower end. The rarity of 'native' wares in the large 'Group 1' assemblage incorporated in construction make-ups under the south range of the forum (Pollard, forthcoming (a)) is taken to imply that they were redundant by the eighties AD to all intents and purposes, though some vessels and even a residue of conservative potters may have survived into the last decades of the 1st century. The assemblage from phase 4 on Site 2 supports the evidence of 'Group 1', indicating that 'native' wares of probable/assured Iron Age origin were declining in usage by the seventies.

The shelly CG1A provides an important exception, its characteristic jar forms current into the middle years of the 2nd century with but minor developments in shape and finish (p. 78). Grog was also a temper favoured for storage jars in the Roman period.

The Wares of the "Belgic" phase

A simple division into "Belgic" and "Romano-British" wares cannot be imposed on the pottery of the 1st century AD in Leicester. On the one hand there are those wares with an Iron Age pedigree that continued to be used with varying degrees of change into the Roman period. On the other hand there are those which, though usually considered as typically 'Roman', appear to have developed from both 'native' and 'alien' traditions in the pre-Flavian to Vespasianic years (the grey and oxidised wares). The term "Belgic" should be explained: it indicates pottery of a style paralleling that current in Belgic Gaul during the centuries immediately either side of the dawn of the Christian era, and prevalent in a 'core area' comprising Kent, Essex and Hertfordshire from at least the final decades of the 1st century BC to the third quarter of the 1st century AD. The East Midlands lie on the northern fringe of the style's distribution, which was well established in south east Britain and it would seem in the East Midlands at the time of the Claudian conquest. It co-existed with fine wares imported from Gallia Belgica and further afield, which undoubtedly exerted some influence on its evolution. These developments, 'native' in the sense that they took places apparently within Iron Age societies in Britain albeit with Gallo-Roman stimuli, were in part disrupted by the introduction of 'alien' traditions in the wake of the conquest, whose manifestations included rusticated jars and reeded rim bowls.

The 'native' wares include grog tempered (GT) wares 1 and 2, mixed gritted (MG) wares 1 and 2, sandy (SW) wares 2 and 3, and calcite gritted (CG) wares 1A, 2A and 3A. These have been defined elsewhere (Pollard, forthcoming (a)). The fine pottery was usually wheel thrown whilst jars were probably mainly coil built: the 'grain' of the shell in CG1A in section often betrays evidence of the coils themselves. This generalisation is upset by the presence of a number of 'fine' jars, usually burnished and often decorated with cordons, grooves or linear motifs, which were, or appear to be, wheel thrown (eg Fig. 50.6, 7; 52.39, 40, 45). The varying techniques of production may reflect differing functions, although for one function at least, the interment of the cremated remains of the deceased, both coiled and wheel thrown vessels were deemed suitable. Shallow 'clamp' kilns and bonfires were used to fire much of the pottery, but rapid advances took place in kiln technology in the mid 1st century AD (Swan, 1984, 53-89), facilitating the production of wares with broadly standardised colours (grey, oxidised and white) whose appearance contrasts with the more 'earthy' browns and red-browns of the bulk of the GT, MG and SW pottery. These technological developments coincided with, and perhaps to some extent precipitated, the demise of grog as a temper.

Transitional Wares

The transformations that overtook the fine wares of the late Iron Age are subtle in both fabric and form. A sequence of 'Iron Age' through 'transitional' to 'Roman' may be constructed, with a decrease in the quantities of calcite or combusted organic matter in, and an increase in hardness of, the fabrics providing rough indicators of a vessel's place in the sequence.

Differentiation of the 'Iron Age' GT2, SW2 and MG2 from untempered or fine sandy early 'Roman' wares (grey wares 2 and 3, oxidised wares 2 and 6 in particular) can be somewhat arbitrary even with this rule of thumb. A Neronian 'transitional' butt beaker may be virtually identical in fabric to the naked eye to an Antonine poppyhead beaker. Moreover, while some forms underwent detectable changes (compare for example nos. 47, 249, 250, 299 and 31 in the report with one from the forum - Pollard forthcoming (a), no. 15), others exhibit extreme conservatism (eg nos. 43, 46, 102, 126, 253 here), frustrating attempts to date individual vessels and distinguish residuals.

Transitional grey wares, with grog, calcite and sand present in varying quantities (GT5, 6; MG3) and their more rare oxidised counterparts (MG4 in particular) probably originated in the principates of Claudius and Nero; they are present in the kiln discards at Great Holme Street, on the left bank of the Soar outside the Roman city (Mellor, 1975-6, Lucas, 1976-7). The robust GT5 and 6, along with GT3, may have survived into the second century alongside CG1 as favoured fabrics for larger jars. These exceptions apart, the transition in fabrics was complete by the end of the Flavian dynasty, and perhaps somewhat earlier. It is to be hoped that further excavation will allow closely-dateable groups of this crucial period to be recorded.

The Forms

The sample includes rims totalling 24.63 EVEs including intrusive sherds of 2nd century samian and a Midlands mortarium. The proportions by vessel class are indicated in Table 6. These classes are, with the exception of flagons, platters, and cups, dominated by 'Iron Age' and 'transitional' wares.

The flagons comprise 3 vessels in white slip ware 1 (Fig. 53.58-59, 61.7% of all flagons), 1 in amphora fabric 25 (Fig. 53.57, 23.4%) and 1 each in white wares 2 and 10, the former a 'Hofheim' collared rim, the latter possibly an early ring-neck variant. 39.8% of the platters are in terra nigra, including Camulodunum types 1, 5, 12, 13, 14 and 16, and there is a possible Cam 5 in terra rubra 1. Samian platters comprise 22.0%, and there are rims also in colour-coat 21 (Fig 50.1) and grey ware 3. The cups include samian Drag 24/25 and Drag 27 (75.7% of contemporary cups), and one rim (2.7%) in terra rubra 2, of Cam 56.

Jars and storage jars are the sole classes represented in CG1, 2A and 3A, GT5 and 6, MG1 and SW3, apart from a single carinated bowl in CG3A. The single vessels in GW9, SW1 and MC1 are also jars. The ledge rim jar and necked storage jar are the characteristic forms in CG1, and plain rim jars (cf Clamp 1985 Fig. 31.23 eg) occur solely in CG wares. Jar forms are more diverse in fabrics other than CG1.

A detailed examination of the 'native Iron Age' wares reveals that, aside from jars and storage jars, the most common forms are butt beakers, carinated bowls, and necked bowls. This reflects the situation on rural sites in Northamptonshire (eg Hall and Nickerson, 1967; Williams 1974) and seemingly at Jewry Wall, Leicester (Kenyon, 1948, 124-135, where the 'mortar-like vessel' type equates with the carinated bowls herein). Platters and neckless (globular or high-shouldered) beakers are less well represented, but all five forms occur in GT2, MG2 and SW2, fabrics at the fine end of the native pottery spectrum (GT2 platters, though not present in the sample, occur in Site 2 phase 2). The fashions of beakers and bowls were passed on to early Roman potters, there being examples of GW2, 3 and 5, and OW2, 6 and 7, again particularly of butt beakers and carinated bowls. The latter can be traced in an unbroken line of descent to the 2nd century vessels of Jewry Wall types A1-2 (*ibid.* 86-87, and Fig. 44.15), and may be thought to provide a 'service' with the somewhat narrower, or more squat, 'biconical beakers' (eg *ibid.* Fig. 21.4, and Pollard forthcoming (a), no. 47). Platters also occur in later 1st century to early 2nd century grey wares (eg herein Fig. 51.19-20, Fig. 57.120), but were in effect superseded by the black-burnished ware style of dish in the Hadrianic period.

It should be acknowledged that there are no simple divisions to be made between carinated bowls and biconical beakers, or between necked bowls, S-shape bowls and necked jars, size, proportions and degree of finesse all being taken into account. The everted rim jar is essentially a Romano-British phenomenon, though 'Iron Age' and 'transitional' ware examples have been noted. The form merges with ledge rim jars in CG1 and OW2 and 3 by the turn of the 2nd century (cf nos. 67, 76, 79 and 140 herein eg).

Imports from the Continent

Detailed accounts of these will be found in the appropriate sections. The following is, therefore, a summary of the types present in the sample.

"Gallo-Belgic" wares are moderately well represented. The terra nigra platters include late Augustan to Tiberian (Cam 12) and post-conquest (Cam 16) forms as well as those spanning the conquest. Terra rubra vessels include platters in TR1 and TR1A, a cup in TR2, and a beaker in TR3. TR1A dates to *c.* 15 BC-AD 25. The white ware butt beakers include rims of a type made up to *c.* AD 60 (eg Fig. 65.242, 243), but not the earlier type (well illustrated by

Table 6 The "Belgic" Pottery Phase : Proportions of vessel classes

Sites 1, 2 and 6: phase 1 (Sites 1 and 2); phase 1D (Site 6); Feature 92, phase 3 (Site 2). Proportions of vessel classes by EVEs (rims), expressed as proportions of total assemblage (column 1) and of 'native' wares assemblage (WS11; CG1, 2, 3A; GT1-3; MG1-2; SW2-3) (column 2).

	1	2
Platters	7.6	2.3
Cups	1.9	0.5
Flagons	6.8	-
Beakers	17.7	20.1
Jars	27.0	27.6
Storage Jars	19.0	24.3
Bowls	18.9	24.0
Lids	0.4	0.5
Dishes	P*	-
Mortaria	0.2*	-
Amphorae	P	-
Vessel type unknown	0.7	0.6
Sample size (EVEs)	24.63	17.63

*entirely intrusive

Clamp 1985, Fig. 31.2 and Pl. 8) which does however occur in Site 2, phase 3.

Central Gaulish wares are represented by the micaceous terra nigra platter with graffito (Fig. 50.2), *c.* 10 BC-AD 25.

South Gaulish wares are confined to samian, including a Tiberian-Claudian Drag 17, and pre-Flavian and Flavian platters and cups, along with a Drag 29 of *c.* AD 30-45 (Fig. 44.1).

Products of the Mediterranean provinces are confined to amphorae, and an Italian flagon (Fig. 53.57). The amphorae may include Dressel 2-4 (fabrics 1, 2, 25) and Richborough 527 (Peacock 1977a). It is of interest to note that the most common types overall in Roman Britain, Dressel 20 and Pelichet 47, are not represented in the sample.

Arretine ware is not present on any of the sites covered by this volume. It has however been found in other areas of Ratae, including Jewry Wall (Kenyon, 1948), Bath Lane (Dannell, 1985), and the south range of the forum (*ibid.*, forthcoming).

Intrusive Pottery in the Sample

The sample includes several fabrics which are clearly intrusive; Central and possibly East Gaulish 2nd century samian, mortarium fabrics 12 and 18, and BB1. Some of the other Romano-British pottery may also be intrusive. One context in particular is comparatively heavily contaminated, F15 I 93 on Site 2, which includes the 1 sherd of MO18, 3 sherds of BB1, 3 out of the 5 sherds of WW2, and 15 out of the 53 sherds of GW2-6 present in the sample. This context also includes 157 sherds of 'native' wares, and 1 of 1st century samian, and comprises 9.3% by weight (10.6% of sherds) of the sample.

Table 7 Sites 1 and 2 : proportions of selected wares by phase

Statistics are percentage presence figures of all wares in the phase : sherd counts left, weight right hand columns
"MC 2-3" includes GT1-4, MG1-2, SW, CG2A, CG3A, CG4
"Trans" comprises transitional Iron Age/Roman wares : GT5-6, MG3-4, MC1
[...] = intrusive

Site 1

Phase	1		2		3		4		5		6		7	
MC2-3	51.5	54.7	52.5	62.1	12.6	10.5	0.6	0.5	4.5	4.2	-	-	2.1	2.5
Trans.	3.2	6.3	0.8	3.4	-	-	0.1	0.3	0.8	1.3	-		-	-
CG1	17.8	24.5	8.5	8.6	2.7	1.9	4.3	8.1	10.2	18.3	3.0	0.9	6.6	6.6
GW	7.9	3.7	11.9	5.2	29.6	27.8	45.9	41.6	38.7	34.7	34.3	49.0	55.8	59.1
BB1	-	-	-	-	-	-	-	-	0.2	0.01	40.3	24.7	0.9	0.9
Total count/ weight (all wares)	466/9406		118/2627		223/6259		715/10968		511/7758		67/668		532/7381	

Site 2

Phase	1		2		3(F11,24,92)		3(F7,49-51,67-8)		4		5	
MC2-3	49.0	45.1	47.8	47.1	42.2	40.4	1.4	2.5	5.0	4.4	1.1	0.6
Trans.	6.9	8.3	5.6	8.1	0.3	0.2	4.2	14.7	0.3	0.7	0.3	1.5
CG1	33.3	42.2	21.5	27.2	25.8	36.3	2.8	3.3	16.8	9.3	12.1	14.6
GW	3.3	1.5	5.6	6.5	0.6	0.4	56.3	56.5	48.6	34.3	45.5	32.0
BB1	[0.4	0.1]	-	-	-	-	-	-	2.1	1.1	4.3	4.0
Total count/ weight (all wares)	842/16564		358/5932		353/8065		71/1289		1170/21194		727/10035	

The Pottery of Leicester in the Flavian to Hadrianic Period c. AD 70-140

Introduction

The report on the pottery from the south range of the forum of Leicester (Pollard forthcoming (a)) includes discussion of two large groups, dated to *c.* AD 70-130 and *c.* AD 100-225. The following notes are intended to amplify some of the observations made therein concerning developments in wares and the currency of certain forms. Table 8 presents statistics of the proportions of wares present, by weight, in ten 'key' groups drawn from recent analyses by the present author. Tables are available from the archive which detail the occurrence of forms by fabric, measured in EVEs, respectively in Site 1 F60+F63, Site 1 V 5 (phase 7C), Site 2 phase 4, Site 2 F46, and Site 5 F35-37, 39-42.

'Fine' Wares

Samian dominated the market for fine pottery cups and platters/shallow bowls throughout this period. The vast increase in volume of imports in the Flavian period (Marsh 1981) coincided with the ultimate demise in importation of Gallo-Belgic and related fine wares and also the end of the Lyon colour-coat and Central Gaulish lead glazed ware industries. The wane of the South Gaulish samian factories resulted in a trough in samian importation (*ibid.*), but even allowing for the secondary/residual nature of the contexts/assemblages that prevail in the data base, it is apparent that late 1st century samian continued to be used into the reign of Hadrian.

Colour-coated and mica dusted wares did not compete with the major samian forms for the most part, although fine grey wares do occur in deep open bowl forms (eg nos. 84 and 98; cf Marsh 1978). The dearth of Hadrianic samian on Sites 1 and 2 is of especial interest in view of the presence of small quantities of BB1 of Hadrianic-Antonine date on both sites in Roman levels, notably Site 2 phase 4, and phase 5 F46. Marsh's assertion (1981) that samian import volumes did not recover significantly until the 130s would seem to be validated by the evidence from Leicester, therefore.

Grey Wares, Calcite Gritted Ware 1A and BB1

A decline in CG1A usage contemporaneous with the development of grey wares in the later 1st century is demonstrated in Table 9. The two were apparent competitors on the market for jars and, to a lesser extent, for large 'storage' jars. It is not known whether special functions were allocated to CG1 vessels rather than to GW, and thus whether the 2nd century 'decline' in CG1 relates to the gradual abandonment of such practices rather than to increasing consumer preference (or potter preference) for GW jars whose functions were identical to those of CG1. The arrival of BB1 from Dorset on the markets of Leicester in the Hadrianic period coincided with a further decline in CG1 and cut significantly into the grey ware trade also. Jars were the main class of vessel produced in grey wares throughout their early history, and the emergence of a strong imported competitor must have been an unwelcome intrusion upon local potters' monopolies. The fashion for BB1-style dishes is thought to have brought about the demise of the reeded rim bowl (cf Marsh and Tyers 1978), a common Flavian to Trajanic form, although the development of flanged bowls in the (?)120s-130s (cf Pollard forthcoming (a), Group 2), may also have been influential.

Large 'storage' jars may have formed an increasingly large proportion of CG1 production in the 2nd century (cf Jewry Wall Cooking pot Types A-C and Storage jar Type K), the traditional everted/ledge rim jar being obsolete by the end of the 2nd century both in CG1 and grey wares, the latter tending more to wide-mouthed and BB1-influenced types.

Rustication and 'en barbotine' Decoration on Grey Wares

These two decorative motifs - assuming the former not to be applied solely to facilitate grip - were commonly applied in mutual exclusion to neckless jars during the period under review. The terms are conveniently defined in Webster (ed. 1976) and respectively by Swan (1975,12) and Green (1978,112). The former is generally dated to between 50 and 120; 'after 70 production and distribution tended to be geared to the northern garrisons' (Swan, *ibid.*; cf Gillam 95-99). The latter, if one sets aside the beakers with panels of small dots in the 'poppyhead' (Tyers 1978) and broadly contemporary beaker traditions (cf Clamp 1985, Fig. 34.107-8), is judged conventionally to be contemporary with rustication (Gillam 67-8), in the north at least. A study of the incidence of the two motifs in the seven Flavian+ 'key' groups (Table 10) brings forth two hypotheses. Firstly, that rustication was a common feature of grey ware jars in the Flavian-Trajanic period in Leicester, and was indeed produced locally (cf Figs. 54.65, and 69.317 herein, conforming respectively to Gillam 98 and 99). Secondly, that the zenith of popularity of barbotine (excluding the small-dot panel motif) may be placed in the early part of the 2nd century (*c.* AD 100-140?), with a median date ten to twenty-five years later than that of rustication. Linear barbotine schemes (eg Clamp 1985 Fig. 33.57, and Fig. 69.315 herein) and 'ring-and-hairpin' schemes (eg Kenyon 1948 Fig. 40.24) may have emerged at the turn of the 1st century, supplementing the Flavian 'ring-and-dot' style (Gillam 67-8; Clamp 1985 Fig. 33.65-65A), and its component derivatives. The extreme rarity of barbotine-decorated sherds in the Flavian-Trajanic forum assemblage (Pollard forthcoming (a), Group 1) suggests that the style was rare before the Trajanic years; the seven sherds belong to only two vessels, one with rings and ribs, the other with dot panels. The transition from rusticated to barbotine jars is accompanied by a slimming-down of the profile of the rim within a general tradition of short, more-or-less straight eversions (cf Kenyon 1948, and Pollard forthcoming (a)). The barbotine jars may thus span the half century that witnessed the superseding of rusticated ware by the influx of black-burnished (BB1) cooking pots (cf Swan 1975, 12).

Oxidised Ware Forms

The earliest, pre-Flavian forms are translations of 'native' beakers, bowls and platters, in 'transitional' ware (see above, p 74). Jars with thick, short everted rims (eg Fig.

Table 8 Part I: Development in Ware usage *c.* AD 1-150 (Miscellaneous Sites)

Proportions of first/second century pottery assemblages by weight and ware (key groups)

Site	Site 1 (653.1965)	Site 2 (163.1969)	Site 2 (163.1969)	Site 1 (653.1965)	Site 1 (653.1965)
Phase	1	1	3	4A	7C
Feature/Layer			F92	F60+63	V 5
Notional pottery date range	1-70/80	1-70/80	1-70/80	70-120	70-120/150
Date of deposition	1-70	1-70	70-120	70-120	120-140/150
Sample size (grams)	9406	16564	7081	8820	4652
Wares					
Arretine (*present) + Samian	1.1	0.4	0.4	10.2	7.0
Colour-coats (*mostly intrusive)	0.2	-	-	0.2	-
Misc. fine (TN,TR,LG,MW,MD,OW4)	3.7	0.2	0.9	0.1	0.1
Mortaria (*intrusive)	-	0.2*	-	5.4	6.2
Amphora fabrics (*Cam 139 only)	1.5	0.1	22.5*	11.1	1.8
White wares	1.7	0.5	0.4	10.5	7.2
White slip wares (*WS1/WS11 only)	0.4*	0.5*	4.1*	3.7	0.5
Oxidised wares	2.2	0.8	-	7.0	1.8
Grey wares	3.7	1.5	0.4	46.2	64.8
BB1 (*intrusive)	-	0.1*	-	-	1.1
R-B coarse imports (BB2,CG3B, Derbys)	-	-	-	-	-
Calcite gritted ware 1	24.5	42.2	28.2	4.9	5.9
Grog tempered wares 1-4	32.4	12.0	9.8	0.2	0.5
Misc. 'native' (CG2-4, MG1-2, SW)	22.4	34.6	33.1	0.3	3.0
Misc. 'transitional' (GT5-6, MG3-4, MC1)	6.3	8.3	0.3	0.4	-

Table 8 Part II: Development in Ware usage *c.* AD 1-150 (Miscellaneous Sites)

Proportions of first/second century pottery assemblages by weight and ware (key groups)

Site	Forum (302.1971) (295.1973)	Site 2 (163.1969)	Site 2 (163.1969)	Temple (164.1969)	Forum (302.1971) (295.1973)
Phase	2B	4	5		4A
Feature/Layer	'Group 1'		F46	II 84+ 109+111	'Group 2'
Notional pottery date range	70-120/130	60-130	60-130/150	100-140	100-225
Date of deposition	120-140	120-150	150-450	120-150	280-320
Sample size (grams)	58660	21194	9603	8841	37013
Wares					
Arretine (*present) + Samian	10.0*	5.5	7.3	1.9	7.4*
Colour-coats (*mostly intrusive)	0.2	0.4*	0.07	0.8	0.9
Misc. fine (TN,TR,LG,MW,MD,OW4)	0.08	0.5	0.6	0.2	0.2
Mortaria (*intrusive)	4.6	2.7	6.3	4.2	16.2
Amphora fabrics (*Cam 139 only)	13.0	24.4	10.1	24.0	33.4
White wares	7.1	11.8	15.4	26.6	18.8
White slip wares (*WS1/WS11 only)	1.5	1.7	2.4	0.4	1.4
Oxidised wares	2.5	3.0	5.1	0.3	3.5
Grey wares	35.4	34.3	32.1	13.2	11.5
BB1 (*intrusive)	0.02	1.1	3.4	6.3	4.3
R-B coarse imports (BB2,CG3B, Derbys)	-	0.07	-	-	0.04
Calcite gritted ware 1	18.6	9.3	15.0	3.4	1.9
Grog tempered wares 1-4	3.1	2.6	0.4	0.2	-
Misc. 'native' (CG2-4, MG1-2, SW)	0.5	1.7	0.2	18.5	0.4
Misc. 'transitional' (GT5-6, MG3-4, MC1)	3.4	0.7	1.6	-	-

Table 9 The relationship between grey wares, calcite gritted ware 1A, and BB1, *c.* AD 1-140

Site	1	2	2	1	1	302.1971 +295.1973 (forum)	2	2	164.1969 (temple)	302.1971 +295.1973 (forum)
Phase	1	1	3	4A	7C	2B	4	5		4A
Feature/layer			F92	F60 + 63	V 5	'Group 1'		F46	II 84 + 109 + 111	'Group 2'
Notional pottery date range	1-70/80	1-70/80	1-70/80	70-120	70-120/150	70-120/130	60-130	60-130/150	100-140	100-225
CG1A as proportion (%) of GW+CG1A +BB1 (weight)	86.8	96.3*	98.8	9.5	11.8	34.6	20.9	31.7	14.9	10.6
Ratio of CG1A: GW (weight)	6.6:1	28.1:1	79.8:1	1:9.5	1:10.9	1:1.9	1:3.7	1:2.1	1:3.9	1:6.2
Ratio of CG1A: BB1 (weight)	-	332.7:1*	-	-	5.3:1	996.6:1	8.3:1	4.5:1	1:1.8	1:2.3
Ratio of GW: BB1 (weight)	-	11.9:1*	-	-	58:1	1885.2:1	30.5:1	9.5:1	2.1:1	2.7:1

*BB1 intrusive

Site 1 653.1965
Site 2 163.1969

54.79-81) and lids (Fig. 51.23) may date from *c.* AD 60-130, whilst broadly similar vessels with white painted decoration (eg. Figs. 52.29 and 54.68; Kenyon 1948 Fig. 38.29) may belong to the first half of the 2nd century. 'Group 2' on the forum (Pollard forthcoming (a)) illustrates the diversity of 2nd century types, the dates of inception of three of which are clarified by the present Sites 1 and 2.

Clay rough cast beakers and rouletted beakers with cornice or short everted rims (*ibid.*, nos. 42, 85, 97, 98 and Figs. 68.298 and 69.311 herein, eg) are entirely unrepresented on these sites with the exception of a rouletted sherd in a medieval level on Site 2, and the same is true of flanged bowls in oxidised ware. Taken together, the Flavian to Hadrianic assemblages on the two sites are quite large enough to permit the inference that had these three forms been in circulation before *c.* 130 they would have been represented; their relative abundance in the forum Group 2, in Hadrianic-Antonine deposits on Silver Street (Pollard forthcoming (c)) and the 'temple' site (*ibid.*, forthcoming (b)) and at the Jewry Wall suggest that the epithet of 'Antonine' is well-deserved as a guide to their peak of fashionability.

The Illustrated Iron Age and Roman Pottery

305 vessels have been drawn, aside from the decorated samian, from Sites 1-6, 8, 9, 11 and 12. There are two elements to this catalogue; firstly, additions to the corpus that is being compiled of pottery types in Leicester, and secondly, representative illustration of the groups from F3 on Site 3, and F21, 22 and 24 on Site 6. These are the only contexts for which the full range of types present is depicted. The content by form and fabric of several other assemblages of key significance for the understanding of the development of pottery is present in tabular form in the archive. The justification for this is multifold. Firstly, our understanding of the chronology of Midlands wares in Leicester is in its infancy, and it is the imports, notably for the first two centuries AD Gallo-Roman and samian wares and BB1, that provide the cornerstones of the dating sequence. The forms these wares take are well known. Secondly, the vast bulk of the pottery comes from secondary deposits, and much will, to some extent, be residual. This is immediately apparent on consideration of Kenyon's "Forum" (Bath house) levels on the Jewry Wall site (1948). Thirdly, the report is one in a series to be published on Late Iron Age and Roman Leicester, commencing with that on the excavations in the Bath Lane area (Clay and Mellor 1985), during which a corpus of illustrations and of key groups will be built up, from which it is hoped to generate a Pottery Type Series volume, providing considered dating where possible for types based upon a much larger data base than any one report could provide. Misconceptions in dating that become enshrined in the literature are not easily dispelled (cf Wilson 1972, 1984). Fourthly, the repetitous illustration of familiar types serves little purpose without exceptionally good independent dating evidence; it is moreover expensive both in time and in the eventual cost of publication. Some repetition is inevitable, as better examples of types come to light. Thus Sites 1-4, 8 and 9 were drawn and mounted before the decision was reached to incorporate Sites 5 and 6 in the report. The range of variation of "Belgic" phase types is illustrated in view of the current

Table 10 Rusticated sherds and 'en barbotine' sherds in grey ware assemblages *c.* AD 50-140

Site	1	2	2	1	1	302.1971 +295.1973 (forum)	2	2	164.1969 (temple)	302.1971 +295.1973 (forum)
Phase	1	1	3	4A	7C	2B	4	5		4A
Feature/layer			F92	F60 + 63	V 5	'Group 1'		F46	II 84 + 109 + 111	'Group 2'
Notional pottery date range	1-70/80	1-70/80	1-70/80	70-120	70-120/150	70-120/130	60-130	60-130/150	100-140	100-225
Total grey ware (sherd count)	37	28	1	282	221	1429	569	318	84	199
Rustic as prop (%) of all GW	-	-	-	6.7	7.2	16.0	8.3	3.8	-	0.5
Barbotine as prop (%) of all GW	-	10.7*	-	8.5	5.9	0.5	4.9	12.6	25	5.0
Barbotine as prop (%) of all GW (excluding small-dot panels)	-	10.7*	-	3.5	5.4	0.5	4.6	10.4	9.5	4.5
Barbotine small-dot panels (sherd count)							2	7		1
Barbotine large-dot panels (sherd count)		2*		6	2	2	12	8	6	9
Barbotine ring-&-dot (sherd count)				14	4		6	2		
Barbotine ring (sherd count)				3	2	3	1	2		
Barbotine ring+ rib (sherd count)								6		
Barbotine large-dot panel + rib (sherd count)							2	2	1	
Barbotine rib (vertical or oblique) (Sherd count)					2	2	4	13	1	
Barbotine hairpin (sherd count)		1*		1	2					
Barbotine uncertain motif (sherd count)							1			

* intrusive (?)

Site 1 653.1965
Site 2 163.1969

interest in the antecedents of Roman towns in Britain, and in the pottery of these (eg Bennett et al 1982; Fulford 1984; Niblett 1985) and of other wealthy early settlements (eg Partridge 1981; Stead and Rigby 1986). The opportunity is taken to publish thirteen vessels from other sites which provide further information on types or wares illustrated in the main body of the catalogue, and which would not otherwise see the light of day. These have been extracted either from the collections of the Jewry Wall Museum, Leicester, or from previously unillustrated material from published sites.

Site 1

Phase 1

Fig. 50

1. C21 Platter, cf Drag 18. See p 54 above for discussion.(884 + 883) F73 + F72: V 49 + V 50, phase 1B.
2. Micaceous TN. Platter, Cam 1, with concentric grooves on base int. See p 69. Graffito incised on base ext (Fig. 49.G1; report, p 72). (217) F47: III 51, phase 1B.
3. CG3A Everted rim (storage) jar, lid-seated. Diameter approximate. Black surfaces. (749) F72: V 58, phase 1B.
4. CG3A Necked storage jar, impressed row over faint combing. Probably coil built. Reddish brown through brown and reddish yellow to light red surfaces, patchy (very dark grey) reduction. Cf nos. 14, 257. (750) F75: V 66, phase 1B.
5. GT1 Ledge rim jar, rilled. Probably coil built. Reddish yellow (5YR) surfaces, partially sooted. Cf no. 52. (767 + 769) F73 + F72: V 59, + V 63, phase 1B.
6. GT1 Narrow-mouthed jar, burnished from lip to girth ext, except in zone of tooled lattice. Possibly wheel thrown. Red to light red surfaces (2.5YR 5/6 to 6/6). Cf Clamp 1985 Fig. 33.86. (770) F75: V 66, phase 1B.
7. GT1 As 6, with light red (2.5YR) surfaces. (768) F72:

V 62, phase 1B.

8. GT2 S-shape bowl. Black to dark brown ext, burnished, surface. Cf nos. 41, 42, 46, 56, 253. (777) F73: V 49, phase 1B.
9. MG2 Platter, Cam 21. Black surfaces, burnished. Cf Clamp 1985 Fig. 33.82, and no. 48. (835 + 836 + 837) IIIA 66 (F51), + IIIA 70 + VI 28; phases 1C + 1C + 2A.
10. SW2 S-shape bowl. Dark grey to black, burnished, surfaces. Cf carinated bowls, eg Clamp 1985 Fig. 31.8, and no. 246, but with rounded girth. (862) F72: V 62, phase 1B.
11. SW2 Lid. Reddish yellow (5YR 6/6) surfaces, burnished ext and partially int. Cf no. 239. (852) IIIA 70, phase 1C.
12. SW3 Jar, burnished chevron. Hole drilled through wall after firing. Probably coil built. Black surfaces. (867 + 868) IIIA 66 (F51), + IIIA 70, phase 1C.

Phase 2.

Fig. 51

13. AM18 Rim of rilled amphora, Cam 189 or possibly Kingsholm 117 (cf Sealey 1985, 87-90; Timby 1985a). Cf Pollard forthcoming (a), no. 170. (275) F135: VI 24, phase 2C.
14. MG1 Storage jar, impressed row above combing, cf nos. 4 and 257, and Clamp 1985 Fig. 31.11. Possibly coil built but finished by turning. Diameter uncertain. Greyish int and upper ext, light red lower ext surfaces. (828 + 829 + 830). VI 25 + VI 26 + VI 28, phase 2A.

14A. Suggested reconstruction of 14, based on form and dimensions of nos. 4 and 110. Scale 1/8.

Phase 3

15. Samian, South Gaulish. Pedestal form of Drag 35/36. Vernhet distinguishes six services, include Drag 35, 42, 46 and three hybrids, each of which has a small bowl, a larger bowl or shallow dish and a pedestal bowl or cup (Vernhet 1976, 1986; this vessel falls under his service A, no. 3, equated with Hermet 29/29A). See also Stanfield 1929, nos. 21-4 (950 + 943) F71 + F63: V 39 + V 21, phases 3B, 4A.
16. MD1C Flanged rim bowl, mica coated int and on upper face of lip and flange. (227) F71: V 39, phase 3B.
17. GW6 Everted rim jar, reeded rim. Cf the waster or second, MacRobert 1987 Fig. 31.12 from St. Peters Lane. (625 + 624) F49 IIIA 68 + IIIA 72, phase 3B.
18. GW10 Lid. (659) F133: VI 17, phase 3C.
19. GW6 Platter, burnished body int and as radial lines on base int. (639 + 630 + 638) V 39 (F71) + V 21 (F63) + V 38; phases 3A, 4A, 4A.

Unstratified

20. GW6 Platter, as 19, with radial decoration encircled by grooves. Both 19 and 20 are knife trimmed ext. The type appears to have been inspired by later terra nigra forms, notably Cam 8, 12, 13 and 16. Cf Cam 32. Midlands parallels include vessels from Northamptonshire (Woods 1972, Fig. 8.1, 6; Fig. 2.2, 3), Warwickshire (Webster 1971-3, Fig. 15.150), and Rutland (Corder 1961, Fig. 14.1-2). See also, from Leicester, Hebditch 1973, Fig. 26.93. Neronian to Flavian floruit. (656).

Phase 4

21. WW2 Ring-neck flagon, cf Jewry Wall Ring-neck Jug Type B.1. (325) F63: V 21, phase 4A.
22. WW7 Carinated cup. (357) VIII 8, phase 4A.
23. OW2 Lid, *c.* 95% present. Cf Clamp 1985 Fig. 33.69, in GW3. (439) F63: V 21, phase 4A.
24. GW2 S-shape bowl. Cf nos. 43, 46, 102 and 253. (687 + 688) F63: V 19 + V 21, phase 4A.
25. GW6 Necked bowl, tooled decoration on shoulder, burnished facets on neck and girth. (626) F63: V 19, phase 4A.

Phase 5

26. MD6 Flanged rim dish, mica coated overall. Cf no. 266. (229 + 230) III 13 + III 23, phases 5C and 5B.
27. MD6 Bowl, groove on rim. Mica coated on rim, and body ext. Cf nos. 131 (grey ware) and 226. (238) VII 4, phase 5C.
28. OW2 Small everted rim jar, knife trimmed body. Cf nos. 49, 81, 145 and Pollard forthcoming (a), no. 8. An early Roman type, pre-Flavian to, at the latest, Hadrianic. Cf nos. 53 and 109 for Iron Age parallels. (424 + 426 + 435 + 433) III 23 + III 24 + IIIC 6 + IIIB 7, phases 5B, 5A, 5B, 7C.

Fig. 52

29. OW6 Globular beaker, everted rim. White painted ring(s) on shoulder, as no. 68, and cf the bowl, no. 284. Possibly Mancetter-Hartshill product, of the early to mid 2nd century. Cf grey ware 'ring-and-dot' jars, such as no. 105, and other oxidised beakers, nos. 174 and 218. (458) IIIC 6, phase 5B.
30. GT6 Everted rim jar, grey. Cf the GW6 and GW9 rims from pre-Flavian contexts, nos. 33 and 245, and Pollard forthcoming (a), no. 67 in GT5. (817). IIIA 52, phase 5A.
31. MG2 Butt beaker, decorated with a diamond-toothed roulette wheel or spring-iron, interrupted by a burnished line. Dark grey to black surfaces. Paralleled at Margidunum (Oswald 1948a, Pl. xii.4), and occurring in MG and grey wares, this variant of the 'butt beaker' tradition may have been introduced around the time of the conquest, with production terminating before the end of the 1st century. A GW5 vessel comes from the same context. (837) IIIC 6, phase 5B.

Phase 6

32. GW3 Hemispherical bowl. 'Compass' scribed arcs and incised lines under rouletting, an unusual combination of these elements (cf Marsh 1978, Type 42, and Marsh and Tyers 1976). The fabric and surfaces are grey, in contrast with the black vessels predominant in the south-east (*ibid.*; Monaghan 1982). The term 'London Ware' is often applied to this style (Marsh 1978, 123-124), but sources other than London itself are known, including possibly the lower Nene Valley (Perrin 1980; Howe et al 1980, 10 and Fig. 2.23). A date range of *c.* 90-150 is likely. (472). III 5, phase 6B.

Site 2

Phase 1

33. GW9 Form as 30, but without obvious grog. A 'very coarse' grey ware, paralleled amongst the material associated with kilns at Great Holme Street, Leicester (Mellor 1975-6, Lucas 1976-7), and classifiable as a 'transitional' ware. Very dark grey surfaces, sooted ext. (741) F71: III 25, phase 1C.
34. CG1A Ledge rim jar, 'finger-nail' impressed lip and shoulder. Coil built. Black surfaces, patchy reddish brown int. The motif is an Iron Age tradition, probably going out of use by the Neronian period. Cf Clamp 1985 Figs. 32.53 and 33.93. (888) F53: II 90, phase 1B.

35. CG3A Knife trimmed(?) lip bead rim jar. Very dark grey ext, light red int (2.5YR) surfaces. Cf no. 39. (944) F15: I 93, phase 1B.
36. GT1 Ledge rim storage jar, burnished ext. Probably coil built, diameter uncertain. Very dark grey surfaces. Cf Jewry Wall Storage Jar Type K. (999) F71: III 53, phase 1C.
37. GT5 Narrow-mouthed jar, knife trimmed lower ext. Light grey core, grey surfaces. Cf no. 113. (1106-1111) I 24 (F3, phase 6A) + F15: I 54 (/89) + I 89 + I 90 (/91) + I 91 + I 93, phase 1B.
38. GT6 Bead rim (storage) jar, combed ext. Probably coil built, diameter approximate. Grey surfaces, partially fire scorched ext (2.5YR 5/4 - 5/6) through firing almost to the point of vitrification. (1091) F15: I 93, phase 1B.
39. MG1 Narrow-mouthed jar, cf no. 35. Very dark grey to reddish brown (5YR) surfaces. (1116) F15: I 54 (/89), phase 1B.
40. MG2 Tall conical jar (?), probably with pedestal base (Thompson 1982, 83-84). Finely tooled chevron on plain surface, burnished zones below. This vessel appears to be unique in Leicester's extant collections. Greyish brown to very dark grey (10YR) surfaces. (1167) F53: II 90, phase 1B.
41. MG2 Necked bowl. Dark grey to black surfaces. Cf nos. 8, 24 etc. (1136 + 1148) I 36 (phase 2) + F18: I 59, phase 1B.
42. MG2 As 41, with black to dark reddish grey ext and grey int surfaces. (1159 + 1160) F15: I 90(/91) + I 93, phase 1B.
43. MG3 S-shape bowl. Virtually identical to nos. 24 (GW2), 102 (GW3), 253 (GT2), and Clamp 1985 Fig. 34.120 (OW2), form and fabric variations are subtle and serve to illustrate the broad continuum in pottery from the mid 1st into the 2nd centuries. (1195) F12: I 39, phase 1B.
44. CG2A Plain rim jar, impressed decoration. Possibly coil built, certainly hand made. Diameter uncertain. An Iron Age vessel, but it does not closely match in either fabric or form the group from F24 on Site 6. Cf Clamp 1985 Figs. 31.23 and 32.39; Kenyon 1948 Figs. 34.9, 35.2 and 14, 36.19. Black ext surface, dark reddish brown int. (1202) F53: II 93, phase 1B.
45. SW2 Base of pedestal jar. Black to reddish yellow surfaces. Cf no. 252. Pedestals are rare in Leicester, and full profiles have yet to be recovered. Necked jars as well as the conical vessel no. 40 probably stood on such bases here, as elsewhere (Thompson 1982, 83-84). (1267) F73: III 50, phase 1A.
46. SW2 As 41, with grey to very dark grey surfaces. One-third complete. Note the unburnished zone on the lower body of 41, 42 and 46. (1233 + 1234) F15: I 90 (/91) + I 93, phase 1B.

Fig. 53

47. SW2 Butt beaker. Fine combed decoration. Very dark grey ext, light brown int surfaces (7.5YR). The 'tubby' shape resembles the earlier Gallo-Belgic form (Rigby 1981a Type 40; Rigby 1989), cf Kenyon 1948 Fig. 36.10, 11 and Clamp 1985 Figs. 31.5 and 32.27. (1241) F12: I 97, phase 1B.
48. SW2 Platter, as no. 9. Surfaces mottled black, reddish brown to yellowish red (5YR), burnished. (1203 + 1211 + 1222 + 1236 + 1238) I 16 (F1) + I 46 (F16) + I 56 + I 93 (F15) + I 94 (F27): phases 4C, 1B, 2, 1B, 1A.
49. MC1 Small jar, cf no. 28, etc. Grey, partially blackened ext. Cf Clamp 1985 Fig. 33.91 (SW2). The fabric finds parallels at Great Holme Street, Leicester, amongst kiln material (cf MacRobert 1987, Figs. 31.5 and 33.55), and is classifiable as a 'transitional' grey ware. (1292) F12: I 97, phase 1B.

Phase 2

50. WS1 Ring-neck flagon, cf Pollard forthcoming (a), no. 123. (440) II 71, phase 2.
51. OW6 Miniature butt beaker, burnished neck and rim. Small vessels also occur in Iron Age fabrics (eg no. 99), but this vessel may be 'transitional'. (521 + 536) II 7 (/8) (F40) + III 30; phases 6A, 2.
52. GT1 Ledge rim jar, cf no. 5. Probably coil built. Very dark grey ext, reddish brown int surfaces. (993) III 30, phase 2.
53. GT1 Small bead rim jar, probably coil built. Very dark grey to dark greyish brown surfaces (10YR), sooted ext. I 76 + I 4 (F3); phases 2, 6A.
54. GT2 Possibly a 'barrel' (neckless butt) beaker. Very dark grey to reddish brown surfaces (5YR). (1028) III 52, phase 2.
55. MG4 Necked jar, cf MacRobert 1987, Fig. 32.22. A 'transitional' fabric, oxidised version of MG3 (cf no. 126). (1201) I 76, phase 2.
56. SW2 Necked bowl, cf Pollard forthcoming (a), nos. 1, 46 in grey ware. Black to reddish brown surfaces (5YR). *c.* 50% present. (1226) I 75, phase 2.

Phase 3, Feature 92

57. AM25 One-handled flagon, Cam 139 (Hawkes and Hull 1947, Pl. xii.2, bottom left, and Pl. lxix) (see above, p 64). (291 - 296) II 84, phase 2; + F92: II 97 + II 98 + II 100 + II 102; + F55: II 103, phase 1C. 64 of the 66 sherds (1596g out of 1622g) are from F92.
58. WS1 Plain collar-rim flagon, Jewry Wall Flagon Type A.15. The latter is in the same ware. (441 + 443) II 97 + II 102.
59. WS1 Grooved collar-rim flagon. (441) II 97.A third vessel similar to nos. 58-9, but refired to the point of vitrification, was also present in F92. (941 + 442 + 443) II 97 + II 100 + II 102.
60. CG1A Necked storage jar, combed. Coil built, finished by turning. The cordon is a variant, uncommon and possibly early in the development of the form, cf Clamp 1985 Fig. 32.41, and nos. 110, 180 and 254 here. Reddish yellow (5YR) to grey ext surface. (893) II 97.
61. CG3A Ledge rim jar, coil built, cf no. 300. Reddish brown int, black ext surfaces. *c.* 50% present. (948-951). II 100 + II 102 + II 107; + F35 II 103, phase 1C.
62. GT2 Necked jar (or bowl). Reddish brown surfaces (5YR). (1104 + 1105) II 100 + II 102.
63. GT2 High-shouldered beaker, combed wavy lines. Profile is reconstructed from local parallels in MG2 (Clamp 1985 Fig. 31.10) and grey ware (*ibid.*, Fig. 34.97) (cf Thompson 1982, 110-113). Reddish yellow (5YR) surfaces, possibly a white slip ext, cf WS11. (1018) II 97.

Fig. 54

64. MG2 Carinated bowl. A remarkably irregular profile and rim, implying poor throwing. Cf Clamp 1985, Fig. 31.8 and 15, and nos. 10, 246 and 294 here. Black surfaces. (1171 + 1172 + 1174) II 97 + II 100 + II 102.

Phase 3, Feature 49

65. GW3 Everted rim rusticated jar. Badly warped and blistered, this may be a genuine waster; although the wall is

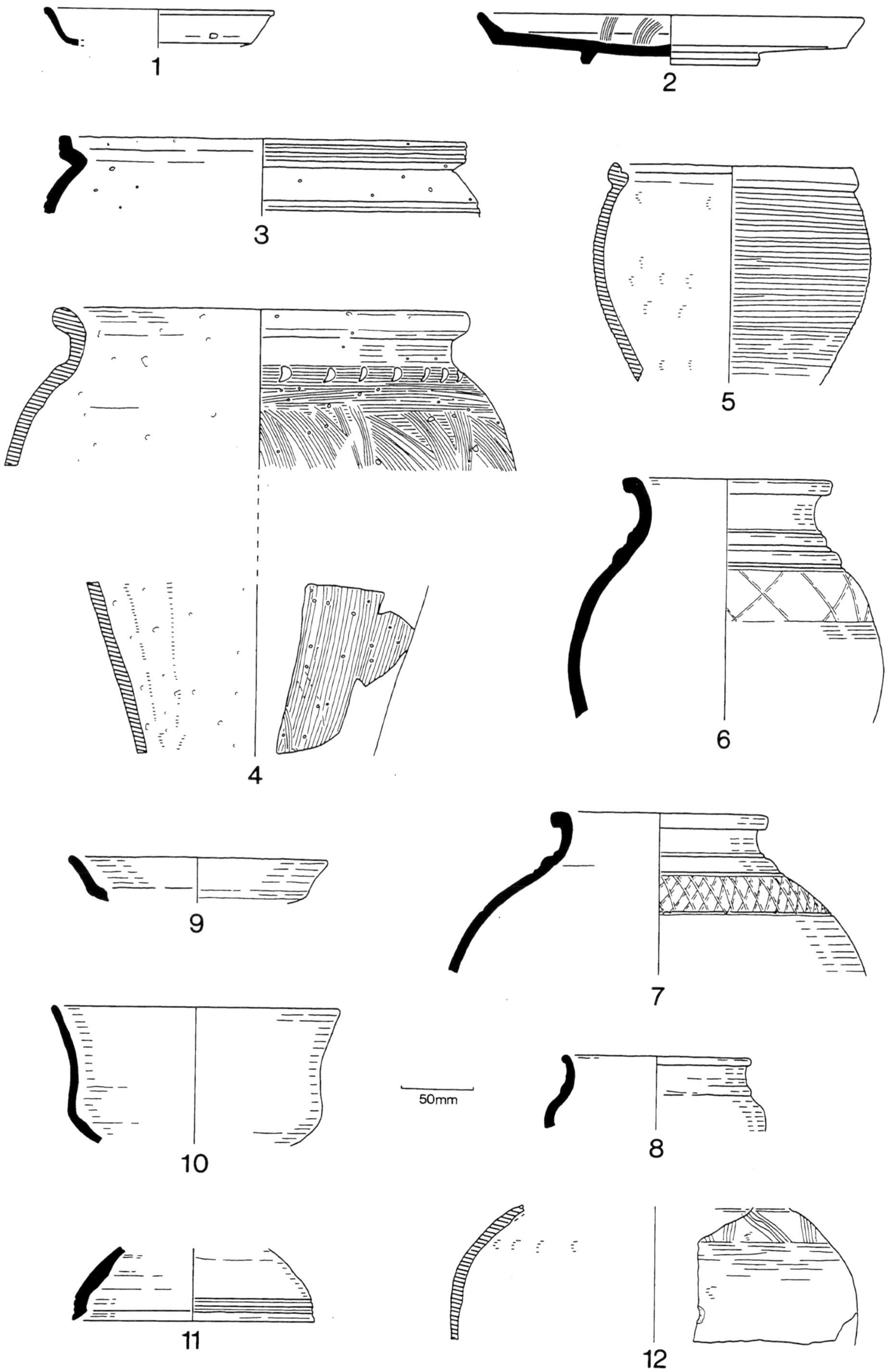

Fig. 50 Iron Age and Roman Pottery Site 1 Phase 1 (1-12) Scale 1:4

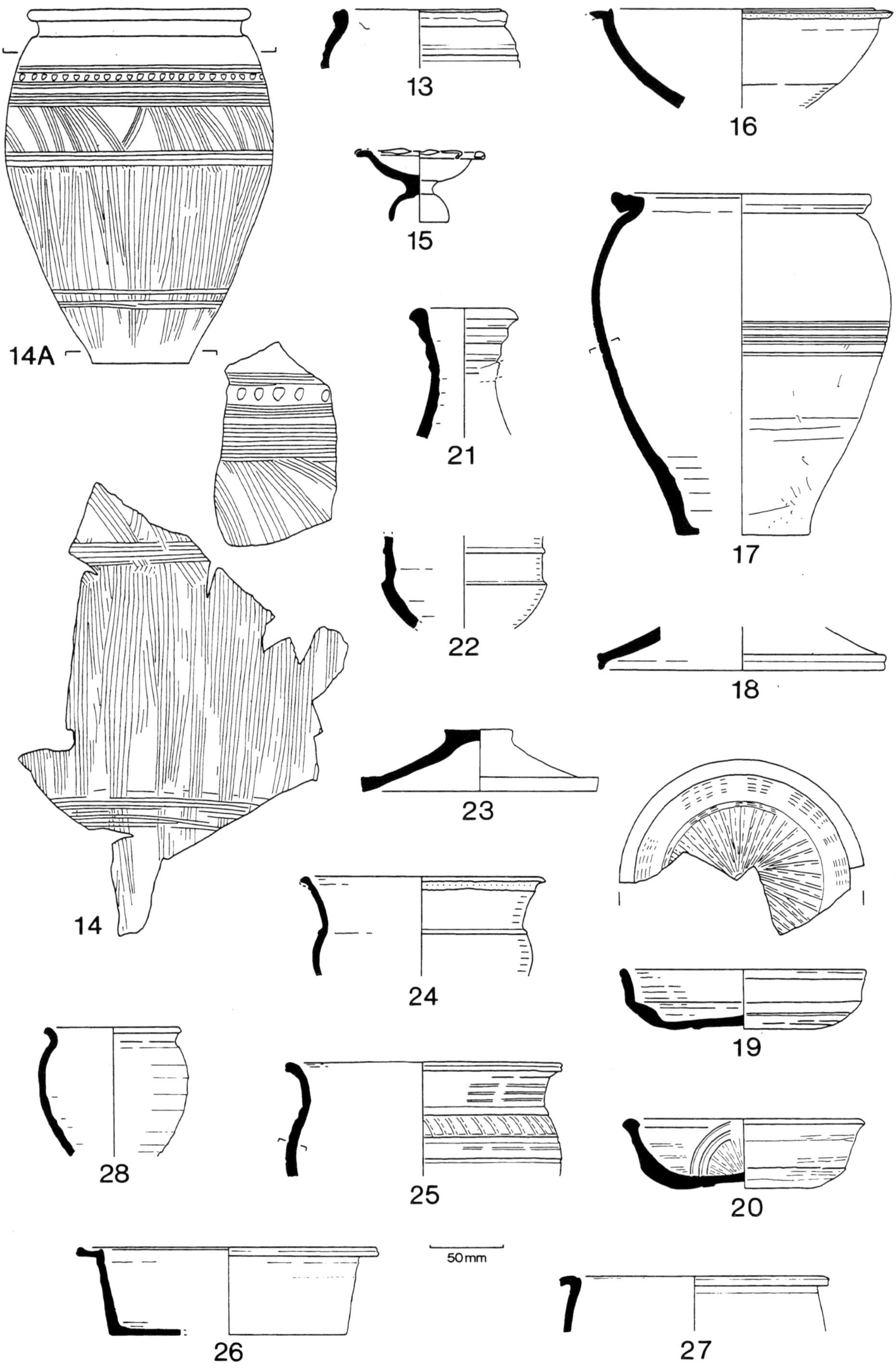

Fig. 51 Iron Age and Roman Pottery Site 1 Phase 2 (13-14); Phase 3 (15-19); u.s. (20); Phase 4 (21-25); Phase 5 (26-28) Scale 1:4 except 14A: Scale 1:8.

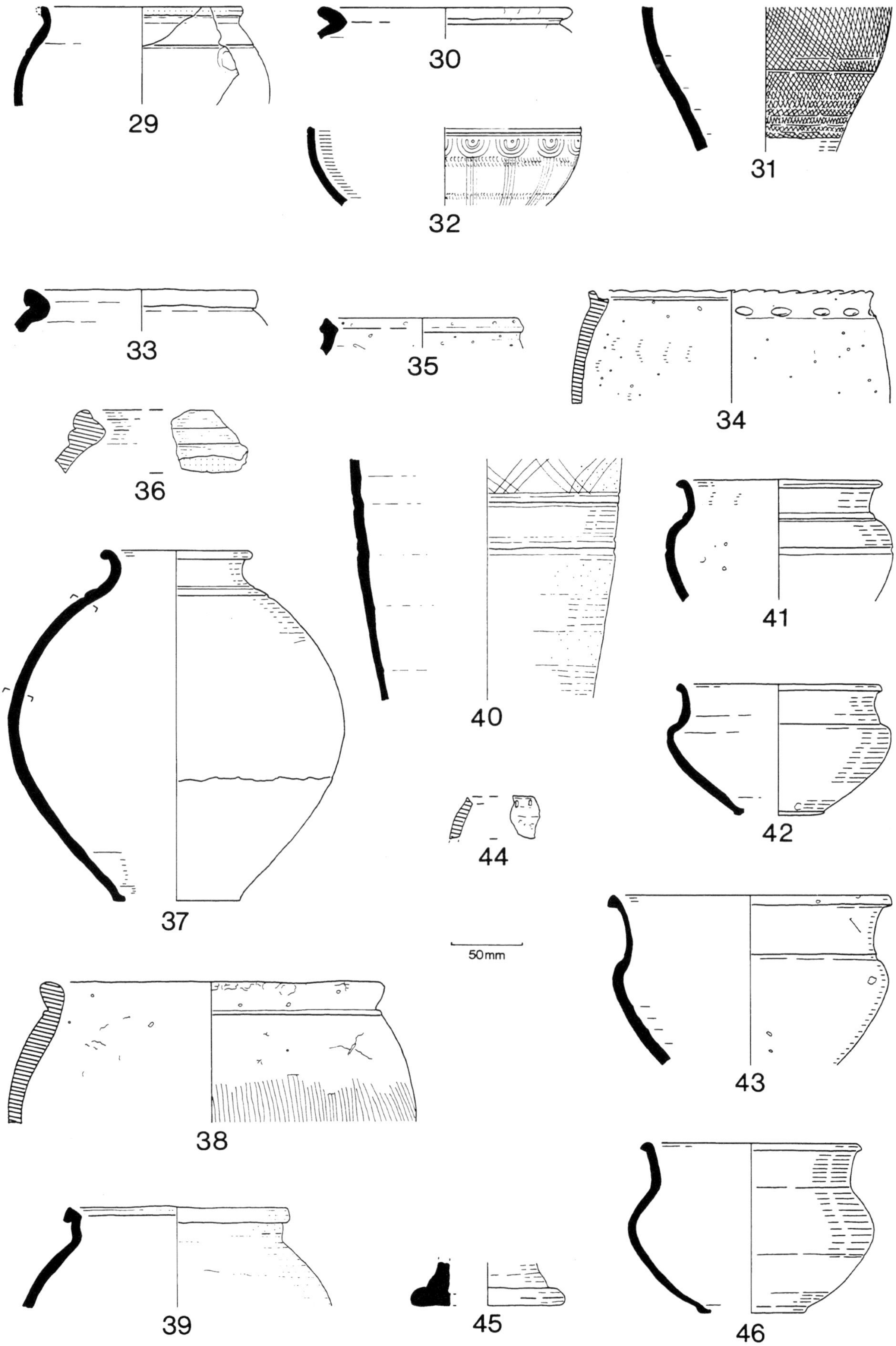

Fig. 52 Iron Age and Roman pottery Site 1 Phase 5 (29-31); Phase 6 (32); Site 2 Phase 1 (33-46) Scale 1:4

nowhere holed in the two-thirds (approximately) of the vessel present, it does not stand freely. (645) II 79.

Phase 4

66. WW2 Ring-neck flagon, Jewry Wall Ring-neck Jug Type E.12 (340). F1: II 57, phase 4B.
67. WW1 Everted rim lid-seated jar, rilled. Cf no. 76, and Clamp 1985 Fig. 33.77. (317). II 118, phase 4B.
68. OW7 Globular beaker, as no. 29. (544). II 67, phase 4B.
69. GW3 Wide-mouthed jar or bowl, cf nos. 8, 41, 42. (614). F1: II 55, phase 4B.
70. GW3 Reeded rim bowl, *c.* 50% present. (615) F1: II 55, phase 4B.
71. GW6 Reeded rim bowl, *c.* 50% present. (672 + 674 + 675 + 679) I 4 (F3) + I 9 (F8) + I 25 (F8) + I 20 (F1); phases 6A, 4B, 4B, 4B.
72. GW6 Necked jar, cf Jewry Wall Necked Jar Type C.6. (682) F8: I 26, phase 4B.
73. GW5 Small necked jar, Jewry Wall Necked Jar Type C.9. Cf no. 103. *c.* 67% present. (678) F8: I 25, phase 4B.
74. GW6 Platter or dish, cf nos. 19, 20 and Kenyon 1948 Fig. 37.11. (714) F1: II 56, phase 4B.
75. GT1 Bead rim jar with tooled lattice and burnished rim. Probably coil built. Black to dark grey surfaces. Cf no. 224, and Clamp 1985 Fig. 32.46. (979) F1: II 57, phase 4B.

Phase 5, Feature 46

76. WW1 As no. 67. (314) II 27.
77. WW2 Flaring carinated bowl, cf nos. 216, 217 and the handled 229, and in WS2 MacRobert 1987 Fig. 32.18. Broadly 2nd century; a similar vessel was associated with late 2nd century pottery at Towcester (Symonds 1980, Fig. 25.113). Cf O'Neil 1928, Pl. xxiv. 9-10. (323) II 27.
78. WW3 Spout, cf no. 219. Spouts or 'vases' occur on the shoulders of large jars, usually in threes (eg Colchester 390: Hull 1958), and in pairs(?) on face jars (eg Verulamium 910: Wilson 1972; Usk: Darling 1977, Fig. 6.4.18). Strainers carry a single spout over a pierced vessel wall (Marsh 1978 Type 46). (372) II 36.
79. OW3 As no. 67, with rilled shoulder. Identical to no. 279, and cf no. 80. Reduced and sooted ext. Presumably derived from the CG1A version established in the late Iron Age (cf Clamp 1985, Fig. 32.26) and current into the first half of the 2nd century, eg nos. 108, 223. (506) II 46.
80. OW7 Form as no. 79, rilled. Diameter uncertain. (543) II 37
81. OW3 Cf. no. 28 etc. *c.* 90% present. (503 + 515) II 11 (F42, phase 6A) + II 117.
82. GW3 Fragment of annular ring. Rings, often skeuomorphs, occur on the handles of the bowl or cauldron type, cf nos. 197, 276 and 305 here (Gillam 174, dated *c.* 120-160, and Colchester 302 (Hull 1958)). A 'honey-jar' variant with girth constriction from Reculver also has handle rings, and was associated with a 2nd century jug (Philp 1958, Fig. 2.1 and 2 respectively). Scale 1/2. (609) II 49.
83. GW10 Flagon or flask. (749). II 49.
84. GW12 Hemispherical(?) bowl, burnished ext. 'Compass'-scribed arcs and lozenge stamp impressions. An S-shape bowl from Margidunum combines scribed arcs with an impressed branch-like stamp (Oswald 1948a, Pl. xvi.8). The stamp (no. 84A, scale 1/1) is not recorded in a recent corpus of East Anglian and south-eastern early Romano-British stamped wares (Rodwell 1978, Fig. 7.20), although other forms of stamp occur on bowls of this type with scribed arcs at Scole (Norfolk) and Colchester (*ibid*) nos. 106, 120). The cross hatch stamp is not known at West Stow (J. Plouviez, in corresp., 1990) (557) II 43.

84A. Detail of stamp, drawn from a composite of the two incomplete impressions in the sherd.
85. GW11 Bowl or dish, cf no. 270. Diameter approximate. (750) II 27.
86. GW3 Globular beaker with diamond panels en barbotine. Cf no. 290 for the delicate moulding of the base. (593) II 40.
87. GW3 Small everted rim jar or beaker; found complete and intact. See no. 315 for a decorated version, and no. 104 for larger vessel. (653) II 117.
88. GW3 Small jar with everted rim, slightly warped. Cf no. 147, and in MG1 Clamp 1985, Fig. 33.56. (581) II 27.

Fig. 55

89. BB1 Pie dish, burnished overall except for zone ext where chevron and zigzag pattern tooled. An unusual deviation from the lattice and arcading that characterise pie dishes and their flanged descendents on sites in the north (Gillam 1970), its occurrence lends support to the evidence of BB1 lids in Leicester (no. 190 is typical) for a Midlands trade distinct from, and perhaps with slightly earlier beginnings than, that with the northern frontier zone. (779) II 27.

Phase 6

90. CG1B Flanged dish, rilled. Flange formed by folding lip back over body. A 4th century form, which in Leicestershire may have been in use mainly in the latter half of the 4th and perhaps into the 5th centuries. The dating at Towcester is supportive (Woodfield 1983, Fig. 18). Forms a 'set' with necked jars and dog dishes (*ibid.* Fig. 30. 254 - 257, and no. 318 below). (902) F64: III 4, phase 6D.
91. MO22 Mortarium, possibly by Coertutinus, cf no. 154. (313) F3: I 24, phase 6A.

Site 3

Phase 2, Feature 3

92. MD6 Indented beaker, mica coated ext and on rim (Marsh 1978 Type 21). *c.* AD 70-130. Number of indentations uncertain. (500) II 10, phase 2A.
93. MO7 Verulamium region mortarium, *c.* AD 50-110 (cf eg Verulamium 2645, 2647, 2648: Wilson 1984). (502 + 503) II 9 + II 10, phase 2A.
94. MO12 Midlands, possibly Mancetter-Hartshill, mortarium, *c.* AD 100-165 (cf eg Pollard forthcoming (a), nos. 200, 202, 203). (505) III 10, phase 2B.
95. WW3 Ring-neck flagon, Neronian to Hadrianic(?). (511 + 512) II 9 + II 10, Phase 2A.
96. OW2 Everted rim lid-seated jar. (525) III 9, phase 2B.
97. OW6 Everted rim high-shouldered beaker. (527) III 12, phase 2A.
98. GW2 Flaring carinated bowl; finely combed, and rouletted. Burnished overall, ext over combing. A substantially complete identical vessel with small bead rim was found at Great Holme Street, with the impression of an elliptical 'herringbone' stamp on the int base. (528 + 529) III 10 + III 12, phases 2B, 2A.
99. GW3 Everted rim globular or high-shouldered beaker, with rouletting and panels of large dots en barbotine. Grey ware 'ring-and- dot' vessels in Leicester are generally larger and lack the rouletting. This vessel may be Flavian. (538) III 10, phase 2B.

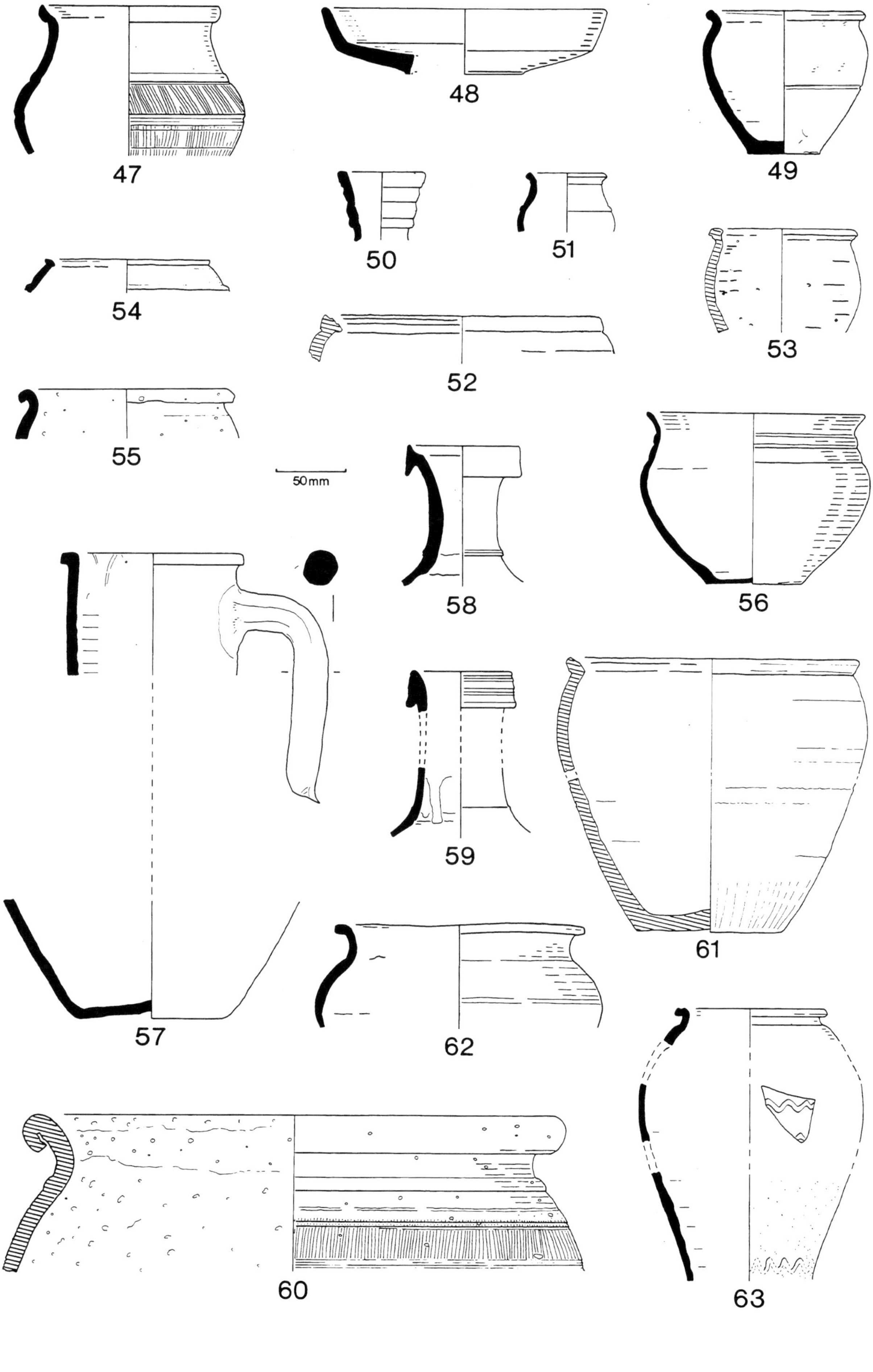

Fig. 53 Iron Age and Roman pottery Site 2 Phase 1 (47-49); Phase 2 (50-56); Phase 3 (57-63) Scale 1:4

100. GW3 Biconical beaker, cf no. 200. (539) III 10, phase 2B.

101. GW5 Biconical beaker. A more narrow version of the cordoned carinated bowl (cf Pollard forthcoming (a), no. 61), with "Belgic" antecedents. Late 1st to early 2nd centuries for 100, 101(?). (548) III 10, phase 2B.

102. GW3 S-shape bowl, as nos. 24, 253 etc. (540) III 10, phase 2B.

103. GW3 As no. 73, but larger. *c.* 67% present. (542) III 12, phase 2A.

104. GW3 As no. 87, but larger, 'jar', size. Cf Clamp 1985, Fig. 33.62. (530 + 536 + 537) I 12, phase 3C; + F3: III 9 + III 10, phase 2B.

105. GW3 As no. 104, with 'ring-and-dot' motif en barbotine. See p 78 for discussion. Sooted. (532). II 10, phase 2A.

106. GW5 Bowl (or platter) with 'cup' in centre, the two vessels presumably formed separately. An unusual form, perhaps an 'hors d'ouevre' or side-dish. It is paralleled at Hartshill (1961 excavations), Kiln 12, in what appears to be the stoke hole fill, in grey ware associated with a small coarse ware assemblage possibly of late 1st to early 2nd century date (P. Booth, K. F. Hartley pers comms). A third vessel resides in Devizes Museum (V. Swan, pers comm). A similar vessel is known from Ham Saltings, near Upchurch, Kent, in a burnished black sandy wheel-thrown fabric (unstratified: British Museum accession no. 1883 12-13, 464). (549) III 10, phase 2B.

Fig. 56

107. (See below, phase 3).

108. CG1A Ledge rim jar, coil built. Light brown surfaces, partially blackened and sooted ext. (558) II 9, phase 2A.

109. GT1 Small jar, recurved everted rim. Possibly coil built, certainly hand made. Very dark grey to dark brown surfaces (7.5 YR). Cf nos. 53, 238. (566) IV 17, phase 2B.

110. CG1A Necked storage jar, combed. Coil built. Light red (2.5YR) to reddish yellow (5YR) surfaces. Cf no. 180, which is somewhat later in date (mid to late 2nd century?) and has 'lost' the combing. (559 - 561) III 9 + III 10 + III 12; phases 2B, 2B, 2A

Miscellaneous contexts, phases 3 and 4

107. GW10 Wide-mouthed necked jar or bowl. (554) I 12, phase 3C (Fig. 56).

111. MO4 Mortarium, stamped by Sarrius (stamp Fig. 48.1, report p 66). (608) II 4, phase 3C.

112. CG2A Large (storage) jar. Probably wheel thrown, an unusual technique for this fabric. Scored chevron. Very dark grey int, greyish brown to dark grey (10YR) ext surfaces. (564 + 565) II 2 + II 5; phases 4B, 3C.

113. GW3 Small narrow-mouthed jar, or flask; cf no. 37. Jewry Wall Necked Jar Type E.17. (651) F22: IV 3, phase 4C.

Site 4

Phase 1

Fig. 57

114. TN Carinated bowl. See p 69 above for discussion. (262) F28: V 5, phase 1A.

115. CG3A Bead rim jar, burnished ext. Black surfaces. (341) F45: V 9, phase 1A.

116. CG3A Large (storage) jar, everted rim, cf no. 281. Probably coil built. Very dark grey to brown surfaces. Likely to be a pre-Roman Iron Age type, but it is not paralleled in the early (F24) group on Site 6, nor amongst 'mainstream' "Belgic" phase types. (342) F45: V 10, phase 1A.

117. MG2 Necked jar. Very dark grey surfaces. A virtually identical vessel comes from Site 9, in the marginally finer GW2. Nos. 117 and 125 are particularly fine examples of late Iron Age potting. (367 + 369 + 374 + 376) II 23 (F10) + II 27 (F13) + V 10 (F45) + V 11 (F49); phases 1A, 1A, 1A, 1B.

120. GW3 Platter, derivative of TN form Cam 16; concentric grooves on int and ext base. Small blisters demand consideration as a second (cf no. 126). Neronian- Flavian? (267) F34: IV 20, phase 1B.

Phase 2

118. WW2 Beaker with delicately formed grooved rim. (229) F33: IV 3, phase 2.

119. WS2 Everted rim beaker with red painted decoration (no. 119A, scale 1/2). Probably Flavian-Hadrianic, the combination of white slip and red paint is unusual in the East Midlands (but cf no. 278). No parallel for the scheme has been traced in the East Midlands either at known production sites (eg Mancetter, Little Chester, Rushden (Woods and Hastings 1984), South Carlton (Webster 1944)) or on major occupation sites (eg Margidunum, Letocetum, Tripontium, Bannaventa, Irchester, Duston and The Lunt). (241) F33: IV 3, phase 2.

Medieval levels

121. GW3 Pie dish, derivative of BB1 type Gillam 220, current *c.* AD 120-160. Burnished overall except for plain zone over which lattice is tooled. (263 + 270) I 2 (F1) + V 20 (F2).

122. GW3 Cylindrical bowl. Barbotine dots over ribs on plain zone; burnished ext above cordon. Cf no. 155. (266) F22: IV 18.

123. GW1 Burnished, tooled chevron ext. The slight groove on the flange recalls the BB1 types Gillam 226 and 227, dated *c.* 200-240 and 210-300 respectively. (259) F1: I 2.

124. GW1 Dog dish, burnished and decorated as no. 121. Possibly BB1, though not conforming to Dorset fabric characteristics; virtually identical to Gillam 316, dated *c.* 125-160. (258) F1: I 2.

125. MG2 Narrow-mouthed jar. A similar vessel in SW2 comes from Stanion, Northants (information from P. Foster). Very dark grey surfaces. An unusual form. (364) F4: II 13.

126. MG3 Necked bowl, cf nos. 117, 102 etc. Blistered as no. 120. (382 + 383). F7: II 18 + II 20.

127. MG3 Bead rim jar. (384) F7: II 20.

Site 5

Phase 1

Fig. 58

128. WS2 'Pulley rim' flagon, the rim formed by folding the wall back onto itself. Probably an import from south east Britain, perhaps north Kent (cf Blumstein 1956, but J. Monaghan (pers comm) does not think it to be in a Hoo fabric). Cf Bushe-Fox 1932 nos. 197, 199, and Green 1981 Fig. 21.40-43. 1st century AD, perhaps Neronian-Vespasianic. (537) IV 22, phase 1A.

129. MD3 Reeded rim ?bowl, mica coated ext and on rim. Sooted overall. Marsh 1978 Type 36.6. (360) III 4, phase 1B.

130. GW3 Biconical beaker or small carinated bowl, rouletted. (31) F104: X 40, phase 1D.

131. GW6 Reeded rim bowl, cf no. 27. (37) F104: X 40, phase 1D.

132. GW5 Bead rim jar with offset shoulder, cf no. 117. (67)

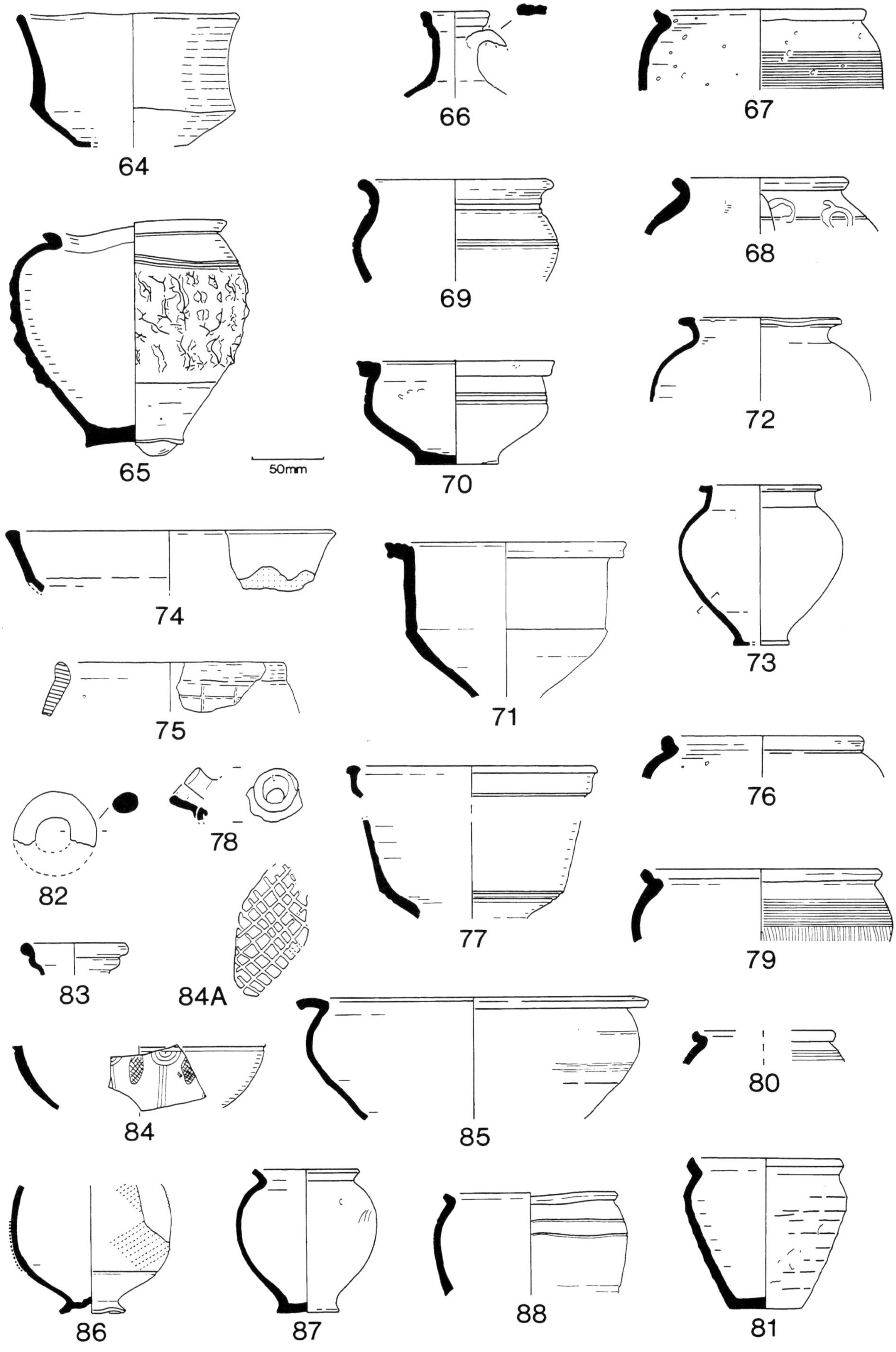

Fig. 54 Iron Age and Roman pottery Site 2 Phase 2 (64); Phase 3 (65); Phase 4 (66-75); Phase 5 (76-88)
Scale 1:4 except 82: Scale 1:2, and 84A: Scale 1:1.

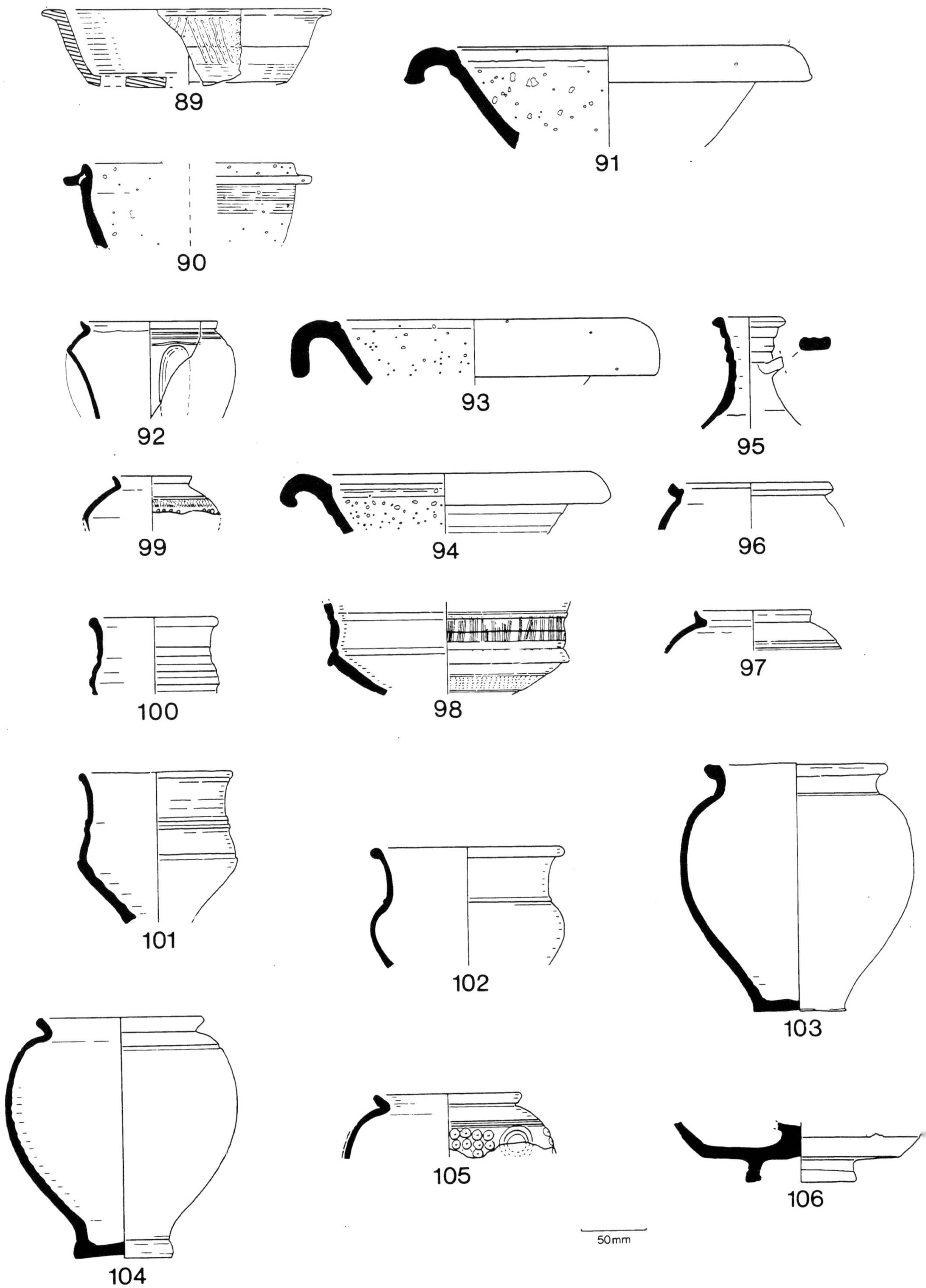

 Fig. 55 Iron Age and Roman pottery Site 2 Phase 5 (89); Phase 6 (90-91); Site 3 Phase 2 (92-106) Scale 1:4

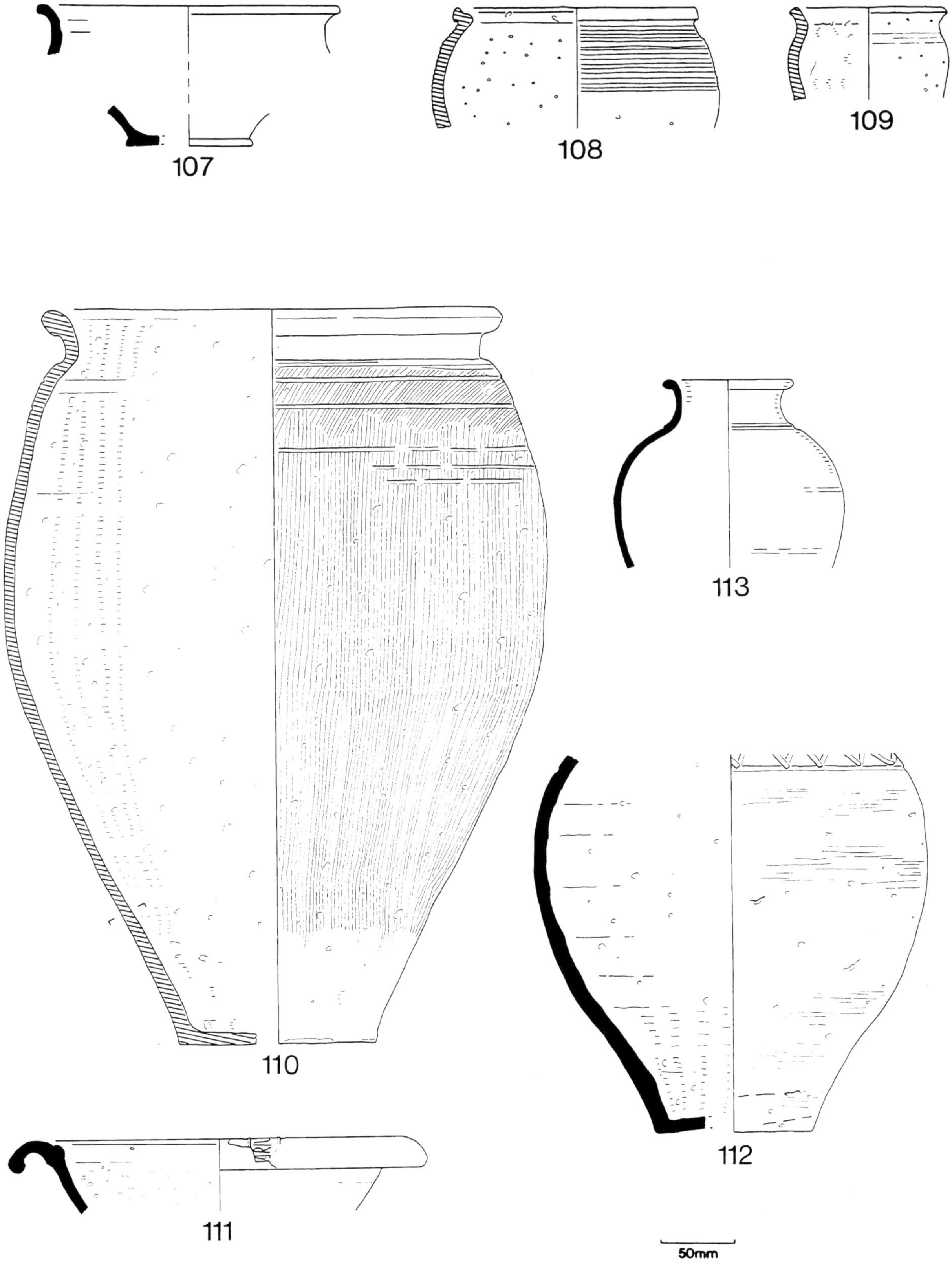

Fig. 56 Iron Age and Roman pottery Site 3 Phase 2 (108-110); Phases 3 and 4 (107, 111-113) Scale 1:4

F104: X 40, phase 1D.

133. GW3 Everted rim jar, lid-seat groove on lip int. (32) F104: X 40, phase 1D.

134. GW3 Everted rim jar, rouletting partially cutting tooled wavy line. Cf Pollard forthcoming (a), no. 110. (68) F104: X 40, phase 1D.

135. GW10 Everted rim jar, burnished upper shoulder and tooled lattice. Probably buried complete and intact, now *c.* 67% complete. Foot possibly thrown separately. Cf Brixworth 177 (Woods 1972). (38 + 926) F104: X 40, phase 1D + VII 4, phase 4C.

Phase 2A

136. C2 Lower Rhineland. Globular beaker with scales en barbotine (Greene 1979, 58, Fig. 24.10). Date range of pre-Flavian to Flavian + (K.T. Greene, pers comm) (345 + 346) F40: VII 44; + F21: VII 45; phases 2A, 6B.

137. GW2 'Eggshell' thickness cf TN. Biconical beaker. (732) F39: VII 3.

138. AM7 Handle, seemingly mounted entirely on shoulder, cf Dressel 21/22 and Kingsholm 117 (Timby 1985a, Fig. 28, and Sealey 1985, 89-90). R. Tomber (pers comm) has suggested an East Mediterranean source having parallels with Palestinian forms. Precise angle of handle, and diameter of body, uncertain. (383) F39: VII 2.

139. MD6 Tripod bowl with plain flanged rim. Abraded int, seemingly mica coated overall, sooted ext and on rim. Marsh 1978 Type 27. (373) F39: VII 42.

140. WW5 Reeded rim bowl, Southwark Type IV A.5-7 (Marsh and Tyers 1978). Verulamium region, mid Flavian to Hadrianic or early Antonine (eg Verulamium 337: Wilson 1972, 1984). (460) F39: VII 3, phase 2A.

141. WS2 Ring-neck flagon, *c.* 95% complete and intact. (266) F39:VII 38.

142. WS2 Small 'honey jar', complete except for loss of one handle. (921) F42: V 28.

143. WW4 'Disc rim' flagon, possibly rim to no. 199. 1st century AD, cf Southwark Type I D (Marsh and Tyers 1978), and Cam 149-150. (446) F35: V 26.

144. WW2 Lamp(?), complete. Pinched basal knob. No sooting. (918) F42: VI 27.

145. OW2 As no. 28 etc. (598) F39: VII 2.

146. GW3 Carinated beaker, Jewry Wall Carinated bowl Type A.1. Burnished ext except where lattice tooled. (718) F39: VII 42.

147. GW3 Everted rim jar, cf. no. 88. *c.* 60% present, with spalling of base. (717) F39: VII 41.

148. CG1A Necked, ledge rim, jar, rilled. Very dark grey ext, very pale brown int surfaces. (864 + 878) F39: VII 3; + F21: VII 45; phases 2A, 6B.

Fig. 59

149. MO7 Mortarium, stamped by Sollus (stamp Fig. 48.2, report p 66). (224) F41: VI 25.

150. MO10 Mortarium, stamped by Doinus (stamp Fig. 48.3, report p 66). (234 + 236) F41: VI 25; + F39, VII 43.

151. MO12 Mortarium, stamped by Erucanus (stamp Fig. 48.4 report p 66). (239) F39: VII 38.

152-153. MO18 Two mortaria with identical double-impressed stamps, same die as no. 151 (stamps Fig. 48. 5-6; report p 67). (250-253) F39: VII 2 + VII 3.

154. MO22 Mortarium, stamped by Coertutinus (stamp Fig. 48.7, report p 67). Cf no. 91. (258) F39: VII 2.

Phase 2B

155. GW3 Cylindrical bowl, white painted crescents and dots over burnished surface. Cf no. 122. (684) VI 11.

156. GW7 Necked jar. (745) VI 11.

157. GW6 Bead rim jar. (36) X 19.

Phase 2C

158. C12 Central Gaulish(?) bag shaped beaker, rouletted. Greene 1978 Fig. 2.3:4. (335) VI 9.

159-161. WW2 Three flanged rim bowls with red paint on flange, possibly overpainted with white on no. 160. A type not previously recognised in Leicester, its origins may lie in Northants (R. Friendship-Taylor, pers comm). Vessels identical to nos. 160-161 have been published from Derby (Dool 1985, Fig. 81.185), and Mancetter (O'Neil 1928 Pl. xxiii.4) The associations are late 1st to early 2nd centuries on Site 5, and Hadrianic to Antonine at Derby with residuals. (431; 433; 436) V 31 (unphased), VI 9, VII 29.

Fig. 60

162. WW4 Two-handled(?) flagon, cf Pollard forthcoming (a), no. 25. (447) VI 9.

163. WW2 Small unguentarium, as no. 191, complete. Possibly Mancetter- Hartshill product. (919) VII 9.

164. WW4 Necked jar, cf MacRobert 1987 Fig. 31.1. (448) VI 9.

165. WW2 Platter or bowl, possibly derived from Drag 18/31. Reddish yellow (7.5YR) surfaces. (434 + 435) VI 9 + VII 26.

166. WW10 Unguentarium, cf Gillam 36/Colchester 389 (Hull 1958). (462) VI 9.

167. WS4 Two-handled flagon, cf Southwark Type I J.1 (Marsh and Tyers 1978). Verulamium region ('red granular white slipped') fabric (*ibid.* p 550), *c.* AD 120-160. (532 + 533) V 36 (unphased) + VI 9.

168. MD5 Reeded rim ?bowl, mica coated body ext. Cf Marsh 1978 Type 36, and no. 203 below. (365) VI 9.

169. AM23 Base of 'carrot' amphora, Cam 189 or possibly Kingsholm 117 (Timby 1985a) (418) VI 30.

170. AM19 Fishbourne 148.3 amphora rim (Cunliffe 1971), as Pollard forthcoming (a), nos. 169, 175. A 1st to early 2nd century type, also illustrated from Kingsholm (Timby 1985a, Fig. 28. 123-125). (416) VI 31.

171. AM9A Haltern 70, pre-Flavian, cf no. 206 (Sealey 1985, 59-65). (395) VII 9.

172. MO7 Mortarium, with counterstamp of Martinus or Marinus (stamp, Fig. 48.8, report p 67). (228) VII 25.

173. MO12 Mortarium, stamped by Vitalis IV (stamp, Fig. 48.9, report p 67). (238) VII 9.

174. OW2 Globular beaker, white painted dot panel and irregular brush strokes over burnished surface. Body scarred with shallow horizontal finger-wiped grooves prior to painting. Cf Nos. 29, 68 and 218. (557) VI 31.

175. GW3 Everted rim jar, lightly scored oblique 'slashes' on plain zone below burnished shoulder. (702) VII 9.

176. GW3 Necked jar, linear rustication. Necked rusticated jars are unusual in Leicester, but commonplace in Norfolk (Thompson 1958, 'Icenian'; Andrews 1985, Type 100). (702) VII 9.

177. GW6 Form as no. 132, possible rilled. (34 + 35) X 6; + F106: X 11; phases 2C, 3A.

178. GW6 (Narrow-mouthed) necked jar, cf no. 156. (707) VII 26.

179. GW3 Cheese press, pierced base. With only some 11% of the rim present, the absence of holes in the wall of this sherd need not be significant; virtually identical to an OW2 vessel (MacRobert 1987, Fig. 32.38). (631 + 709)

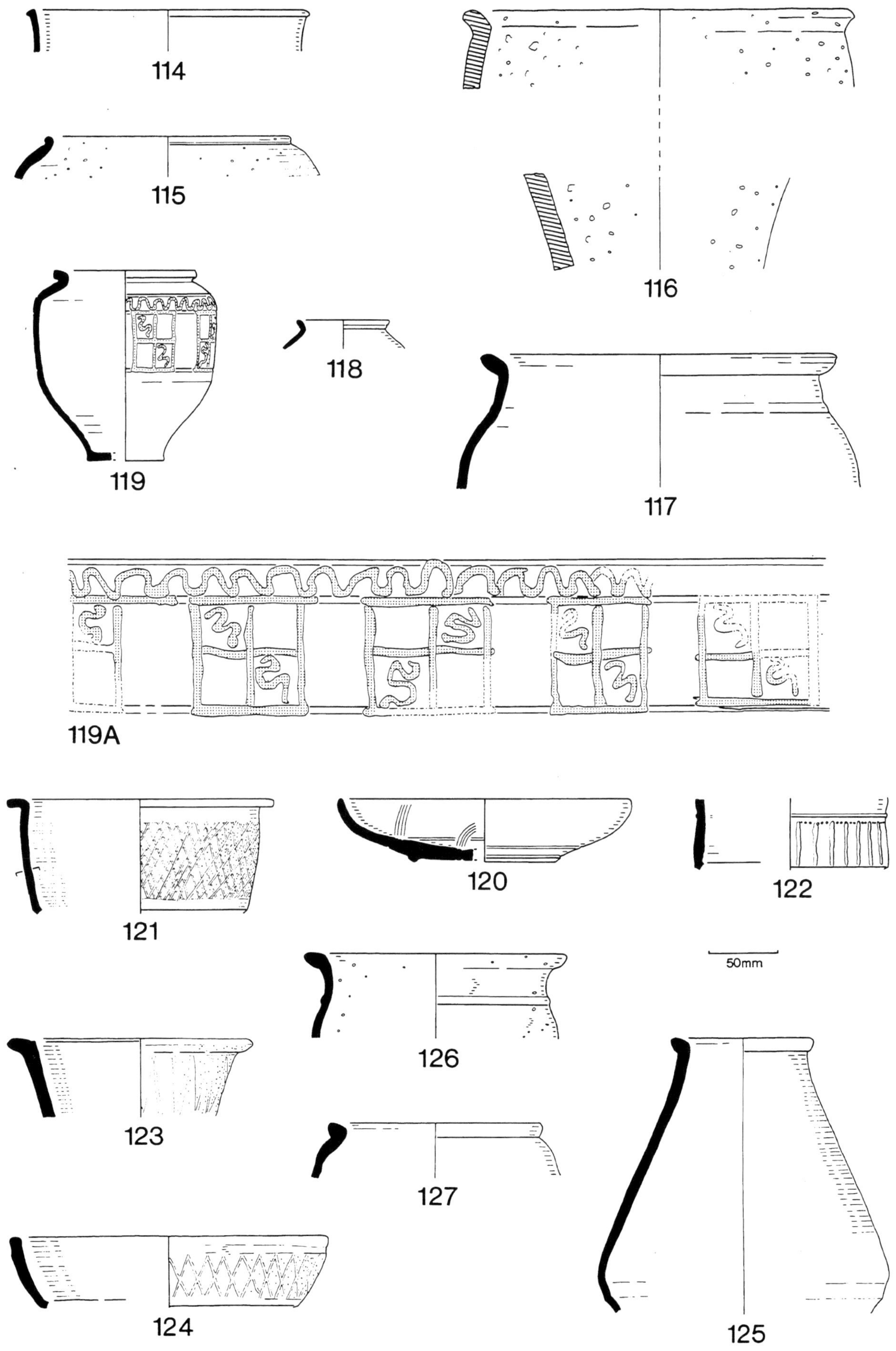

Fig. 57 Iron Age and Roman pottery Site 4 Phase 1 (114-117, 120); Phase 2 (118-119); Medieval levels (121-127) Scale 1:4 except no 119A: Scale 1:2

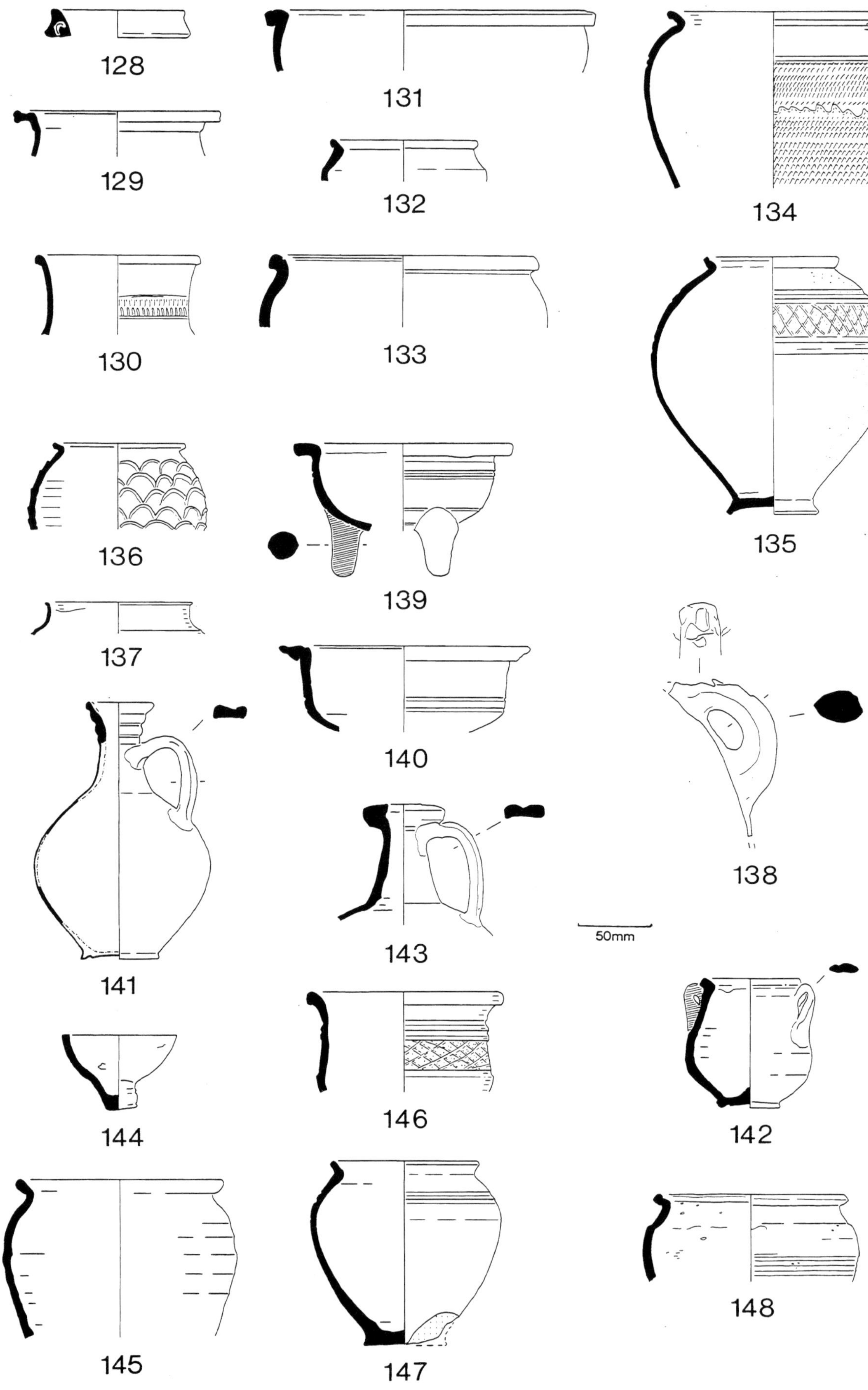

Fig. 58 Iron Age and Roman pottery Site 5 Phase 1 (128-135); Phase 2A (136-148) Scale 1:4

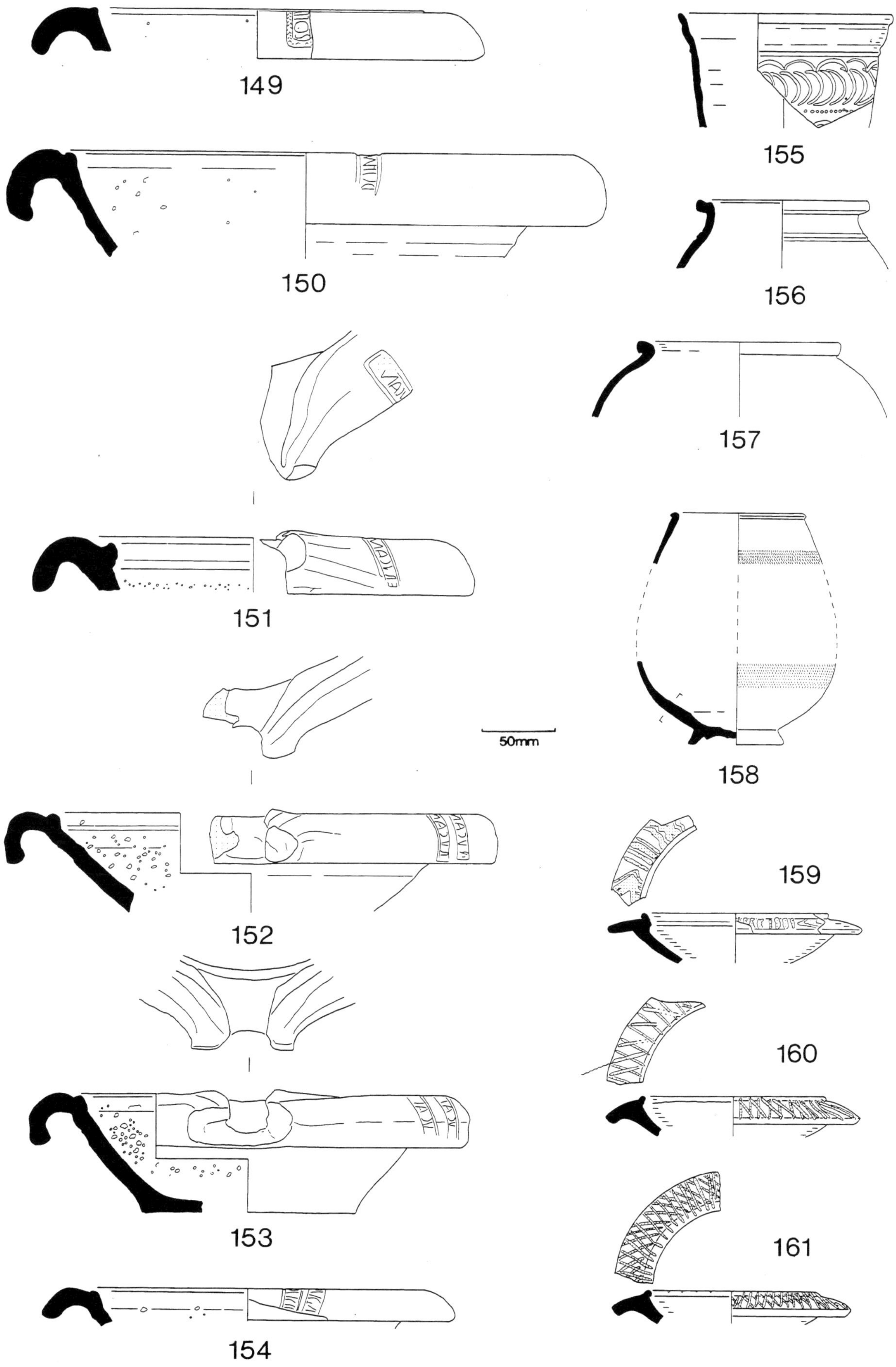

Fig. 59 Iron Age and Roman pottery Site 5 Phase 2A (149-154); Phase 2B (155-157); Phase 2C (158-161) Scale 1:4

II 16 F64: + VII 28; phases; 6C, 2C.

180. CG1 Necked storage jar, possibly coil built. Reddish yellow surfaces (5YR). Identical vessel in the unphased V 30. The three grooves on the shoulder may be a 2nd century deviation from the established rilling or combing (cf nos. 60, 100), possibly outliving the former. The squared rim to a large extent supplanted the rounded version (eg. no. 60) perhaps around the end of the 1st century (cf Jewry Wall Storage Jar Types E-G, A-C respectively). (829) IV II.

Phase 3A

Fig. 61

181. Samian, Central Gaulish, possibly Antonine. Drag 34. Cf Oswald and Pryce 1920 Pl. lii.8, and Stanfield 1929 nos. 43 and 61. The flange was notched on its outer face prior to slipping. (131) V 7.

182. C2 Waisted beaker(?), rough cast clay ext. Source uncertain: very pale brown (10YR 8/4) fabric with very dark grey to black slip (N 3/0 to 2/0) overall, appearing yellowish red (5YR) where thin on outer edge of lip and on cornice of shoulder. 2nd century? (292 + 308) VI 7 + VII 48; phases 3A, 3C.

183. AM9A Type uncertain. MacRobert (1983) illustrates an identical rim (Fig. 20.20), identified by Sealey as Beltran IV. However, Williams considers this ascription improbable (pers comm), thereby ruling out Dressel 14 also, which is equated with a subdivision of Beltran IV (Peacock and Williams 1986, Class 20). Sealey compares the rim with Beltran Lloris (1970) Fig. 184.12. The type also occurs on the Leicester Norfolk Street Villa (Pollard forthcoming (e)). (390) V 7.

184. WW2 Two-handled flagon with two 'rings' on neck, cf Jewry Wall Flagon Type A.19. One of a pair from the context, the other identical but smaller (rim diameter 550mm). (429) V 7.

185. MO7 Mortarium, with counterstamp of Albinus (stamp, Fig. 48.10, report, p 67). The spout has become detached from the flange, which lacks keying. (215) V 7.

186. GW7 Flask, or beaker, cf Anderson 1980 Form 5 (8, and Fig. 10.3), Hull 1963 Fig. 47. 11-16 and Type 404, and Stanfield 1929 nos. 29-34. (907) V 7.

187. GW3 Larger version of no. 186, burnished on 'ridges'. This form has not been recognised previously in Leicester. (661) V 7.

188. BB1 Dorset fabric. Trefoil mouthed jug, coil built, burnished ext. The type does not appear in Gillam's corpus (1970) with a BB1 ascription (see Type 61 however). It has recently been described by Wallace and Webster (1989), who suggest a broadly mid 1st to late 2nd century date range; an example from Vindolanda comes from a context dateable to *c.* AD 223-225 (Bidwell 1985, Fig. 67.55). Limescale on neck and body int. (789) VI 7.

189. (See below, phase 4).

Phase 3B

190. BB1 Dorset fabric. Lid, tooled int. Jewry Wall Lid Type A.1. (782) V 13.

Phase 3C

191. WW2 As no. 163, complete, with damaged lip. (920) V 4.

192. WW3 Pinched-mouth jug. Southwark Type I C.1, dated Hadrianic to Antonine (Marsh and Tyers 1978); Verulamium 580, dated *c.* AD 130-200 + (Wilson 1972, 1984). This vessel could be a fine fabric product of the Verulamium region. (439) V 4.

193. WW4 Hemispherical bowl. (442 + 443) V 9; + F33: V 25; phases 3C, 4A.

194. WW4 Reeded rim bowl. (451) VII 24.

195. GW6 Everted rim jar. High-fired, giving burnish a 'graphite' appearance. 2nd to early 3rd century, cf Todd 1968 Fig. 2.10 and 11. (660) V 4.

196. GW5 Reeded rim dish, cf Pollard forthcoming (a), no. 60. Probably within late 1st to mid 2nd century, parallels can be cited from Canterbury (eg Jenkins 1960, Fig. 5. 13-14), although a more local source is likely. (33) X 5.

Phase 3D

197. OW2 S-shape bowl or cauldron, smoothed overall, with pricked decoration. May have borne handles as no. 305; cf also no. 276. (554) F64: I 39.

Phase 4B

198. MO24 Mortarium, Rhineland origin. See discussion, p 67. (259) IX 3.

Fig. 62

199. WW4 Flagon base, possibly of no. 143. (452) IX 3.

Phase 4C

189. GW6 Everted rim jar, tooled lattice; surfaces otherwise plain. (618) I 28.

200. GW3 Biconical beaker, cf no. 100. (699) VII 4.

201. GW6 Wide bowl. Sooted ext. Cf no. 291. (723) VII 47.

Phase 6

202. C3 Platter, possibly derived from Drag 18. Slipped overall, red to light red (2.5YR 5/6-6/6), with reddish yellow (5YR) fabric. Identical to Clamp 1985 Fig. 32.51, and presumably mid to late 1st century AD. The fabric resembles pre-Flavian Colchester colour-coated ware in general, though the form is not associated with this ware in the *colonia* (Hawkes and Hull 1947, 283; Greene 1978, 26-29). (316) IV 1, phase 6A.

203. OW5 Reeded rim; wide bowl (?). (29) F101: X 47, phase 6A.

204. GW5 Small countersunk-handle jar, cf Gillam 40-41, and Swanpool Type F (Webster and Booth 1947). (687) F27: VI 18, phase 6A.

205. C13 Oxfordshire source? Appliqué mask, fired reddish yellow (5YR 7/8 with surfaces 5YR 6/6) with dusky red to dark reddish brown (2.5YR 3/2-3/4) paint emphasising hair, eyebrows, irises and pupils of eyes, and mouth. Young 1977 Type C11, dated *c.* 350-400+. (341) F21: VII 45, phase 6B.

206. AM9A Haltern 70, cf no. 171. (397) F21: VII 45, phase 6B.

207. C19 Swanpool source likely (M. Darling, pers comm). Low-flanged bowl, pinkish white (7.5YR 8/2) paint on flange. Grey core (N5/0 - N4/0), red margins (2.5YR 5/8) and red to light red surfaces (int 2.5YR 6/6-6/8, ext 2.5YR 4/6-5/6). Swanpool Type D33-36 (Webster and Booth 1947). (356) F21: VII 45, phase 6B.

208. GW5 Wide bowl, burnished zones ext. (721) F21: VII 45, phase 6B.

209. C13 Oxfordshire. Young 1977 Type C51, dated *c.* 240-400+. Rim broken off in antiquity and resulting edge smoothed down. Flange and int body burnt. (337) F30: V 23, phase 6C.

210. WW2 Two-handled flagon or narrow-mouthed jar. (437) F32: VII 35, phase 6C.

211. WW4 Tazza, grooved and impressed upper face of frilled rim. (449) F22: VI 14, phase 6C.

212. WW4 Flanged rim bowl, cf Jewry Wall Flanged bowl Type E.22, but no paint on sherd. (450) F23: VI 15,

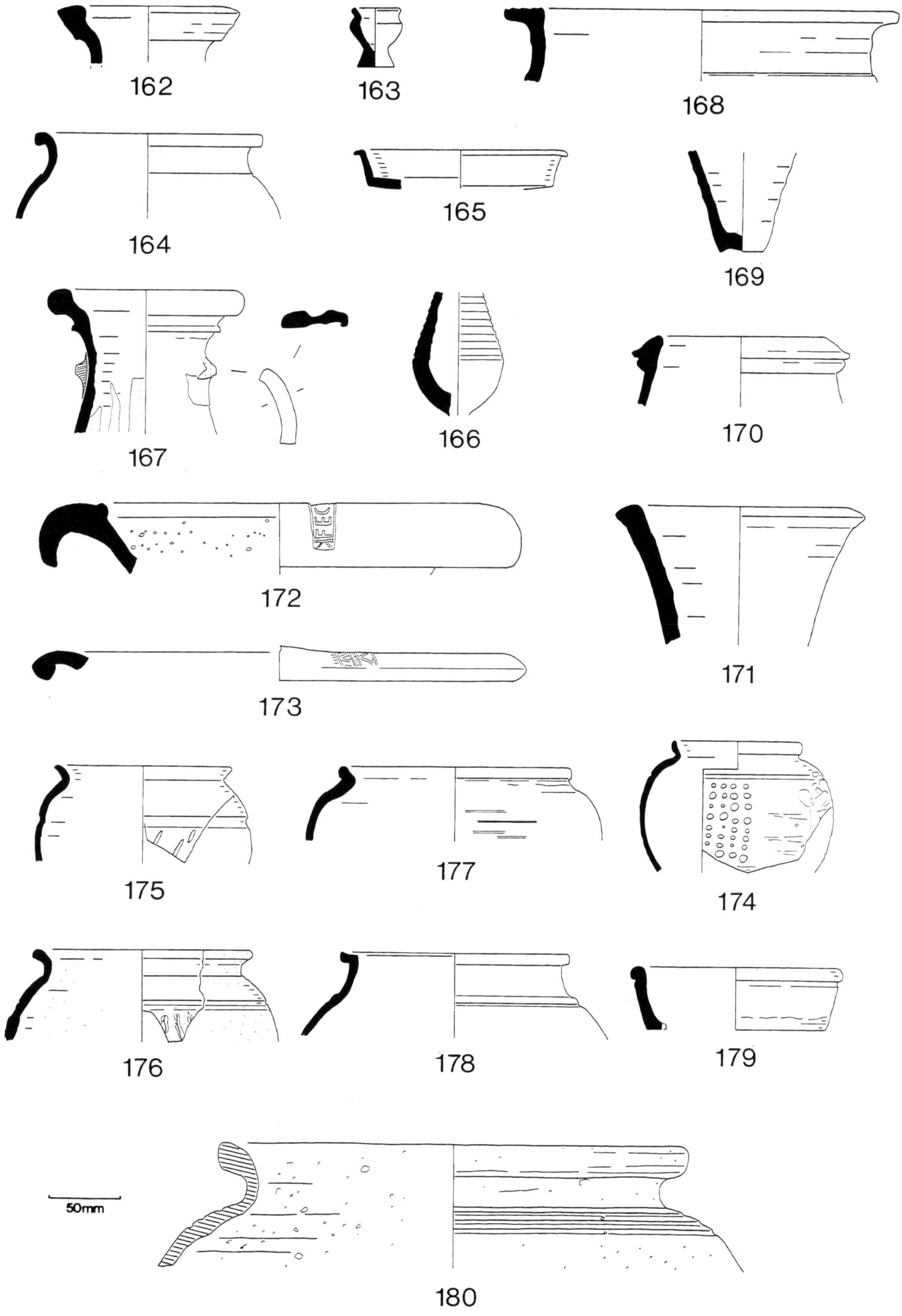

Fig. 60 Iron Age and Roman pottery Site 5 Phase 2C (162-180) Scale 1:4

phase 6D.

Area 5, unphased.

Fig. 63

213. AM10 Rhodian(?) amphora, possibly Rhodian Fabric 1 (Peacock 1977a; Sealey 1985, Cam 184). (402) V 34.
214. MO7 Mortarium, stamped by Marinus (stamp Fig. 48.11, report p 67). (219) V 36.
215. WW4 Cylindrical bowl. (444) V 30.
216. WW4 Vertical sided carinated bowl, cf nos. 77, 217, 229. (445) V 31.
217. WW2 Flaring wall carinated bowl. (432) V 39.
218. OW2 Globular beaker, white painted dots and ribs; cf nos. 29, 68, 174. (556) V 31.
219. OW2 Spout, formed separately from its vessel; cf no. 78. (555) V 30.
220. GW5 Flanged rim bowl, cf no. 290. Burnished rim. (673) V 34.
221. GW3 Platter, cf no. 120. Identical to Kenyon 1948, Fig. 41.24. Smoothed overall. (675) V 36.
222. GW3 Reeded rim bowl, rilled. Cf Jewry Wall Reeded rim bowl Type B.10. (669) V 30.
223. CG1A Ledge rim jar, coil built. Light brown surfaces (7.5YR 6/4). Graffito (Fig. 49.G4, p 72). (844) V 29.
224. MG1 Bead rim jar, as no. 75 but tooled verticals. (895) V 37.

Area 8, unphased.

225. GW3 Reeded rim bowl or dish, grooved and stabbed on upper face of rim, cf Pollard forthcoming (a), no. 55. (225) VIII 10.
226. MD6 Reeded rim bowl, mica coated ext and on rim int; cf no. 27. Marsh 1978 Type 36. (375) VIII 8.
227. WW5 Tazza, Verulamium region. Verulamium 924 type dated to *c.* 110-170 (Wilson 1984), but very similar vessels occur in levels of *c.* 75-105 (Wilson 1972, nos. 309-311). (461) VIII 8.

Unstratified

228. WW3 Nene Valley? Rear of face jug, with non-functional strap handle. White fabric (10YR 8/2) and surface, the latter partially fired to reddish yellow (7.5YR 7/6-8/6). Red paint (10YR 5/6) on handle, neck, and side of rim. (16) X u.s.
229. WW2 As no. 217. (428) I - IX.

Site 6

Phase 1B, Feature 24 (see p 72-4 for discussion)

Fig. 64

230-234. MC4 Jars, 231-233 possible from one vessel. (407, 411, 410, 412, 413).
235-236. MC5 Jars. (415, 414).
237-238. SW1 Jars. (406, 405).
239. SW1 Lid. (404)
240. GT7 Shoulder of jar. (403).
241. CG1A Jar, combed. Grey to dark grey int, dark grey through light reddish brown to pink (5YR) ext surfaces. (352).

Phase 1D

Fig. 65

242-243. WW3 North Gaul. Butt beakers, Cam 113 (see discussion, p 71). (168, 169) F21: 98; F22: 104.
244. GW3 Small jar, recurved to lip. Cf Pollard forthcoming (a), no. 17. Sparse coarse calcite inclusions, cf MG3. (250) F21: 98.
245. GW6 Everted rim jar, cf nos. 30, 33. (252) F22: 100.
246. SW2 Carinated bowl, cf nos. 10, 64, 294, and Clamp 1985, Figs. 31.8 and 15, 32.33. Very dark grey (10YR 3/1) surfaces. (397) F22: 100.
247. GT2 Carinated bowl, pairs of grooves, cf Clamp 1985, Fig. 32.31. Very dark grey to grey (10YR 3/1-6/1) surfaces, with slight reddish yellow scorching on rim. (375) F22: 100.
248. GT2 Girth beaker, burnished, fine combing over. Cam 85E, cf no. 261. Dark brown to brown ext surface, cf TR3A; int surface lost. (374) F22: 100.
249. GT2 Butt beaker, cf no. 47, with references. Very dark grey (5YR 3/1) to reddish brown (5YR) and brown (7.5YR) surfaces, burnished except where combed. (369 + 374) 11 + F22: 100; phases 7A, 1D.
250. GT2 Butt beaker, burnished in zones. Girth cordon abraded through wear. Light reddish brown to reddish yellow surfaces. (369 + 374) 11 + F22: 100; phases 7A, 1D.
251. MG2 Narrow-mouthed jar, or possibly butt beaker, burnished cordons. Pinkish grey (int and ext) (7.5YR) to reddish yellow (ext) (5YR) surfaces. (395) F22: 100.
252. GT2 Base of pedestal jar, cf no. 45. Very dark grey to black surfaces. (373) F22: 100.
253. GT2 Necked bowl, cf nos. 24, 43 and 102. Rim and body possibly from different vessels. Very dark grey to dark reddish grey (5YR 3/1 - 3/3, 4/2). (375) F22: 100.
254. CG1A Necked storage jar, cf nos. 60, 110, 180 eg. Coil built. Greyish brown (10YR) to light brown (7.5YR) surfaces, combed. (350) F22: 100.
255. CG1A Ledge rim jar, two grooves on int rim, cf Kenyon 1948, Fig. 30.18. Light brown surfaces, rilled. (350) F22: 100.
256. CG1A Storage jar, everted rim, slightly cupped int. Very dark grey surfaces. (344 + 350) 42 + F22: 100; phases 2B, 1D.
257. CG2A Necked storage jar, cf nos. 4, 14. Weak red int (2.5YR 4/2), light red (2.5YR) to light reddish brown and light brown (5YR - 7.5YR 6/4) ext surfaces. (354 - 356) F22: 100 + 104, + unstratified.

Fig. 66

258. CG2A Plain rim jar, with fine scored oblique lines upper ext. Hand made, possibly coil built. Dark to very dark grey int, dark grey to light brown ext surfaces. Cf Clamp 1985, Fig. 31.23, and nos. 259-160. (354 + 355) F22: 100 + 104.
259. CG3A As no. 258, combed obliques more emphasised. Colour as no. 258. (364) F22: 100.
260. SW3 Bead rim jar, combed ext. Coil built? Dark grey (5YR 4/1) surfaces. (399) F22: 100.

Phase 2

261. TR1A Beaker, cf no. 248. See p 71 for discussion. (97 + 98) 42 + 60, phase 2B.
262. GW3 Biconical beaker, cf no. 316. Flavian to Hadrianic. (248) 42, phase 2B.
263. OW2 Low-flanged bowl, Jewry Wall Flanged bowl Type D.17. (234) 37, phase 2C.
264. BB1(?) Lid. Burnished on rim ext. (315) 37, phase 2C.

Phase 4

265. MD6 Bevelled rim jar or bowl, mica coated body and cordon ext. (105) 25, phase 4A.
266. MD5 Reeded rim dish, mica coated and sooted overall. Cf no. 26. Marsh 1978 Type 26. (103) 25, phase 4A.
267. GW3 Cylindrical bowl, finely incised oblique lines and

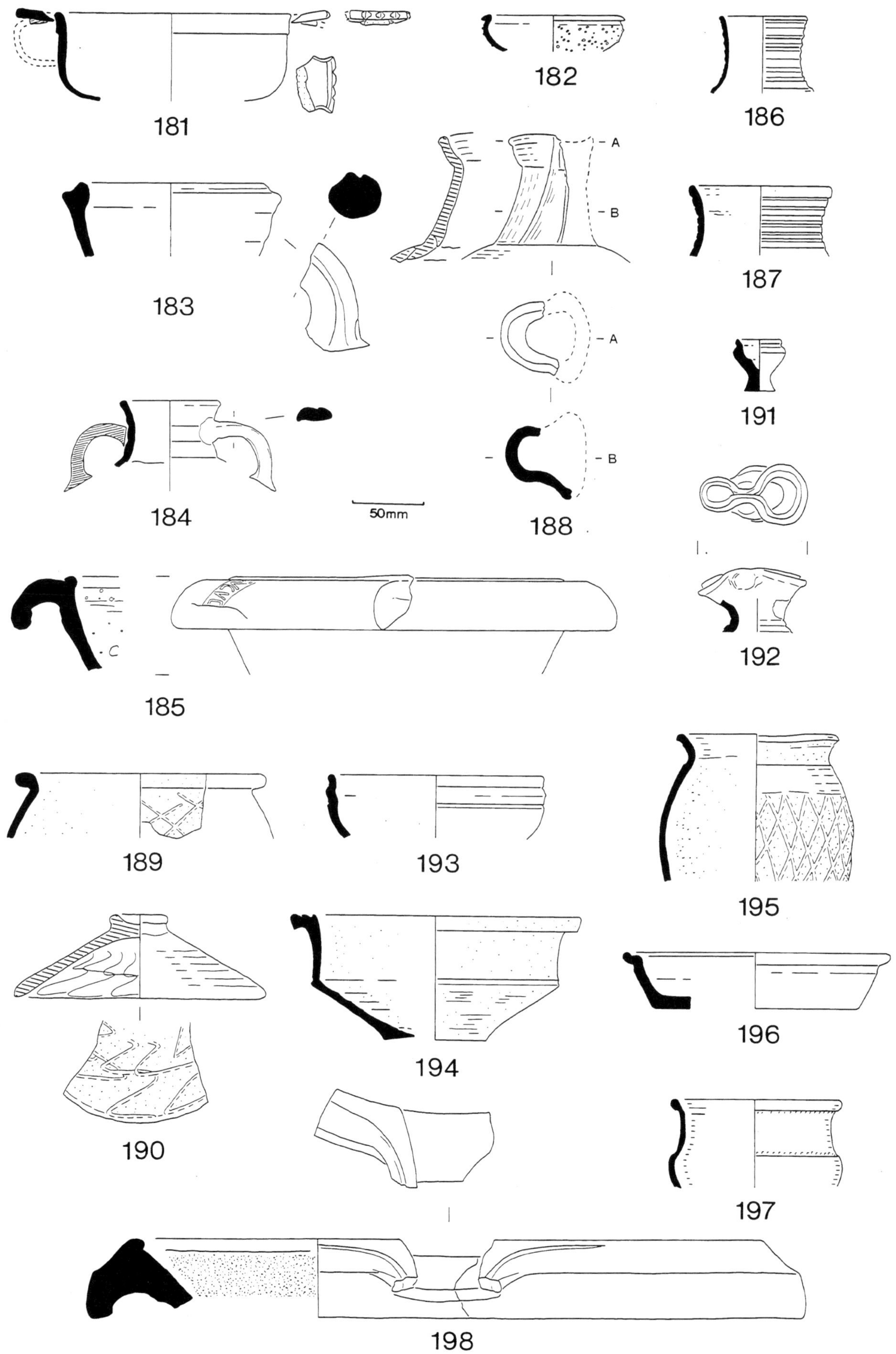

Fig. 61 Iron Age and Roman pottery Site 5 Phase 3A (181-188); Phase 3B (190); Phase 3C (191-196); Phase 3D (197); Phase 4B (198); Phase 4C (189) Scale 1:4

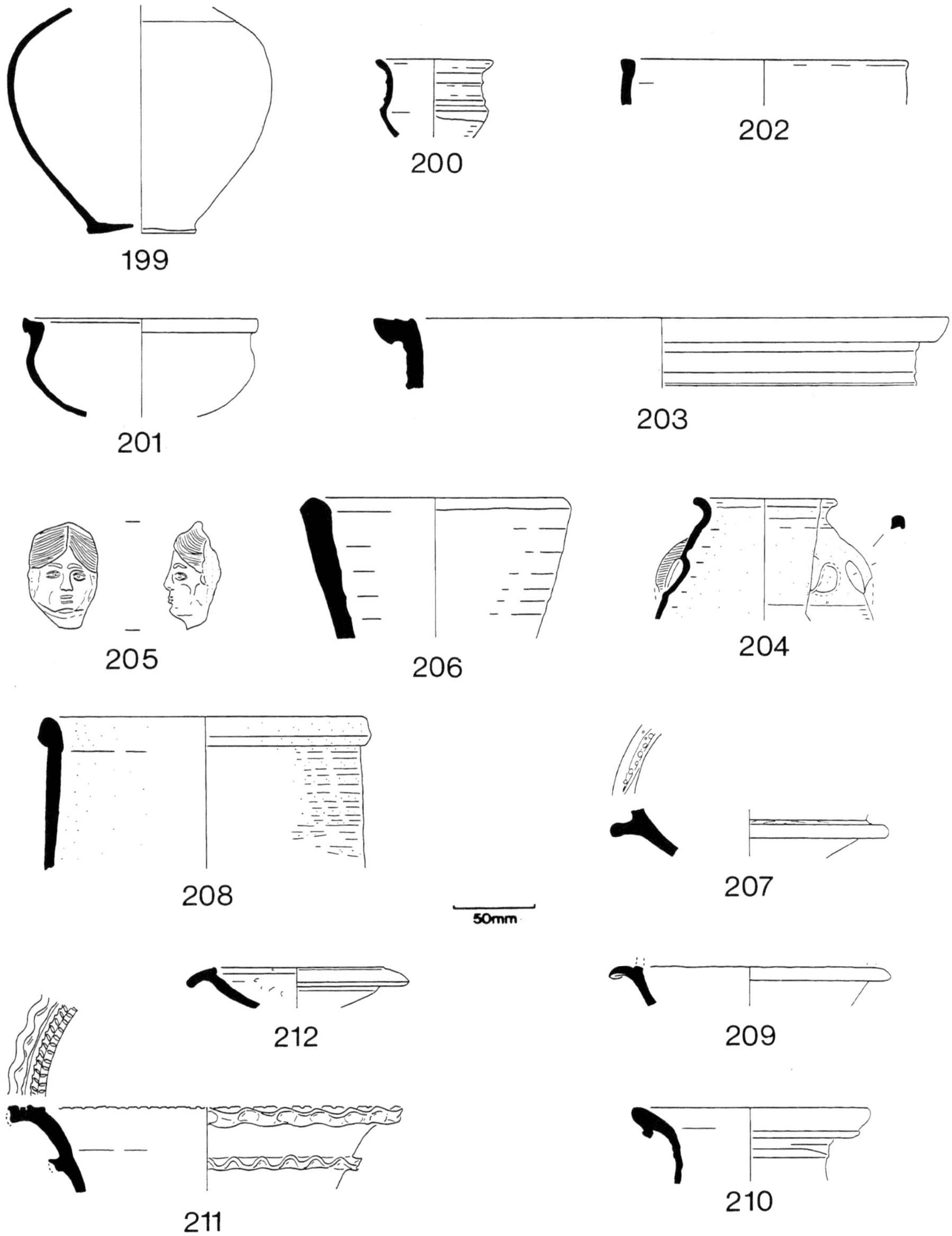

 Fig 62 Iron Age and Roman pottery Site 5 Phase 4B (199); Phase 4C (200-201); Phase 6 (202-212) Scale 1:4

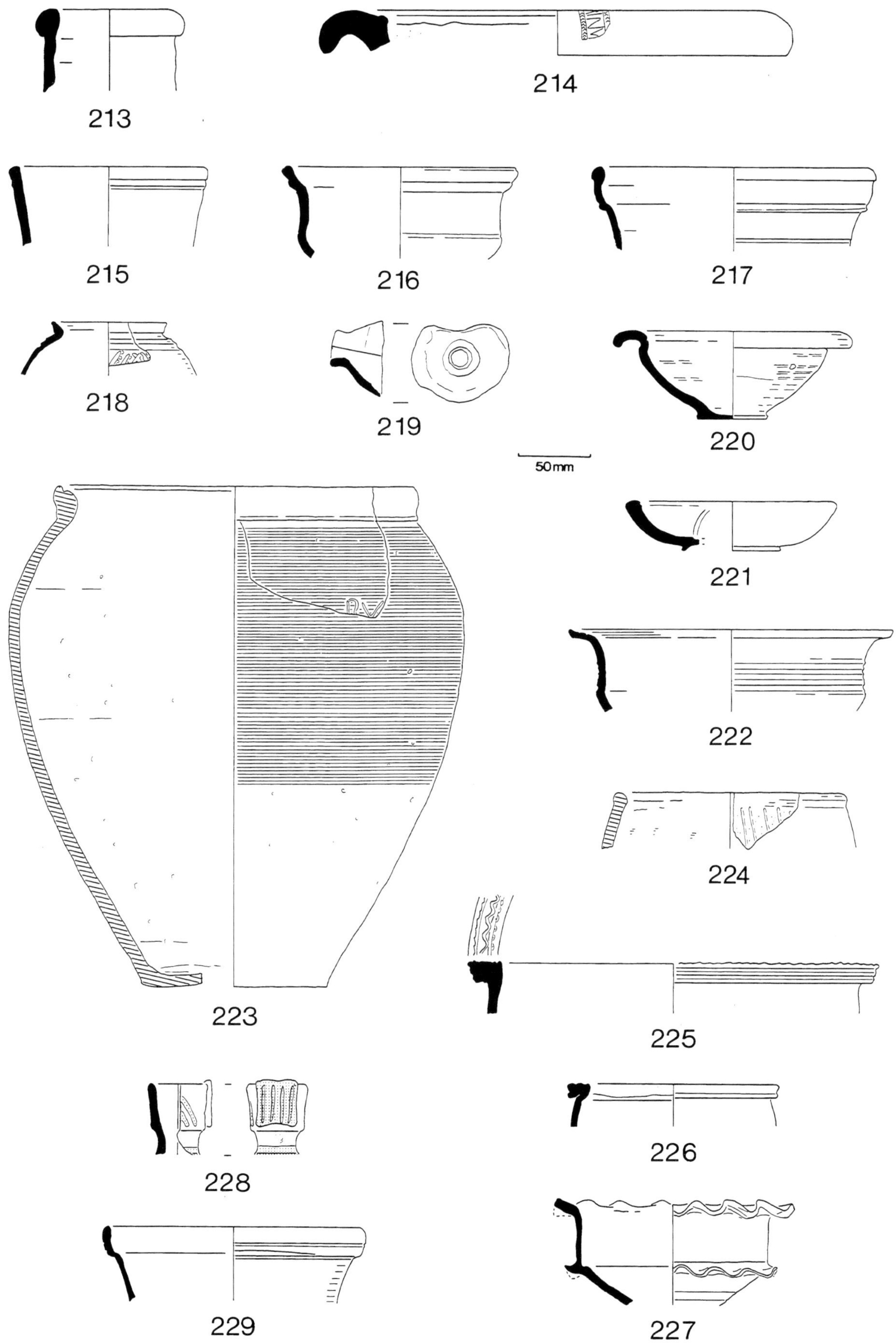

Fig. 63 Iron Age and Roman pottery Site 5 Unphased: Area 5 (213-224); Area 8 (225-227); u.s. (228-229) Scale 1:4

pricked decoration in burnished surface. (247) 25, phase 4A.

268. WW2 High-shouldered beaker, bosses pressed out by fingers into cylindrical 'former'. Fired reddish yellow (5YR) ext: this colour can occur on other forms, including flagons and mortaria, in this fabric, but it is possible that a deliberate attempt was made here to imitate mica coated pottery or bronze (Marsh 1978 Type 20). (164 + 197 + 165) 22 + 23 + 25; phases 4C, 4C, 4A.

269. GW11 Reeded rim bowl, burnished on upper face of flange. Southwark Type IV A.2 (Marsh and Tyers 1978); early to mid 2nd century? (278 + 279) 22 + 25; phases 4C, 4A.

270. GW11 Pie dish, burnished as no. 269 and also lower body ext. Southwark Type IV F.4, there *c.* AD 85-140. Slight groove on rim int. (257) 23, phase 4C.

271. GW1 Dog dish. Burnished overall, fine scored arcading; cf Gillam 329, dated *c.* 190-340. Wheel thrown. (299) 22, phase 4C.

272. GW3 Flask. (273) 22, phase 4C.

Phase 7

273. GW3 Globular beaker. (266) 10, phase 7A.

274. GW1 Pie dish. Burnished overall, tooled lattice. cf Gillam 220, 306, dated *c.* 120-160. Probably wheel thrown. (298) 2, phase 7E.

Phase 8

275. OW9 Much Hadham. Face jug, cf no. 205 and Kenyon 1948, Fig. 57.7, also in OW9. Neck of vessel, and face, seemingly formed in one process, in contrast with no. 205, with features sculpted by burnishing and incision. The eyelids are emphasised quite strongly, but the slit mouth exhibits little attention paid to the lips. The internal aperture of the vessel at the neck is *c.* 30mm. Vessels from Burgh Castle, Norfolk are handled (S. Johnson 1983, Fig. 39.43, 44, 46). (222) F12: 80, phase 8A.

276. GW3 S-shape bowl or cauldron with stumps of one handle. Roughly one quarter of the vessel present, so two or three handles could have existed. Cf Gillam 174 with rings as no. 82 and lattice, and the plain Gillam 175, Hadrianic-Antonine and nos. 197 and 305 herein. Burnished ext except where lattice tooled. (249) F6: 68, phase 8A.

Unstratified

277. GW7 Narrow mouthed jar. (253).

Site 8

Fig. 67

278. WS5 Bodysherd of closed form, probably beaker. Slipped ext, with red painted stripes and band. Cf no. 119. (40) F9: IX 57, phase 3C.

279. OW2 Everted rim jar, as no. 79. (48) VII 71, phase 4A.

280. CG2A cf no. 279. Coil built, rim and rilling turned. Very dark grey to dark reddish grey (5YR) surfaces. (98) II 77, unphased.

281. CG3A As no. 116, coil built. Diameter uncertain. Black surfaces. (101) F13: VI 70, phase 3A.

282. SW3 Everted rim jar, formed probably as no. 280. A late Iron Age plain form found in sandy fabrics of variable coarseness but always reduced; cf Kenyon 1948, Fig. 36.22, and Clamp 1985, Fig. 33.83-84. Very dark grey surfaces. (108) IV, unstratified.

Site 9

283. WW2 Unguentarium, or possibly flagon rim. Possibly a Mancetter-Hartshill product. (13).

284. OW3 Form as no. 77, white painted rings over burnish, cf nos. 29 and 68. (17).

285. OW2 Flagon(?), burnished ext with graffito (Fig. 49.G5, p 72). (16).

286. OW3 Low-flanged bowl. Badly abraded and partially burnt. Dark grey core, yellowish red (5YR) margins; traces of red (10YR 5/6) on the surfaces may result from burnishing rather than slip. The fabric incorporates moderate combusted organic matter, cf SW2. Jewry Wall Flanged bowl Type D. 18/19. (18).

287. C2 Lower Rhineland. Indented globular beaker, Colchester 396 (Hull 1963), Anderson 1980 Form 3, as Fig. 8.3. Rough cast clay. *c.* 85% complete and intact, with rim damaged before firing. (37).

288. GW6 Everted rim jar. Tooled obliques bordered by groove below and tooled line above. (25).

289. GW6 Small everted rim jar, rusticated. Thick-walled, indifferently potted. Cf Pollard forthcoming (a), no. 37. (24).

290. GW3 Flanged rim bowl, Jewry Wall Flanged bowl Type A.1, 2nd century. Cf no. 86 for the delicate base, turned separately from the body. (21).

291. GW3 Wide bowl, cf no. 201. Facet burnished ext. (22).

292. GW4 Jar. Fine rouletting. Cf Howe et al 1980, Fig. 1.1, second quarter of 2nd century. (23).

293. BB1 Gillam 316, dated *c.* 125-160. Burnished except where decoration tooled on ext wall and base, cf Gillam 1976, no. 73. (29).

294. MG2 Carinated bowl, as no. 64, etc. Very dark grey (5YR) through reddish brown (5YR) to brown (7.5YR) surfaces. (32).

295. MO4 Mortarium, stamped by an unidentified potter, two impressions (stamp Fig. 48.12, p 67). (12).

Fig. 68

296. WW2 Two-handled flagon, frilled cordon. Neck plugged into body. (47).

297. OW2 Globular or bag-shaped beaker, cornice rim; cf Clamp 1985, Fig. 34.105. (48).

298. OW2 Bag-shaped beaker, rough cast clay ext; cf Clamp 1985, Fig. 34.104, 117, and Pollard forthcoming (a), nos. 97, 98. (49).

299. MG2 Butt beaker, cf no. 249, and Clamp 1985, Fig. 31.5 eg. Reddish yellow (5YR) surfaces, lightly scored over burnish ext. (51).

300. CG3A Ledge rim jar, cf no. 61. Black to light reddish brown (5YR) int, greyish brown and sooted ext surfaces. Coil built (50).

Site 11 (all A20.1939)

301. MO4 Mortarium, Mancetter-Hartshill. Red painted spout (10R 5/7 red); cf Pollard forthcoming (a), nos 217 and 200, dated respectively by K. F. Hartley to *c.* AD 180-240 and 180-250. Diameter of int beading *c.* 350mm, of flange tip *c.* 420mm. (9) I 19.

302. MO7 Mortarium, Verulamium region. Stamped (report no. 13 p 67, not illustrated separately). Neronian-Flavian. (10) I 3.

303. GW7 Dog dish; Nene Valley? Howe et al 1980, Fig. 2.20 provides a close parallel dated to the 2nd and 3rd centuries. (17) I 2.

Site 12

304. OW3 Triple vase, one vase and fragment of ring present. Horizontal burnish overall on vase and ring. A larger frag-

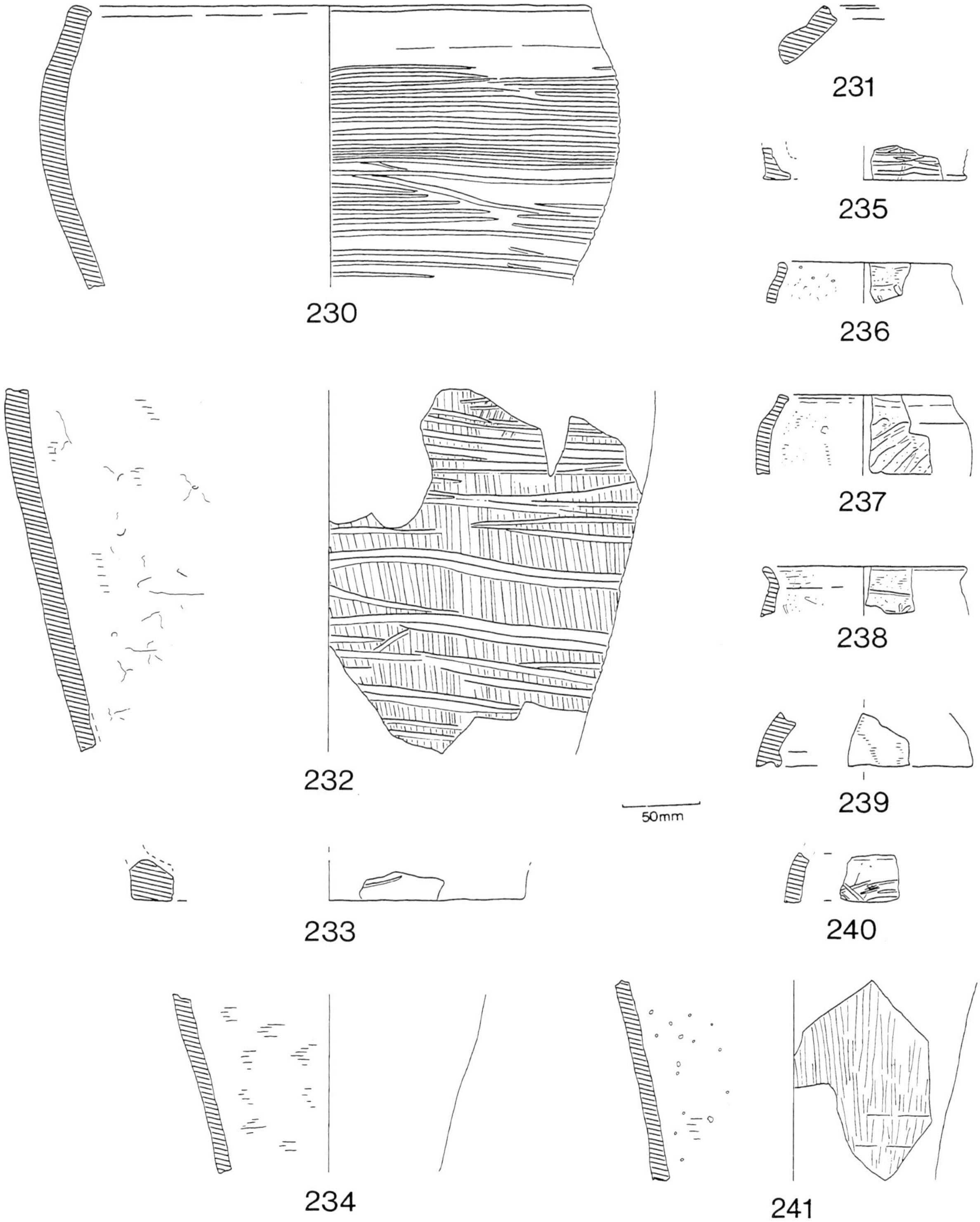

Fig. 64 Iron Age and Roman pottery Site 6 Phase 1B (230-241) Scale 1:4

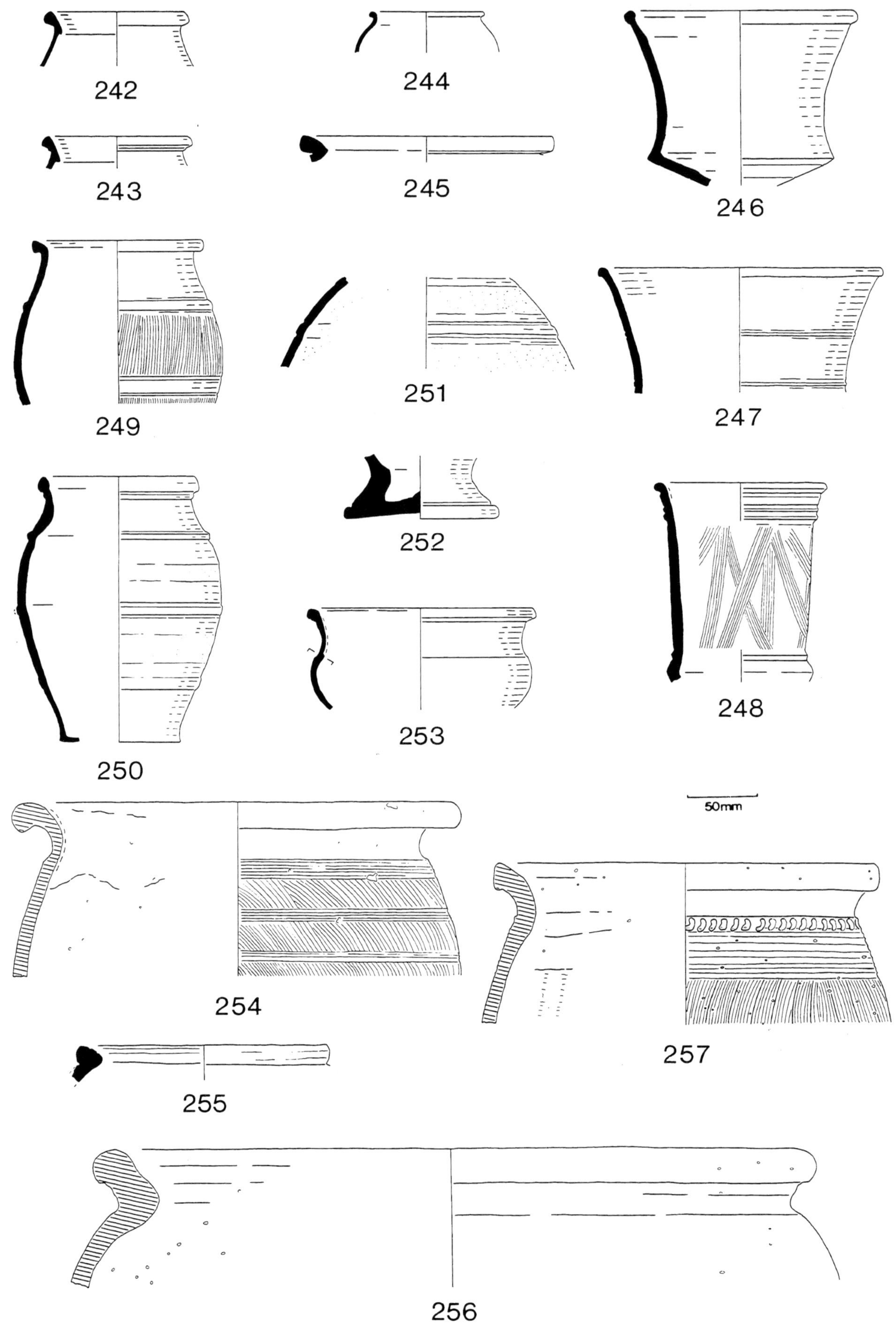

 Fig. 65 Iron Age and Roman pottery Site 6 Phase 1D (242-257) Scale 1:4

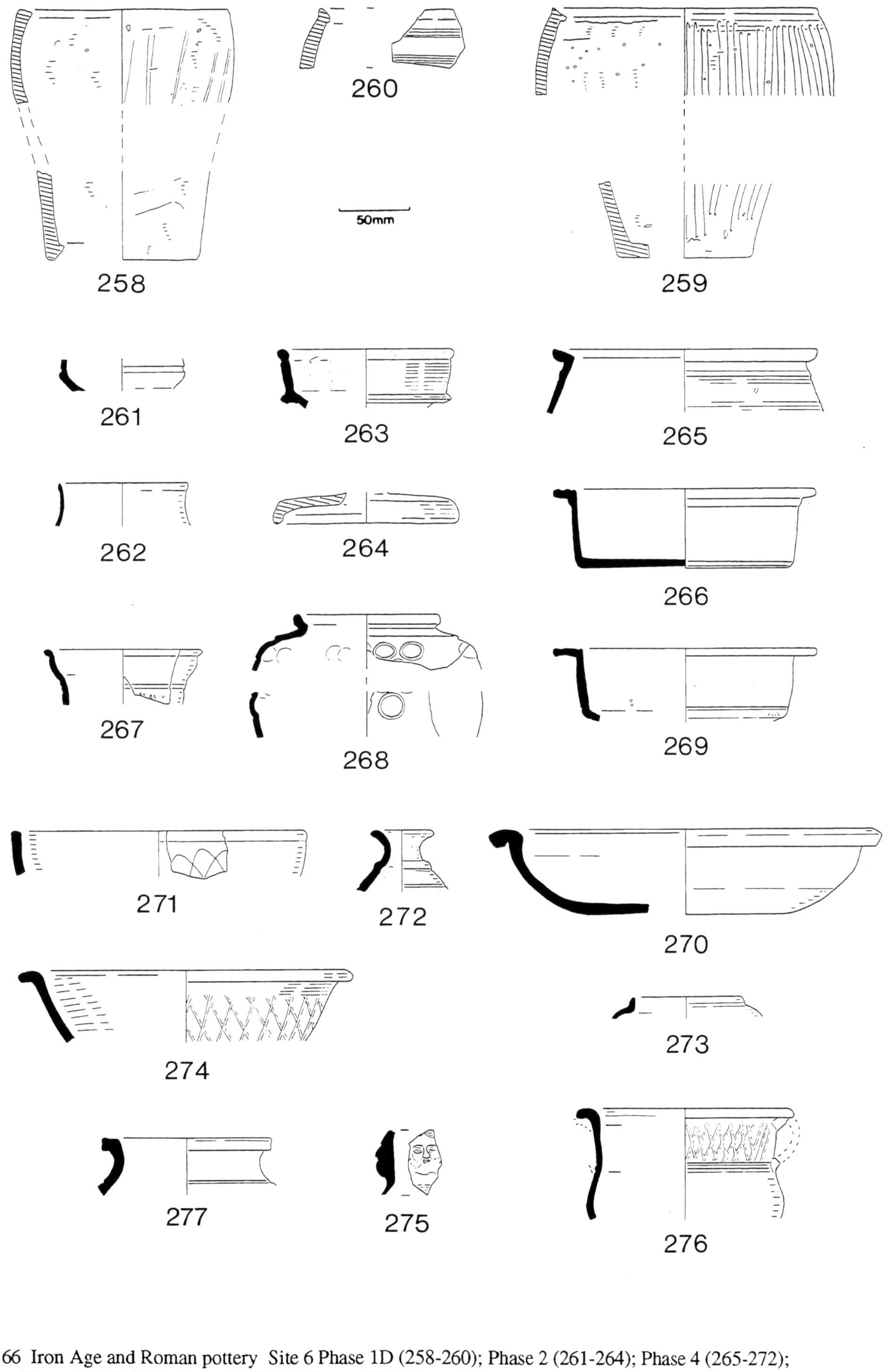

Fig. 66 Iron Age and Roman pottery Site 6 Phase 1D (258-260); Phase 2 (261-264); Phase 4 (265-272); Phase 7 (273-274); Phase 8 (275-276); u.s.(277) Scale 1:4

ment, identical, with two vases present, was found on Causeway Lane in 1979 (MacRobert forthcoming).

305. OW2 Bowl, or cauldron, cf nos. 197 and 276, with two dowelled handles present; both handles and shoulder are pricked, probably a skeuomorphic representation of rivets to be found on metal progenitors. The type is known from kiln sites at Chelmsford (Going 1987, 73-78 and Fig. 35.20) and Brampton (Knowles 1977, Fig. 5.3), the latter with fixed attachment loops, again skeuomorphs (cf no. 82). The Leicester examples lack the slight cordon at neck/body junction of these vessels, and are in a different fabric certainly to the Chelmsford (Moulsham Street) vessel and possibly also to the Brampton vessel. Described by Hull as being 'not common' at Colchester (Colchester 302, Hull 1963, Fig. 105), but occurring in a late 3rd century grave there. A broad 2nd to 4th century range seems likely in Essex, East Anglia and Leicester.

Comparative material from various sites in Leicester (unless otherwise specified), in Jewry Wall Museum.

306. C19 Swanpool(?) Segmental bowl or platter, Swanpool Type D24-32 (Webster and Booth 1947). Reddish grey core (10R 5/1), red margins (10R 5/8); slip dark reddish grey int (10R 3/1), weak red (10R) to very dark grey (N3) to reddish brown (2.5YR 4/4) ext. White painted decoration (10YR 8/2). M. Darling considered the sherd to be 'almost certainly from Swanpool' (pers comm). (A365.1964). Hebditch and Mellor 1973 ('St. Nicholas Street 1964') F6: III, robbing of wall.

307. OW9 Much Hadham. Flanged neck flagon. (3179.1887, Weatherhead Collection) Royal Arcade, found in 1877.

308. OW9 Much Hadham. Ring-neck flagon. Nos. 307 and 308 exhibit the vertical burnish of the neck that is typical of Much Hadham ware. A 'face mask' flask or flagon rim in this ware was found on the Jewry Wall site (Kenyon 1948, Fig. 57.7) (see also no. 275 above). (3178.1887, Weatherhead Collection) 'probably Leicester'.

309. OW9 Much Hadham. Hemispherical bowl. Facet-burnished horizontally ext and rim, plain int. Pink (5YR 8/4) painted decoration. (A654.1964) Blue Boar Lane.

Fig. 69

310. WW4 Vertical sided carinated bowl, cf no. 77 and others. One handle present on roughly half of the vessel (cf Darling 1977, 60, Usk Type 20, for discussion). (A354.1957) Friar's Causeway, hearth 1 (R D Abbott in Clarke 1958, 77-78; no. 310 illustrated therein as Fig. 1, p. 78).

311. OW2 Bag-shaped beaker, nearly complete, rouletted. cf MacRobert 1987, Fig. 32.37, and Pollard forthcoming (a), nos. 42 and 85. Possibly a Mancetter-Hartshill product. Antonine floruit, possibly current into the early 3rd century. (A269.1951) Belgrave Gate, found in 1866.

312. GW12 Cylindrical bowl, with rouletted or stabbed decoration. A vessel from Margidunum is similar (Oswald 1948a, Pl. xiii.8). Possibly a lower Nene Valley or East Anglian product. (A116.1962.1) East Bond Street.

313. GW12 Carinated bowl or beaker, stamped with an eleven-petal 'rosette' die. This die is similar to Rodwell's (1978) dies Ros. 1 and Ros. 5. Possibly an East Anglian product, although J.Plouviez states that overall rosette stamps do not occur at West Stow (in corresp. 1990). Nos. 312-313 are likely to fall within a late 1st and 2nd century range. (A365.1964) Hebditch and Mellor 1973, ('St. Nicholas Street 1964'). F5: III, medieval pit.

313. A,B. Two impressions from the die used on no. 313. Scale 1/1.

314. GW3 Beaker with high relief barbotine studs (or 'spines') partially cut by rouletting. (A116.1962.32) Freeschool Lane.

315. GW3 Globular beaker with barbotine ribs over burnish, cf the plain no. 87. A complete vessel. (A277.1955) Provenance unknown.

316. GW3 Biconical beaker, probably a product of the north Kent Upchurch Marshes potteries (cf Noel Hume 1954, Fig. 3.1; Monaghan 1983, Fig. 9.71-77; Monaghan 1987, 68-70, Type 2G1). Late 1st to early 2nd century. (A405.1955) Jewry Wall site, not published by Kenyon (1948). Site notes indicate that this vessel came from the northern group of buildings, specifically NII/NV, a pre-"Forum" (i.e. pre-baths) level (context LP 38.4).

317. GW3 Everted rim jar, rusticated ribs (cf no. 315). Badly bloated, with warped rim. None of the blisters have burst, so the vessel may have been a serviceable second. *c.* 75% complete. Gillam 99, dated *c.* 110-130. (A296.1957) Town Hall, Horsefair Street, found 1874. Stukeley's Map of Leicester, dated 1722, bears the tantalising legend "Brick kilns where was antiently [sic] a Roman Pottery" in the area now bounded by Oxford Street/Newark Street/Granby Street, just to the south of Horsefair Street (South Gate, unnamed, London Road and Milston [sic] Lane on Stukeley's map) (Buckley and Lucas 1987, Fig. 28). Photograph published in Blank 1971, 13.

318. CG1B Dog dish. Wiped or rilled ext. Late 4th century, cf no. 90. These two types may have been used as a casserole in combination. (A247.1968. 484) Butt Close Lane: Buckley and Lucas 1987, Site 4, F20: I 9, phase 7A (medieval robber trench); see also *ibid.* Figs. 33.47-48 and 34.8 for other pottery from this context.

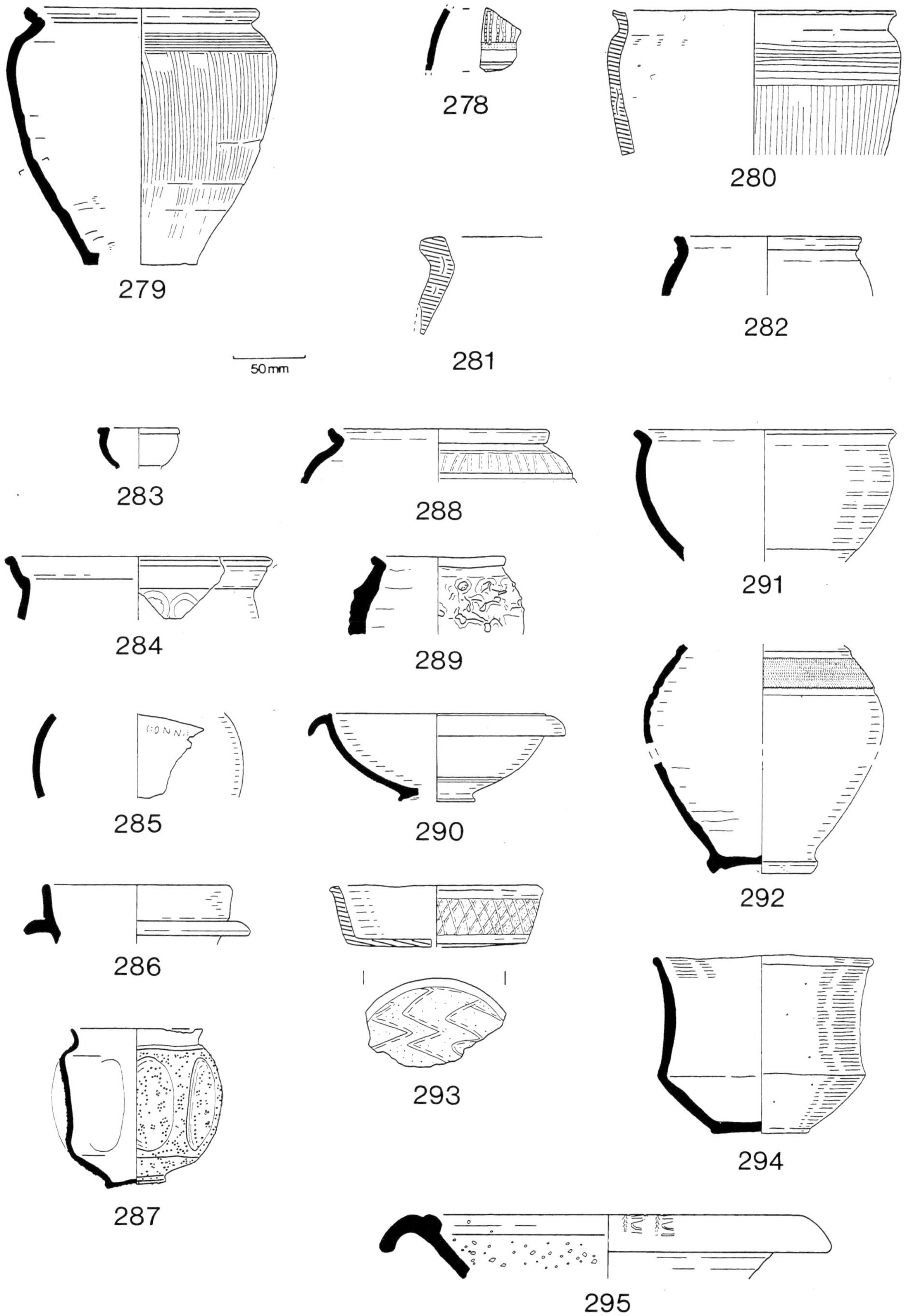

Fig. 67 Iron Age and Roman pottery Site 8 (278-282); Site 9 (283-295) Scale 1:4

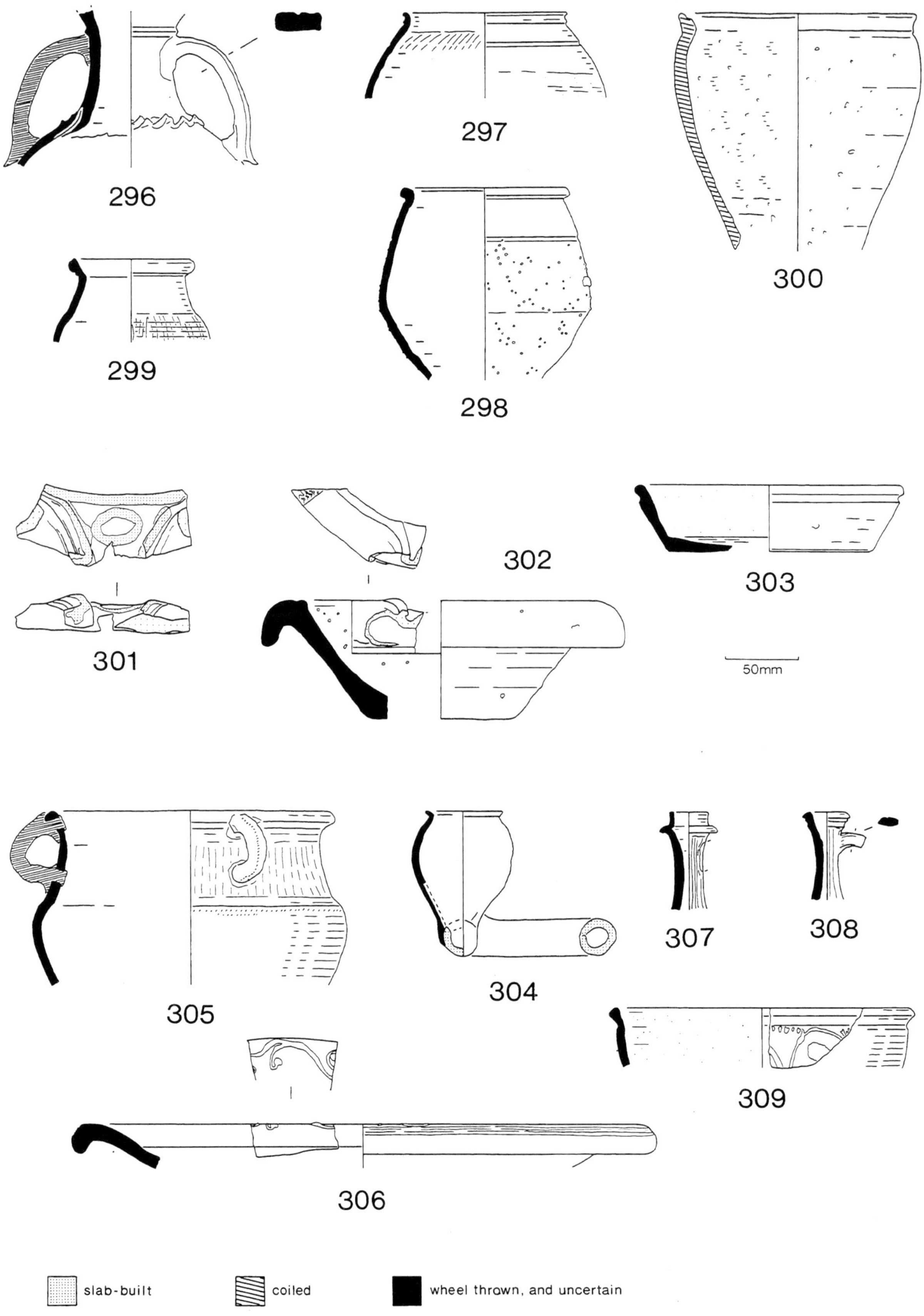

Fig. 68 Iron Age and Roman pottery Site 9 (296-300); Site 11 (301-303); Site 12 (304-305); Comparative material (306-309) Scale 1:4

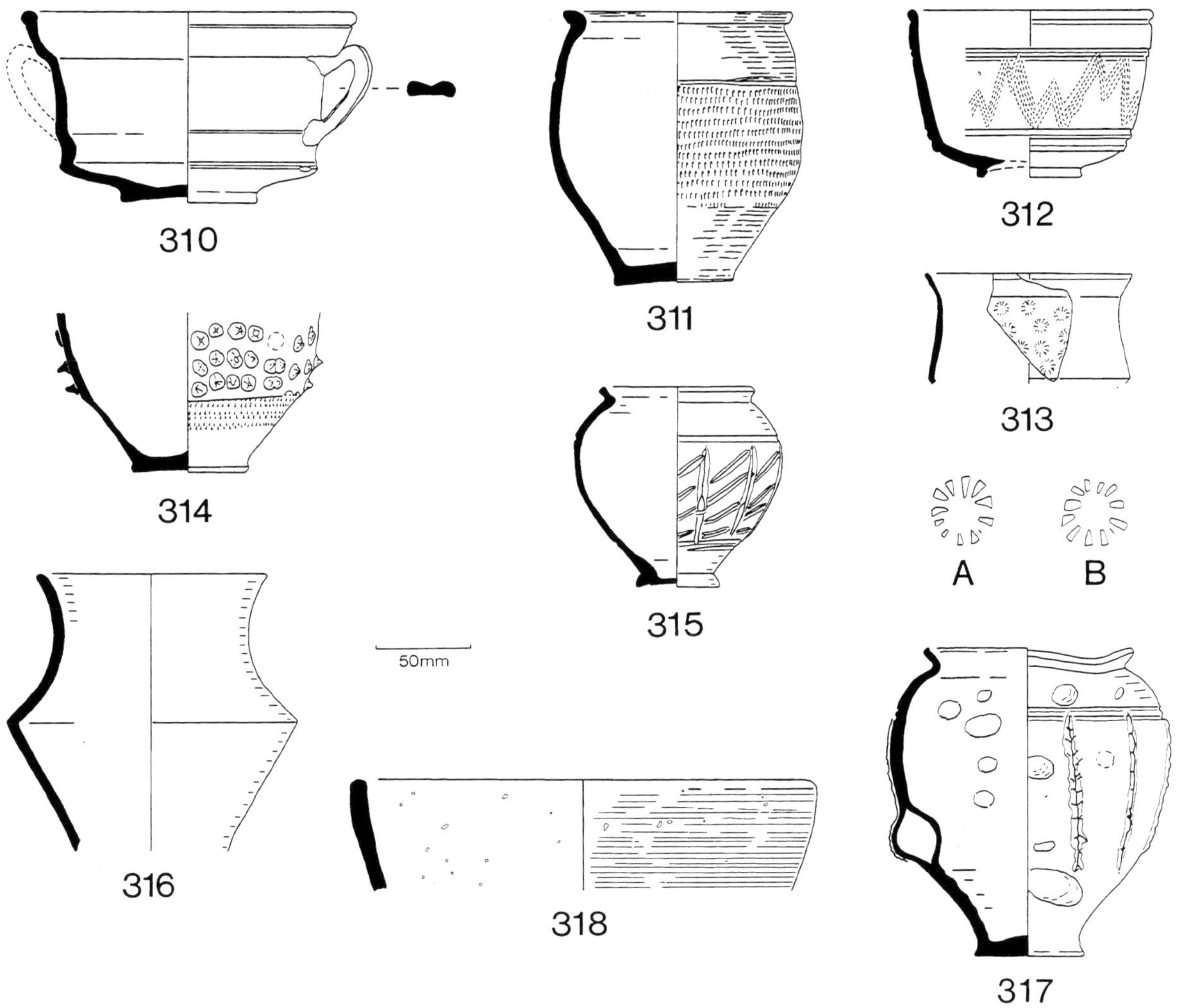

Fig. 69 Iron Age and Roman pottery. Comparative material (310-318). Scale 1:4 except 313A-B: Scale 1:1.

Concordance of Leicester Fabrics (Table 11)

The first major publication of Late Iron Age and Roman pottery by the Leicestershire Archaeological Unit featured a Fabric Type Series devised by the Unit's first Roman Pottery Assistant, Helen Clamp (Clamp 1985). This Type Series was redesigned by the present author during analysis of the pottery from the forum (Pollard forthcoming (a)) to take account of the wide range of wares present especially of the later Roman period, and of re- identifications of early 'native' wares (eg grog tempered). The facility offered by a monograph series for developing concepts whilst hopefully retaining a faithful readership is felt to justify the publication of a table of 'Pollard' Fabrics corresponding to the vessels illustrated by Clamp in a separate volume, thereby maintaining the integrity of the latter's report. Abbreviations follow the codes set out above (p 51). The left hand numbers in each column refer to the illustration numbers of Figs. 30-34 of the Bath Lane report (Clay and Mellor 1985).

Table 11. Revised Fabric Codes for the Late Iron Age and Roman Pottery from the Bath Lane Excavations (Clamp 1985)

Revision by Pollard (cf *ibid.*, forthcoming (a))

Fig.31.	1	Micaceous TN		35	WS1		69	GW3		103	OW3
	2	WW3 (Gaulish)		36	CG3A		70	GW3		104	OW2
	3	MD1A (Gaulish)		37	CG1A		71	GW7		105	OW3
	4	WW10 (Gaulish)		38	CG2A		72	GW7		106	OW2
	5	GT2		39	SW1		73	WW3		107	GW11
	6	GT2		40	GT2		74	WW2		108	GW11
	7	SW2		41	CG1A		75	WW3		109	GW3
	8	SW2		42	CG1		76	MG2		110	GW3
	9	MG1		43	WW2		77	WW1		111	GW3
	10	MG2		44	MD4		78	PR2		112	GW3
	11	MG1		45	GT2		79	PR2		113	GW6(5)
	12	MG1		46	MG2		80	WS1 (Central Gaul)		114	GW3
	13	SW2		47	GW3		81	GT1		115	GW3
	14	MG2		48	GW3		82	SW2		116	OW2
	15	GT2		49	PR6		83	SW3		117	OW2
	16	SW2		50	TR1C		84	SW3		118	WS2
	17	CG1A		51	C3		85	GW3		119	GT2
	18	CG1A		52	CG1A		86	MG2		120	OW2
	19	CG1A		53	CG3A		87	GW6		121	GW3
	20	CG1A		54	CG1		88	GT5		122	GW6
	21	CG1A		55	CG3A		89	PR1		123	GT3
	22	CG3A					90	WS1		124	GW6(5)
	23	CG2A	Fig.33.	56	MG1		91	SW2			
				57	GW3		92	CG1A	Fig.35.	125	GW6(5)
Fig.32.	24	CG2A		58	GW3		93	CG1A		126	GW6
	25	CG3A		59	GW6					127	GW3
	26	MG1		60	GW2	Fig.34.	94	GW6		128	GW2
	27	GT2		61	GW3		95	GW2		129	TN
	28	SW2		62	GW3		96	GW6		130	GW12
	29	MG2		63	GW3		97	GW6		131	GT6
	30	MG2		64	MG3		98	C4		132	WS2
	31	SW2		65	GW3		99	GW6		133	MO4
	32	SW2		66	GW8		100	CG1A		134	AM9A
	33	MG2		67	GW6		101	OW2		135	AM12
	34	MG2		68	GW6		102	OW3			

Correlation Between Illustrated Vessels From Leicester and Thompson's Type Series of "Belgic" Pottery (Tables 12-13)

The following two tables list the relevant illustrated vessels from the present report and from Bath Lane (Clamp 1985), with the types in which they belong in the series developed for south-east England by Thompson (1982). Whilst not a comprehensive list of Thompson's types found in Leicester, it may be useful for summary comparison with areas covered by that author.

Table 12. "Belgic" and other late 1st century BC to mid-1st century AD pottery: correlation with Thompson's typology (Thompson 1982).

* denotes grog tempered ware 1-6
** denotes mixed gritted ware 1-2

Fig.	No.	Type
Fig.50.	3	C5-1
	4	C6-1
	5	C5-1 *
	6	B3-8 *
	7	B3-8 *
	8	D1-1 *
	9	G1-1 **
	10	E1-4
	11	L5
Fig 51.	14	C6-1 **
Fig.52.	30	C2-3 *
	31	G5(-2) **
	34	C5-2
	35	C1-4
	36	C5-1/C6-1 *
	37	B3-8 *
	38	C1-2 *
	39	B1-1 **
	40	A10 **
	41	D1-3 **
	42	D1-2 **
	43	D1-4
	44	C3
	45	A8
	46	D1-1
Fig.53.	47	G5-5
	48	G1-1
	49	C5-1
	51	G5-3
	52	C5-1 *
	53	C1-2 *
	54	D1-2/G5 *
	55	C2-3
	56	D2-4
	60	C6-1
	61	C5-1
	62	B1-1 *
	63	B1-6 *
Fig.54.	64	E1-4 **
	75	C1-2 *
Fig.56.	108	C5-1/C5-3
	109	C2-2 *
	110	C6-1
Fig.57.	115	B5
	116	C1-3/C2-1
	117	B3-10 **
	125	B5-1(cf) **
Fig.58.	148	C5-1/C7-1
Fig.63.	223	C5-1
	224	C1-2 **
Fig.64.	230	C3
	231	C3
	236	C3
	237	C3
	238	C2-3
	239	L2(cf)
Fig.65.	246	E1-4
	247	E1-2 *
	248	G4 *
	249	G5-5 *
	250	G5-4 *
	251	B3/G5-1 **
	252	A8 *
	253	D1-4 *
	254	C6-1
	255	C5-1
	256	C6-1
	257	C6-1
Fig.66.	258	C3
	259	C3
	260	C1-2/C1-3
Fig.67.	280	C4(cf)/C7-1
	281	C1-3/C2-1
	282	C5-1(cf)
	294	E1-4 **
Fig.68.	299	G5-5 **
	300	C5-1

Table 13. "Belgic" and other late 1st century BC to mid-1st century AD pottery from Excavations in Bath Lane (Clamp 1985): correlation with Thompson's typology (Thompson 1982)

* denotes grog tempered ware 1-6

** denotes mixed gritted ware 1-2

Fig.	No.	Type	Fig.	No.	Type
Fig.31.	5	G5-2/G5-5 *		45	E1 *
	6	B1-1 *		46	C2-3**
	7	G5-2		52	C5-1
	8	E1-4		53	C5-2
	9	C6-1 **		54	C6-1
	10	cf G3-4 **		55	F5
	11	C6-1 **			
	12	C6-1 **	Fig.33.	56	C1-2 **
	13	B1-1		64	C1-2/C2-3
	14	E1-1 **		76	G5-6(?) **
	15	E1-4 *		81	C6-1*
	16	E1-1/F3-2		82	G1-1
	17	C5-1		83	C2-3
	18	C6-1		84	C2-3
	19	B1-1		86	B3-2 **
	20	C6-1		88	S2 *
	21	C5-1		91	C1-1
	22	C1-1		92	C5-1
	23	C3		93	C5-2
Fig.32.	24	C1-2	Fig.34.	100	C5-1
	25	C5-1		119	B1-1 *
	26	C1-1 **			
	27	G5-6 *	Fig.35.	131	C6-2 *
	28	D1-4			
	29	D1-1 **			
	30	C1-2 **			
	31	F3-2			
	32	E1-1			
	33	E1 **			
	34	G5-6 **			
	37	C1-3/C5-1			
	38	C1-2			
	39	C3			
	40	E1-2 *			
	41	C6-1			
	42	C6-1			

The Iron Age And Roman Pottery Fabrics: Summary Descriptions

Colour-coated wares

C2. 'White' fabrics, generally fine, including products from the Lower Rhineland, the lower Nene Valley and Central Gaul.

C3. Pale oxidised fabrics, generally fine. Material from Colchester, Central Gaul (Greene 1979, 43) and the lower Nene Valley, as well as that described as 'North Gaul Fabric 2' (Anderson 1981, 335-336) falls in this range.

C4. Described elsewhere (Pollard, in Clamp 1985, 46).

C5. Grey fabrics with dark grey to black slips. Some material may be classified as grey ware, with which group there is an obvious overlap. C5 fabrics are generally fine.

C7. Oxidised, fine sandy, fabrics, possibly a variant of C11.

C11. Dark oxidised fabrics, sometimes with reduced layers in the 'sandwich' visible in the fracture. Generally dark slips and fairly sandy clays.Material from Colchester, Oxfordshire and the lower Nene Valley, as well as 'North Gaul Fabric 1' (Anderson 1981, 332-335) falls in this range.

C12. 'Rhenish' wares from Central Gaul and Trier (Greene 1978).

C13. Oxfordshire red- and brown- slipped fine ware (Young 1977).

C14. Lyon ware (Greene 1979).

C15. Light red, fine, very hard fabric, probably late in date. Rare.

C17. An 'umbrella' group for fabrics bordering on C2, C3 and C11, including possible Colchester and lower Nene Valley products; e.g. very pale oxidised with pink or grey 'sandwich'. Generally fine.

C18. Described elsewhere (MacRobert 1987, 65). The thick red slip is diagnostic. Sources may be diverse, date range wide.

C19. Described above (p 54).

C21. Described above (p 54).

Lead glazed wares

LG1. Central Gaulish; Greene's Fabric (a) (1979, 90).

LG4. Described above (p 51).

LG5. Described above (p 54).

Terra Nigra and Terra Rubra.

Rigby's classification is used (1981a, 159); TN1 is not distinguished from TN, and 'mica-dusted' TN is more accurately described here as 'micaceous'.

Pompeian Red wares

Peacock's classification is used (1977b).

Micaceous wares

MW1. Skeleton Green Fabric 1 (Williams 1981). See also Rigby and Freestone 1986, Fabric 1C.

MD4. Resembles the above in some instances, especially the variant Blue Boar Lane (Leicester) Fabric 69 (MacRobert 1983, 38).

Mica dusted wares

MD1A.Similar to WW3, known in Cam 114 jars (Clamp 1985, Fig. 31.3) from Gallia Belgica.

MD1B.Resembles C2 and WW2, with mica 'dusting' over a slip. Probably lower Nene Valley.

MD1C.Described above (p 54).

MD3. Oxidised, fine fabric possibly including Rhineland bossed beakers (Marsh 1978, Type 20; MacRobert 1983 Fabric 45 and Fig. 22.93).

MD4. Oxidised generally with reduced core, fine sandy, including Blue Boar Lane Fabrics 69 and 74, and Clamp 1985, Fig. 32.44. May include Central Gaulish and London (Marsh 1978, 123) products.

MD5. Oxidised, sometimes with reduction in 'sandwich', coarse sandy. Possibly from London and/or more local, as yet unrecognised, sources.

MD6. Oxidised, sometimes with a 'sandwich', fine; cf OW2. Includes Blue Boar Lane Fabric 73. Unrecognised Midlands source(s)? The most common MD fabric in Leicester.

Mortarium fabrics

The classification is based upon Kay Hartley's report on the forum material (in Pollard forthcoming (a)).

MO1-3. Oxfordshire white (1), white-slip (2), and red/brown colour-coated (3) wares (Young 1977).

MO4. The fine, white, 'pipeclay' fabric used by Mancetter-Hartshill potters; as WW2, with grog trituration grit.

MO6. Pale oxidised or 'off-white', fine sandy fabric from the lower Nene Valley, with ironstone trituration grit.

MO7. Equates with WW5. Verulamium region. Flint and quartz trituration grit.

MO8. Fine, pale oxidised to buff fabric from Gallia Belgica, *c.* AD 50-150. Trituration grit of Fr-Ab quartz supplemented by concentric scoring.

MO9. Fine sandy buff to pinkish white with Sp 'gold' mica distinguishing it from (eg) MO14, MO18 and Little Chester ware. Trituration grit of Fr/Ab quartz plus concentric scoring. Rare.

MO10. Finer version of MO7, cf WW3-4. Similar fabrics known from Verulamium region.

MO12. Cf MO4, but more sandy (as WW4), and with quartz grits dominating the trituration grit, along with grog, flint and rock fragments. Used at Mancetter-Hartshill and possibly by other Midlands potteries.

MO13. Coarse sandy fabric, pale oxidised to buff. Midlands? Rare.

MO14. Fine sandy, pale oxidised to buff and pink. Quartz trituration grit. Cf MO9 and MO12. Probably Midlands, including Little Chester. Rare.

MO15. Fine, white or 'off-white', often powdery. Includes products of north-east Gaul, Kent and Colchester (eg Hartley 1977, 'Groups I and II'; Hartley 1982, 150-151, Fabrics 1A-D), with flint and quartz trituration grit where present.

MO17. Fine sandy, oxidised, trituration grit mainly quartz. South-west Britain or Midlands?

MO18. As MO4 fabric, with MO12 trituration grit.

MO19. As MO12 fabric, with MO4 trituration grit.

MO22. Described above (p 67).

MO24. Described above (p 67).

Amphora fabrics

AM1. Cf PR1, and Dressel 1 fabric 2 (Peacock 1971, 164), but finer, with Sp/Mo 'black sand'.

AM2. Very fine, highly micaceous, oxidised fabric. Cirencester Fabric 77 carries a similar description (Rigby 1982a).

AM3-6. A group of oxidised fabrics with variable quantities of quartz, feldspar, granite and mica, often with salt-whitened surface. May include Baetican, Catalonian and North African products.

AM7. Characteristic of Cam 186 (Peacock 1971, 168-169), generally pale, fine to coarse sandy.

AM8. Buff, lime-rich, with Fr inclusions resembling baked serpentine.

AM9A and 9B. Variants of the Dressel 20 fabric, the latter generally finer, redder, and with a more prominent salt-whitening, characteristics apparently confined to later vessels (late Antonine +). AM9A is the standard, grey-buff, often laminar fabric.

AM10. Rhodian fabric 1? (Peacock 1977a, 266-267).

AM11. Fine, pale oxidised, with sparse inclusions, of which brown rock fragments are distinctive.

AM12 and 13. Buff fine fabrics, often powdery, the latter lacking (apparently) the 'gold' mica of the former (cf Green 1981, 42). Typical of South Gaulish vessels, notably Pelichet 47 (Peacock 1978); cf WW7.

AM16. The distinctive 'volcanic glass' fabric of Richborough 527 (Peacock 1977a, 264-265).

AM18. Oxidised, coarse sandy, typical of the 'carrot' amphora Cam 189, but also associated with other 'rilled' types.

AM19. Distinguished from AM18 by higher (i.e. paler) chromas and an absence of rilling. Associated with Fishbourne 148.3 (Cunliffe 1971).

AM23. Oxidised, soapy, medium sandy with Sp-Mo calcite and Mo-Fr grey and white rock fragments characteristic. Associated with weakly rilled vessels, cf British Bii (eg Peacock 1970, Fig. 28.4-5) and Verulamium 1918 (Wilson 1984).

AM25. Described above (p 64), and by MacRobert (1987, 66).

AM28-30. Described above (pp 64-5).

White wares

WW1. Coarse, generally sandy, characterised by very coarse lumps of clay and limestone; fabric colours vary from 'white' to 'red' and grey. Jars, possibly imported from Northamptonshire, with a Flavian to Antonine floruit in Leicester.

WW2. Fine; cf MO4. Sources may include Mancetter-Hartshill and the lower Nene Valley.

WW3. Fine sandy. Includes northern Gaulish imports (described above, p 71) and possibly upper and lower Nene Valley painted and other wares (e.g. Fig. 63.228).

WW4. Medium sandy; cf MO12. Sources may include the Verulamium region and Mancetter-Hartshill; cf. the fabric of medieval Chilvers Coton ware from near Nuneaton (Warks).

WW5. Coarse sandy; cf MO7. Verulamium region.

WW7. Fine, characterised by 'gold' mica; cf AM12.

WW9. Described above (p 54).

WW10. Miscellaneous fine and fine sandy fabrics; cf (eg) MO15.

White-slip wares

WS1. Clamp's 'Flagon fabric 1' (1985, 41); described also by Rigby and Freestone (1983; 1986; Fabric 1B). See discussion of "cream slipped" flagons above, p 71.

WS2. Fine and fine sandy fabrics; cf OW2.

WS4. Coarse sandy; cf OW3. Sources may include Verulamium region.

WS5. Very fine; the slipped version of OW6.

WS6. Fine sandy, cf OW9. Much Hadham slipped oxidised ware. (Going 1987, Fabric 14). A flagon in this fabric has been found at Little Lane, Leicester (A39.1988).

WS8. Fine, generally reduced with 'white' slip, cf GW3.

WS11. Described above (p 54).

Oxidised wares

OW1. Fine and fine sandy fabrics, can have reduced core and/or surfaces. May include TR3, and certainly 'Gallo-Belgic' derivatives.

OW2. Fine and fine sandy fabrics, often with a colour 'sandwich'.

An umbrella for the bulk of unprovenanced Midlands oxidised wares, probably including Warwickshire and Northamptonshire products; cf MD6, WS2, slipped variants. Some OW2 may have a 'self' slip, brown or other colours, especially on 2nd century beakers. This may be referred to as a colour-coat by some writers.

OW3. Coarse sandy; cf WS4 and AM19. Sources may include the Verulamium region and the Midlands.

OW5. Medium sandy; may include unrecognised medieval and later sherds, the oxidised wares being imperfectly understood for all periods.

OW6. Very fine; at the finer end of the OW2 spectrum, this fabric embraces early Roman derivatives of Iron Age types; cf WS5 and GW2, and the essentially Late Iron Age MG2.

OW7. Fine; cf OW2 but with 'gold' mica diagnostic. General similarity to C4 (Pollard, in Clamp 1985, 46) and the Severn Valley wares (e.g. Rigby 1982b, Fabric 106).

OW9. The 'salt and pepper' Much Hadham burnished ware (Orton 1977b, 37, Fabric (i); see also Going 1987 Fabric 4); white quartz and black iron ore speckle the matrix.

Grey wares

GW1. Medium and coarse sandy fabrics, possibly both hand made (coiled) and wheel thrown. An umbrella for 'BB1 imitations' which adhere closely to the fabric and style of BB1, this may inadvertently include some BB1 itself. South Yorkshire BB1 may be included in this group. Other BB1-derived vessels are classified under GW3-7.

GW2. Fabric as GW12 (described above, p 55), embracing forms without the distinctive decoration of the latter, often derived from Iron Age types; cf OW6, GW8, MG2.

GW3, 5, 6, 9. A gradation from fine to very coarse sandy, some of the coarsest GW9 may be hand-made (cf GT5-6). An umbrella group for grey to black fabrics of unknown or uncertain source, and visually indistinguishable fabrics including Leicester, Ravenstone and possibly Mancetter-Hartshill.

GW4, 7. Fine and sandy white and light grey fabrics, typical of the NeneValley potteries but also produced at Mancetter-Hartshill.

GW8. A fine to fine sandy fabric distinguished by a high (Fr) white mica content. Rare.

GW10. Coarse sandy, high firing temperatures often to the verge of vitrification of the surfaces, but otherwise within the GW6 range. Several similarities with Brixworth forms suggest a possible source in the upper NeneValley's early industries.

GW11. Described above (p 55)

GW12. Described above (p 55)

Dales-type ware

The fabric may fall within any one of GW3, 5 and 6; the form is described and discussed by Loughlin (1977). Rare in Leicester.

Black-burnished wares

BB1 and BB2 follow the definitions of Farrar (1973). many sherds of the former have shale, which may be unique to Dorset ware, but other sources for Leicester cannot be ruled out (eg Rossington Bridge: Buckland *et al* 1980). BB2 is rare and apparently restricted to dishes and jars (cf Pollard 1987, 198-200, Fabric 57), including possible Kent vessels (Pollard 1983, Form V eg). GW1 may include some BB1.

Derbyshire ware

Described by Gillam (1939) and Kay (1962). Rare in Leicester, as is the calcite gritted Dales ware.

Calcite gritted wares

CG1, 1A, 1B. Fr-Ab fossil marine shell, low quartz content. CG1A is early (late Iron Age to 2nd century), CG1B the "Late Roman shelly" ware widespread over the Midlands and the south-east. CG1 embraces sherds whose attribution to A or B is uncertain, or which belong to the relatively small group of vessels that date to the intervening period.

CG2,2A. More sandy than CG1; CG2A is generally hand made. CG2 in the present report covers early, hand made vessels only, the wheel thrown (and late?) CG2B having been recognised on other sites after the writing of this report.

CG3, 3A, 3B. Mo-Fr calcite, mostly platy shell, low quartz content. CG3A is mainly hand made and early; CG3B is wheel thrown and mid-Roman in date. The latter was made in Rutland, south Lincolnshire and possibly the lower Nene Valley and is usually black, more rarely brown.

CG4. Mo calcite, SA and platy, Fr-Ab quartz. Cf SW2. Wheel thrown and possibly also hand made. Early.

Grog tempered wares

GT1-4. GT1 and 2 are respectively coarse and fine fabrics, but with "Belgic" forms diagnostic; GT3 and 4 are coarse and fine again, but without distinctly "Belgic" features. GT3 may include a Midlands fabric (GT3A) of mid to late Roman date, defined by Booth and Green (1989) and Woodfield (1983, 78 Fabric 35b) and recognised subsequent to the preparation of this report.

GT5-6. Generally grey fabrics, with Mo-Fr grog, differentiated from each other by quartz content (Mo-Fr, and Sp, respectively). Recognised amongst wasters from Great Holme Street, Leicester. Cf GW9.

GT7. Described above (p 73).

Mixed gritted wares

MG1-2. Coarse and fine fabrics respectively; as GT1-2, but with grog Sp or absent, and Sp-Mo quartz and calcite. MG2 is slightly coarser than GW2 and OW6. "Belgic" styles.

MG3. A fine to medium sandy grey ware with Mo calcite. Probably local and of early date, a grey ware of 'experimental' nature seems a reasonable interpretation. Probably amongst the range of 'transitional' wares made at Great Holme Street.

MG4. An oxidised variant of MG3, described by MacRobert (1987, 65).

Sandy wares

SW1. Described above (p 73)

SW2-3. Respectively fine and coarse sandy, the former in "Belgic" style, the latter jars of late Iron Age and 1st century AD date. SW2 generally wheel thrown, SW3 hand made.

SW4. Coarse sandy, with no diagnostic features. May include some GW as well as Iron Age and post-Roman material.

Miscellaneous coarse wares

MC1. Described by MacRobert (1987, 65).

MC2-5. Described above (pp 55, 73).

The Post Roman Pottery
Deborah Sawday

The pottery from Site 4 and Site 8 will be discussed in conjunction with other excavations at Leicester Castle (Buckley forthcoming); no post Roman pottery survives from Site 9 and only one sherd from Site 10. Some of the pottery from the other sites was apparently discarded during the excavations, hence the data on the Tables should be treated with some caution.

The pottery (1342 sherds) has been examined under a x 10 binocular microscope and catalogued by fabric, vessel form and context. Quantification is by minimum vessel number, sherd number and weight (grams), the latter and the detailed fabric description being retained in the archive. Where sherds join with pot from other phases, the minimum vessel number is given in the earliest phase in Tables 16-2. Similar material from Leicester has already been described and illustrated (Woodland 1981 and 1987, Sawday forthcoming). Tables and text refer to the general period categories as follows:-
late Saxon/early medieval *c.* 850-1100; early medieval *c.* 1100-1250; medieval *c.* 1200-1450; late medieval *c.* 1400-1550; post-medieval *c.* 1500+. The following abbreviations have been used:- cp/stj - cooking pot/storage jar; stj - storage jar; vtu - vessel type unknown. The Stamford ware vessel forms catalogued in Table 23 are described in Kilmurry 1980, the Potters Marston vessel forms catalogued in Table 24 are described in Sawday 1989 and 1991, and will be described in more detail in Sawday forthcoming.

The Saxon Pottery

Six sherds from four vessels are residual from Site 5, Phase 6 - all would appear to date from the 6th or 7th centuries. Vessel number 2144, Fig 70.1 from the pit, F25, Phase 6C, is in a highly fired reduced fabric with a range of mineral inclusions, including fine mica. The sherd is burnished externally and internally, and decorated with incised horizontal and diagonal lines at the shoulder. Vessel number 2051, represented by three joining body sherds, is in a reduced mineral and (?)calcareous fabric. The two remaining vessels, numbers 2050 and 2052, are both reduced, the former with coarse mineral inclusions including quartz, the latter is highly fired and tempered with fine quartz. Vessels 2050-2052 are from the spread, IV 1, Phase 6A.

The Late Saxon, Medieval and Post Medieval Pottery

Site 1 Table 16 (27 sherds)

The pottery which includes a form 4 cp/stj in PM from Phase 9A all lies within a late Saxon/early medieval date range.

Site 2 Table 17 (347 sherds)

The four sherds in Phases 2, 4B, 4D and 5 are presumed intrusive.

Phase 6A - Robber Trench F3, - Pits F25, F35, F37, F38, F40, F41, F42, F43, F48, F66 and Gully F44 (61 sherds)

Fabrics ST70, TO, LE and LI2 dating from the mid or late 10th century occur in small quantities in the pits F35, Phase 6Ai, and F40, F48 and F66, Phase 6Aii together with pottery dating from 11th to the late 12th or possibly early 13th centuries.
The identifiable forms comprise three cp/stj or spouted pitchers and a bowl in Stamford ware, a socketed or spouted bowl in fabric TO, two cp/stj in PM - forms 3 and 4 respectively, and a cp/stj and jug in LY4.

Phase 6B - Pit F4 (18 sherds)

The presence of a splayed jug base in NO3 suggests a terminal date towards the end of the 13th century for this small group, which also contains a residual jug or tubular spouted pitcher twisted handle fragment in ST31, of a type apparently unique to Leicester (Kilmurry pers comm), (Rahtz 1959, Fig. 15.ST3). A similar but not identical handle occurs on site 5, Fig. 71.27. A form 3 jug base in PM and an internally glazed sherd, probably from a bowl in CC1 also occur in F4.

Phase 6C - Pits F2 and F5, Robber Trench - F36 (86 sherds)

These contexts all produced the late medieval midland purple wares MP1 and MP2 as well as residual pottery dating from the late 10th or 11th centuries onwards - Potters Marston ware in particular occurring in a range of vessel forms apparently typical of the industry spanning the period from *c.* 1100 to *c.* 1300. F2 and F5 in Area 1 contained fragments from the same vessels in CC2 and MP1 suggesting, not surprisingly, that these pits only reveal part of what must have been a much wider pattern of rubbish dispersal in the locality.

Phase 6D - Pits F39, F63 and F90 (94 sherds)

The bulk of the pottery is residual; F63 contained a sherd of LY4 in the late St Neots tradition, with two lines of diamond rouletting on the exterior body, whilst F39 produced two cp/stjs and a spouted pitcher in Stamford Ware. The cistern with the pouring lip, a previously unparalleled feature on this vessel form in Leicester in MP2, Fig. 70.9 occurs in F90, together with a possibly three handled cup with a belled rim in CW2, Fig. 70.10.

This Phase is dated to the 16th or 17th centuries by the presence of sherds of MY and EA in F63 and F39: F90 contained no post-medieval pottery but has been assigned a similar date range on morphological grounds.

Site 3 Table 18 (437 sherds)

Late Saxon/early medieval pottery is presumed intrusive in Phases 3B and 3C.

Phase 4A - Beam Slot F4 (47 sherds)

The forty seven fragments of PM comprise mainly undiagnostic body sherds - save one form 4 cp/stj rim, and body sherds from another similar vessel, which suggests a 12th or early 13th century date for this pottery.

Phase 4B Garden Soil I 13, III 3, II 2 (21 sherds)

The PM cp/stj form 7 probably dates from the late 12th or 13th centuries, whilst the sherd of NO2 may date from the first half of the 13th century.

Phase 4C - Pits F39, F8, F9, F28 (41 sherds)

The bulk of the pottery lies within a 12th century date range, though earlier residual material may include the sherds in TO and ST72, the spouted pitcher, form 5.38 in ST30, and an inturned bowl rim in developed St Neots type ware in LY4, Fig. 71.25. The 12th century material includes a PM jug form 2, and PM cp/stj forms 4 and 6, whilst the Stamford wares include a form 1.57 bowl in ST71, and a form 4/5.41 vessel in ST30. A cp/stj rim in LY4 and a sherd in LY3, both from II 3, F9, may be 13th century in date (McCarthy 1979).

Table 14: Key to Saxon and Medieval Fabrics

Code	Name	Main Inclusion	Production	Sources/Kiln and Fabric Equivalent	Approx. Date Range
SX	Saxon	Various	hb	?Local	
ST2	Stamford ware 2	quartz	wt	Stamford fabrics B/C) }	1150-1250
ST3	Stamford ware 3	quartz	wt	Stamford fabric G } + glazes 1, 3, 5, 6(1)	1050-1200
ST7	Stamford ware 7	quartz	wt	Stamford fabric A }	900-1050
LI2	Lincoln ware 2	calcareous	hb/cb/wt	Lincs (2)	850-1050
TO	Torksey type ware	quartz	hb/wt	Local/East Anglia (3)	900-1200
TH	Thetford type ware	quartz	hb/wt	Lccal/East Anglia (4)	900-1100
LE	Leicester ware	quartz	hb/wt	Leicester, Southgate St (5)	850-1100
PM	Potters Marston ware	igneous	hb/cb/wt	SW Leics, Potters Marston (6)	1100-1300
SP1	Splashed ware 1	quartz	hb/cb	Nottingham (7)	1180-1250
SP2	Splashed ware 2	quartz	hb/cb	Nottingham (*ibid*)	1100-1180
SP3	Splashed ware 3	quartz	hb/cb	? Local/Leicester	1100-1250
LY3	Stanion/Lyveden type ware 3	calcareous	hb/cb	SE Leics/Stanion,Lyveden/Yardley Hastings Northampton fabric T6 (8)	1200-1400
LY4	Stanion/Lyveden type ware 4	calcareous	hb/cb/wt	SE Leics/Stanion,Lyveden/Yardley Hastings Northampton fabric T1-2. T2 (*ibid*)	1100-1400
OS1	Oxidised Sandy ware 1	quartz	hb/cb/wt?	S.E. Leics/Northants/Beds Brackley fabric T68(?)(9)	1100-1250
OS2	Oxidised Sandy ware 2	quartz	hb/cb/wt	? Northants/Beds/Oxon	1100-1250
OS3	Oxidised Sandy ware 3	quartz	wt	? Local	1100-1250
CC1	Chilvers Coton ware 1	quartz	wt	Chilvers Coton fabric A(10)	1200-1400
CC2	Chilvers Coton ware 2	quartz	wt	Chilvers Coton fabric C (*ibid*)	1200-1475
NO2	Nottingham ware 2	quartz	wt	Nottingham (7)	1230-1300
NO3	Nottingham ware 3	quartz	wt	Nottingham (7)	1250-1350
LI3	Lincoln ware 3	quartz	wt	? Lincoln	1250-1400
MS1	Medieval Sandy ware 1	quartz	wt	? Local/Chilvers Coton	1200-1400
MS2	Medieval Sandy ware 2	quartz	wt	? Local/Chilvers Coton/Nottingham/Derbys	1200-1400
MS3	Medieval Sandy ware 3	quartz	wt	? Local/Chilvers Coton/Derbys	1250-1450
MP1	Midland Purple ware 1	quartz	wt	Chilvers Coton fabric D(10)	1375-1550
MP2	Midland Purple ware 2	quartz	wt	? Local/Ticknall (Derbys)	1375-1550
TG	'Tudor Green' type	quartz	wt	Surrey/Hants	1400-1550
CW2	Cisterican ware 2	quartz	wt	? Local/Ticknall (Derbys)	1475-1550

(1) Kilmurry 1980, Leach 1987
(2) Young J pers comm
(3) Barley 1981
(4) Rogerson and Dallas 1984
(5) Hebditch 1967-8
(6) Haynes 1952
(7) Nailor V pers comm
(8) McCarthy 1979, Bellamy 1983
(9) Mellor M pers comm
(10) Mayes and Scott 1984

Abbreviations
hb - hand built
cb - coil built
wt - wheel thrown

Production - primary method of manufacture

Table 15: Key to the post-medieval fabrics

Code	Name	Production	Sources	Approx. Date Range
MY	Midland Yellow ware	wt	? Local/Ticknall(Derbys)	1500-1725
EA1	Earthenware - slipped and lead gl.	wt	? Local/Chilvers Coton/Ticknall	1500+
EA2	Earthenware - slipped and lead gl.	wt	? Local/Chilvers Coton/Ticknall	1600+
EA3	Earthenware - mottled	wt	Staffs	1650-1780
EA6	Earthenware - lead gl. incl. Blackwares	wt	?Local	1500-1750
EA7	Earthenware - slip wares	-	? Local/Chilvers Coton/Ticknall	1600-1850
EA8	Earthenware - cream wares	-	Staffs etc.	1730-1850
EA9	Earthenware - pearl wares	-	Staffs etc.	Late 18th-mid 19th c.
EA	Earthenware - unclassified	-	-	post med
FR	Stoneware - Frechen	wt	Frechen	1550+
SW4	Stoneware - while salt gl.	-	Staffs	1730+
SW5	Stoneware - brown salt gl.	-	Nottingham/Derbys etc	18th-19th c.

gl = glaze

Table 16 Site 1 - minimum vessel numbers/sherd numbers by Phase

Fabric	Phase			
Late Saxon/ Early Medieval	4A	9A	9B	Totals
ST31			1/1	1/1
PM	1/1	10/12	8/12	19/25
SP3		1/1		1/1
Totals	1/1	11/13	9/13	21/27

Phase 5A - Pits F2, F16 and F42 (153 sherds)
The group includes obviously residual sherds in PM and LY4 redeposited from F28 and F39 respectively in Phase 4C, as well as sherds in PM from F16 - linking with material presumed intrusive in IV 5, Phase 3. Other early pottery includes a PM cp/stj in form 4, sherds of ST30, ST31 and ST70 - dating from the 12th century if not earlier. The sherds of developed Stamford ware, ST23, including the jug or tubular spouted pitcher, form 6/24, a jug form 6.17 and the bowl, form 1.53, date from the mid 12th century. The 13th century pottery includes the PM cp/stj in forms 7 and 8, a cp/stj in LY4 and sherds in CC1, CC2 and MS1, whilst a jug fragment in NO3 with a heavily reduced interior dates to *c.* 1300.

Phase 5B - Spreads I 2, III 4, V 3 (101 sherds)
The bowl in ST70, form 12/13.21 may date to the 11th or 12th centuries, however most of the pottery appears to lie within the 13th to the 15th century date range - including a dripping dish in CC1 and two wide mouthed bowls in CC2. Very similar forms occurred in Phase 3 at the Austin Friars (Woodland 1981, Fig. 31.74).

The sherds of MY and EA9, dating from the 16th and 18th centuries respectively, may be intrusive in V 3.

Phase 6 - Modern IV 1, I 8, III 2, I 1.
The pottery spans the period from the 11th to the 18th or 19th centuries and is predominantly residual, some having links with material from Phases 4C and 5A. Interesting forms include a cp/stj, form 2.12 in ST70, and a PM bowl in form 2, both possibly dating to the 11th or 12th centuries.

Site 5 Table 19 (365 sherds)
A sherd from a form 3 cp/stj in PM, and a vtu in ST31 are intrusive in II 6 and X 3 in Phase 3C.

Phase 6A - Spread IV 1 (79 sherds) - Well F27 (28 sherds) - Pit F101 (1 sherd)
Five sherds of Saxon pottery are residual in IV 1, which also produced quantities of late Saxon/early medieval pottery dated from the 10th to the 12th centuries. Interesting forms included two cp/stj forms 3.31 and 11.06 in ST70, a bowl, form 1.54 in ST30, and a cp/stj, form 3.12 in ST36, whilst PM cp/stj occur in forms 3, 4 and 6. Possible 13th century pottery included a stj fragment in PM - and the sherds in SP2, SP3 and OS2. These fabrics all continued in production into the mid 13th century. The sherd in NO3 dating from the second half of the 13th century and the three sherds of post medieval earthenware are presumed to be intrusive in this context.

The well contained a predominance of Stamford table ware forms - jugs and tubular spouted pitchers, though none with the classic developed copper glaze 3. Two PM cp/stj in form 4, and several decorated jug fragments in SP3 are also present. The absence of any of the glazed medieval sandy wares may suggest a 12th century date for this group.

The pit, F101 produced one sherd in ST31.

Phase 6B - Robber Trenches F6, F21, F102 (19 sherds)
The pottery, which dates to the 12th or early 13th centuries, includes two PM cp/stj in form 3 and one in form 4, as well as cp/stj and jug fragments in SP3 and LY4. The sherds of the post medieval fabrics MY and EA2 are presumed intrusive in F21.

Phase 6C - Pits F2, F7, F9, F11, F22, F25 and F26 (63 sherds)
One sherd of Saxon pottery occurs in F25, this and much of the rest of the pottery is obviously residual, several sherds from F22 join with late Saxon/early medieval material from the well, F27 Phase 6A. Later PM forms include a dripping dish and a cp/stj form 8, whilst the presence of sherds in CC1 would suggest a terminal date in the 13th century for this group.

Phase 6D - Pits F4, F17, F18, F23 and F28 (76 sherds)
Much of this pottery joined with sherds from Phases 6A and 6C and is residual in all these contexts. Interesting vessels included a cp/stj form 11.07 in ST31, and a tubular spouted pitcher fragment also in ST31 from F17 and F23 respectively. F4 produced a sherd of MS3 dating from the 14th century, and F17 and F18 sherds of the late medieval fabric MP2, whilst F23 contained a single sherd of MY dating from the 16th century.

Site 6 Table 20 (147 sherds)
Fourteen sherds of late Saxon/early medieval pottery are intrusive in F22 100 Phase 1D, 37 Phase 2C, and 32 and 34 Phase 3A.

Phase 8A - Pit F6 68, - Robber Trench F12 80 (9 sherds).
The pit, F6 contained one sherd of Stamford ware with the developed copper glaze 3, dated *c.* 1150-*c.* 1250, whilst the sherd of MS1 in F12 dates from *c.* 1200 plus.

Phase 8D - Wells F3 66 and F8 72 (37 sherds)
The wells contained predominantly late medieval pottery dating from the late 14th or 15th centuries. Identifiable vessel forms included a wide mouthed bowl in MS3, two cisterns - both with cut outs above the rim in MP2, a pedestal cup base fragment in TG, and two two-handled cups in CW2, with short and tall rims respectively - both forms being paralleled at the Austin Friars (Woodland 1981, Fig. 41, 207 and 209).

Phase 8E - Pits F7 70, 187 and F1 62 (79 sherds)
Whilst the majority of the pottery dates to the medieval period, the presence of the late medieval fabrics MP and CW in all three layers, suggests a high degree of residuality. F1 also contained three sherds of post medieval pottery dated from the 16th and 17th centuries.

Interesting forms include two PM cp/stj forms 4 and 7, a wide mouthed bowl in CC2, a possible costrel fragment and part of a corrugated jug or cup, both in CW2. The Frechen vessel is probably a jug and has the wire cut base typical of this ware.

Site 7 Table 21 (18 sherds)

Phase 4 - Clay/Loam Deposits I 1, II 1 (11 sherds)
Pottery dating from the 13th to the 18th centuries was recovered, vessels of note included a candlestick base or salt lid in MY, a chamber pot in EA2 and a mug in EA3.

Site 10 (1 sherd)
One sherd of pottery was retained from the watching brief - a fragment of a face jug or tubular spouted pitcher in NO3, of a type previously recorded at Nottingham (Coppack 1980, Fig. 71,144).

Discussion

Whilst the small quantities of Torksey and Thetford type wares may be of local origin, the presence of significant quantities of Stamford ware constitutes convincing evidence of trade links to the north east of Leicester during the late Saxon/early medieval period (Fig. 72). The Leicester ware sherd is interesting in that this is the first time that a product of the Saxo Norman Southgate Street kiln has been identified, albeit tentatively, from an excavation in the town (Hebditch 1967-8).

Potters Marston ware represents a major local industry situated approximately 11km to the south west of Leicester.This ware dominates the pottery groups during the latter part of the 12th century, if not before (Fig. 72). This relatively coarse, hand-made pottery, was made in a wide range of forms, whilst the Stamford potters continued to supply culinary wares and increasing numbers of fine table wares throughout the 12th and early 13th centuries (Tables 22-23). The presumed local splash glazed ware, SP3 appears during this period but unlike its Nottingham counterparts, which seem to have ousted Stamford ware from that town by *c.* 1150 (V Nailor pers comm), the Leicester splashed ware here, typically only occurs in relatively small quantities.

Unfortunately evidence of the medieval and late medieval periods is limited here but pottery of this date has been extensively described from the Austin Friars, Leicester (Woodland 1981). Suffice it to say that the trading bias towards the north east during the late Saxon/early medieval period, which appears to predate the trade links documented between Leicester and the ports of the Wash during the 12th and 13th centuries (Carus-Wilson 1962-3), is followed by a shift to the west of Leicester during the medieval period proper with Chilvers Coton as the major supplier of pottery to the town. Similarly, whilst the origin of the most common pottery of the late medieval period, fabrics MP2 and CW2 is uncertain, again a source to the west, possibly Ticknall in Derbyshire has been suggested.

Table 17: Site 2 - minimum vessel numbers/sherd numbers by Phase.

Fabric	Phase									
	2	4B	4D	5	6A	6B	6C	6D	U/S	Totals
Late Saxon/ Early Medieval										
ST20					1/ 1			2/ 2		3/ 3
ST21					1/ 1			1/ 1	1/ 1	3/ 3
ST30					20/22		2/ 2	9/10	1/ 1	32/ 35
ST31				1/1	7/ 9	1/ 1		4/ 4	4/ 8	17/ 23
ST33							1/ 1	1/ 1		2/ 2
ST70					4/ 4			1/ 2	1/ 1	6/ 7
TO					4/ 4			1/ 1	2/ 2	7/ 7
TH								1/ 1		1/ 1
LE					1/ 1					1/ 1
LI2					1/ 4					1/ 4
PM	1/1	1/1	1/1		9/ 9	14/14	22/25	22/22	26/34	96/ 107
SP3					1/ 1			1/ 1	1/ 1	3/ 3
LY4					5/ 5		1/ 1	2/ 5	2/ 2	10/ 13
OS1									1/ 1	1/ 1
OS2							1/ 1	1/1		2/ 2
OS3							1/ 1			1/ 1
Medieval										
LY3						1/ 1				1/ 1
CC1						1/ 1	6/ 9	1/ 1	3/ 6	11/ 17
CC2							10/14	1/ 1		11/ 15
NO3						1/ 1	1/ 1		3/ 5	5/ 7
LI3							1/ 1			1/ 1
MS1							1/ 1			1/ 1
MS2							2/ 4		1/ 1	3/ 5
MS3							10/10		1/ 1	11/ 11
Late Medieval										
MP1							7/ 9		1/ 1	8/ 10
MP2							5/ 6	2/20	1/ 1	8/ 27
CW2								8/19	2/ 4	10/ 23
Post Medieval										
MY								1/ 1	1/ 1	2/ 2
EA1									1/ 1	1/ 1
EA2									5/ 5	5/ 5
EA6									1/ 7	1/ 7
EA								1/ 1		1/ 1
Totals	1/1	1/1	1/1	1/1	54/61	18/18	71/86	60/94	59/84	266/347

Table 18: Site 3 - minimum vessel numbers/sherd numbers by Phase.

Fabric	Phase							
	3B	3C	4A	4B	4C	5A	5B	6(mod)	Totals
Late Saxon/ Early Medieval									
ST20						1/ 1			1/ 1
ST23	1/ 1					3/ 18		1/ 5	5/ 24
ST30					3/ 4	1/ 1			4/ 5
ST31				1/ 1		2/ 8		0/ 1	3/ 10
ST70						1/ 1	1/ 1	1/ 1	3/ 3
ST71					1/ 2				1/ 2
ST72					1/ 1				1/ 1
TO				3/ 3	1/ 1	1/ 1			5/ 5
TH				1/ 1					1/ 1
PM		5/ 5	13/47	15/15	20/25	40/ 83	19/29	22/37	134/241
SP1							1/ 1		1/ 1
SP3		1/ 1			3/ 3	6/ 14		5/ 5	15/ 23
LY4					4/ 4	7/ 13	1/ 1	5/ 6	17/ 24
Medieval									
LY3					1/ 1				1/ 1
CC1						5/ 6	4/ 4	3/ 3	12/13
CC2						3/ 3	18/62	3/ 4	24/69
NO2				1/ 1					1/ 1
NO3						1/ 2			1/ 2
MS1						1/ 2		1/ 1	2/ 3
MS2							1/ 1		1/ 1
Late Medieval									
CW2								1/ 1	1/ 1
Post Medieval									
MY							1/ 1		1/ 1
EA2								1/ 1	1/ 1
EA7								1/ 1	1/ 1
EA9							1/ 1		1/ 1
SW5								1/ 1	1/ 1
Totals	1/ 1	6/ 6	13/47	21/21	34/41	72/153	47/101	45/67	239/437

Table 19: Site 5 - minimum vessel numbers/sherd numbers by Phase.

Fabric	Phase						
	3C	6A	6B	6C	6D	U/S	Totals
Saxon							
SX		5/ 5		1/ 1			6/6
Late Saxon/Early Medieval							
ST21			3/ 3	1/ 1	2/ 2		6/ 6
ST30		2/ 2				2/ 2	4/ 4
ST31	1/ 1	6/ 14	1/ 1	7/14	18/28	2/ 2	35/ 60
ST32		2/ 3		0/ 1	0/ 8		2/ 12
ST35		1/ 1		0/ 5	0/ 4		1/ 10
ST36		3/4					3/ 4
ST70		2/2					2/ 2
ST71					1/ 1		1/ 1
TO		4/4				1/ 1	5/ 5
PM	1/1	28/40	5/ 5	22/30	14/17	19/26	89/119
SP2		3/ 3					3/ 3
SP3		17/23	1/ 1	4/ 4	4/ 7	4/ 5	30/ 40
LY4		2/ 2	6/ 6	5/ 5	1/ 1	4/ 5	18/ 19
OS2		1/ 1					1/ 1
OS3						1/ 1	1/ 1
Medieval							
CC1				2/ 2		1/ 1	3/ 3
CC2					1/ 1		1/ 1
NO3		1/ 1				2/ 2	3/ 3
MS3					1/ 1		1/ 1
Late Medieval							
MP1						2/ 7	2/ 7
MP2					2/ 5		2/ 5
CW2						3/ 4	3/ 4
Post Medieval							
MY			1/ 1		1/ 1		2/ 2
EA2			1/ 2				1/ 2
EA6						1/ 1	1/ 1
EA8						1/ 1	1/ 1
EA		3/ 3					3/ 3
SW5						4/39	4/ 39
Totals	2/ 2	80/108	18/19	42/63	45/76	47/97	234/365

Table 20: Site 6 - minimum vessel numbers/sherd numbers by Phase.

Fabric	Phase							
	1D	2C	3A	8A	8D	8E	U/S	Totals
Late Saxon/Early Medieval								
ST23				1/ 1	1/ 1			2/ 2
ST30						1/ 1		1/ 1
ST31			1/ 1			2/ 2		3/ 3
PM	1/ 1	4/ 5		5/ 7		16/16	1/ 3	27/ 32
SP3							1/ 1	1/ 1
LY4						2/ 3		2/ 3
OS1			1/ 1					1/ 1
Medieval								
CC1		1/ 2			1/ 1	2/ 2		4/ 5
CC2						5/ 5	1/ 1	6/ 6
NO3		2/ 3					1/ 1	3/ 4
MS1				1/ 1		2/ 3		3/ 4
MS2					3/ 3			3/3
MS3					1/ 1	1/ 1		2/ 2
Late Medieval								
MP1						1/ 1		1/ 1
MP2			1/ 1		6/21	9/27		16/ 49
TG					3/ 3			3/ 3
CW2					6/ 7	8/15	1/ 1	15/ 23
Post Medieval								
EA2						1/ 1		1/ 1
FR						1/ 2		1/ 2
SW5							1/ 1	1/ 1
Totals	1/1	7/10	3/3	7/9	21/37	51/79	6/ 8	96/147

Table 21: Site 7 - minimum vessel numbers/sherd numbers by Phase.

Fabric	Phase		
	4	U/S	Totals
Late Saxon/Early Medieval			
ST31		1/ 1	1/ 1
PM		2/ 2	2/ 2
Medieval			
CC1	1/ 1		1/ 1
Late Medieval			
MP2	1/ 1	1/ 1	2/ 2
CW2	1/ 1		1/ 1
Post Medieval			
MY	4/ 4		4/ 4
EA2	1/ 1	1/ 1	2/ 2
EA3	2/ 2		2/ 2
EA7		1/ 1	1/ 1
SW4		1/ 1	1/ 1
SW5	1/ 1		1/ 1
Totals	11/11	7/ 7	18/18

Table 22: All Sites Minimum vessel numbers and sherd numbers by form

Form (Fabric ST:- Kilmurry forms 2,3,4/5 and 11 = cp/stj; 1,12/13 = bowl; 6/24 = jug; 24 = tubular spouted pitcher).

Fabric	cp/stj	stj	bowl	cauldron	dripping dish	spouted pitcher	jug	tubular spouted pitcher	bottle	cisten	jar	dish	cup	mug	posset pot	costrel	chamber pot	candlestick	vtu	Totals
Saxon																				
SX																			6/6	6/6
Late Saxon/Early Medieval																				
ST2			1/11				3/12												15/15	19/38
ST3	15/21		2/2			1/1	8/33	3/19											80/95	109/17
ST7	3/3		2/3																9/10	14/16
LI2																			1/4	1/4
TO	2/2		2/2																13/13	17/17
TH	1/1																		1/1	2/2
LE																			1/1	1/1
PM	87/133	2/2	8/11		1/1		31/44												238/335	367/52
SP1																			1/1	1/1
SP2							2/2												1/1	3/3
SP3	5/5			1/1			7/7												37/55	50/68
LY4	17/20		4/4				5/6												21/29	47/59
OS1																			2/2	2/2
OS2																			3/3	3/3
OS3	1/1																		1/1	2/2
Medieval																				
LY3																			2/2	2/2
CC1			1/1		1/1		11/17												18/20	31/39
CC2	1/1		10/49				7/9												24/32	42/91
NO2																			1/1	1/1
NO3							7/11												6/6	13/17
LI3																			1/1	1/1
MS1							2/4												4/4	6/8
MS2							3/5												4/4	7/9
MS3			6/6				1/1												7/7	14/14
Late Medieval																				
MP1							2/7												9/11	11/18
MP2							1/1			5/29									22/53	28/83
TG													2/2						2/2	4/4
CW2							1/8						5/10		1/2	1/7			22/25	30/52
Post Medieval																				
MY																		1/1	8/8	9/9
EA1-3																				
EA6-9			3/3								1/1	2/2	1/7	2/2			1/1		13/14	23/30
EA																				
FR							1/2													1/2
SW4																			1/1	1/1
SW5			1/1						1/10										5/31	7/42
Totals	132/187	2/2	40/93	1/1	2/2	1/1	92/169	3/19	1/10	5/29	1/1	2/2	8/19	2/2	1/2	1/7	1/1	1/1	579/794	875/134

Table 23: All sites - Stamford ware - the occurrence of Kilmurry vessel forms

Site	Context	Phase	Fabric	Cooking Wares						Table Wares		Illus No.
				2	3	4/5	11	1	12/13	5	6/24	
2	F35	6A	ST31			4/5.41						
2	F40	6A	ST31			4/5						
2	F41	6A	ST30			4/5.41			12/13.13			
2	F4	6B	ST31								6/24	
2	F36	6C	ST30		3.12							
2	F39	6D	ST30		3.12	4/5.46						
2	F90	6D	ST30		3.27							
2	u/s		ST30			4/5.64						
2	u/s		ST31								6/24	
3	F1	3B	ST23								6/24	
3	F28	4C	ST30			4/5.41				5.38		
3	F28	4C	ST30			4/5						69.20
3	F28	4C	ST71					1.57				
3	F16	5A	ST23					1.53			6.17	
3	F16	5A	ST23								6/24	
3	V 3	5B	ST70						12/13.21			
3	I 1	6	ST70	2.12								
5	IV 1	6A	ST30					1.54				
5	IV 1	6A	ST36		3.12							
5	IV 1	6A	ST70		3.31		11.06					
5	F27	6A	ST31								6/24	
5	F27	6A	ST32								24.08	
5	F27	6A	ST32								6/24	
5	F27	6A	ST35								24.02	
5	F27	6A	ST36								6.19	
5	F101	6A	ST31								6/24	
5	F22	6C	ST31								6/24	
5	F17	6D	ST31				11.07					
5	F23	6D	ST31								24	
5	u/s		ST30			4/5						71.36
5	u/s		ST30			4.13						
6	I 32	3A	ST31	2/8								71.39
7	u/s		ST31								6.13	
Totals (vessel nos.)				2	5	9	2	3	2	1	14	

Table 24: All sites - the occurrence of Potters Marston ware forms by minimum vessel numbers

			cp/stj							stj	dri	bowl		jug			
Site	Context/Phase		2	3	4	6	7	8	u/c			1	2	1	2	3	u/c
1	F2	9A			1												
2	F3	6A		1													
2	F43	6A			1												
2	F4	6B														1	
2	F2,36	6C		3	1			1					1	1	1		
2	F39,90	6D		1	2							1					
2	u/s			4					1			1	1		2		2
3	IV 5	3C				1											
3	I 19	4A			1				1								
3	III 3	4B	1	1	1	1	1										
3	II 2	4B							1								
3	F8	4C			1												
3	F9	4C				1									1		
3	F28	4C			5	1											
3	F39	4C				1											1
3	F2	5A			1			1	1								
3	F16	5A						1									2
3	F42	5A					1										
3	V 3	5B										1					4
3	I 1	5B												1			
3	IV 1	6					1	1									1
3	I 8	6										1					
5	F64	3C		1													
5	IV 1	6A		1	2	1				2							4
5	F27	6A			2												
5	F6	6B		1	3												
5	F21	6B		1													
5	F2,9,11	6C		7	1	5	2				1		1		2		1
5	F4,18,23	6D		4	1	4						1			1		2
5	u/s				1	1		3									2
6	L37	2C			1												
6	F1,7	8E			1		1										2
7	u/s			2													
Totals			1	27	26	16	6	7	4	2	1	5	3	2	7	1	21

u/c - unclassified

Illus. Number	Fabric	Pot Number	
Site 5			
Phase 6C - F25			
Fig.70			
1	SX	2144	vtu, body sherd, burnished with incised decoration on the exterior.
Site 1			
Phase 9A - F2			
2	PM	1512	cp/stj form 4, rim top sooted on exterior.
Site 2			
Phase 6Ai - F3			
3	PM	2056	cp/stj form 3
Phase 6Ai - F44			
4	LY4	2095	jug
Phase 6Aii - F40			
5	TO	2086	socketed/spouted bowl
Phase 6Aii - F41			
6	PM	2093	cp/stj form 4, or cauldron/spouted pitcher? Distortion on rim suggests possibly near a handle.
Phase 6Aii - F38			
7	LY4	2082	cp/stj, sooted exterior rim
Phase 6B - F4			
8	PM	2148	jug form 3
Phase 6D - F90			
9	MP2	2145	cistern with pouring lip, no evidence for/against handles, glazed interior base
10	CW2	2128	three handled cup with belled rim, glazed
u/s			
11	TO	2200	cp/stj
12	PM	2185	jug
13	LY4	2198	bowl, sooted in patches, rim top and ext
Site 3			
Phase 4B - III 3			
14	TO	958	cp/stj
15	TH	960	cp/stj
16	PM	963	cp/stj form 2
17	PM	979	cp/stj form 3
18	PM	962	cp/stj form 6, sooted exterior rim
19	PM	964	cp/stj form 7
Phase 4C - F28			
20	ST30	984	cp/stj or spouted pitcher, Kilmurry form 4/5, or possibly a jug form 6
Phase 4C - F8			
21	PM	973	cp/stj form 4
Phase 4C - F9			
22	PM	978	jug form 2
23	LY4	980	cp/stj
Phase 4C - F39			
24	LY4	972	cp/stj, irregular thumbing and sooting on exterior
Fig. 71			
Phase 4C - F28			
25	LY4	992	bowl
Phase 6 - I 8			
26	PM	1056	bowl form 1

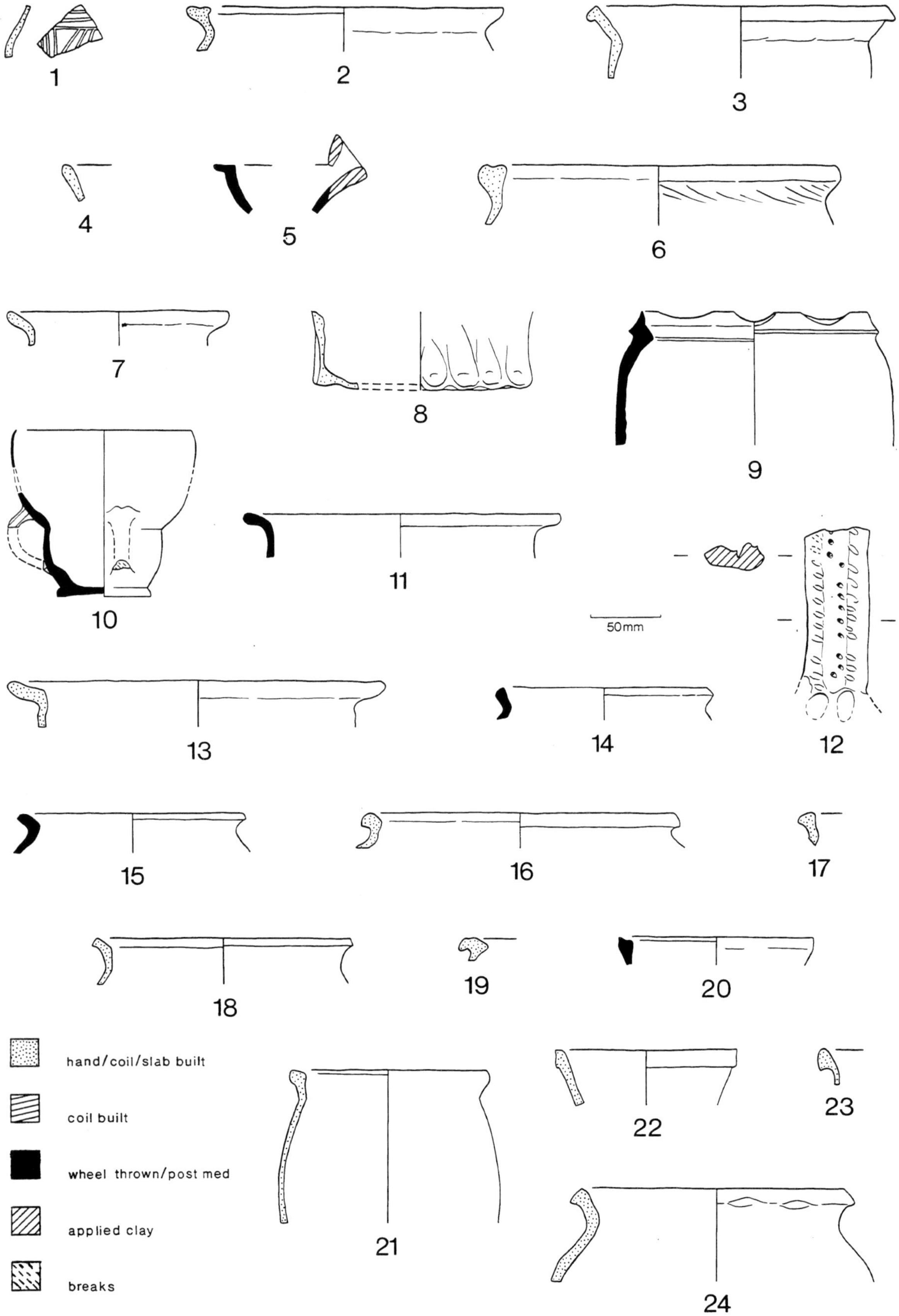

 Fig 70 Post Roman Pottery Site 5 (1); Site 1 (2); Site 2 (3-13); Site 3 (14-24) Scale 1:4

Site 5			
Phase 6A - F101			
27	ST31	102	jug/tubular spouted pitcher handle, Kilmurry form 6/24
Phase 6A - IV 1			
28	SP3	2069	cp/stj or cauldron
Phase 6A - F27			
29	SP3	2089	jug, glazed
Phase 6C - F9			
30	PM	2120	bowl, form 2
Phase 6C - F2			
31	SP3	2113	jug, glazed exterior
32	LY4	2115	cp/stj
Phase 6C - F25			
33	LY4	2143	bowl
Phase 6D - F4			
34	SP3	2159	jug
Phase 6D - F18			
35	PM	2147	bowl form 2, sooted interior and rim top
u/s			
36	ST30	2184	cp/stj or spouted pitcher Kilmurry form 4/5? Sooted exterior and rim top
37	TO	2158	bowl
38	OS3	2191	cp/stj
Site 6			
Phase 3A - 32			
39	ST30	748	cp/stj Kilmurry form 2/8?
Phase 8B - 62			
40	CW2	726	costrel, glazed exterior wall
Phase 8E - F7			
41	PM	740	jug
42	LY4	741	cp/stj
u/s			
43	LY4	753	jug
Site 7			
Phase 4 - I 1			
44	MY	6	candlestick or salt/savory dish, glazed
Phase 4 - II 1			
45	EA2	10	chamber pot?, glazed
46	EA3	9	mug, glazed interior and exterior wall
u/s			
47	EA2	2	bowl, glazed
Site 10			
u/s			
48	NO3	1	tubular spouted pitcher, glazed handle top

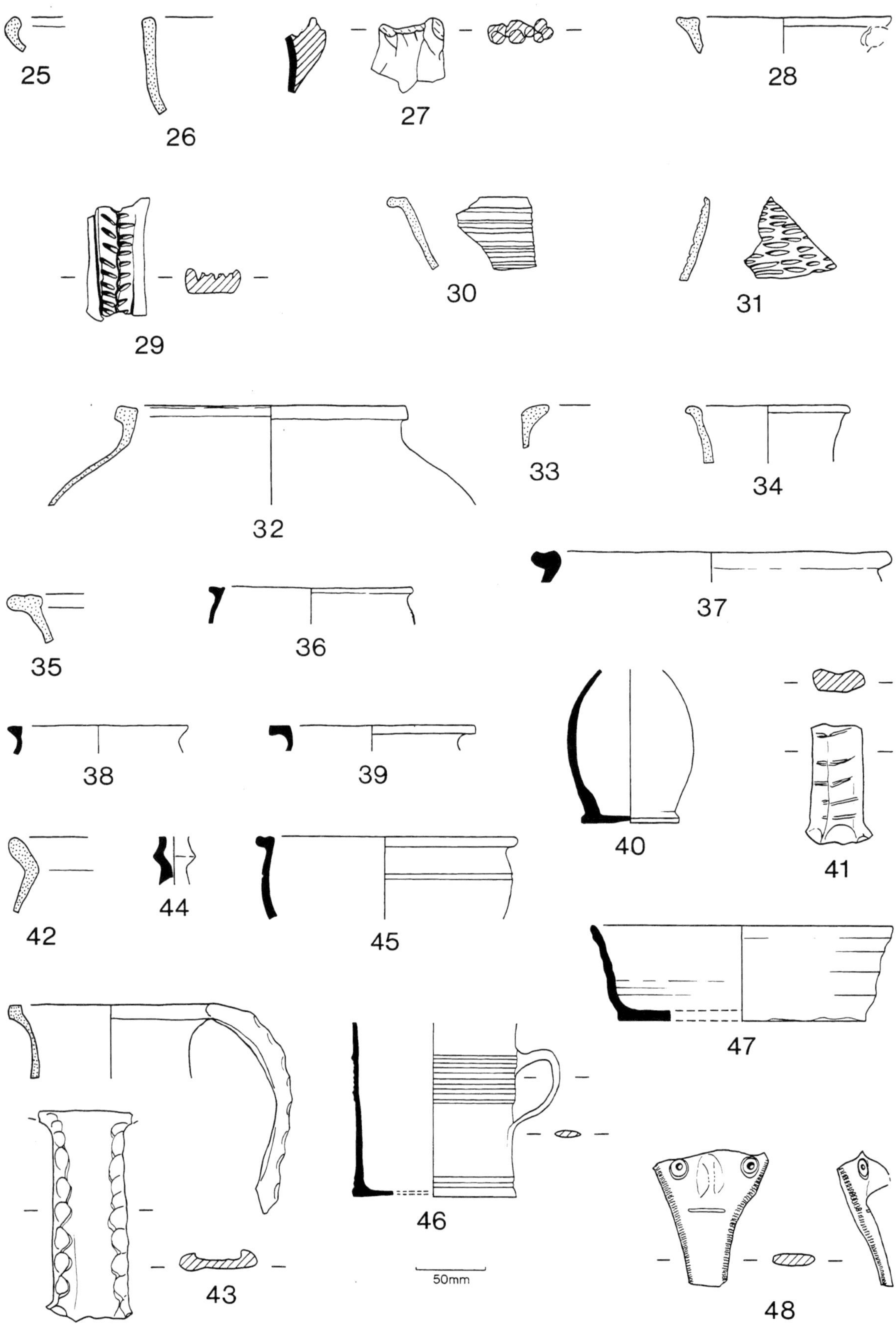

 Fig 71 Post Roman Pottery Site 3 (25-26); Site 5 (27-38); Site 6 (39-43); Site 7 (44-47); Site 10 (48) Scale 1:4

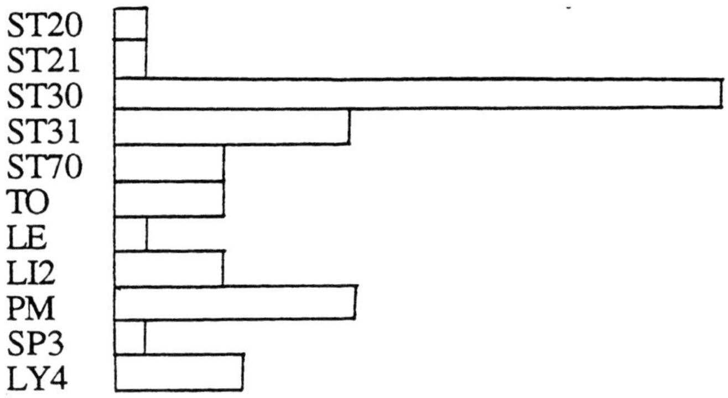

Total - 61 sherds

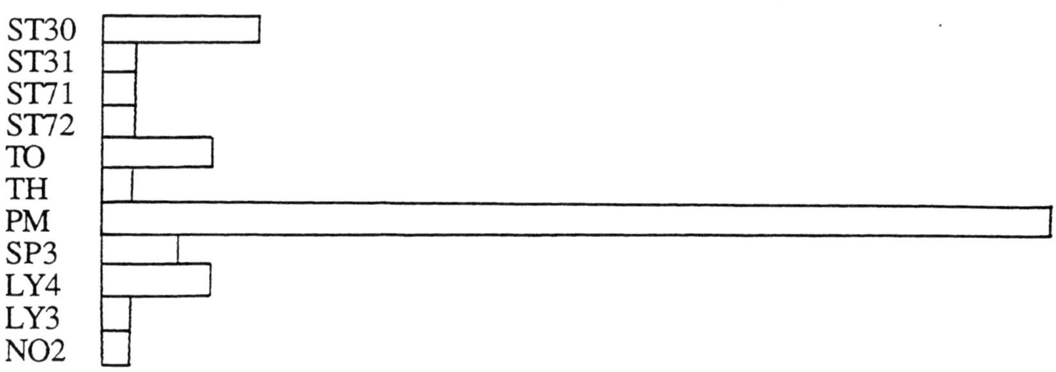

Total - 62 sherds

Fig. 72 The relative proportions of fabrics present by sherd numbers.
Top: Site 2 Phase 6A - Late Saxon/early medieval
Bottom: Site 3 Phases 4B and 4C - early medieval

Medieval Ridge Tile *Richard Buckley*

Only 32 fragments, weighing 1.61 kg, of medieval ceramic roofing furniture were recovered from the group of sites under consideration. All were from ridge tiles, with the exception of two unclassified fragments from Site 3. None of the tile was definitely associated with medieval structures and the fabric range present is fairly typical for excavations of medieval sites in the Leicester area. The crests have been classified according to the typology proposed by Allin (1981, 56-62).

Table 25 Medieval Ridge Tile

Site	Phase	Context	Fabric	Type	Crest	Frags	Weight(g)
2	6A	F40(II 7)	MS2	RT	-	1	15
	6B	F4 (I 5)	SP3	RT	-	1	20
	"	F90(II 15)	PM	RT	-	1	60
	"	"	CC1	RT	-	1	20
	6C	F2 (I 3)	SP3	RT	-	1	25
	"	"	CC1	RT	V	2	65
	"	"	CC2	RT	-	1	10
	"	F2 (I 7)	CC1	RT	-	1	45
	6D	F39(II 6)	CC1	RT	-	1	20
	u/s	-(III u/s)	CC1	RT	-	2	170
3	5A	F16(III 5)	PM	RT	-	1	75
	5B	- (I 2)	PM	RT	-	2	75
	"	"	u/c	u/c	-	1	35
	"	(V 3)	PM	RT	-	1	40
	"	"	u/c	u/c	-	1	100
	MOD	"(I 1)	CC1	RT	-	1	95
	"	"	SP3	RT	-	1	35
	"	(III 2)	CC2	RT	-	1	25
5	3C	- (V 4)	CC2	RT	-	1	20
	5A	- (IV 1)	CC1	RT	-	1	15
	u/s	u/s	CC2	RT	VI	2	140
6	8D	F3 (66)	MS2	RT	-	2	45
	8E	- (187)	MS2	RT	-	1	50
	8E	F1 (62)	CC2	RT	VII	1	270
	u/s	u/s	CC1	RT	-	1	90
	"	"	CC5	RT	-	1	25
	"	"	SP3	RT	-	1	25
				TOTAL		32	1.610kg

Abbreviations:

(fabrics)	SP3	Splashed ware 3
	CC1	Chilvers Coton ware 1
	CC2	Chilvers Coton ware 2
	CC5	Chilvers Coton ware 5 (Mayes and Scott 1984 (fabric B))
	MS2	Medieval Sandy ware 2
	PM	Potters Marston
	u/c	Unclassified
(type)	RT	Ridge tile
	u/c	Unclassified
(Crest)	V	Type V, looped (Allin 1981,59)
	VI	Type VI, pinnacle (*ibid.* 59)
	VII	Type VII, spiked knob (*ibid.* 62)

The Celtic Coins

Andrew P. Fitzpatrick

Two Celtic coins were recovered, one each from the Redcross Street (Site 5) and Peacock Pavement (Site 1) excavations.

1. South Ferriby Type - Allen (1963a) ZA/Mack455/van Arsdell 879-1 'Half' denomination.
   Obv: Blank.
   Rev: Horse to right with a rosette of pellets enclosing a larger pellet above.
   Weight: 0.41 gm.
   Site 5 Phase 1A (1040) IV. 24.

2 Obv: cp. Mack 464/van Arsdell 950-1.
   Rev: Mack 456/cp. van Arsdell 889-7.
   Weight: 0.47 gm.
   Site 1 Phase 4A (35) F63 V. 21.

The obverse of this coin is comparable to a rare silver unit apparently inscribed VEP CO (Allen 1963a, no. 396, Pl. VIII, 396; 396A, illus. on p. 39). On the present example the horse is apparently not to the right as on most other VEP CO coins but to the left. In this and also typologically, the horse is comparable to Allen's South Ferriby ZB 'half' denomination (*ibid* nos. 361-73; Mack 456; van Arsdell 889-7). The legend on the obverse of the two coins published by Allen is uncertain and it is illegible on the present example but the design is related to those on gold and silver coins inscribed VEP CORF (Mack 459-60) (Mossop 1968) so the reading seems plausible, although it should be remembered that one of the coins in this group is inscribed VEPOC COMES or OMES (May 1976, 199; van Arsdell 1989, 252-3).

It should also be noted, however, that the best parallels for the design are on coins inscribed VOLISIOS DUMNOCOVEROS (Mack 463) and VOLISIOS DUMNVOLLAU[NOS] (Mack 466).

These two coins bring the total of Celtic coins provenanced as being from or 'near to' Leicester to 13 (below), six of which were found in the Jewry Wall excavations (only four are presently in the Leicestershire Museums Collection; Nos. 2, 7, 9 and 11 below). Six of the Leicester coins certainly belong to the north-eastern British or 'Corieltauvian' series (nos. 1-6). It is possible that one of the other coins, a silver one (no. 12) whose identification is uncertain may also have been a Corieltauvian issue.

Before examining the significance of these coins to the origin and status of Iron Age Leicester it is necessary to consider their dating and the reliability of the provenances of some of the coins.

The Chronology of the Celtic Coins from Leicester.

On presently accepted chronology, the earliest of the coins is a Gaulish piece, the Gallo-Belgic E gold stater (no. 10) although the reliability of its 'Leicester' provenance is far from certain. These coins were issued in north-east France and Scheers has argued convincingly that the bulk of them were issued by the Belgic confederacy during Caesar's Gallic Wars (1972: 1977, 65-8). A statistical study of the dies used to strike the coins has shown clearly the prodigious size the issue (Haselgrove 1984, 87-94). Because of the Caesarian date of the coins most commentators interpret those found in Britain as representing the payment of British allies and mercenaries.

The earliest British coins (Allen's British A and B (Allen 1960)) derive typologically from the predecessor of Gallo-Belgic E, the Gallo-Belgic C. In considering the date of these British coins, Kent has attempted to resolve the apparently contradictory evidence of an early type (Gallo-Belgic C) being chosen for the prototype for British A and B with their weight range, which is appropriate to a later type (Gallo-Belgic E). Kent suggests that the majority of the Gallo-Belgic coins in Britain arrived at the same time, that is during the Gallic Wars. The various types of Gallo-Belgic gold coins are associated in hoards in Britain and this might seem to support Kent's argument (1978a; 1978b). In Belgic Gaul, however, the different types are not found together in hoards and this suggests that the circulation of the coins in Britain and continental Europe differed. The earlier Gallo-Belgic A and C coins may have arrived in Britain at the time of their issue and they may then have continued to circulate until the 50s B.C. In continental Europe by contrast, the coins were recoined to make the later types. This would also help to account for the worn state of Gallo-Belgic A and C in Britain noted by Kent. It should also be remembered that despite Scheers' confidence, the first Gallo-Belgic E coins may have been struck rather earlier than 57 B.C. (cf. Haselgrove 1984) so the similarity in weight between British coins and Gallo-Belgic E does not *prove* a date in the Gallic Wars.

It should also be borne in mind that Scheers' chronology for the coinage of Belgic Gaul is itself based on a chronology which attempts to correlate historical and numismatic evidence and which dates most coins to after c. 120 B.C. Recent archaeological work in central Europe, notably by Polenz (1982) has demonstrated beyond reasonable doubt that this chronology is incorrect and that a much longer history is likely. The full implications for the coinage of Belgic Gaul of Polenz's research have not yet been appreciated but the possibility is raised that some of the major British regional series started as early as the beginning of the 1st century B.C.: much as Allen argued in 1960.

Certainty is elusive but the earliest Corieltauvian coins (Allen's Corieltauvian 'Prototypes' (1963a, 9-10) or British H (1960, 107-8)) which derive from the later varieties need not necessarily be dated to the Gallic Wars or their aftermath. Haselgrove (1987, 264, Tab A2:7) has suggested that British H and I have a more subtle and complex relationship with both Gallo-Belgic C and south-eastern British issues than is generally appreciated, with the British issue called HA by Allen (1960) providing the prototype for the north-eastern H and I issues (Haselgrove 1987, 87, 264). British I may take both features and metrology from Gallo-Belgic E and perhaps also features from other south-eastern (Kentish?) coins (*ibid*). Van Arsdell sets the origin of the Corieltauvian series about 70 B.C., suggesting that they derive directly from Gallo-Belgic C and that they were replaced by British I during the Gallic Wars (1987, 215, his 'North East Coast' and 'Reduced Weight' types). In contrast Nash dates British H and I to the Gallic Wars (1989, 124).

Possibly contemporary with, but probably slightly later than, these staters are silver coins which are quite different typologically, having a boar on the obverse (Allen 1963a, 10). Because of these differences it is difficult to associate them with the gold coins. It has been suggested by van

Arsdell (1985) that the obverse of the earliest of the silver coins copies the boar on a Republican coin of C. Hosidius C. f. Geta in the 60s B.C., thus providing a *terminus post quem* for the series. Even if this is correct, and it is debatable, it is not particularly helpful as a number of British Celtic coins imitate Republican coins which must have been several decades old when they were copied (Scheers 1982; Haselgrove 1987, 92-4, Fig 5:5). Van Arsdell suggests that the silver coins are the counterpart to British I (his 'Reduced Weight' type (1989, 236)).

The second phase of Corieltauvian coinage is represented by Allen's (1963a) South Ferriby types named after the hoard discovered there (Allen 1963b). Two of these uninscribed silver coins have been found in Leicester (no. 3 = South Ferriby U and no. 4 = South Ferriby ZA). Contemporary with them is the "Whorl" type/South Ferriby L gold stater (Allen 1963a) (no. 1) but this was found c 2.5km to the south-west of the known late Iron Age settlement and so may be of little relevance here. A silver coin first described as 'Gaulish' (no. 7) is also probably contemporary with the South Ferriby types.

These coins are followed at Leicester by the inscribed, third phase, issues of AVN AST or COST (No. 5) and VEP CORF? (no. 6, both silver) which probably date from the last 25 years B.C. onwards.

A fourth and final phase 4 includes the issue of VOLISIOS DUMNOVELLAV[NOS] (no. 2 gold plated) which may date to the Roman conquest period (May 1987, 70; van Arsdell 1989, 247, 263).

Contemporary with these phase 3 and 4 coins is the bronze coin of Eppillus (no. 9), which was probably issued in Kent. THE GERMANVS INDITVLLI L coin (no. 11) may also be grouped with these inscribed issues. These coins imitate a Quadrans of Augustus issued at Lyon and probably date to the last two decades B.C., although where they were struck remains uncertain (Scheers 1977, 180-1; Castelin 1985, 115-16). Six other of these coins have been found in Britain; three from Colchester-Sheepen (not one *contra* Scheers 1977, 821) and singletons from Canterbury, Lancing Down (Sussex) (Hoard) and Silchester (Allen 1960, 278). The AVN AST or COST and VEP CORF? coins lie at the beginning of these third phase issues (May 1976, 199). Reservations have been expressed about the reliability of the identification of number 12 as a certainly or possibly Gaulish issue. If, however, the identification was correct then it is likely to have been broadly contemporary with the uninscribed second phase Corieltauvian coins. The gold coin of Tasciovanus (no. 8) is uncertainly provenanced and so of doubtful value but it belongs to the earliest phase of Tasciovanus' coins and probably dates to the last quarter of the 1st century B.C. (Fitzpatrick 1985, 59).

Discussion

As the number of Celtic coins from Leicester is so small and because of the possibility that the dates of the issue of the coin, its loss, and the archaeological context in which it is ultimately incorporated may vary appreciably, the evidence provided by the Leicester finds must be treated cautiously.

At present none of the Celtic coins from Leicester can be shown to have been found in a pre-Conquest context. In considering this subject May has argued that it is unreasonable to assume that most of the Corieltauvian coins from Lincolnshire are Roman losses, even though it is difficult to demonstrate this (1984, 18). While this may be true, it is noteworthy that the major period of loss/deposition at some late Iron Age and early Roman sites in Essex was in the early Roman period (Fitzpatrick 1985, 63), and it is also extremely difficult to identify Dobunnic coins from Iron Age contexts (Sellwood 1984a, 203). In part this may be due to circular arguments over the date of the coins and the date of the contexts, and the redeposition of coins will probably also have been a significant factor. Nonetheless it is possible that the introduction of Roman currency had a major effect on the value(s) and use(s) of Celtic coins (Reece 1979) and that the large number of Celtic coins from early Roman contexts does represent a change in their circulation. Despite this, even if the early Roman period was a time of major loss and/or deposition of Celtic coinage, it is still possible that it may be an accurate reflection of Iron Age coin circulation, if not loss (Haselgrove 1987, 204-8).

However, as May also points out, the proportions of uninscribed to inscribed Corieltauvian silver coins from many sites in the East Midlands are such as to suggest that the sites are not Roman foundations (May 1984, 18). If this were to have been the case it would be expected that the Celtic coins would be dominated by the later inscribed issues. To the contrary, the general trend is for uninscribed coins to outnumber inscribed coins by a ratio of between 3 and 2:1 on certain or probable major settlements of the later Iron Age in the East Midlands. This trend may not be entirely of chronological origin, however, and in part it may relate to the size of the issues for it is not known if Celtic coinage was issued regularly (Fitzpatrick 1985, 61). However, Whitwell observes that the third phase coins inscribed VEP CORF appear to be the largest issue (1982, 16).

With due reservation over the small number (6) of Corieltauvian coins from Leicester, which is well below the mean, and the uncertain relationship between the dates of issue and loss, the 1:1 ratio of uninscribed to inscribed coins and the presence of coins which were issued early in the third phase and also the non-Corieltauvian coins all point to the adoption of coinage in Leicester in the late 1st century B.C.

This dating is compatible with the dates of the earliest imported pottery from the Jewry Wall (Jarvis 1984-85; 1986) and the Bath Lane sites (Clay and Mellor 1985, 41-62). It is noticeable that the reliably provenanced and identified coins from Leicester nearly all (8 of 9) come from excavations which have produced early 1st century A.D. (and possibly in part late 1st century B.C.) pottery assemblages (*ibid*, Fig. 29). It is the limited opportunities to examine Iron Age deposits in these excavations which is the most likely explanation for the present small total of Celtic coins from Leicester. If the imported Iron Age pottery is considered, the number of vessels represented is small but the variety of types and sources represented is noteworthy and as they comprise c 16% of the maximum [sic] number of vessels present at Bath Lane (*op cit*, Tab. 1-2), this is probably of some significance.

It should be recognised, however, that the so-called Iron Age 'coin-moulds' may have little to do with the issuing of coins rather than with alloying (cf. May 1984, 21: Collis 1985). Thus the 'coin-mould' fragments from Leicester (Clay and Mellor 1985, 69-70, Fig. 39, 18-20) need not be taken to indicate that coins were issued there. Equally, the discovery of large quantities of 'coin-moulds' at Old Sleaford (Jones *et al* 1976) but only a handful of Celtic coins (cf. also Brown and Simmons 1984-85), indicates that there is no direct correlation between 'coin-moulds' and coin finds. As it is still not known if the issuing of Corieltauvian coins was under centralised control - none of the coins appear to have the names of mints as some of the south-eastern ones do - the expectation that the issue of coins was appropriate to a capital may be misplaced (*contra* Allen 1963a, 37; Clay 1985, 31-2). However, the broad correlation in space and time of Celtic coins and the 'moulds' (Tournaire *et a*l 1982; Fischer 1983, 44, Abb. 1) is suggestive of a link and the recent discovery of what appears to be a mint at Villeneuve-Saint-Germain (Aisne) in northern France (Debord *et al* 1985) adds further support.

As is well known, the inscribed coins of the Corieltauvi bear two names and in one case, DVMNOC TIGIR SENO [sic], three (van Arsdell 1983; 1989, 260-1). Allen (1963a, 30) and Clay (1985, 31-2) both favour the interpretation of the names as those of magistrates responsible for different areas within the tribe's control but as May has observed it is questionable whether such a sophisticated administrative system existed amongst the Corieltauvi (May 1976, 200). The interpretation of the names as those of moneyers also seems unlikely (Allen 1963a, 29; cf. Sellwood 1984b, 410). Although Allen did not support the ideas (1963a, 29-30), other possibilities are that the names represent paramount and subordinate kings (cf. Nash 1982) or a 'dynastic' relationship of the kind known in south-eastern England (Fitzpatrick 1985, 59-62). In the latter hypothesis the Corieltauvian coins and also those of the Iceni inscribed CANS DVRO and ALE SCA (May 1976, 200) could state a sibling relationship in a distinctive eastern English form which contrasts with the use of *filius* in the south-eastern series. Kimes, Haselgrove and Hodder have suggested that the strength of the boundary discovered in their analysis of the distribution of Corieltauvian coins recorded in 1982 reflected the existence of a divided territory and that the two names on the inscribed coins are those of the joint rulers of this territory (1982, 123-4). However, the strength of the boundary notwithstanding, the location of the transects used in the analysis (*ibid*, Fig. 5) make it difficult to accept this interpretation. Instead the subsequent finds from Lincolnshire summarised by May (1984, 21-2) do suggest a continuous geographical distribution of the coins rather than a divided one, as Kimes, Haselgrove and Hodder themselves anticipated. Even so, it still remains possible that the names do represent a divided territory with joint rulers perhaps succeeding through inheritance. Elsewhere in Britain such a divided territory seems identifiable in the coins of the Dobunni (Sellwood 1984b, 411-13; 1986, 206, Pl.10). If the coins circulated in both parts of the territory or were manufactured in one place and distributed *en bloc* to other areas, a divided territory would not necessarily be recognisable in the distribution of the coins (cf. Collis 1971; 1981). A final possibility is that the names reflect a federation of the kind suggested elsewhere in Europe, for example in Noricum (Mackensen 1975, 268-9; cf. Nash 1987, 141).

Conclusion

At present, while the Celtic coins from Leicester are compatible with the earliest imported pottery in suggesting that occupation may have started by the last 10 or 20 years B.C., they do not provide proof. At the same time the nature of the evidence provided by the so-called 'coin-moulds' and the inscriptions on coins does not provide decisive evidence that Leicester was either a mint or a capital of the Corieltauvi in the Iron Age. It is important, however, to bear in mind the limited nature of the exploration of Iron Age Leicester which has so far been possible. Because of this the numbers of coins and also imported pottery vessels is small but their variety is suggestive and they combine to hint that such a development and status for Iron Age Leicester seems likely.

Acknowledgements

I should like to thank Bob Rutland for his help with the coins held in the Jewry Wall Museum and Colin Haselgrove for his comments on an earlier draft of the text.

Celtic Coins from Leicester.

1. Corieltauvi

Gold

a) Uninscribed

1.Type:	'Whorl' type stater/South Ferriby L (Allen 1963a)/British KA (Allen 1960)/Mack 448/van Arsdell 829.
Weight:	81.9 gr. 5.32 gm.
Findspot:	88 Waltham Avenue, Leicester, around 1940.
Reference:	Allen 1963a, 15, PL. VI, 224; Gunstone 1971, Pl. II, 53.

b) Inscribed

2. Type:	Mack 466, VOLISIOS/DVMNOVELLAV[NOS]. Gold plated with bronze core 'stater'/van Arsdell 988-1.
Weight:	60.8 gr. 3.96 gm (This corrects that given in Gunstone 1971).
Findspot:	Jewry Wall, levels disturbed by the building of the baths.
Reference:	Kenyon 1948, 279; Allen 1963a, 19, PL. VIII, 430; Gunstone 1971, Pl. II, 61: Jewry Wall Archive No. 705.

Silver

a) Uninscribed

3.Type:	South Ferriby Type U (Allen 1963a)/Mack 410a?/van Arsdell 875-1 'Full' denomination.
Weight:	21.6 gr. 1.4 gm
Findspot:	Bath Lane excavation.
Reference:	Allen 1963a, 16, 39, no. 304A: Clay and Mellor 1985, 62; Gunstone 1971, Pl. II, 57; Haselgrove 1978, 104.

4. Type:	South Ferriby ZA (Allen 1963a)/Mack 455/van Arsdell 879-1. 'Half' denomination.
Weight:	0.41 gm.
Findspot:	Redcross Street excavation.
Reference:	p 131. no.1 above

b) Inscribed

5. Type:	Mack 458 var?, AVN (AST or COST), van Arsdell 914-1 or possibly South Ferriby ZB (cf. Allen 1963a, Pl. VIII). 'Half' denomination.
Weight:	Not known.
Findspot:	Jewry Wall, excavation.
Reference:	Kenyon 1948, 279. Probably the same coin as Allen 1963a, 17, no. 378; Gunstone 1971, Pl. II, 59; The coin is not in the Leicestershire Museums collections but can be correlated with the silver coin of the Brigantes mentioned in the Jewry Wall report (Kenyon 1948, 279).

6. Type:	Obv. cp. Mack 464; van Arsdell 950-1, Rev. Mack 456 cp. van Arsdell 889-7 (VEP CORF?).
Weight:	0.47 gm.
Findspot:	Peacock Pavement excavation.
Reference:	p 131. no.2 above

II. Other British Coins

Gold

7. Type:	Mack 437/van Arsdell 1552-1.
Weight:	15.71 gr. 1.02 gm.
Findspot:	Jewry Wall, contemporary with the baths.
Reference:	Kirkman 1940, 24; Kenyon 1948, 24, 279; Jewry Wall Archive No. 373.

Described as being a 'Galloping Horse with three dot-in-circle symbols in field' by Kirkman (1940, 24) but only as 'Gallic Silver' in the Jewry Wall report (Kenyon 1948, 279). The piece is a Mack 437 but is typologically more advanced than the Mack type specimen and is similar to some Central Gaulish coins (e.g. Nash 1978, 201-2, 216, Pl. 21, 512-14) which may explain why it was ascribed to Gaul by Kirkman. The Central Gaulish coins may have provided the prototype for the British coins. The present example appears to be gold-plated.

8. Type:	Mack 149-50, van Arsdell 1680-1, 1682-1. TASCIAV[ANVS].
Weight:	Not known.
Findspot:	'near Leicester'.
Reference:	Evans 1890, 535; Allen 1960, 223.

Bronze

9. Type:	Mack 311, van Arsdell 452-1, EPPI[LLVS].
Weight:	40.5 grm. 2.63 gm.
Findspot:	Jewry Wall, levels disturbed by the building of the baths.
Reference:	Kenyon 1948, 279; Gunstone 1971, Pl. II, 35; Allen 1960, 214; Jewry Wall Archive No. 704.

III. Gaulish Coins

Gold

10. Type:	Scheers (1977) Series 24/Gallo-Belgic E/Mack 27/van Arsdell 50-56.
Weight:	90.2 gr. 5.86 gm. (This corrects that given in Gunstone 1971), s.g. 13.26.
Findspot:	'Leicester'
Reference:	Gunstone 1971, Pl. I, 6; Haselgrove 1978, 18.

This coin was purchased, possibly at the same time as a stater of Philip of Macedon, and the reliability of its provenance is suspect.

Bronze

11. Type:	GERMANVS INDITVLLI L. Described as 'Gallo-Roman temp. Augustus' in the Jewry Wall report (Kenyon 1948, 279) but Kirkman correctly identified the coin as a Germanvs Inditulli issue (Scheers Series 216 (1977, 809-21, Pl XXVI, 739-42)).
Weight:	28.5 gr. 1.85gm.
Findspot:	Jewry Wall, Unstratified.
Reference:	Kirkman 1940, 24; Kenyon 1948, 36, 279; Jewry Wall Archive No. 687.

IV. Uncertain British or Gaulish Coins

Silver

12. Type:	Scheers Series 87 (1977)/De la Tour XXXIV, 8519 approx.
Weight:	Not known.
Findspot:	'Leicester'. Apparently found in the demolition of a cottage.
Reference:	Allen 1960, 277; Scheers 1977, 126-7, 555-6, Fig. 142, Pl. XV, 416-18. Not mentioned in Allen 1963a, 35-6.

V. Uncertain Coins

13. An 'uncertain' British coin is mentioned in the Jewry wall report (Kenyon 1948, 279). The coin is not in the Leicestershire Museums collections.

The Roman Coins

Richard Buckley

Site 1

1. Phase 9C (10) V 3 — Tetricus I

Obv:	[ ]TETR[ ]
Rev:	illegible
Antoninianus	AD 270-273
Axis:	-
Weight:	0.79g
Diameter:	17.0mm
Condition:	Very Worn

2. U/S (126) VI U/S — ?Radiate Copy

Obv:	? Radiate bust r.
Rev:	illegible
Antoninianus	c. AD 270+

Axis: -
Weight: 0.60g
Diameter: 12.0mm
Condition: Worn and corroded

Site 2

3. Phase 4B (17) F8 I 25 — Illegible
Weight: 5.29g
Diameter: 26.0mm
Condition: Very worn and corroded
Material: Copper alloy

4. Phase 4C (9) F1 I 16 — Vespasian
obv: [IMP CAES VESPA]S[IAN]AV[G COS VIII]PP
rev: Victory stg.l. holding shield inscribed SPQR. S.C.
As RIC 599 Rome AD 77-79
Axis: 225°
Weight: 9.03g
Diameter: 29.0mm
Condition: Worn and corroded

5. Phase 5 (70) F46 II 49 — Domitian
obv: CAESAR AVG F DOMITIANVS[C]OS V
rev: Spes dr. adv. l. holding up flower in r. hand, and lifting up dress with l. S.C.
As RIC 791a Lugdunum AD 77-78
Axis: 225°
Weight: 8.03g
Diameter: 26.0mm
Condition: Worn

6. Phase 5 (71) F46 II 50 — Vespasian
obv: IMP C[AESAR V]ESPASIAN[ ] Radiate bust r.
rev: A[EQVITAS] AVGVST S.C.
Dupondius as RIC 557a, 568, 580a AD 74-76
Axis: 180°
Weight: 9.20g
Diameter: 26.0mm
Condition: Worn

7. Phase 6A (87) F48 II 68 — Constantine I
obv: CONST[ANTINVS IVN NC] Radiate bust r.
rev: [BEATA TRANQVILLITAS] MM illegible
AD 321-323
Axis: 180°
Weight: 2.52g
Diameter: 18.0mm
Condition: Worn

8. Phase 6A (90) F48 II 72 — ?Antoninus Pius
obv: Laureate bust r.
rev: illegible
Sestertius AD 138-161
Axis: -
Weight: 22.44g
Diameter: 31.0mm
Condition: Very worn

9. Phase 6C (16) F36 II 3 — Tetricus I
obv: [ ]TETR[ICV]S P[F AVG] Radiate bust r.
rev: illegible
Antoninianus AD 270-273
Axis: -
Weight: 3.19g
Diameter: 18.0mm
Condition: Worn

Site 3

10. Phase 4B (12) WB III 3 — ?Carausius
obv: Radiate bust r.
rev: illegible
Antoninianus AD 286-293
Axis: -
Weight: 3.49g
Diameter: 22.0mm
Condition: very worn and corroded

11. U/S (14) WB IV 1 — Irregular Fel Temp Reparatio
obv: bust r.
rev: Fel Temp Reparatio, fallen horseman type *c.* AD 357-367
Axis: -
Weight: 0.65g
Diameter: 9.0mm
Condition: worn

Site 4

12. Medieval levels (21) F16 II 10 Irregular Fel Temp Reparatio
obv: illegible
rev: Fel Temp Reparatio, fallen horseman type *c.* AD 357-367
Axis: -
Weight: 0.61g
Diameter: 13.0mm
Condition: Very worn

13. Medieval levels (23) F22 IV 18 — Valentinian I, Valens or Gratian
obv: bust r.
rev: GLORIA NO[-VI SAECVLI]
AD 367-375
Axis: 180°
Weight: 2.37g
Diameter: 16.0mm
Condition: Very worn and corroded

14. Medieval levels (31) V 19 — Constantinopolis
obv: [CONSTAN-TINOPOLIS]
rev: Victory stg.l. on a prow, holding spear and shield [ ]PLG[ ]
As RIC 241 AD 330-331 Lugdunum
Axis: 180°
Weight: 1.24g
Diameter: 16.0mm
Condition: Worn and corroded

Site 5

15. Phase 3A (1331) V 7 — 1st-2nd Century
obv: bust r.
rev: illegible
As/Dupondius 1st-2nd Century
Axis: -
Weight: 7.31g
Diameter: 26.0mm
Condition: Very worn and corroded

16. Phase 3C (1307) I 13 — Domitian
obv: [ ]COS XI[ ] bust r.
rev: Figure standing
As AD 85
Axis: 225°
Weight: 7.80g

Diameter: 28.0mm
Condition: Very worn and corroded

17. Phase 6B (1305) F6 IV 30 Carausius
obv: IMP CARAVSIVS PF AV
rev: LAETITIA A[VG]
Laetitia Stg. l. holding wreath and javelin
Antoninianus AD 286-293 as RIC 882,836
Axis: 180°
Weight: 2.99g
Diameter: 21.0mm
Condition: Worn

18. Phase 6B (1304) F12 I 30 Antoninus Pius
obv: ANTONINVS AVG PI- VS PPTRPCOS III
rev: [ITALIA SC]
Sestertius RIC 746 Rome AD 140-144
Axis: 360°
Weight: 20.17g
Diameter: 33.0mm
Condition: Slightly worn

19. Phase 6B (1333) F21 VII 45 Maximinus II
obv: IMP MAXIMINVS PF AVG T | F
rev: GENIO - POP ROM PTR
RIC 845b Treveri AD 310-313
Axis: 360°
Weight: 3.45g
Diameter: 22.0mm
Condition: Slightly worn

20. Phase 6B (1332) F21 VII 45 Claudius II
obv: [DIVO CLAV]DIO
rev: CONSECR[ATIO]
Antoninianus RIC 261 Mediolanum AD 268-270
Axis: 135°
Weight: 1.88g
Diameter: 17.0mm
Condition: Worn

21. Phase 6B (1334) F21 VII 45 Tetricus I
obv: [IMP(C)TETR]ICVS P F AVG
rev: illegible
Antoninianus AD 270-273
Axis: -
Weight: 1.67g
Diameter: 17.0mm
Condition: Very worn

22. Phase 6C (1301) F2 II 14 Radiate Copy
obv: Radiate head r.
rev: illegible
Antoninianus, copy *c.* AD 270+
Axis: -
Weight: 0.35g
Diameter: 9.0mm
Conditon: Worn and corroded

23. Phase 6C (1302) F2 II 14 Radiate Copy (Tetricus)
obv: [ ]TE[ ]
rev: illegible, blundered legend - Possibly Fides Militum type
Antoninianus, copy *c.* AD 270+
Axis: 180°
Weight: 2.35g
Diameter: 18.0mm
Condition: Worn and corroded

24. Phase 6C (1309) F17 VII 30 illegible
Fragment only, copper alloy.

25. Phase 6C (1310) F17 VII 30 Irregular Fel Temp Reparatio
obv: head r.
rev: Fel Temp Reparatio, fallen horseman type *c.* AD 357-367
Axis: -
Weight: 0.35g
Diameter: 8.0mm
Condition: Worn and corroded

26. Phase 6C (1311) F17 VII 30 illegible
Fragmentary, copper alloy.

27. Phase 6C (1323) F22 VI 14 Marcus Aurelius
obv: [AVREL]IVS CAE-SAR[AVG...]
rev: Figure standing [ ] SC
Sestertius AD 146-161
Axis: 135°
Weight: 20.61g
Diameter: 29.0mm
Condition: Very worn

28. Phase 6C (1319) F25 VII 34 Theodora
obv: FL MAX THEODORAE AVG
rev: PIETAS [ROMANA] |
as RIC 79 Treveri AD 337-40 [ ]TR[ ]
Axis: 180°
Weight: 1.22g
Diameter: 15.0mm
Condition: Worn

29. Phase 6C (1320) F25 VII 34 Claudius II
obv: [IMP C]LAVDIVS AV[G]
rev: [AEQV]ITAS AVG
Antoninianus RIC 14 AD 268-270
Axis: 315°
Weight: 2.46g
Diameter: 17.0mm
Condition: Worn

30. Phase 6C (1321) F25 VII 34 Constantine I
obv: CONSTANTINVS PF AVG
rev: [SOLI INVIC - TO COMITI T | F
RIC 42 Treveri AD 313-315 PTR
Axis: 180°
Weight: 2.88g
Diameter: 20.0mm
Condition: Slightly worn

31. Phase 6D (1303) F4 III 5 Constantine I
obv: CONSTA-NTINVS AVG
rev: BEATA TRAN-QVILLITAS PTR
RIC 303 Treveri AD 321
Axis: 180°
Weight: 2.92g
Diameter : 19.0mm
Condition: Slightly worn

32. Phase 6D (1312) F23 VI 15 illegible fragment
Copper alloy

33. Phase 6D (1314) F23 VI 15 illegible fragments
Copper alloy

34. Phase 6D (1322) F23 VI 15 Theodora

obv:	[THEO-]DORAE AVG
rev:	[P]IETAS ROMANA
	AD 337-340
Axis:	180°
Weight:	1.90g
Diameter:	14.0mm
Condition:	Worn

35. Phase 6D (1313) F24 VII 33 Radiate Copy

obv:	?Radiate head
rev:	illegible
Antoninianus	*c.* AD 270+
Axis:	-
Weight:	0.66g
Diameter:	12.0mm
Condition:	Worn and corroded

36. Phase 6D (1315) F24 VII 33 Radiate Coin

obv:	Radiate head
rev:	illegible
Antoninianus	*c.* AD 270+
Axis:	-
Weight:	2.06g
Diameter:	17.0mm
Condition:	Worn and corroded

37. Phase 6D (1317) F24 VII 33 Constantine II

obv:	CONSTANTINVS IVN NOB C
rev:	GLOR-IAEXERCITVS 2 standards
	AD 330-334
Axis:	180°
Weight:	2.13g
Diameter:	17.0mm
Condition:	Worn

38. Unphased (1324) VIII 5 Septimius Severus

obv:	L SEPT SEV PERT AVG IMP VIIII
rev:	PM TRP V COS [II PP]
Denarius RIC 105	Rome AD 197
Axis:	360°
Weight:	2.26g
Diameter:	15.0mm
Condition:	Slightly worn

39. Unphased (1325) VIII 8 ?Nero

obv:	Radiate bust r.
rev:	illegible
Dupondius	AD 54-68
Axis:	-
Weight:	5.91g
Diameter:	26.0mm
Condition:	Very worn and corroded

40. Unphased (1326) VIII 5 Domitian

obv:	IM[P CAES DOMIT AVG GERM]
	COS XI CENS POT PP
rev:	illegible
Sestertius	Rome AD 85
Axis:	-
Weight:	18.54g
Diameter:	33.0mm
Condition:	Worn and corroded

41. Unphased (1327) VIII 5 Marcus Aurelius

obv:	[ ]VS[ ] bare head, r.
rev:	Figure stg., holding spear and making offering
Sestertius	AD 146-180
Axis:	360°
Weight:	(incomplete coin) 11.82g
Diameter :	31.0mm
Condition:	Very worn; incomplete

42. Unphased (1328) V 34 ?1st-2nd century

obv/rev:	illegible
?As/Dupondius	1st-2nd century
weight:	3.31g
Diameter:	25mm
Condition:	Very worn and corroded

43. Unphased (1329) V 34 Hadrian
obv: IMP CAESAR TRAIANVS HADRIANVS AVG
rev: MONETA AVGVSTI SC
Sestertius RIC 586c Rome AD 119-121

Axis:	180°
Weight:	24.21g
Diameter:	33.0mm
Conditon:	Slightly worn

44. U/S (1308) Irregular Fel Temp Reparatio

obv:	
rev:	Fel Temp Reparatio, fallen horseman type *c.* AD 357-367
Axis:	180°
Weight:	1.39g
Diameter:	14.0mm
Condition:	Very worn

45. U/S (1330) Constantine I/II

obv:	CONSTANTINVS[ ]
rev:	[GLORIA EXERCITVS] 2 standards
	AD 330-334
Axis:	360°
Weight:	1.32g
Diameter:	16.0mm
Condition:	Very worn

46. U/S (1335) Caracalla

obv:	laureate bust r. [IVLIA AUGUSTA]
rev:	[VOTA SUSCEP]TA X

Plated *denarius;* mule - obv. Julia Domna as RIC 539, Rev. Caracalla RIC 151. AD 206+

Axis:	180°
Weight:	2.16g
Diameter:	18.0mm
Condition:	Worn

Identified by P. J. Casey.

47. X U/S (3) Victorinus

obv:	[IMP C V]ICTORINVS P F AVG
rev:	[FIDES MILITVM]

Antoninianus RIC 110 Cologne AD 268-270

Axis:	180°
Weight:	3.08g
Diameter:	19.0mm
Condition:	Slightly worn

Site 6

48. Phase 7C (12) 6 Faustina I

obv: [DIVA AVGVSTA] FAVSTINA
rev: AETER[NITAS] SC
Sestertius RIC 1108 Rome AD 141
Axis: 360°
Weight: 20.11g
Diameter: 30.5mm
Condition: Worn and corroded

Other coins are recorded from this site, but remain unlocated.

Site 7

49. Phase 4 (3) 1 Licinius
obv: IMP LICI-NIVS AVG
rev: DN LICINI AVGVSTI VOT XX $\frac{}{RS}$
RIC 233 Rome AD 321
Axis: 180°
Weight: 3.76g
Diameter: 20.0mm
Condition: Slightly worn

The Medieval Coin Robert A Rutland

Site 2

Phase 6C (1) F2 I 3 Edward III
obv: EDWARDVS REX ANGLI Facing crowned bust
rev: CIVITAS LOMDOM Long cross, three pellets in each quarter, amulet in one quarter.
Silver penny North type 1205 Edward III 4th coinage Pre Treaty (1351-61) Series G (1356-61)
Diameter: 18.0mm
Weight: 0.84g
Condition: worn

The Brooches
D.F. Mackreth and Sarnia Butcher

Part 1 Sites 1-4, 6 and 8 — *D.F. Mackreth*

The brooches in this report are numbered in sequence to suit the text, not in site order. (All are made from a copper alloy)

Colchesters

Fig. 73

1 Half the six-coil spring survives. The hook just begins to straighten out to lie flat on the head of the bow. The wings are short and plain. The bow is plain and has a rounded front and back with a slight arris down the sides and a flat face on either side of the head. Behind the head of the bow can be seen the forging marks. The catch-plate is hammered out and had three piercings with a poorly fretted bar separating them.
Site 8 Unphased (3) IV u.s.

2. The spring has six coils. The hook is a little longer than in Brooch 1 and has a pointed end. The wings are very short and plain. The bow is plain and has a square section with very slightly rounded corners. The marks of forging can be seen on the back of the bow. The catch-plate was hammered out and has two small rectangular holes.
Site 2 Phase 3 (31) F11 I 37

3. The spring has 16 coils. The hook is again a little longer than on the last brooch and has a small nib on the end. The wings are heavily damaged by corrosion, but seem to have been plain and are curved to seat the spring. The bow is much wider than thick and has a shallow flute down the centre. The lower part of the bow is missing with only the very top of the catch-plate surviving.
Site 4 Phase 1B (29) RC F27 V 12

Brooches 1 and 2 are standard examples. Neither shows any sign of being early in the typological sequence, the rounded profiles of the bows and the general proportions show that these are of British manufacture. Neither displays any feature which is late in the sequence either, as Brooch 3 does. The earliest Colchesters which show definite signs of their continental origins should be contemporary with those which would make them Augustan in date. As the latest Colchesters had ceased to be made by the Conquest, Brooches 1 and 2 should belong to the middle range and date from *c.* 10 to *c.* 30/5 A.D. Brooch 3 shows, by the length of its wings designed to cope with the uncharacteristically long spring, the hook with its nib and the groove down the bow along with its section, that it is late in the series. A plain groove down the bow is uncommon and the writer has only come across one group with this feature and all save one from Barton Court (Miles 1986, 5, mf. D6, Fig.102.5 No. 5) come from the King Harry Lane cemetery at St. Albans FN1 (Stead and Rigby 1989, published after this section was written). While there are signs that the hook was becoming more elaborate, none has the exaggerated proportions of the wings found here. However, all should belong to the period after *c.* 30 and, in the case of the present item, the end of its *floruit* may be as late as 55/60.

Colchester Derivatives

4. The spring is missing. It had been held in place firstly, by a broken rearward-facing hook behind the head of the bow and, secondly, by solder behind the left-hand wing. The wings are long and curved to seat the spring. The better preserved wing has a vertical groove at its end and in the middle. There is a curved diagonal groove on each side of the latter forming a V. The rest of the brooch is hideously corroded and all the lower part is missing.
Site 2 Phase 1C (65) F71 III 25

The brooch is badly corroded and, while the description laid emphasis on the diagnostic features, the final demonstration that the type is the Rearhook lies in the clear presence of solder. Examples seldom have this preserved and it once appeared that the type was short-lived precisely because of what seemed to be an inefficient method of holding the spring and it is true that the spring is very seldom found in position. However, the distribution and the dating available for the type suggest another reason for its restricted date-range. The type is overwhelmingly at home in Norfolk with examples spreading across the Fens to the western margins and also to the south, but in limited numbers. The only major extension to the basic distribution is a sporadic occurrence in Gloucestershire, and south into Dorset. The dating is: Bagendon, two examples, *c.* 40-50 (Clifford 1961, 172, Fig.31.1, 4); Hod Hill, before 50 (Brailsford 1962, 7, Fig.6,C13; Richmond 1968, 117-9); Puckeridge, Herts, *c.* 40-65 (Partridge 1979, 38, Fig.6.10); Colchester, three examples 49-61 (Hawkes and Hull 1947, 311-2, Pls. xci.44,46, xcii.51), three examples, *c.* 50/55-60/1 (Crummy 1983, 12-3, Fig.6.56, 57; Fig.8.62), 50-65 (*ibid*, 12-3, Fig 7.61); Bagendon, 50-60, Clifford 1961, 172, Fig. 31.2): Lockleys, Welwyn, Herts, before 60/70 (Ward-Perkins 1938, 352, Fig.2.1): Colchester, 61-*c.* 65 (Hawkes and Hull 1947, 311, Pl. xci.45); The Lunt, Baginton, Warks., 64-70 (Hobley 1971-3, 13; Hobley 1966-7, 108, Fig. 19.3); Harlow, ?80-100 (France and Gobel 1985, 79, Fig.41.68). Only the one from Harlow falls later than the decade 60-70 and most are earlier than 65. This is a remarkable archaeological record when residual items abound in practically every other type of brooch. The conclusion is that the type is specifically Icenian and the workshops or craftsmen failed to survive the suppression of the Boudican revolt. The absence of dated specimens from Norfolk itself is a product of the general lack of excavation and publication of relevant sites.

5. The body of the brooch is in two pieces which are covered with corrosion accretions, the brooch itself is eaten away in many places. The six-coil spring is mounted on an axis bar running through a plate behind the head of the bow, the chord passes through an upper hole in the plate. No decoration can be seen. The bow appears to have a straight profile and a sharp bend at the head.
Site 1 Phase 7B (104) F119 VI 7

Little can be said about this badly damaged piece. The spring-fixing arrangement occurs so close to the Conquest that there should be little doubt that it had come into being before then. However, there is no need to argue for an early date for this example. The straight profile is unusual; practically all Colchester Derivatives have a curve, but there is no reason to think that the profile here has any chronological significance. Only the broadest date-range can be proposed; mid 1st century to mid 2nd, although it is doubtful whether

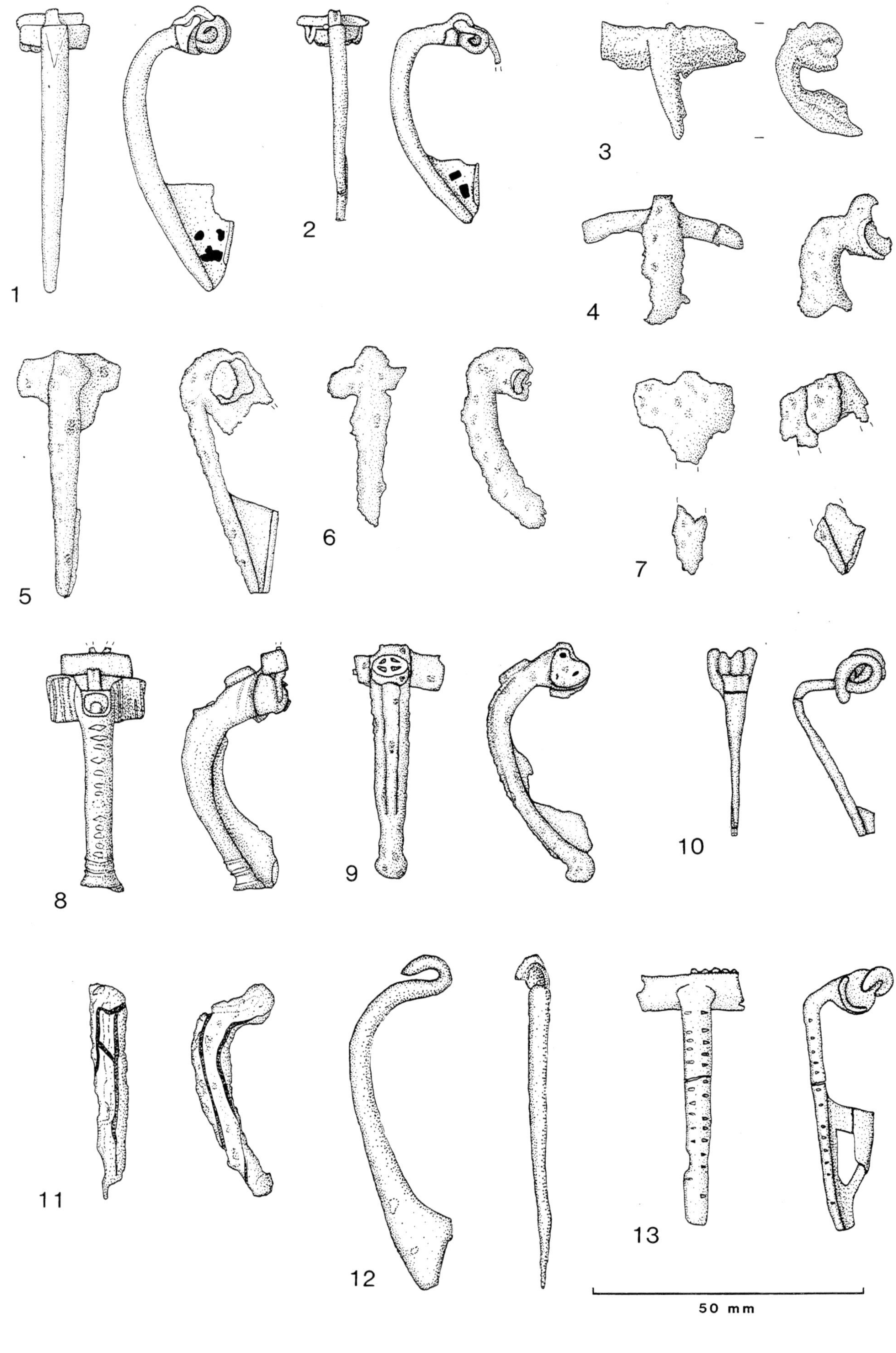

Fig. 73 The Brooches 1-13 Scale 1:1

this spring-fixing system lasted as late as this.

6. A brooch covered with corrosion products, definitely a Colchester Derivative, but one whose pin-fixing arrangement is far from certain.
   Site 1 Phase 1B (55) F73 V 55
7. Two very corroded fragments one of which is the head of a Colchester Derivative with a sprung-pin.
   Site 2 Phase 2 (101) II 84

Neither of these brooches has any identifiable datable features and both can only be assigned to the general range of mid-1st century to *c.* 150/75.

Headstuds

8. The pin was hinged, the axis bar being housed in a half-cylinder behind the wings. In the ends of these is mounted a damaged wire loop which passes through a cast collar on whose front are four triangular recesses top and bottom leaving a line of reserved lozenges between. Each wing has a groove at each end and, between, a repeat of the decoration on the collar. On the head is a crest with a groove along its top. Below the crest is the stud which is wide and deep. All that survives of the setting is a rivet passing through the bow with a broad head on which can be seen a berried rosette. The rest of the bow has a groove down each side with a line of lozenge-shaped recesses down the middle with infilling triangular ones on each side. Pale blue enamel survives in the lozenges. At the foot of the bow is a triple moulding under which is a flute and the splayed foot. Under this is a shallow recess with a hole for rivet, now missing, running through to the catch-plate.
   Site 6 Phase 4C (22) 23
9. The pin was hinged, the axis bar being housed in a half-cylinder behind the wings. These are damaged, but part of a flute is preserved. The stud has a reserved four-petalled motif in its top. The bow had a groove down each side with a line of reserved lozenges down the middle. The foot is damaged, but seems to have at least two mouldings separated by a flute from a double cross-moulding at the foot of the bow.
   Site 2 Phase 5(49) F46 II 27

Despite being a well known type, the Headstud is not particularly common and discussion of it is aggravated by the varieties in which it occurs, including those without studs yet which are patently of the same family (e.g. Miket 1983, 119, Fig. 77.165), However, both of the present examples belong to well defined groups. Brooch 8 has a minor variation in which the separate loop and collar is replaced by a cast-on loop. It is found all over Roman Britain and the temptation to see it as being northern is more the product of several coming from one site (e.g. Traprain Law; Burley 1955-6, 157, Nos. 21, 22, 23) where there were extensive excavations than of a real appreciation of where the bulk lie, principally because of a lack of publication. Dating: Chichester, after early 2nd century (Mackreth 1978, 279-80, Fig. 10.26,11); Derby, second half of the 2nd century (Brassington 1980, 18, Fig. 8.a); Barry, Cold Knap, after 150? (Evans *et al*, 1985, 109, Fig. 15.1). Amongst those with cast-on loops, only one from Harlow has a date; before 80 (France and Gobel 1985, 79, Fig. 41.73).

Brooch 9 also belongs to a definite group, this time with the distribution lying in southern England. The variations are fewer and concern the motif on the stud; the four petals may be replaced by a plain sunken annulus or, occasionally, a reserved lozenge with concave sides. The dating is sparse; Nettleton, *c.* 70-120 (Wedlake 1982, 128, Fig. 53.61). The picture which emerges from the available dating of both groups is the wide time span suggested. In each there is the single specimen which may date as early as 70/75 and this would certainly suit the general appearance of the Headstud well before the end of the 1st century (e.g. Gould 1963-4, 43, Fig. 18.3; Crummy 1983, 13, Fig. 9.65), but whether this should dictate that the bulk of the dated examples of the group to which Brooch 8 belongs should be regarded as residual is another matter, there are still not enough dated specimens to establish a secure range. Perhaps the best *floruit* which can be proposed is that both groups may run from the later 1st century into the second.

La Tene III

10. The spring has four coils and an internal chord. The upper bow is broad with a groove down each side, a curve across the bottom. The swelled area between has two curved grooves which meet in the middle. The rest of the bow is very thin and most of the catch-plate is missing. The profile is straight beneath a sharp curve at the head.
    Site 2 Phase 1C (78) F71 III 25

At best, this brooch could be described as a Nauheim Derivative. The diagnostic feature in this case would be the decorated panel at the top of the bow and the overall taper to what should be presumed to have been a pointed foot. The loss of most of the catch-plate is unfortunate; the style of the brooch is early enough for it to be important to know whether the catch-plate had been solid or had a single large piercing. The latter would place the brooch in the middle of the 1st century B.C. and make it a variety of Nauheim. While the classic Nauheim has, in effect, a sheet metal bow, the more sturdy section of the present specimen is not unknown and not much reliance should be put on such a detail. Similarly, to insist on a markedly framed catch-plate is out of place. However, the dating of Brooch 10 has to rely on other factors. The chief of these is that, although the spring-fixing arrangement carried on until near the end of the 1st century A.D., bows of this pattern are not to be expected after the Conquest. Perhaps the best range which can be suggested is from the later 1st century B.C. into the 1st century A.D.

11. The first coil only of the four-coil-internal-chord system survives. The brooch is very corroded, but seems to have a rounded section and a tight bend at the top masking the front of the spring.
    Site 2 Phase 2 (93) II 71
12. An almost exact repeat of the last brooch, but much better preserved.The bow has a round section. There is no sign of a piercing in what is left of the catch-plate.
    Site 1 Phase 4 (20) F63 V 19

There is very little to provide any guidance over the dating of these brooches. The style of their profiles might suit the earlier 1st century A.D., but the basic type can date to almost the end of the same century.

Langton Down

13. The spring is housed in a poorly preserved spring-case which seems to be plain along its front. The junction of the bow with the case is marked by a small moulding on each side. The bow has a triangular section with an arris down the centre. On each side is a series of narrow triangular recesses

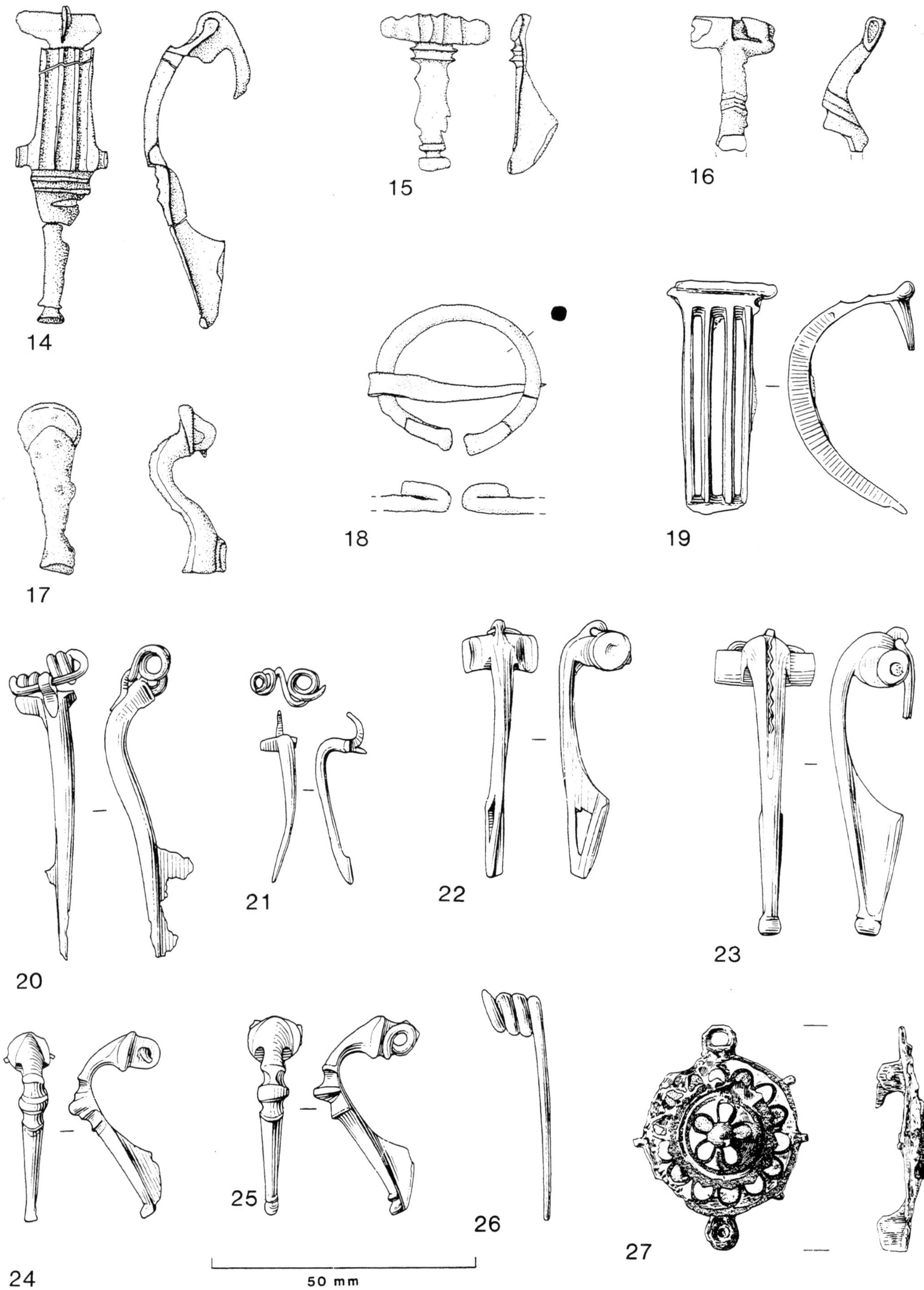

 Fig. 74 The Brooches 14-27 Scale 1:1

probably once filled with niello. The catch-plate has a return parallel with the bow, but with a cut-away to the bottom of the bow.

Site 2 Phase 2 (67) III 26

This is not the classic form of Langton Down which has a plain reeded bow. The design occurs rarely and there is no good evidence to suggest that it must be thought of as a form later than the general run. In Britain, an example from Colchester was dated *c.* 50-61 (Hawkes and Hull 1947, 319, Pl. xcv.108) and another from Eccles appears to be mid 1st century A.D. (excavations, A Detsicas, to be published). Of the four from Augst, two were undated and another clearly residual, the fourth was mid 1st century (Riha 1979, 97, Taf.17.453). The best that can be said is that this pattern was to be found in the second quarter of the 1st century and that it had probably largely passed out of use, like nearly all other Langton Downs, by the time of the Conquest.

Hod Hill

Fig. 74

14. Four pieces making up a brooch complete with pin whose axis bar is housed in the rolled-over head. The upper bow has four ridges separated by flutes, the ridges are cross-cut. Attached to each of the lower corner is a small wing with a boss at its end. The lower bow has two cross-mouldings at the top, has a flat front face and tapers to the usual two-part foot-knob.

    Site 8 Phase 3C (2) F9 IX 57

15. Most of the upper bow is missing. It had five ridges, the middle three grouped together. There are wings of better shape attached to the lower corners. There are also two cross-mouldings at the top of the lower bow the rest of which is damaged, but seems to have been a flat plate shaped to look like a leaf (cf. Bushe-Fox 1932, 76 Pl. viii.3) although this feature is more typical of a single-part design (cf. Riha 1979, 137, Taf.37.1008, 1009). There is a line of punched dots down the middle and traces of others on each side set at angles suggesting the veining on a leaf. The foot-knob is in the usual two parts.

    Site 2 Phase 1C (34) F14 I 44

These are standard Hod Hills. The type arrives for the first time in numbers in Britain after the Conquest and its distribution here shows that it was passing out of use in the decade 60 to 70, very few indeed surviving much later.

16. The rolled over head is tucked in close behind a cross-ridge. The head is wide and the upper bow very narrow with a triangular section and a marked arris down the front where it is stopped by two cross-mouldings which lie above a sharp step back to the lower bow. Only the very top of this is present and appears to be a flat plate.

    Site 1 Phase 7B (120) F119 VI 7

An uncommon design, another example comes from Leicestershire (High Cross, Jewry Wall Museum, 177.1955 (51)) and this shows that the full form has a fantail lower bow. The chief feature which places this brooch amongst the Hod Hills is the rolled-over head, the two-part design of the bow being of lesser importance when both parts are to a great measure uncharacteristic. Examples are few in Britain and none is dated. That the common date for Hod Hills may be inappropriate here rests not so much on the unusual design, but in the ridge against which the rolled-over head rests. There is a suggestion here of the later development of the Hod Hill found on the continent which leads to enamelled designs. The most likely date range for the present brooch is the second half of the 1st century.

Knee

17. The spring has an internal chord and is mounted between two pierced lugs behind the semi-circular head plate. On the front of this is a crescent-shaped cell full of discoloured enamel. The bow is cabriole-shaped and covered with corrosion products which, however, are not thick enough to hide the presence of a strip of white metal appliqué down the centre, two beaded ridges can be seen. The catch-plate is very small.

    Site 6 Phase 5C (34) 17

The method of holding the spring, the shape of the head-plate and the overall shape of the bow coupled with the use of enamel and decorated appliqué white metal show that this brooch is British in manufacture. There is no reason to think that there was much in the way of development within the series as it was almost certainly a copy of the general type on the continent and only made when that became popular. The dating, including the group with proper spring cases, is: Canterbury, 100-180 (Frere *et al*, 1982, 121, Fig. 59.7); Wroxeter, ?130-150 (Bushe-Fox 1914, 13, Fig. 4.6); Baldock, 180-220 (Stead and Rigby 1986, 113, Fig. 46.103); Bignor, 190/200-225/250 (Frere 1982, 179, Fig. 26.6); Gadebridge, late 2nd or early 3rd century (Neal 1974, 127, Fig. 55.25). The indicated dating is from 125 into the 3rd century. A note of caution, however, is needed. These sites lie in southern Britain where, without the aid of reconstructed military history, dating is difficult from the latter part of the 2nd century, therefore, to press for a definite continuation into the 3rd century may be unwise, although the possibility exists.

Penannulars

18. The ring has a circular section. Each terminal is turned back along the top of the ring. The design on the terminals is not clear, but there are faint indications of two cross-grooves. The pin has a slight hump and a simple wrap-round.

    Site 1 Phase 7C (59) V 5

As the form of the terminals is not entirely certain, little discussion is possible. In general, penannulars are most popular in the 1st and 2nd century A.D. and there is nothing present here to suggest that the brooch should be later.

19. Fragments only of a ring with a circular section survive.

    Site 1 Phase (60) F51 IIIA 66

Also, not illustrated, corroded remains like the last from Site 1 Phase 1B (54) F73 V 59 and Phase 5A (57) IIIA 54. No comment can be offered about these three brooches.

Part 2 Site 5 Sarnia Butcher

19. The upper part only of a Bagendon brooch. The head consists of a narrow tube in which the pin is hinged; a knob survives at one end of the axial rod. The upper bow is divided into four ribs. Corrosion obscures most details but it is clear that the ribs were threaded by transverse rods. Surviving length 45mm. Brass.

    Site 5 Unphased (1135) V 30

A smaller brooch from Bagendon itself shows the same features (Clifford 1961, 177, Fig. 31.1). Another apparently similar brooch comes from Switzerland (Ettlinger 1973, Taf. 9, 11, p. 95). The Bagendon evidence suggests that the type reached its floruit in the second quarter of the 1st cen-

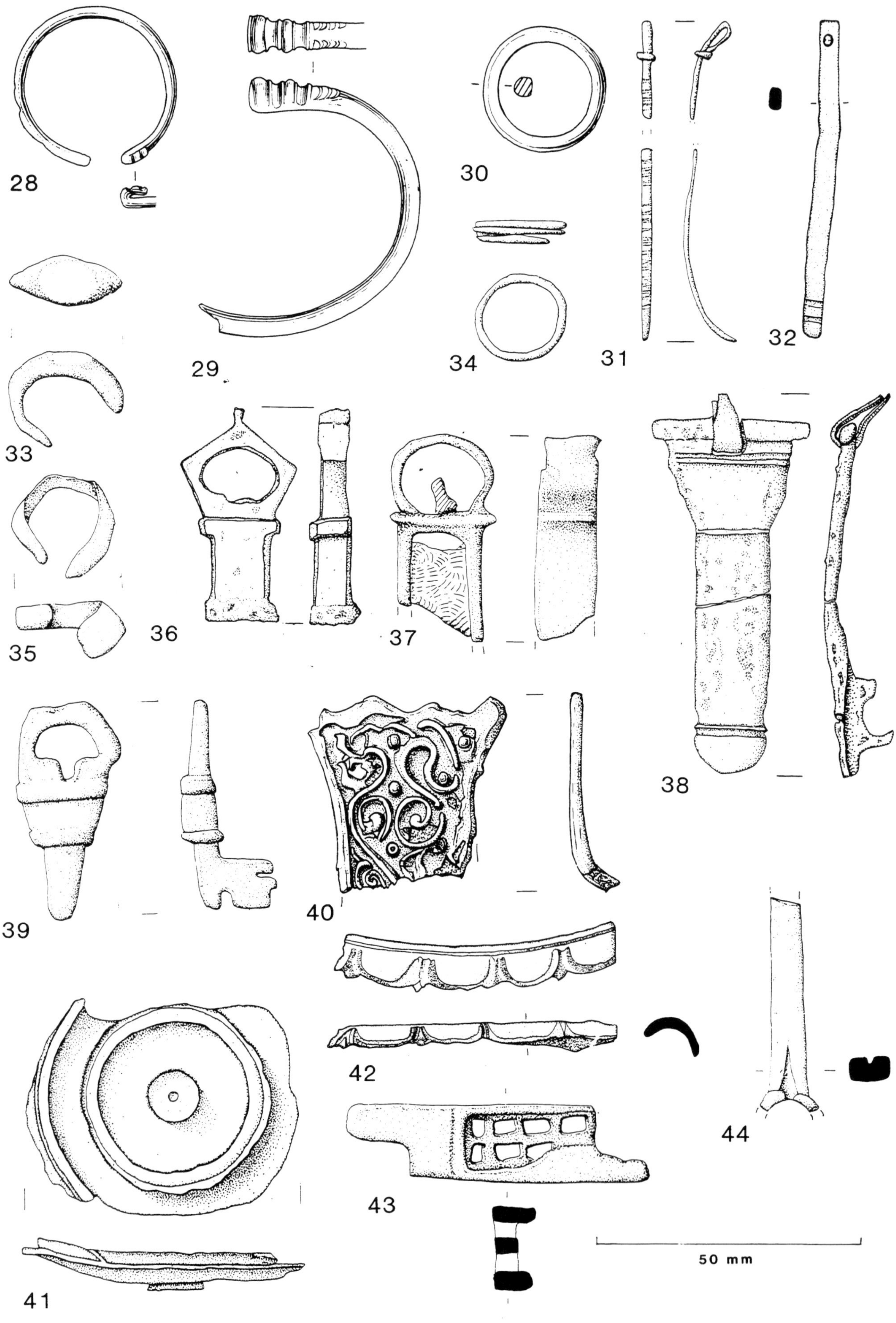

 Fig. 75 The Brooches and Small Finds 28-44 Scale 1:1

tury AD.

20. A one-piece spring of six coils is secured by the chord passing through a hook on the head of the brooch and is protected by a short plain crossbar. The bow is plain and tapers to the foot, behind which is a catchplate which though broken, shows traces of openwork. Length excluding spring 55mm. Brass.
Site 5 Phase 3C (1092) V 4

This is a typical Colchester brooch; the type was first discussed by M R Hull (Hawkes and Hull 1947, 308-309) and his general dating still stands, although there is now an emphasis on its occurrence in the first half of the 1st century AD. However it also occurs frequently in post-conquest levels down to the Flavian period.

21. A similar brooch to 20., though smaller and more damaged. Surviving length 28mm. Brass.
Site 5 Phase 1A (1041) IV 25
22. The spring of four or more turns is held on a rod secured in discs at the end of the crossbar and by the chord passing through a crest on the head of the brooch. The bow is plain and tapers to the foot from which the catchplate is worked at a right angle; this has a triangular opening. Length overall 49mm. Leaded gunmetal.
Site 5 Phase 2C (1017) IV 10

The method of securing the spring defines this as a "Polden Hill" type in M R Hull's classification (British Academy, unpublished). The type is particularly common in the West Midlands and Wales, and by analogy with brooches of related type from Wroxeter should be dated to the second half of the 1st century AD.

23. A more developed version of the "Polden Hill" type than No.17 above. This has a heavier head with flanges beside the bow, grooves down the bow and a small foot-knob which is integral with the harp-shaped catchplate. Length overall 59mm. Leaded gunmetal.
Site 5 Phase 3A (1002) VI 7

Wroxeter provides a closer parallel for this brooch: Bushe-Fox 1914, 11, Fig.4.1, contexts AD 80-120.

24. A small brooch of the Backworth or trumpet group. The spring, which is missing, was held on a rod passing through a lug behind the trumpet-shaped head. It probably once had a loose wire shackle, as there is no trace of a cast tab at the head. At the centre of the bow there is a triple moulding, not carried round to the back as in some brooches of this group. Length 36mm. (Leaded) bronze.
Site 5 Phase 1C (1034) I 25

M R Hull distinguished this as the "Chester" type as it was so common there: one was from a deposit of late 1st to early 2nd century date (Hull 1967, 42).

25. Very similar to No.24 above, but slightly longer and the central moulding differs. The spring of 3-4 turns survives. Length 38mm. Leaded bronze/gunmetal.
Site 5 Phase 6D (1047) F18 VII 31
26. The pin and half of the spring (three turns) of a brooch. Surviving length 44mm. Most likely of the later 1st or 2nd centuries AD.
Site 5 Phase 1A (1039) IV 24
27. Disc brooch with concentric decoration of crescent-shaped enamelled cells, alternately yellow and turquoise with red in the triangles between them, surrounding a central boss which bears five petal-shaped cells; these are of the same colours. There are six plain metal lugs round the rim, and a loop opposite a larger lug with concentric rings which covers the catchplate. The pin is hinged between two lugs and there is a slight hollow behind the central boss. Diameter, excluding lugs, 30mm. Brass.
Site 5 Phase 3B (1004) V 13

This brooch was first published with others of the type in 1977 (Butcher 1977, No.6, pp.51-53). Parallels were cited which showed a distribution mainly in southern and midland Britain and a date around 100 AD. Since then others have been seen from Wicklewood (Norfolk, courtesy of Norwich Castle Museum) and Carlisle, Blackfriars Street excavations 1977.

Others from northern Britain have been published: Watercrook (Potter 1979, 211, Fig. 84.16) and Chester (Grosvenor Museum 1972). The distribution evidently covers most of Britain, but still none of this exact type is known from the continent.

Fig.75

28. Broken penannular brooch: a thin ring with the terminals turned back and cross-ribbed. The pin is missing. Diameter approximately 32mm. Gunmetal.
Site 5 Phase 4C (1048) VII 4

This belongs to the commonest type of penannular brooch from Roman Britain. Examples can be quoted from contexts in the 1st century AD but many come from later sites.

29. Slightly more than half survives of a stout ring with one terminal consisting of multiple ribbed mouldings with side flanges. Fine grooves run along the outer face of the ring. Diameter approximately 48mm.
Site 5 Phase 2A (1003) F40 VII 44

This might be a bracelet rather than a brooch (no pin survives) but other brooches are known with multiple-knobbed terminals, though none very similar to this.

30. Plain ring with gap and no terminals; perhaps a finger-ring but could be a small annular brooch. Diameter 23mm.
Site 5 Phase 1C (1042) I 27

The Small Finds — Patrick Clay

Part 1 Roman

Objects of Copper Alloy

31. Fragments from a bracelet decorated with transverse grooves in groups. 3rd-4th century.
Site 2 Unphased (41) II u.s.
32. Strip with eye at one end and two transverse grooves at the other. This item which is apparently complete may have served as a pendant or clasp.
Site 5 Unphased (1012) I u.s.
33. Finger ring fragment with yellow glass setting.
Site 1 Phase 4A (32) F63 V 21
34. Coiled finger ring. These items were common at Sheepen (Hawkes and Hull, 1947, 330) perhaps suggesting a 1st century date (Crummy, 1983, 47 Fig.50.1759).
Site 2 Phase 4B (94) I 75
35. Penannular plain finger ring with rectangular section.
Site 5 Phase 3C (1093) V 4
36. Cast handle probably for a key or knife.
Site 2 Phase 6A (28) II 7
37. Cast handle for an iron knife consisting of a hollow suspension loop and cut out area with the remains of an iron blade. This has some similarities to a handle found at Colchester used for a knife or razor (Crummy, 1983, 110 Fig.

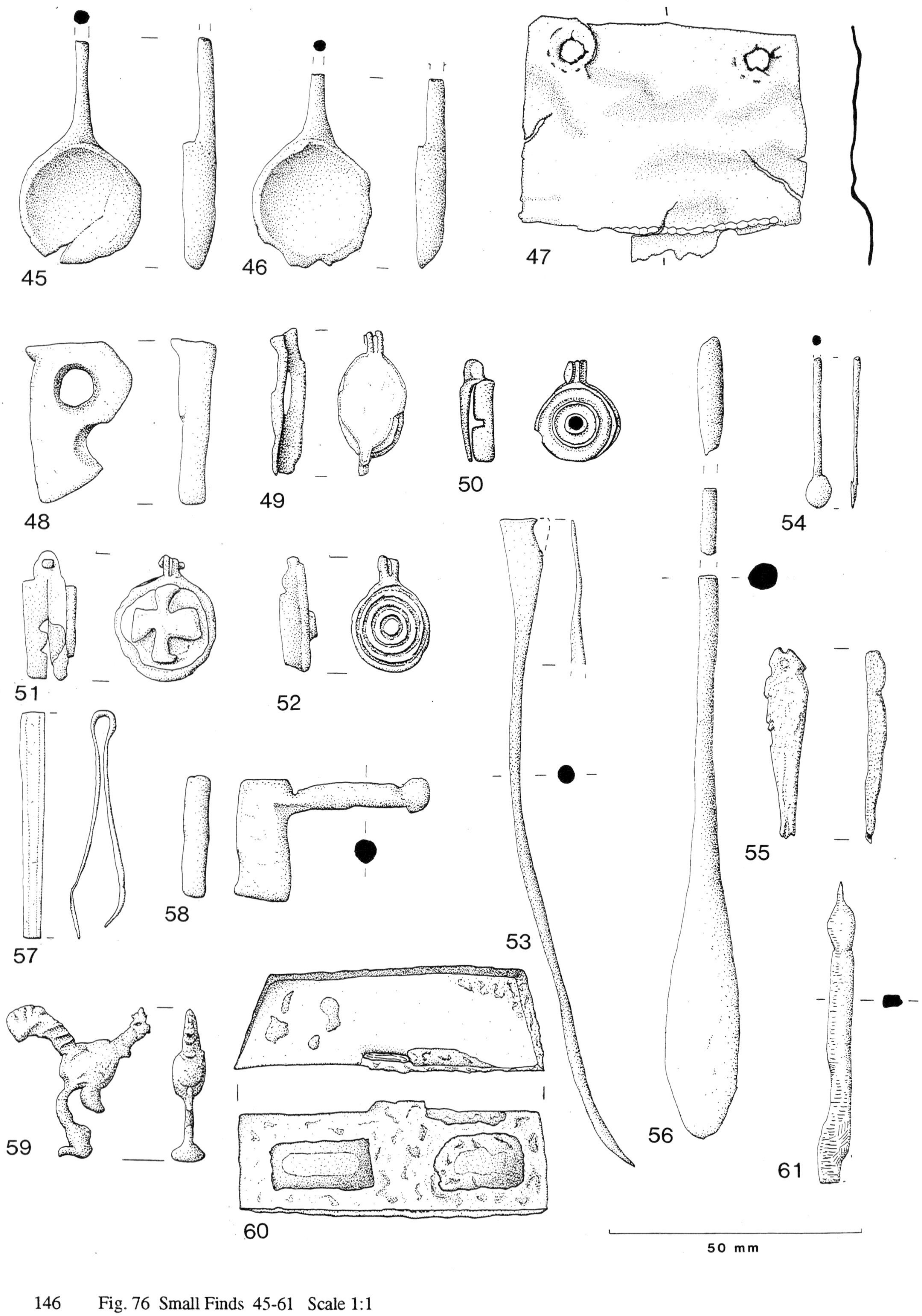

 Fig. 76 Small Finds 45-61 Scale 1:1

112.2939).
Site 5 Unphased (1241) VI u.s.

38. Hinged hasp for a lock, possibly emulating the shape of a brooch (cf. an example from Richborough, Cunliffe, 1968, 103 Pl.45, 194).
A similar object was found attached to a wooden box containing gaming pieces at Mansell Street, London (L. Blackmore pers comm)
Site 2 Phase 4B (7) F8 I 27
39. Lever lock key possibly for a casket.
Site 5 Phase 3A (16) F106 X 11
40. Lock bolt used with tumbler locks (cf. Crummy, 1983, 124 Fig.136).
Site 5 Phase 2A (1105) F41 VI 4
41. Decorated strip possibly from a vessel handle with dot and curvilinear decoration. Traces of blue enamel are present (stippled on drawing).
Site 1 Phase 4B (127) VII 7
42. Base from a patera (saucepan) with two foot rings and a central stud.
Site 1 Phase 3C (36) F101 V 17
43. Rim from a bowl, with ovolo decoration, of 180mm diameter. This may be from the same vessel as 42.
Site 1 Phase 3C (41) F101 V 17
44. Handle, possibly from a small vessel.
Site 5 Phase 2A (1159) F36 V 27

Fig.76

45. Spoon with round bowl (cf. Crummy, 1983 69 Fig.73, 2008 type 1; Goodburn, 1984, 41 Fig.15.120). Late 1st-2nd century.
Site 6 Phase 5A (16) 50
46. Spoon with round bowl, most of handle now missing. Late 1st-2nd century.
Site 6 Phase 6C (18) F14 84
47. Sheet with rivet holes and embossed decoration, possibly box inlay.
Site 1 Phase 3C (135) F101 V 17
48. Cast letter 'P' possibly from an inscription(?) (cf. Crummy, 1983, 145, Fig.179 4285-4286).
Site 5 Phase 3A (1340) VI 7
49. Seal box. This shows no trace of enamelling or decoration and is similar in shape to Crummy's Acorn-shaped type 1 (Crummy, 1983, 103, Fig.106.2517). 1st-2nd century.
Site 1 Phase 5B (53) III A 50
50. Base of a round seal box (Crummy, 1983, type 2, 103). 1st-2nd century.
Site 5 Phase 2A (1164) F36 V 27
51. Round seal box with a stylised bird in flight decoration. This was probably originally enamelled (cf. Cunliffe, 1968, 201 Fig.44.183) 2nd-3rd century.
Site 5 Phase 3A (1142) VI 7
52. Round seal box with concentric circle decoration showing some traces of enamel. 2nd-3rd century.
Site 5 Phase 4B (1007) I 1
53. Stylus.
Site 9 (6) u.s.
54. Toilet spoon with flat scoop, part of the stem now missing.
Site 1 Phase 6A (72) III 8
55. Nail cleaner, similar to Crummy's type 16 (1983, 58 Fig.62.1871) of mid to late 1st century date.
Site 2 Phase 3 (102) F92 II 97
56. Spatula-probe, part of the shaft now missing.
Site 5 Phase 4B (1035) I 4
57. Tweezers with incised grooves along the edges.
Site 5 Phase 6B (1161) F21 VII 45
58. Miniature votive axe. This is a flag shaped axe similar to others found at Woodeaton, Oxfordshire (Green 1975, 68 Fig.30 a-b) although no decoration is discernible on this example. These items have a widespread distribution (Green 1975, Faudet 1983) and are often associated with Romano-Celtic temple sites. (For other Leicestershire examples see Pirie 1986).
Site 9 (3) u.s.
59. Head from a pin in the shape of a cockerel (cf. Hawkes and Hull, 1947 Pl.100.21; Crummy, 1983, 30 Fig.31.501).
Site 5 Phase 4C (1019) II 12
60. Rectangular block with two recesses. Casting blank or weight (?).
Site 1 Phase 3B (44) F71 V 39

Object of Iron

61. Stylus, bent and corroded.
Site 1 Phase 7C (105) VI 3

Objects of Lead

Fig. 77

62. Handle (?) with moulded terminals and central collar.
Site 5 Unphased (1226) V 37
63. Handle for drawer or vessel (?). Similar copper alloy handles are known, cf. Hawkes and Hull, 1947, 332 Pl.99.9 and 10.
Site 5 Phase 6B (1157) F90 VI 61

Objects of Bone

64. Toggle, broken longitudinally with incised line decoration. This has some affinities with decorated examples from Cirencester (Webster, 1982, 109 Fig.35.95) and Richborough (Bushe-Fox, 1949, Pl.54.227). Pre-Flavian.
Site 5 Phase 1D (5) F104 X 40
65. Toggle (?) with narrow, crudely cut, transverse hole and raised terminals.
Site 5 Phase 2C (1166) VI 9
66. Spoon with round bowl, part missing. Late 1st-2nd century (cf. Corney, 1984, 115 Fig.38.2; Down and Rule, 1971, Fig.5.16.171; Cunliffe, 1964, Fig.24.16).
Site 1 Phase 8A (101) F48 IIIB 4
67. Pin, part missing with crude sub-spherical head having some similarities to an example from South Shields (Allason-Jones and Miket, 1984, 68 Fig.2.290).
Site 5 Phase 1C (1024) F12 I 30
68. Pin with point missing. Crummy type 1 (1979, 159; 1983, 20 Fig.17). *c.* 50-200.
Site 5 Phase 4B (1343) IX 3
69. Pin, Crummy type 5 (1979, 162; 1983, 23 Fig.21.395) with one reel beneath ovoid head. 4th century.
Site 5 Phase 6C (1061) F22 VI 14
70. Pin, with part missing. Crummy type 3 (1979, 161; 1983, 21 Fig.19). 3rd-4th century.
Site 5 Unphased (1235) u.s.
71. Pin, Crummy type 2 (1979, 160; 1983, 21 Fig.18.162), with two grooves below the head. *c.* 50-200.
Site 6 Phase 5C (21) 17

Fig. 78

72. Needle with spatulate head (cf. Crummy, 1983, 65 Fig.70.1982 type 2; Allason-Jones and Miket, 1984, 65 Fig.2.269).
Site 5 Phase 2C (1155) VI 31
73. Object resembling a spindle whorl although the hole is not central and is very narrow for a spindle.
Site 2 Phase 5 (60) F46 II 40

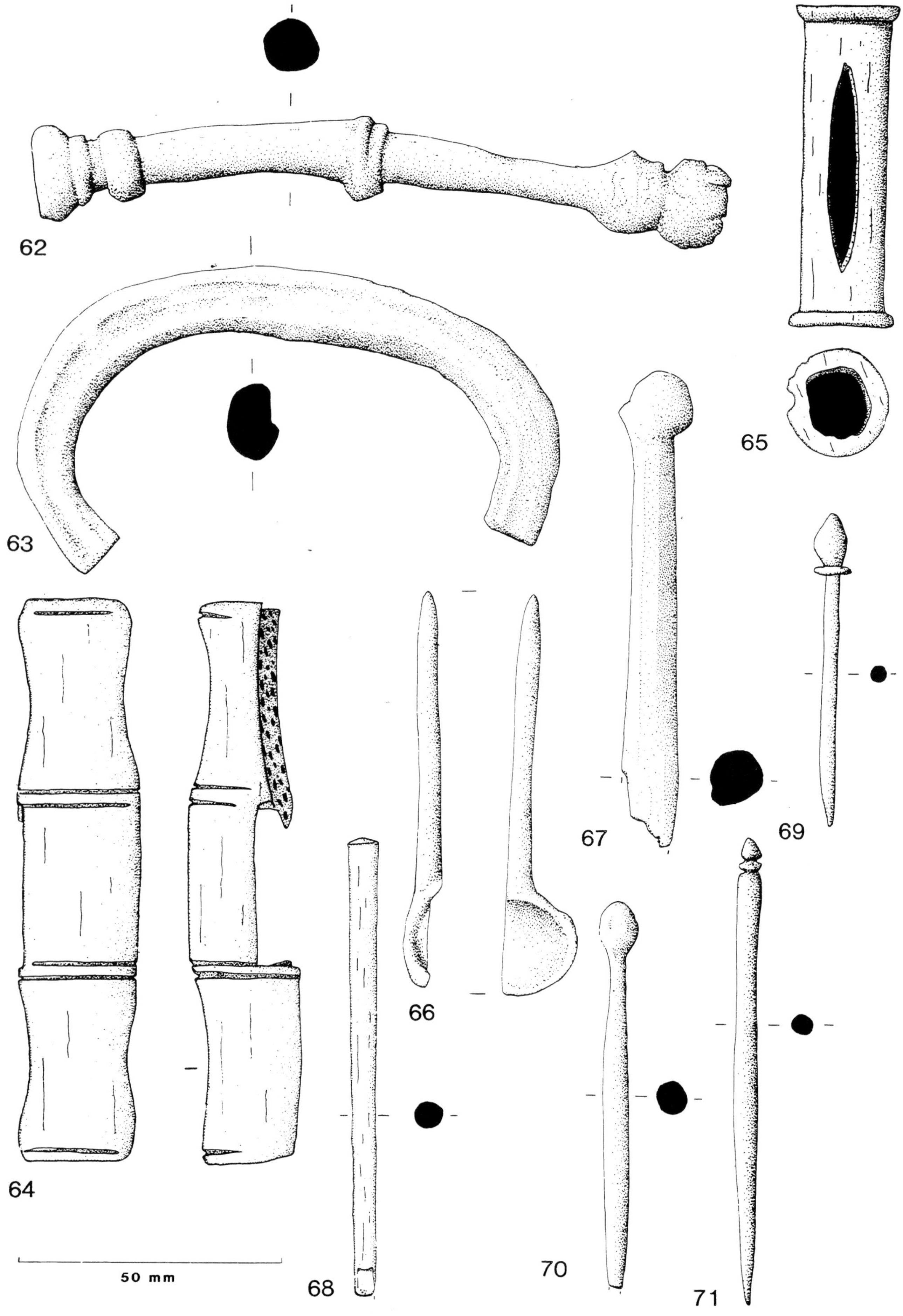

 Fig. 77 Small Finds 62-71 Scale 1:1

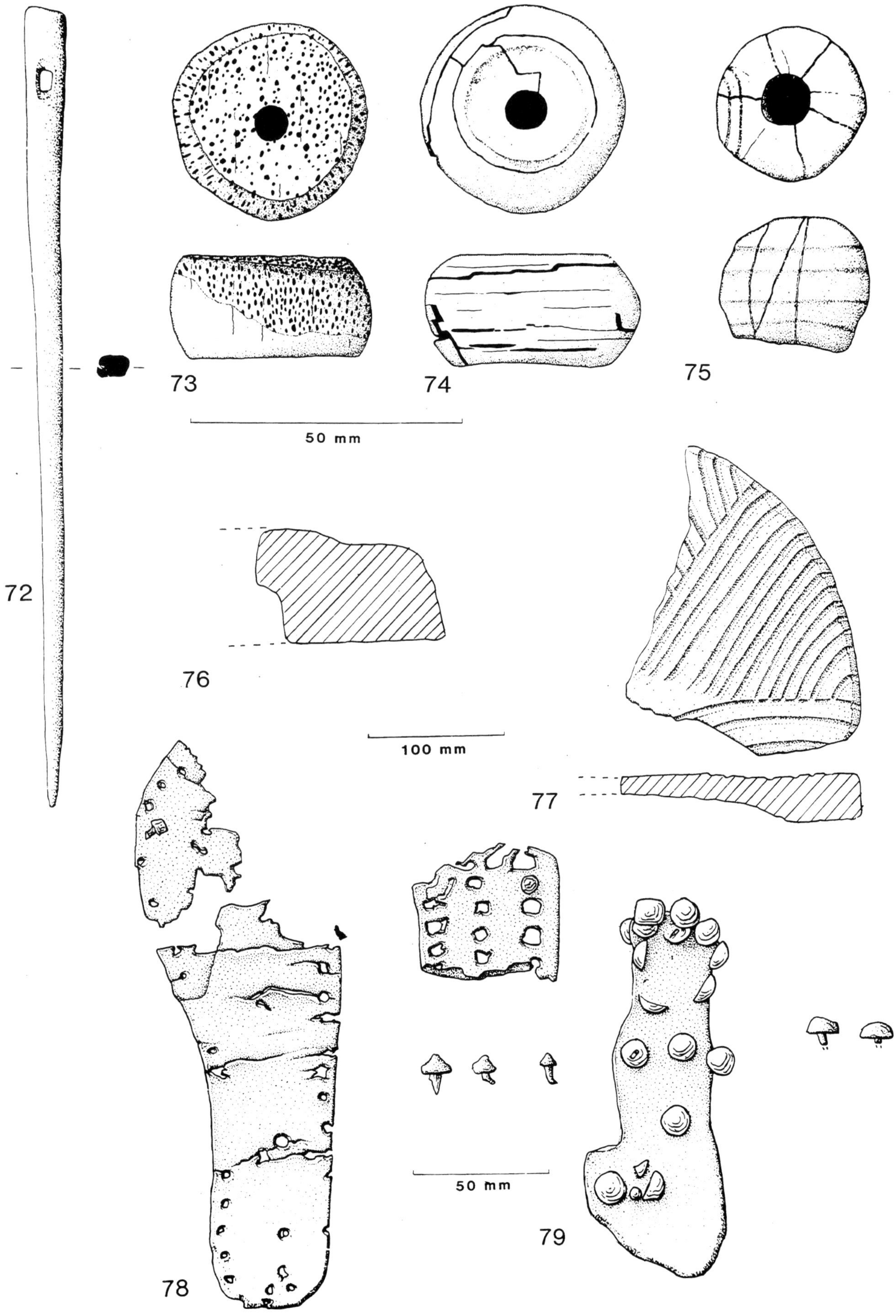

Fig. 78 Small Finds 72-75 Scale 1:1; 76-77 Scale 1:4; 78-79 Scale 1:2

Object of Shale

74. Spindle whorl of biconical section. These items are usually dated to the 3rd century (Lawson, 1975, 272).
Site 5 Phase 6C (1339) F17 VII 30

Objects of Stone

75. Spindle whorl, with crudely scratched vertical lines, formed from an ironstone nodule.
Site 9 Unphased (7) u.s.
76. Fragment of dressed bottom stone from an RB domestic quern. Mayen Lava.
Site 1 Phase 7B (167) F119 VI 7
77. Fragment of bedstone from a Hunsbury type quern. Millstone Grit -Derbyshire/Yorkshire area.
Site 8 Phase 3C (5) F9 X 54

Objects of Leather

78. Boot fragments possibly from a left foot of a calceus consisting of two fragments of an insole and a fragment of the outer sole or packing with fourteen hobnail holes. Fifteen iron hobnails were found associated with these fragments (underside, drawn after conservation - estimated shrinkage 20%) cf. Keppie, 1975, 68-83; Thornton, 1977, Fig.23.515.
Site 3 Phase 2A (11) WB. F3 II 9 and Phase 5A (50) WB. F42 IV 4
79. Fragment (drawn in situ) with twenty two dome shaped copper alloy studs in association. This may be a fragment of upholstery decorated with studs.
Site 1 Phase 4A (22) F63 V 21

Part 2 Post-Roman

Objects of Copper Alloy

80. Buckle with incised decoration.
Site 3 Phase 5A (2) F2 I 7
81. Fragments from a circular strainer cf. Clay, 1981, 133 Fig.46.20; Hurst and Golson, 1955, 99, Figs.24.8 & 14; London Museum, 1940, 206 Fig.68.8.
Site 2 Phase 4B (18) I 25

Object of Iron

82. Box padlock. This has copper alloy traces on its surface possibly resulting from the brazing process used in its manufacture (Richardson, 1959, 81). Cf. Goodall, 1979, 268 Fig.116.1.
Site 2 Phase 6D (37) F90 II 15

Objects of Bone

83. Apple corer decorated with incised line and ring/dot motifs, cf. Baker et al 1979, 290 Fig.179.1518 and 1521.
Site 2 Unphased (22) u.s.
84. Bodkin manufactured from a pig fibula, cf. Oakley and Harman, 1979, 311, Fig.138.48; Platt and Coleman-Smith, 1975, 271 Fig.247.1921 & 1929 and 248.1931.
Site 2 Unphased (46) IV 2
85. Bodkin similar to 134 but with an offset hole and broken shaft.
Site 2 Unphased (47) u.s.
86. Parchment Pricker with lathe turned spherical head. 13th-14th century (Macgregor, 1985, 121 with refs), see also Platt and Coleman-Smith, 1975, 271, 274 Figs.247.1928 and 248.1936. (described as pins)
Site 3 Phase 6 (15) IV 1
87. Hipped pin with spherical head, cf. Coad and Streeten 1982. Head dress pin. 11th-12th century
Site 5 Phase 6A (4) F101 X 47

Objects of Stone

88. Spindle whorl cf. Oakley and Hall, 1979, 288 Fig.126.11.
Site 3 Phase 5A (1) F2 I 3
89. Disc possibly used as a lid. Slate.
Site 5 Phase 6C (1354) F2 II 14

A complete catalogue of small finds is available from Leicestershire Archaeological Unit.

The Glass Louise Monk

Site 1

Forty-eight fragments including three from two beads (one faience) were examined. Three fragments from Phases 4A, 5A and 7C were from window glass. All the glass belonged to the first three centuries AD and included parts of four pillar moulded bowls, one being a rare colourless specimen (9) and another of deep blue (6), probably made before AD 75 , although it should be observed that these vessel fragments are extremely durable. Also notable are the five fragments (2) including part of a handle from flasks, flagons or jars of the later 1st-mid 2nd century from the Seine-Middle Rhine area (Harden, 1967 238-40), the small colourless jar (13) of Isings Form 94 small type of the 2nd century and the fragment of a colourless cup (10).

1. One body fragment from a pale blue-green pillar moulded bowl, one wide flattish rib extant. Isings Form 3a. 1st century.
Phase 4A (33) F60 V29.
2. One fragment of neck with basal constriction of a jug or flask. This is of thick blue-green metal, decorated with optic-blown swirling ribs fading on the neck. Isings Form 52 from the Seine-Rhine area. Late 1st-mid 2nd century.
Phase 5A (92) III 27. See also 3B (51) F71 V 39, Phase 4A (19) F63 V 19, Phase 4B (17) 13, and a handle fragment from Phase 7C (12) V 5.
3. One fragment from the rim of a flask, diameter 50 mm. The rim is formed by folding outwards, down and upwards. Pale blue-green, rather bubbly metal, somewhat distorted. 1st century onwards.
Phase 5A (93) III 26.
4. One fragment from the rim of a flask or unguentarium in deep blue-green metal. The rim, estimated diameter 40 mm, is formed by folding outwards, up and inwards. 1st century onwards.
Phase 5A (94) III 25.
5. One fragment from the base and lower body of an unguentarium with a possibly conical body. The vessel is poorly made of a blue-green, thick and bubbly metal possibly of Isings Form 28b. 1st century onwards.
Phase 5B (77) III 23.
6. One fragment from a deep blue pillar moulded bowl with a large wide vertical rib. The exterior above the ribbing is ground while the ribs and interior are fire polished. Isings Form 3b, probably dating from before AD75.
Phase 5C (74) III 13.
7. One handle and body fragment from a small bath-oil flask with a "dolphin" handle in blue-green metal. Isings Form 61 of later 1st-early 3rd century date.
Phase 5C (128) VII 4.
8. One fragment from the rim and body of a pillar moulded bowl of blue-green metal with part of two ribs extant. Isings Form 3b of later 1st century date.
Phase 7A (110) VI 8.

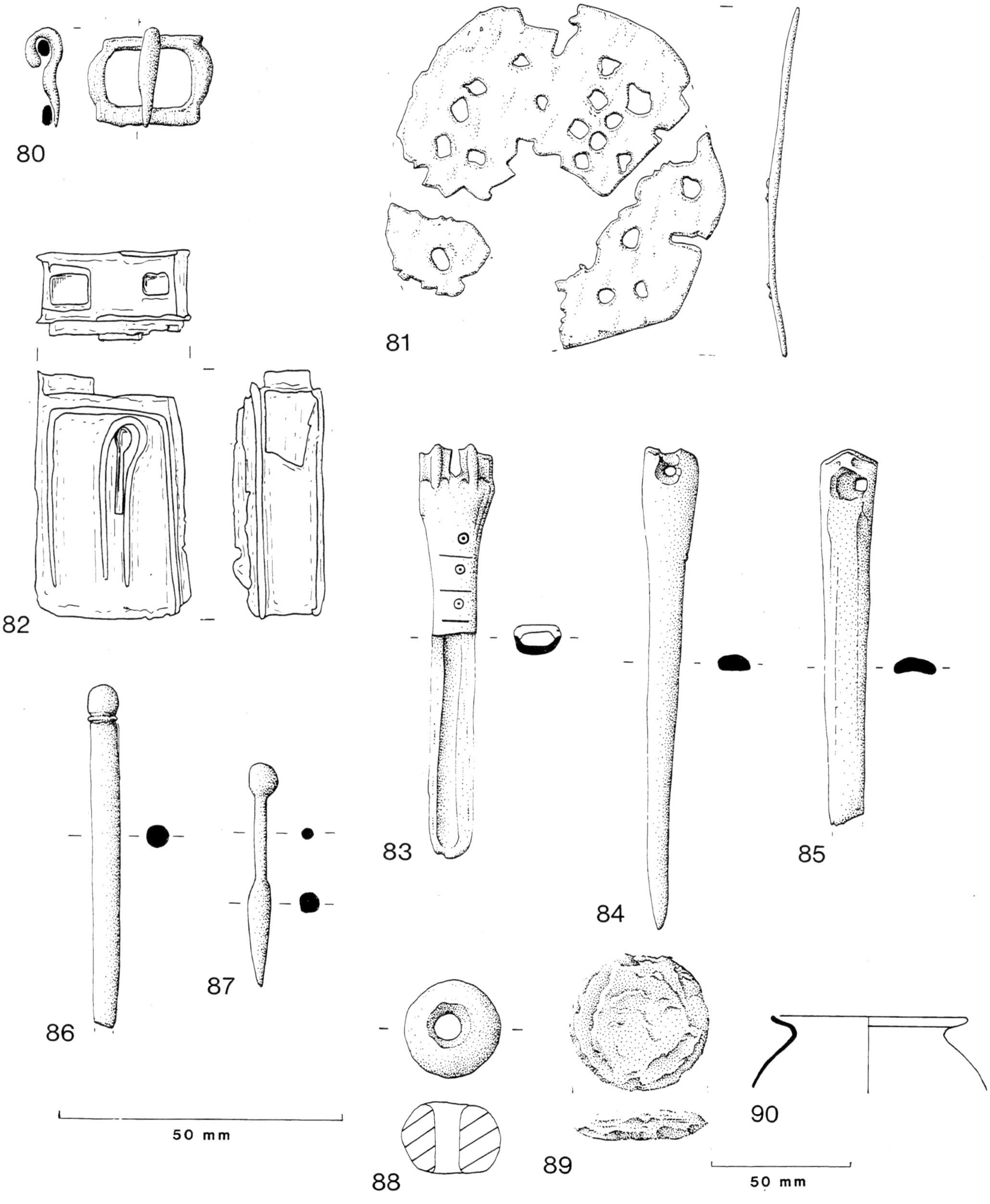

Fig. 79 Small Finds and Glass 80-81, 86-87 Scale 1:1; 82-85, 88-90 Scale 1:2

9. One body fragment from a colourless pillar moulded bowl with a fine, narrow slightly curving rib. This is possibly Isings Form 3a of later 1st century.
Phase 7C (121) IIIB 7.
10. One rim fragment from a small cup with an upright rim decorated on the exterior with two parallel incised lines and a slightly convex body. The blown metal is colourless, very fine and thin now dulled and weathered. Late 1st-2nd century.
Phase 7C (39) IIIB 10.
11. Two fragments from the base and shoulder of a small square bottle in blue-green metal. *c*. 70-130
Phase 7C (69) III 4.
12. One fragment from the tubular rim of a jar or bowl, the rim (estimated diameter 160mm) folded outwards and down in blue-green metal now weathered. Later 1st-early 2nd century.
Phase 7C (130) VI 4.
13. Fragment from the rim and body of a small jar. The rim (estimated diameter 80 mm) is everted and flattened while the body is bulbous. The interior of the rim is lightly ground. The undecorated colourless metal is very thin, now dulled and cracked. Isings Form 94, small type. 2nd century. (Fig. 79.90).
Phase 8A (99) F48 IIIB 4.
14. One fragment from the rim of a funnel mouthed flask. The rim is tubular folded up and inwards, the very thin metal pale blue-green in colour. Isings Form 92. 2nd century.
Phase 8A (100) F48 IIIB 4.

Beads

15. One fragment from a faience 'melon' bead.
Phase 6A (118) VI 11.
16. Two fragments of red glass possibly from a cylindrical bead.
Phase 7C (16) V 5.

Site 2

Forty-two fragments were examined, including parts of three beads (one probably not Roman). Seven fragments of window glass were found from Phases 4B and 6A, all of the matt/glossy type of the 1st-2nd centuries.

17. One fragment possibly from the upper body of a flask or jug decorated with parts of two slightly converging trailed-on ribs. Blown metal of golden-brown colour. Later 1st-early 2nd centuries.
Phase 4B (26) F8 I 25.
18. Large fragments from the lower part of the body of a bowl decorated with faint, slightly divergent, fine ribs. Mould blown greenish/colourless metal now dulled and weathered. Late 1st-early 2nd century.
Phase 4B (89) II 67.
19. One fragment from the lower part of a double spur handle from a flagon or jug in blue-green metal. Later 1st-early 2nd century. Similar to 20 but with no ribbing visible on the body fragment.
Phase 4B (108) II 67.
20. One fragment from a lower handle attachment as 19 with traces of optic-blown ribbing on the body.
Phase 4B (125) II 67.
21. One body fragment from a flask, jug or jar showing part of one optic-blown rib possibly from the same vessel as 19 and 20. Pale blue/green metal probably made in the Seine-Middle Rhine area (Charlesworth 1972, 202). Later 1st-mid 2nd century.
Phase 6A (19) F35 II 2.

Beads

22. One fragment from a deep blue bead with wide and irregular hole.
Phase 1B (53) F15 I 89.
23. Small faience melon bead.
Phase 5 (59) F 46 II 38.
24. Spherical bright blue bead with the exterior ground smooth. Post-medieval?
Unphased (32) III 5.

Site 3

25. Cylindrical bead, 25mm long, in dark green metal made by drawing a rod and perforating with a wire. 4th-5th century or later.
Unphased (3) I 8.

Site 5

168 fragments were examined including parts of four beads and nine fragments of window glass from Phases 2A, 2C, 3C, 4B, 4C, 6B and 6D the latter showing part of the edge of the pane. An unstratified fragment of window glass showed signs of rudimentary chipping for re-use. Forty nine fragments were from bottles of natural blue-green glass of which three were definitely cylindrical. One of the square bottles (39) has a patterned base.

The vessel forms represented covered all periods from the 1st to the 3rd-4th centuries although only three (35, 50 and 52) were specifically later types. Most of the fragments represented vessel forms of the later 1st-2nd centuries with a wide variety of domestic usage, notable forms being the colourless dish or plate (54), a Hofheim type cup (48), a small jar or bowl with short pinched ribs (35) and the small 3rd century type jug (51).

26. Fragment of body and 'Dolphin' handle from an oil flask in blue-green metal. The handle has been drawn up the shoulder and on to the neck, then drawn backwards to form a circular opening to carry a cord or chain. For a discussion of these flasks see Harden and Price 1971, 336. Isings Form 61 1st-4th century.
Phase 1C (1114) IV 17
27. Body fragment from a pillar moulded bowl in plain blue-green metal with part of one narrow vertical rib extant. Isings Form 3b of 1st century date.
Phase 2A (1122) F41 VI 25.
28. Two base and body fragments from a pillar moulded bowl, same vessel as 36.
Phase 2A (1182) F36 V 27.
29. Three base and body fragments from a pillar moulded bowl.
Phase 2A (1192) F36 V 27.
30. Three body and base fragments from a flask or flagon in golden brown metal with a possibly conical body showing traces of optic-blown ribs. Later 1st-2nd century.
Phase 2A (1193) F36 V 27.
31. One body fragment from the neck and upper handle of a long-necked one handled jug or flagon. The neck narrows slightly towards the top. Bright green metal with slight weathering. Isings Form 52 a-c. Later 1st-early 2nd century.
Phase 2C (1118) VII 9.
32. Part of the lower end of a handle from a prismatic bottle in blue-green metal. The handle (width 60 mm) has been drawn into sixteen sharp claws to grip the bottle shoulder. Later 1st-mid 2nd century.
Phase 2C (1120) VII 25.
33. One fragment from the rim and body of a jar or bowl in blue-

green metal. The upright tubular rim (diameter *c.* 190 mm) is folded out and under while the body is decorated with a pattern of swirling optic-blown ribs, parts of three being extant. Later 1st-early 2nd century.
Unphased (1130) V 33.

34. One fragment of the lower body of a pillar moulded bowl in blue green metal with parts of two slender rounded ribs visible. The vessel is cast with a ground interior decorated with two concentric abraded bands whilst the exterior is fire polished. Isings Form 3a. Later 1st century possibly before AD 80. Concentric abraded bands and the junction of the side and base of the vessel are believed to be early in the Vindonissa series (Berger 1960, 10, 18).
Unphased (1137) V 34.
35. One body fragment from a vessel (jar?) with fine pinched and tooled short vertical ribs on the widest part of the globular body. Pale grey-blue very poor quality metal with large and small bubbles and dirty inclusions. 3rd-4th century.
Unphased (1153) V 36.
36. One fragment from the base/body of a pillar moulded bowl. The pale blue-green metal is rather thinner than usual with small prominent closely spaced ribs. The exterior is fire polished while the interior is finely ground with one abraded band near the body/base junction. Isings Form 3a of later 1st century date.
Phase 2C (1191) VI 10.
37. One fragment from the base and base ring (estimated diameter 40mm) of a small cup or bowl in very weathered blue-green metal. A tooling mark is present on the inside of the base ring. Later 1st-2nd century.
Phase 3C (8) X 2.
38. One body fragment from a pillar moulded bowl in blue-green metal with parts of two broad straight ribs extant. Isings Form 3b of later 1st century date.
Phase 3A (9) F106 X 13.
39. One base fragment from a mould blown square bottle in blue-green metal, now dulled and weathered. The base is decorated with two concentric circles (outer circle diameter *c.* 60mm) and a central raised dot
Phase 3C (1145) V 10.
40. One fragment of rim and body from a bowl with an upright tubular rim (estimated diameter 200 mm) folded out and down in pale greenish metal
Unphased (1152) V 32.
41. One small body fragment from a blue green pillar moulded bowl, now very dulled and weathered.
Unphased (1181) V 32.
42. Two fragments from the body of a flask or jug in blue-green metal, one fragment decorated with four concentric abraded bands while the other has one fine applied rib. Later 1st-2nd century.
Phase 3C (1096) IV 5.
43. One fragment of the base and body of a pillar moulded bowl in weathered pale blue-green metal showing heavy wear on the base. The exterior is fire polished with traces of fine ribs on the lower body whilst the interior is very finely ground. 1st century.
Phase 4C (1185) VII 4.
44. One fragment from the rim and body of a small jar in very thin colourless blown metal, now slightly weathered. The fire-smoothed upright rim is decorated with one incised line on the exterior while the sharply constricted neck is similarly treated. Later 1st-early 2nd century.
Phase 6A (1113) IV 1.
45. One body fragment from an unguentarium in pale blue-green metal. Isings Form 8. 1st century onwards.
Phase 6B (1056) F12 I 30.
46. One fragment from the plain base and lower body of a bulbous-bodied flask in blue-green metal. A wear mark is present around the edge of a slight indentation. Later 1st-2nd century.
Phase 6B (1060) F12 I 30.
47. One fragment of handle with a central rib from a long necked jug or flagon in pale greenish metal.
Phase 6B (1112) F12 I 30.
48. One fragment from the body of a hemispherical colourless cup now very dulled and weathered. Estimated rim diameter: 90 mm. Hofheim type of later 1st-2nd century.
Phase 6B (1116) F12 I 30.
49. Body fragment from a pillar moulded bowl in pale blue metal with a broad ill defined rib. Both interior and exterior are fire polished. Isings Form 3a. Later 1st century.
Phase 6C (1150) F17 VII 30.
50. Body fragment from a pillar moulded bowl in pale green - blue metal. This has a fire polished exterior and ground interior with one abraded band near the junction of the base and side similar to 34 above. Isings Form 3b. Later 1st century possibly before AD 80 (Berger 1960, 10, 18).
Phase 6C (1177) F17 VII 30.
51. One fragment of a 'chain' handle from a jug with parts of three 'links' extant in dark blue-green metal. 3rd century.
Phase 6C (1188) F26 V 18.
52. One fragment of a flask rim, everted, bent down, up and inwards to form a tube. Pale greenish metal with some patches of irridescence. Isings Form 101. 3rd-4th century.
Unphased (1031) I u.s.
53. One fragment from the lower neck of a flask or jug decorated with wrythen ribbing partly smoothed away on the neck. Blown into a mould and then free inflated.
Unphased (1126) I u.s.
54. Two fragments from a colourless plate or dish, the base almost flat and of even thickness, the other fragment being slightly curved. Cast, ground and polished, the base decorated with a raised concentric circle to form a base ring. Later 1st-mid 2nd century.
Unphased (1117) u.s.
55. A base fragment from a small bowl in colourless metal. The flat base (estimated diameter 50mm) has an applied central pad and a tubular base ring.
Unphased (1189) VIII 6.

Beads

56. Small 'melon' bead with oblique decorative grooves. Possibly 1st century.
Phase 2C (1023) IV 10.
57. Small semi-spherical bead in deep purple metal, formed round a rod. Possibly 4th century or later.
Phase 6C (1001) F2 II 14.
58. Large faience 'melon' bead
Unphased (1053) u.s.
59. Fragment of faience 'melon' bead
Unphased (1250) u.s.

Site 6

Thirty eight Roman fragments were examined datable to the 1st-3rd centuries. These included three fragments of window glass from Phases 4B, 5C and 7A and a fragment of faience bead (70).

60. Body and handle fragment from large jar or bottle in blue-green metal, flattened with three different sized ribs. This is possibly from a jar with "M" shaped handles such as Isings Form 63. Later 1st-2nd century.

Phase 1D (661) F24 108.

61. Five fragments from the body of a thin colourless beaker or cup with slightly outsplayed sides decorated with a wheel-cut line above another band of six. Some irridescence is present. Late 1st-end of 2nd century.
Phase 2C (724) 37.

62. A fragment of tubular, slightly everted rim (ext. diam. 160mm) from a bowl in blue-green metal. Late 1st century onwards.
Phase 4C (31) 22.

63. Body fragment of colourless vessel decorated with a pair of fine wheel-cut lines. Late 1st-2nd century.
Phase 6B (44) 15.

64. Several fragments from the rim and body of a small colourless cup, with an upright rim and slightly curving body decorated with a fine wheel-cut line. Late 1st-2nd century.
Phase 6B (670) 15.

65. Seven fragments (three joining) from the body of a straight sided cup or beaker with outcurving rim, the lower body curving in towards the base. The metal is blown, yellowish-colourless now abraded and scratched. The body is decorated with at least one row of long oval cut facets (max length 120 mm; max width 5mm) three of which survive. A narrow wheel-cut line borders the upper edge of the decoration. 3rd century (cf. Harden, 1962, 137 Fig. 88 Nos 205.1 and 205.3).
Phase 7A (50) 12.

66. Base and footring fragment from a small cup or bowl in blown colourless metal with some irridescence. The base (est. diam. 41mm) exterior and footring are ground and polished, the footring being set at an obtuse angle to the base. Later 1st-early 2nd century.
Phase 7A (651) 9.

67. A fragment of handle and lower attachment from a globular bodied jug or flagon in bright green metal. The flat strap handle has a prominent rib on the left-hand edge, its lower end being drawn into three unequal sized spurs. Later 1st-2nd century.
Phase 7A (671) 14.

68. Two fragments from the rim and body of a straight-sided cup with slightly incurving, fire rounded rim (est. diam 70mm) in blown blue-green metal now in poor condition with patches of irridescence. Later 1st century onwards.
Phase 8E (653) F1 62.

Beads and Counter

69. Fragments of faience bead
Phase 4C (943) 24.

70. Counter, circular (max. diam. 14mm) with D shaped section in deep green glass appearing black now scratched and dulled with slight irridescence. This type was used throughout the Roman period.
Phase 4B (25) F13 82.

Site 9

71. Completely opaque pale blue spherical bead. Probably Victorian.
Unphased (1) u.s.

Roman Tile — John Lucas

It seems probable that on most of these excavations the Roman tile was not usually retained, hence Sites 1, 3, 4, 5 and 6 yielded a total of 4.70kg of tile. No meaningful interpretation of this material can be made. The same is true of the tile from Site 2 despite the recovery of 53.24kg of tile. The problem on this site is aggravated by the lack of any tile from any structural contexts. Over 70% of the tile came from the gravel deposits of F1 in Phase 4B and a further 20% came from the pit F46 in Phase 5. It would seem that most of this tile is from residual contexts and this is attested to by the great variety of types of tile identified. No interpretation of any value can be made for all that is represented here is a typical collection of Roman tile from Leicester that could be expected from any small residual group.

The only facet worth noting is the atypical:

Fig. 49. G6 (p 70).

Site 1 Phase 4A F60 (1501): graffito cut before firing on one fragment of wall tile (*parietalis*) [...] IC IIIV [...] (or) IC IIM possibly for [FI] IC IIIV[...], *[f]ec(i)[...]viii* 'I have made ... eight (tiles)' (see *Britannia* xx (1989), 340).

The Wall Plaster — Richard Buckley

Wall plaster fragments were recovered from Sites 1, 2, 5 and 6 and a full report is available from Leicestershire Archaeological Unit. Of note are roller impressed fragments from Site 1 Phases 7A-B and 8A falling into the diamond and lattice group (Lowther 1948). Architectural features are present from Site 2 Phase 4B possibly from window or door areas. A fragment from Phase 4B features a background with overpainted plant(?) motifs in yellow, green and red which may be part of a candelabrum feature.

Site 5 records indicate that the north western room in Area V was repainted and replastered, firstly red and later dull green and that there were quarter round fillets at the junction of the floor and wall. The south western room was apparently only plastered and painted once, in plain red (p 28). Unfortunately none of the plaster from these rooms was retained.

The Human Skeletal Material Anthony J. Goudwell (Sites 2, 3) and Ann Stirland (Site 5)

Site 2

A fragment of an ilium was recovered from Phase 3, F92 II 107. It would be reasonable to suppose this represents a disturbed, earlier inhumation, and warns of the likelihood of other derivative material.

Site 3

Eight bones overall were recovered from three phases (Phase 2B F3; Phase 5A F 16 and Phase 6). These are mixed and must have originated from disturbed burials (Stirland, 1981, 168).

The group from 5A (F16) contains articulating humerus, radius and ulna. These bones are not considered as good indicators of sex or stature so any such deductions are tentative. The humeral head vertical and transverse diameters respectively are 44.8 and 41.5mm. which lie between the figures given by Dwight (In Bass, 1979) for male and female sizes, being nearer the female value in respect of the vertical diameter, but the transverse is nearer that of the male. The ratio between the two measurements, for what it is worth, is closer to that implicit in Dwight's figures for males.

Site 5

These scanty remains consist of some fragments from a possible three individuals. They are:

> A skull belonging to an adult, probably female; a mandible and the distal portion of a right adult humerus, probably male; a fourth left metacarpal belonging to a child of less than 16 years.

Although the maxilla is separate and broken, it presumably goes with the female skull and the age based on tooth attrition is 35-45 years. The age for the male mandible, using the same criteria, is 25-40 years, and the female would appear to be a little older. The teeth are poor and somewhat caried, particularly in the mandible where there is also an abscess round the root of the missing left first molar. Apart from these dental conditions, there is no other visible pathology present. The humerus has a supracondylar process or 'hook' of bone on the lateral side, above the articulation for the elbow. This is considered to be a non-pathological morphological trait.
Phase 6B F21 V 17

The Animal Bone Anthony J. Gouldwell

Deposits from these sites were not sieved and retention policies are not now known; some bone was undoubtedly discarded. In view of this a summary of the identified animal bone is given in Table 26 and detailed reports are available in the site archive. All the assemblages are dominated by sheep/goat and pig bones, with smaller numbers of chicken bones and occasional bones of horse, dog, cat, deer (red, roe and fallow), hare, goose, duck and pigeon.

Measurements of a group of cattle metapodials from 16th century deposits at Site 6 (Phase 8) are given in Table 27 with estimated withers heights ranging from 105 to 133cm (n=17).

Industrial Residues and Mortar Analysis Graham C. Morgan

Detailed reports are available in the site archive. Furnace slag and lining was present on Sites 1-3 suggesting some iron smelting activity. Lead working was evident from Site 2 Phase 4B.

Mortar analysis from Site 1 confirmed three different types of mortar used below Mosaics 1 and 2. These consisted of 1) foundation layers (pebbles, flint, quartz, dolerite, tile, limestone fragments, sand and silica). 2) *Opus Signinum* (tile, quartz, flint, dolerite, sandstone, sand and silica). 3) White mortar bedding for tesserae (tile, flint, quartz, sand, silica).

Table 26: Summary of animal bones from Sites 1-6

	Site 1	Site 2				Site 3	Site 5	Site 6					
	Ph.1B-7E	Ph.1-3	Ph4	Ph5	Ph6	Ph1-3	Ph.2-4	Ph1	Ph2-3	Ph4-5	Ph6-7	Ph8A	Ph8B-E
	C1-2 AD	C1 AD	eC2 AD	C4	C11-13	C1-3 AD	C2-3 AD	C1 BC-1 AD	C1-2 AD	C2	C3-4	C11-13	C16
Horse	-	10	1	-	1	1	-	-	-	-	-	-	1
Cattle	7	134	118	89	31	6	31	26	4	53	34	10	265
Sheep/Goat	5	164	33	96	24	4	59	16	3	11	11	2	104
Pig	5	73	34	55	11	4	4	16	1	17	11	1	100
Red deer	-	-	1	1	1	-	-	-	-	-	3	-	-
Fallow deer	-	-	-	-	-	-	-	-	1	-	-	-	-
Roe deer	-	-	1	-	-	-	-	-	-	-	-	-	-
Hare	-	1	1	1	-	-	-	-	-	-	-	-	-
Fox	-	-	58	-	-	-	-	-	-	-	-	-	2
Dog	-	1	1	-	-	-	-	-	-	-	1	-	-
Cat	-	-	-	-	-	-	-	-	-	-	-	-	27
Fowl	-	2	18	20	6	-	16	-	1	10	9	-	7
Goose	-	-	2	1	-	-	-	-	-	2	-	-	3
Whitefronted Goose		-	3	-	-	-	-	-	-	-	-	-	-
Duck	-	-	1	-	-	-	-	-	-	-	-	-	1
Pigeon	-	-	1	-	-	-	-	-	-	-	-	-	-

Table 27 Site 6: Cattle withers height estimates

Phase	Context	L/R	Bone	Measurement (mm)	Factor (upper & lower*)	Withers Height (m) Female/male
8B	F2 64	r	metacarpus	178.0	5.98-6.05	1.06-1.08
					6.24-6.33	1.11-1.13
8B	F2 64	r	metatarsus	207.+	5.28-5.35	1.09-1.11+
					5.55-56.2	1.15-1.16
8B	F2 64	r	metatarsus	222.0	5.28-5.35	1.17-1.19
					5.55-5.62	1.23-1.25
8D	F8 72	l	metacarpus	189.5	5.98-6.05	1.13-1.15
					6.24-6.33	1.18-1.20
8D	F8 72	r	metacarpus	197.5	5.98-6.05	1.18-1.19
					6.24-6.33	1.23-1.25
8D	F3 66	l	metatarsus	199.0	5.28-5.35	1.05-1.06
					5.55-5.62	1.10-1.12
8D	F3 66	r	metatarsus	207.0	5.28-5.35	1.09-1.11
					5.55-5.62	1.15-1.16
8D	F3 66	r	metatarsus	217.5	5.28-5.35	1.15-1.16
					5.55-5.62	1.21-1.22
8D	F3 66	r	metatarsus	212.0	5.28-5.35	1.12-1.13
					5.55-5.62	1.18-1.19
8E	187	r	metacarpus	176.0	5.98-6.05	1.05-1.06
					6.24-6.33	1.10-1.11
8E	187	r	metacarpus	195.5	5.98-6.05	1.17-1.18
					6.24-6.33	1.22-1.24
8E	187	r	metacarpus	195.0	5.98-6.05	1.17-1.18
					6.24-6.33	1.22-1.23
8E	187	l	metatarsus	237.0	5.28-5.35	1.26-1.27
					5.55-5.62	1.32-1.33
8E	187	r	metatarsus	227.0	5.28-5.35	1.20-1.21
					5.55-5.62	1.26-1.28
8E	187	l	metacarpus	182.5	5.98-6.05	1.09-1.10
					6.24-6.33	1.14-1.16
8E	F1 62	l	metatarsus	214.0	5.28-5.35	1.13-1.14
					5.55-5.62	1.19-1.20
8E	187	l	metatarsus	212.5	5.28-5.35	1.12-1.14
					5.55-5.62	1.18-1.19

NB: *: conversion factors are the upper and lower estimates for males and females respectively pooled from the studies of Fock (1966), Matolcsi (1970) and Zalkin (1960) as cited by von den Driesch and Boessneck (1974). Ranges are given for male (on upper line for each two-line entry) and female (lower) animals in all cases.

+: the length measurement "207.+" (Phase 8B, F2 64) applies to a metatarsus whose proximal surface has been scraped during butchery to remove a sliver of bone possibly less than 1mm thickness.

Underlined values emphasise the withers height estimates for bulls. These particular specimens are distinctly stouter than others in the table (measurements in archive).

Abbreviations

Cam.	Hawkes and Hull 1947
CIL	*Corpus Inscriptionum Latinarum*
D.	Dechelette 1904
De La Tour	La Tour, H, de 1892
Gillam	Gillam 1970
Jewry Wall Types	Kenyon 1948
Mack	Mack 1975
O.	Oswald 1936-7
Rogers	Rogers 1974
S & S	Stanfield and Simpson 1958
Tacitus	Tacitus, *Agricola*
Van Arsdell	van Arsdell, 1989

Bibliography

Allason-Jones, L, and Miket, R, 1984 *The Catalogue of Small Finds from South Shields Fort* (Soc Antiq Newcastle-upon-Tyne Monograph 2, Newcastle-upon-Tyne)

Allen, D F, 1960 The Origins of Coinage in Britain: A Reappraisal *in* Frere S S, (ed) 1960 *Problems of the Iron Age in Southern Britain* (Inst Archaeol Univ London Occas Pap 11) 97-308

Allen, D F, 1963a *The Coins of the Coritani* (Sylloge Coins Brit Isles, 3, Brit Academy, London)

Allen, D F, 1963b *Celtic Coins from South Ferriby* Hull Mus Pub 214, 33-6

Allin, C E, 1981 The Ridge Tiles *in* Mellor, J E, and Pearce, T, 1981, 52-64

Anderson, A C, 1980 *A Guide to Roman Fine Wares*, (VORDA Res Ser Highworth, Wilts)

Anderson, A C, 1981 Some Continental Beakers of the First and Second Centuries AD *in* Anderson, A C, and Anderson, A S, (ed) 1981, 321-47

Anderson, A C, and Anderson, A S, (eds) 1981 *Roman Pottery Research in Britain and North-West Europe* (Brit Archaeol Rep (Int Ser) 123, Oxford)

Andrews, G, 1985 The Romano-British Pottery from the 1974 and 1977 excavations *in* Hinchliffe, J, and Sparey Green, C, 1985, *Excavations at Brancaster 1974 and 1977*, 71-125 (E Anglian Archaeol 23 (Norfolk Archaeol Unit, Dereham))

Arthur, P A, 1978 The Lead Glazed Wares of Roman Britain *in* Arthur, P A, and Marsh, G, (eds) 1978, 243-355

Arthur, P A, and Marsh, G, (eds) 1978 *Early Fine Wares in Roman Britain* (Brit Archaeol Rep (Brit Ser) 57, Oxford)

Baker, D, Baker, E, Hassall, J, and Simco, A, 1979 Excavations in Bedford 1967-77 *Bedfordshire Archaeol J* 13, 1-309

Balmelle, C, 1985 *Le Decor Geometrique de la Mosaique Romaine* (Paris)

Bass, W M, 1979 *Human Osteology: A Laboratory and Field Manual of the Human Skeleton.* (2nd edition Missouri Archaeol Soc, Columbia, Missouri)

Beltrán Lloris, M, 1970 *Las Anforas Romanas en Espana* (Zaragosa)

Bennett, P, Frere, S S, and Stow, S, 1982 *Excavations at Canterbury Castle* (Archaeol of Canterbury 1, Kent Archaeol Soc, Maidstone)

Berger, L, 1960 *Romische Glaser aus Vindonissa* (Basel)

Bidwell, P T, 1979 *The Legionary Bath-house and Basilica and Forum at Exeter* (Exeter Archaeol Rep 1, Exeter City Counc and Univ Exeter)

Bidwell, P T, 1985 *The Roman Fort of Vindolanda, at Chesterholm, Northumberland* (English Heritage Monograph Ser 1, Historic Buildings and Monuments Commission for England, London)

Bird, J, Graham, A H, Sheldon, H L, and Townend, P, (eds) 1978 — *Southwark Excavations 1972-74* (Joint Publication 1, London Middlesex Archaeol Soc and Surrey Archaeol Soc)

Blank, E, 1971 — *Ratae Coritanorum* (Ginn, London)

Blumstein, M, 1956 — Roman Pottery from Hoo *Archaeol Cantiana* 70, 1956 (1957), 273-7

Blurton, T R, 1977 — Excavations at Angel Court, Walbrook, 1974 *Trans London Middlesex Archaeol Soc* 28, 14-100

Bonsor, G E, 1931 — *The Archaeological Expedition along the Guadalquivir River 1889-1901* (New York)

Booth, P M, and Green, S, 1989 — The Nature and Distribution of Certain Pink Grog tempered vessels *J Roman Pottery Stud* 2, 77-84

Brailsford, J W, 1962 — *Hod Hill, volume one, Antiquities from Hod Hill in the Durden Collection* (London)

Brassington, M, 1971 — A Trajanic Kiln Complex near Little Chester, Derby, 1968 *Antiq J* 51, 36-69

Brassington, M, 1980 — Derby Racecourse Kiln Excavations 1972-3 *Antiq J* 60, 8-47

Brown, G, and Simmons, B B, 1984-5 — Old Sleaford, Excavations 1984 *Fenland Res* 2, 1984-5 (1985), 31-5

Buckland, P C, Magilton, J R, and Dolby, M J, 1989 — The Roman Pottery Industries of South Yorkshire *Britannia* 11, 145-64

Buckley, R J, forthcoming — *Leicester Castle*

Buckley, R J, and Lucas, J N, 1987 — *Leicester Town Defences* (Leicestershire Museums, Art Galleries and Records Service, Leicester)

Burley, E, 1955-6 — A catalogue and survey of the metal-work from Traprain Law *Proc Soc Antiq Scot* 89, 1955-6 (1958), 118-26

Burnham, B C, and Johnson H B, (eds) 1979 — *Invasion and Response. The Case of Roman Britain* (Brit Archaeol Rep (Brit Ser) 73, Oxford)

Bushe-Fox, J P, 1914 — *Second Report on the Excavations on the Site of the Roman Town at Wroxeter, Shropshire 1913.* (Rep Res Comm Soc Antiq London 2, Oxford)

Bushe-Fox, J P, 1932 — *Third Report on the Excavation of the Roman Fort at Richborough, Kent.* (Rep Res Comm Soc Antiq London 10, London)

Bushe-Fox, J P, 1949 — *Fourth Report on the Excavation of the Roman Fort at Richborough, Kent* (Rep Res Comm Soc Antiq London 16, London)

Butcher, S A, 1977 — Enamels from Roman Britian *in* Apted, M R, (ed) 1977, *Ancient Monuments and their Interpretation* (Philimore, London), 41-70

Callender, M H, 1965 — *Roman Amphorae* (Univ Durham Publications, Oxford Univ Press)

Carus-Wilson, E M, 1962-3 — The Medieval trade of the ports of the Wash *Medieval Archaeol* 6-7, 1962-3 (1964), 182-201

Castelin, K, 1985 — *Keltische Münzen. Katalog der Sammlung des Schweizerischen Landesmuseum Zürich. Bd II. Kommentar*

Charlesworth, D, 1972 — The Glass *in* Frere, S S, 1972, 196-215

Clamp, H, 1985 — The Late Iron Age and Romano-British Pottery *in* Clay, P, and Mellor, J E, 1985, 41-59

Clarke, D T-D, 1952 — Archaeology in Leicestershire 1939-51 *Trans Leicestershire Archaeol Hist Soc* 28, 17-47

Clarke, D T-D, 1958 — Archaeology in Leicestershire 1957-1958 *Trans Leicestershire Archaeol Hist Soc* 34, 77-84

Clay, P, 1980 — Seven Inscribed Leaden Sealings from Leicester *Britannia* 11, 317-20

Clay, P, 1981 — The small finds - non structural *in* Mellor, J E, and Pearce, T, 1981, 130-44

Clay, P, 1984-5 — An excavation at Grove Farm, Enderby (SK551002) -

Interim Report *in* Liddle, P, 1984-5, Archaeology in Leicestershire and Rutland 1984 *Trans Leicestershire Archaeol Hist Soc* 59, 1984-5 (1985), 86-103 (86-7)

Clay, P, 1985 — The Pre-Roman Iron Age Settlement *in* Clay and Mellor, 1985, 29-32

Clay, P, 1992 — An Iron Age Farmstead at Grove Farm, Enderby, Leicestershire *Trans Leicestershire Archaeol Hist Soc* 66, 1-82

Clay, P, and Mellor, J E, 1985 — *Excavations in Bath Lane, Leicester* (Leicestershire Museums, Art Galleries and Records Service, Leicester)

Clifford, E M, 1961 — *Bagendon: A Belgic Oppidum. A record of the excavations of 1954-56* (Cambridge)

Coad, J G, and Streeten, A D F, 1982 — Excavations at Castle Acre Castle, Norfolk 1972-1977 *Archaeol J.* 139, 1982 (1983), 138-301

Collis, J R, 1971 — Functional and Theoretical Interpretations of British Coinage *World Archaeol* 3, 71-84

Collis, J R, 1981 — A Typology of Coin Distributions *World Archaeol* 13, 122-8

Collis, J R, 1985 — Iron Age 'Coin Moulds' *Britannia* 16, 237-8

Coppack, G, 1980 — *The Medieval Pottery of Lincoln, Nottingham and Derby* (unpublished PhD thesis, Univ Nottingham)

Corder, P, 1961 — *The Roman town and villa at Great Casterton, Rutland. Third Report* (Univ Nottingham)

Corney, M, 1984 — Objects of Bone *in* Fulford, M G, 1984, 115-6

Crummy, N, 1979 — A chronology of British Bone Pins *Britannia* 10, 157-63

Crummy, N, 1983 — *The Roman Small Finds from excavations in Colchester 1971-9* (Colchester Archaeol Rep 2, Colchester Archaeol Trust Ltd)

Crummy, P, 1982 — The Origins of some major Romano-British Towns *Britannia* 13, 125-34

Cunliffe, B W, 1964 — *Winchester Excavations 1949-60 Vol 1* (City of Winchester Museums & Libraries Comm)

Cunliffe, B W, (ed) 1968 — *Fifth Report on the Excavations of the Roman Fort at Richborough, Kent.* (Res Rep Comm Soc Antiq London 23, Oxford)

Cunliffe, B W, 1971 — *Excavations at Fishbourne 1961-1969, Volume II : the Finds* (Rep Res Comm Soc Antiq London 27, Leeds)

Cunliffe, B W, 1978 — *Iron Age Communities in Britain* (2nd edition Routledge and Kegan Paul, London)

Dannell, G B, 1971 — The Samian Pottery *in* Cunliffe, B W, 1971, 260-316

Dannell, G B, 1985 — The Arretine and Samian Pottery *in* Clay, P , and Mellor, J E , 1985, 59-61

Dannell, G B, forthcoming — The Arretine and Samian Pottery in Mellor J E, forthcoming (a)

Darling, M J, 1977 — Pottery from early military sites in Western Britain *in* Dore, J, and Greene, K T, (eds) 1977, 57-100

Darling, M J, forthcoming — *The Roman Pottery from East Gate, Lincoln* (provisional title) (City of Lincoln Archaeol Unit fascicule)

Debord, J, Giroussens, C, Gruel, K, Romero, P, and Tarrats-Saugnac, A, 1985 — Étude métallographique et analyse de matérial monetaire de l'atelier de Villeneuve-Saint-Germain (Aisne) *in* Bonnamour, L, Duval, A, and Guillaumet, J-P, (eds) 1985, *Les Ages du Fer dans la Vallée de la Saone. Paléométallurgie du Bronze* (Rev Archéol Est Centre Est Supp 6/Actes du VIIe colloque sur les Ages du Fer en France non-Méditerraneane), 271-8

Dechelette, J, 1904 — *Les Vases ceramiques ornes de la Gaule Romaine* (Paris)

Detsicas, A P, (ed) 1973 — *Current Research in Romano-British Coarse Pottery* (Counc Brit Archaeol Res Rep 10, London)

Dool, J, 1985 Derby Racecourse: Excavations on the Roman Industrial Settlement, 1974 *in* Dool, J, Wheeler, H, et al. 1985, Roman Derby: Excavations 1968-1983 Derbyshire *Archaeol J* 105, 1985 (1986), 2-348 (155-221)

Dore, J, and Greene, K T, (eds) 1977 *Roman Pottery Studies in Britain and Beyond* (Brit Archaeol Rep (Supp Ser) 30, Oxford)

Down, A, and Rule, M, 1971 *Chichester Excavations Vol 1* (Chichester Civic Society Excavation Comm, Oxford)

Driesch, A, von den, and Boessneck, J, 1974 Kritische Anmerkung zur Widerristhohenberechnung aus Langenmassen vor - und fruhgeschichtlicher Tierknochen *Saugetierkundliche Mitteilungen* 22, 325-48

du Plat Taylor, J, and Cleere, H, (eds) 1978 *Roman shipping and trade: Britain and the Rhine provinces*(Counc Brit Archaeol Res Rep 24, London)

Dunbabin, K M O, 1978 *The Mosaics of Roman North Africa: studies in iconography and patronage* (Oxford Monographs on Classical Archaeol, Oxford)

Elsdon, S M, 1992 The Iron Age Pottery *in* Clay P, 1992, 38-52

Ennaifer, M, 1983 Le theme chevaux vainqueurs a travers la serie des mosaiques africaines *Melanges de L'ecole francaise de Rome* 95, 817-58

Esmonde-Cleary, S, 1985 The quick and the dead: suburbs, cemeteries and the town *in* Grew, F, and Hobley, B, (eds) 1985, *Roman urban topography in Britain and the western empire* (Counc Brit Archaeol Res Rep 59, London), 74-7

Ettlinger, E, 1973 *Die romischen Fibeln in der Schweiz* (Bern)

Evans, E, Dowdell, G, and Thomas, H T, 1985 A third-century Maritime Establishment at Cold Knap, Barry, South Glamorgan. *Britannia* 16, 57-125

Evans, J, 1890 *The Coins of the Ancient Britons, Supplement* (London)

Farioli Campeneti, R, (ed) 1984 *Atti del III colloquio Internazionale sul Mosaico Antico, Ravenna 1980* (Ravenna)

Farrar, R A H, 1973 The Techniques and Sources of Romano-British Black-Burnished Ware, *in* Detsicas, A P, (ed) 1973, 67-103

Faudet, I, 1983 Miniature 'Ex-voto' from Argentomagus (Indre) *Britannia* 14, 92-102

Fischer, F, 1983 Das Handwerk bei den Kelten zur Zeit der Oppida *in* Jankuhn, J, Janssen, W, Schmidt-Wiegand, R, and Tiefenbach, H, (eds) 1983, *Das Handwerk in Vor-und Frühgeschichtlicher Zeit. Teil 2. Archäologische und philologische Beitrage* (Abhandl Akad Wissenschaft Göttingen, Phil-Hist Klasse, Folge 3,123) 34-49

Fitzpatrick, A P, 1985 The Celtic Coins *in* France, N E, and Gobel, B M, 1985, 49-66

Fock, J, 1966 *Metrische Untersuchungen an Metapodien einiger europaischer Ruiderrassen* (Dis, Munchen)

Ford, T D, 1972 Geology, *in* Pye, N, (ed) 1972, Leicester and its region (Leicester Univ Press), 19-58

France, N E, and Gobel, B M, 1985 *The Romano-British Temple at Harlow, Essex* (ed F R Clarke and I K Jones; West Essex Archaeol Group; Alan Sutton, Gloucester)

Freestone, I C, 1989 The petrography of the pottery from the Iron Age Cemetery, *in* Stead, I M, and Rigby, V, 1989, 264-6

Freestone, I C, and Rigby, V, 1988 The introduction of Roman ceramic styles and techniques into Britain: a case study from the King Harry Lane Cemetery, St. Albans, Hertfordshire *Materials Res Soc Proc.* 123, 109-15, Pittsburgh

Frere, S S, 1966 The end of towns in Roman Britain *in* Wacher, J S, (ed) 1966 *The Civitas Capitals of Roman Britain* (Leicester Univ Press), 87-100

Frere, S S, 1972 *Verulamium Excavations Volume I* (Rep Res Comm Soc

Antiq London 28, Oxford)

Frere, S S, 1984a — Roman Britain in 1983; I Sites Explored *Britannia* 15, 265-332

Frere, S S, 1984b — *Verulamium Excavations Volume III* (Oxford Univ Comm Archaeol Monograph 1)

Frere, S S, Stow, S, and Bennett, P, 1982 — *Excavations on the Roman and medieval defences of Canterbury* (Archaeol of Canterbury 2, Kent Archaeol Soc, Maidstone)

Fulford, M G, 1984 — *Silchester. Excavations on the Defences 1974-80* (Britannia Monograph Ser 5, Soc Promotion Roman Stud, London)

Gillam, J P, 1939 — Romano-British Derbyshire Ware *Antiq J* 19, 429-37

Gillam, J P, 1970 — *Types of Roman Coarse Pottery Vessels in Northern Britain* (3rd edition, Oriel Press, Newcastle-upon-Tyne)

Gillam, J P, 1976 — Coarse Fumed Ware in North Britain and Beyond *Glasgow Archaeol J* 4, 57-80

Goddard, H, 1870 — The Jewry Wall, Leicester *Trans Leicestershire Architect Archaeol Soc* 2, 202-04

Going, C J, 1987 — *The Mansio and other sites in the south-eastern sector of Caesaromagus : the Roman pottery,* (Chelmsford Archaeol Trust Rep 3.2/Counc Brit Archaeol Res Rep 62, London)

Goodall, I H, 1979 — The Iron Objects *in* Williams, J H, 1979, 268-77

Goodburn, R, 1984 — The Non-Ferrous Metal Objects *in* Frere, S S, 1984b, 19-67

Gould, J, 1963-4 — Excavations at Wall (Staffordshire) 1961-3 *Trans Lichfield S Staffordshire Archaeol Hist Soc* 5, 1963-4 (1964), 1-50

Green, C M, 1978 — Flavian 'ring and dot' beakers from Londinium: Verulamium Form 130 and allied types, *in* Arthur, P A, and Marsh, G, (eds) 1978, 109-18

Green, C M, 1981 — Roman Pottery *in* Jones, D, and Rhodes, M, 1981, *Excavations at Billingsgate Buildings ('Triangle') Lower Thames Street, 1974* (London Middlesex Archaeol Soc Spec Paper 4), 39-79

Green, M J, 1975 — Romano-British Non-ceramic model objects in south-eastern Britain *Archaeol J* 132, 1975 (1976), 54-70

Greene, K T, 1978 — Imported Fine Wares in Britain to AD 250: a Guide to Identification *in* Arthur, P A, and Marsh, G, (eds) 1978, 15-30

Greene, K T, 1979 — *The Pre-Flavian Fine Wares, (Report on the Excavations at Usk, 1965-1976,* Univ of Wales Press, Cardiff)

Grosvenor Museum, 1972 — *Newsletter*

Gunstone, A J H, 1971 — *Ancient British, Anglo-Saxon and Norman Coins in Midlands Museums* (Sylloge Coins Brit Isles 17, Brit Academy, London)

Hall, D N, and Nickerson, N, 1967 — Excavation at Irchester, 1962-3 *Archaeol J* 124, 1967 (1968), 65-99

Hammerson, M J, and Murray, C, 1978 — Other Roman Pottery *in* Dennis, G, 1978, 1-7 St. Thomas Street *in* Bird, J *et al*, (eds) 1978, 291-422 (337-375)

Harden, D B, 1962 — Glass in Roman York *in* RCHME, 1962, *An Inventory of the Historical Monuments in the City of York 1 Eboracum, Roman York* (Roy Comm Hist Monuments England, London), 136-41

Harden, D B, 1967 — The Glass Jug *in* Biddle, M, 1967, Two Flavian Burials from Grange Road, Winchester *Antiq J* 47, 238-40

Harden, D B, and Price, J, 1971 — The Glass *in* Cunliffe, B W, 1971, 317-68

Hartley, B R, 1972 — The Samian Ware *in* Frere, S S, 1972, 216-62

Hartley, B R, 1979 — The use of samian tesserae in Romano-British mosaics *Mosaic 1* (April), 5-6

Hartley, K F, 1972 — The Mortarium Stamps *in* Frere, S S, 1972, 371-81

Hartley, K F, 1973a — Stamped Mortaria *in* Hebditch, M, and Mellor, J E, 1973, 58-9

Hartley, K F, 1973b — The Marketing and Distribution of Mortaria *in* Detsicas, A P, (ed) 1973, 39-51

Hartley, K F, 1977 — Two Major Potteries producing Mortaria in the First Century AD *in* Dore, J, and Greene, K T, (eds) 1977, 5-17

Hartley, K F, 1981 — The Mortaria *in* Partridge, C R, 1981, 196-9

Hartley, K F, 1982 — The Mortaria *in* Bennett, P, Frere, S S, and Stow, S, 1982, 150-8

Hartley, K F, 1984 — The Mortarium Stamps *in* Frere, S S, 1984b, 280-91

Hartley, K F, 1986 — Mortarium Stamps from the Civil Settlement, Doncaster, *in* Buckland, P C, and Magilton, J R, 1986, *The Archaeology of Doncaster. 1. The Roman Civil Settlement* (Brit Archaeol Rep (Brit Ser) 148, Oxford), 143-53

Haselgrove, C C, 1978 — *Supplementary Gazetteer of Find-Spots of Celtic Coins in Britain, 1977* (Inst Archaeol Univ London Occas Pap 11a)

Haselgrove, C C, 1984 — Warfare and its Aftermath as Reflected in the Precious Metal Coinage of Belgic Gaul *Oxford J Archaeol* 3, 81-105

Haselgrove, C C, 1987 — *Iron Age Coinage in South-East England : The archaeological context* (Brit Archaeol Rep (Brit Ser) 174, Oxford)

Haverfield, F J, 1903 — Report of the Cumberland Excavation Committee for 1902 *Trans Cumberland Westmorland Antiq Archaeol Soc* 3 (N.S.), 328-49

Haverfield, F J, 1918 — Roman Leicester *Archaeol J* 75 (2nd ser, vol 25), 1-46

Hawkes, C F C, and Hull, M R, 1947 — *Camulodunum* (Rep Res Comm Soc Antiq London 14, Oxford)

Hebditch, M, 1967-8 — A Saxo-Norman pottery kiln discovered in Southgate Street, Leicester, 1964 *Trans Leicestershire Archaeol Hist Soc* 43, 1967-8 (1968), 4-9

Hebditch, M, 1973 — Coarse Pottery *in* Hebditch, M, and Mellor, J E, 1973, 59-71

Hebditch, M, and Mellor, J E, 1973 — The Forum and Basilica of Roman Leicester *Britannia* 4, 1-83

Hermet, F, 1934 — *La Graufesenque* (Paris)

Hildyard, E J W, 1952 — A Roman Site at Dere Street *Archaeol Aeliana (4th ser)* 30, 223-38

Hobley, B, 1966-7 — A Neronian-Vespasianic Military Site at 'The Lunt', Baginton, Warwickshire *Trans Proc Birmingham Archaeol Soc* 83, 1966-7 (1969), 65-129

Hobley, B, 1971-3 — Excavation at 'The Lunt' Roman Military Site, Baginton, Warwickshire. 1968-71. Second Interim Report *Trans Proc Birmingham Warwickshire Archaeol Soc* 85, 1971-3 (1973), 7-92

Howe, M D, Perrin, J R, and Mackreth, D F, 1980 — *Roman Pottery from the Nene Valley: a Guide* (Occasional Pap 2, Peterborough City Mus)

Hull, M R, 1958 — *Roman Colchester* (Rep Res Comm Soc Antiq London 20, Oxford)

Hull, M R, 1963 — *The Roman Potters' Kilns at Colchester* (Rep Res Comm Soc Antiq London 21, Oxford)

Hull, M R, 1967 — The Nor'Nour brooches *in* Dudley, D, 1967, Excavations on Nor'Nour in the Isles of Scilly 1962-6 *Archaeol J* 124, 1967 (1968), 1-64 (28-64)

Hurst, J G, and Golson, J, 1957 — Excavations at St. Benedicts Gates, Norwich 1951-3 *Norfolk Archaeol* 31, 5-112

Jarvis, P A, 1984-5 — The Origin and Status of Iron Age Leicester - the Evidence from the Jewry Wall Site *Trans Leicestershire Archaeol Hist Soc* 59, 1984-5 (1985), 92-3

Jarvis, P A, 1986 — The Early Pits of the Jewry Wall Site, Leicester *Trans Leicestershire Archaeol Hist Soc* 60, 7-15

Jenkins, F, 1960 — Two Pottery Kilns and a Tilery of the Roman Period at Canterbury *Archaeol Cantiana* 74, 1960 (1961), 151-62

Johnson, A, 1983 — *Roman Forts of the 1st and 2nd centuries AD in Britain and the German Provinces* (Adam and Charles Black, London)

Johnson, P, 1979-80 — The mosaics of Roman Leicester *Trans Leicestershire Archaeol Hist Soc* 55, 1979-80 (1981), 1-10

Johnson, S, 1983 — *Burgh Castle: Excavations by Charles Green, 1958-61* (E Anglian Archaeol 20, Norfolk Archaeol Unit, Dereham)

Jones, M U, Kent, J P C, Musty, J, and Biek, L, 1976 — Celtic Coin Moulds from Old Sleaford, Lincolnshire *Antiq J* 56, 238-40

Kay, S O, 1962 — The Romano-British Kilns at Hazelwood and Holbrook, Derbyshire *Derbyshire Archaeol J* 82, 1962 (1963), 21-42

Kent, J P C, 1978a — The Origins and Development of Celtic Gold Coinage in Britain *Actes du congrès international d'archéologie: Rouen*, 3,4,5, juillet, 1975 (Rouen) 313-24

Kent, J P C, 1978b — The London Area in the Late Iron Age: An Interpretation of the Earliest Coins *Collectanea Londiniensia: Studies in London Archaeology and History Presented to Ralph Merrifield* (London Middlesex Archaeol Soc Spec Pap 2) 53-8

Kenyon, K M, 1948 — *Excavations at the Jewry Wall Site, Leicester* (Rep Res Comm Soc Antiq London 15, Oxford)

Keppie, L J F, 1975 — Catalogue of Finds: Stone to Clay *in* Robertson, A, Scott, M, and Keppie, L J F, 1975 *Bar Hill: A Roman Fort and its Finds* (Brit Archaeol Rep (Brit Ser) 16, Oxford)

Kimes, T, Haselgrove, C C, and Hodder, I R, 1982 — A method for the Identification of the Location of Regional Cultural Boundaries *J Anthrop Archaeol* 1, 113-31

Kirkman, J S, 1940 — New Varieties of Roman Coins from the 1936-1938 Excavations at Leicester *Numis Chron* 77 (5th ser, vol 20), 24-31

Knorr, R, 1912 — *Sudgallische Terra-Sigillata-Gefasse von Rottweil* (Stuttgart)

Knorr, R, 1919 — *Topfer und Fabriken verzierten Terra-Sigillata des ersten Jahrhunderts* (Stuttgart)

Knorr, R, 1942 — Fruhe und spate Sigillata des Calus *Germania* 26, 184-91

Knorr, R, 1952 — *Terra-Sigillata-Gefasse des ersten Jahrhunderts mit Topfernamen* (Stuttgart)

Knowles, A K, 1977 — The Roman Settlement at Brampton, Norfolk: Interim Report *Britannia* 8, 209-21

La Tour, H, de, 1892 — *Atlas des monnaies gauloises* (Paris)

Lawson, A J, 1975 — Shale and jet objects from Silchester *Archaeologia* 105, 241-76

Leach, H N, 1987 — Stamford Ware Fabrics *Medieval Ceramics* 11, 69-74

Leicester Museums, 1959 — Archaeology in Leicestershire and Rutland 1958-9 *Trans Leicestershire Archaeol Hist Soc* 35, 78-86

Leicester Museums, 1960 — Archaeology in Leicestershire and Rutland 1959-60 *Trans Leicestershire Archaeol Hist Soc* 36, 49-54

Leicester Museums, undated — *Roman Pavements* (Leicester Mus Dept of Antiquities leaflet)

Levi, D, 1947 — *Antioch Mosaic Pavements* (Princetown Univ Press)

Liddle, P, 1982 — *Leicestershire Archaeology. The Present State of Knowledge. Vol 1 to the end of the Roman Period* (Leicestershire Museums, Art Galleries and Records Service, Leicester)

Loeschke, S, 1942 — Die Belgische Keramik aus Oberaden, *in* Albrecht, C, 1942, *Das Romerlager in Oberaden 2*

London Museum, 1940 — *Medieval Catalogue* (HMSO, London)

Loughlin, N, 1977 — Dales Ware: a contribution to the study of Roman coarse pottery *in* Peacock, D P S, (ed) 1977, 85-146

Lowther, A W G, 1948 — *A study of patterns on Roman flue-tiles and their distribution* (Res Papers Surrey Archaeol Soc 1)

Lucas, J N, 1976-7 Excavations at Great Holme Street, Leicester *Trans Leicestershire Archaeol Hist Soc* 52, 1976-7 (1978), 86-7

Lucas, J N, 1980-1 The Debris of History: An Archaeological Survey of Leicester *Trans Leicestershire Archaeol Hist Soc* 56, 1980-1 (1982), 1-9

Lucas, J N, 1989 An excavation in the North-East quarter of Leicester: Elbow Lane 1977 *Trans Leicestershire Archaeol Hist Soc* 63, 18-47

Lucas, J N, forthcoming *The Norfolk Street Roman Villa, Leicester*

McCarthy, M, 1979 The Pottery *in* Williams, J H, 1979, 151-242

Macgregor, A, 1985 *Bone, Antler, Ivory and Horn* (Croom Helm, London and Sydney : Barnes and Noble Books Totowa, New Jersey)

Mack, R P, 1975 *The Coinage of Ancient Britain* (3rd edition, Spink, London)

Mackensen, M, 1975 The State of Research on the 'Norican' Silver Coinage *World Archaeol* 6, 249-75

Mackreth, D F, 1978 The Roman Brooches *in* Down, A, 1978 *Chichester Excavations III* (Phillimore, Chichester Civic Society Excavation Comm,Chichester), 277-87

Macphail, R I, 1981 Soil and Botanical Studies of the 'dark earth' *in* Jones, M, and Dimbleby, G,(eds) 1981, *The Environment of Man; the Iron Age to the Anglo-Saxon Period* (Brit Archaeol Rep (Brit Ser) 87, Oxford), 309-31

MacRobert, E, 1983 *The Pottery from Blue Boar Lane, Leicester* (unpublished thesis for Diploma in Post-Excavation Studies, Univ Leicester)

MacRobert, E, 1987 The Roman Pottery (excluding samian) *in* Buckley, R J, and Lucas, J N, 1987, 65-75

MacRobert, E, 1989 The Roman Pottery, *in* Lucas, J N, 1989, 25-33

MacRobert, E, forthcoming The Roman Pottery from the 1979 excavations *in* Buckley, R J, and Connor, A, forthcoming *Excavations on Causeway Lane, Leicester* (provisional title)

McWhirr, A D, 1971-2 Archaeology in Leicestershire and Rutland 1970-72 *Trans Leicestershire Archaeol Hist Soc* 47, 1971-2 (1973), 62-76

Marsh, G, 1978 Early second century fine wares in the London area, *in* Arthur, P A, and Marsh, G, (eds) 1978, 119-224

Marsh, G, 1981 London's Samian supply and its relationship to the development of the Gallic Samian Industry *in* Anderson, A C, and Anderson, A S, (eds) 1981, 173-238

Marsh, G, and Tyers, P A, 1976 Roman Pottery from the City of London *Trans London Middlesex Archaeol Soc* 27, 228-44

Marsh, G, and Tyers, P A, 1978 The Roman Pottery from Southwark *in* Bird, J, et al, (eds) 1978, 533-82

Martin, J, 1981 The documentary evidence *in* Mellor, J E, and Pearce, T, 1981, 1-5

Matolsci, J, 1970 Historische Erforshung der Korpergrosse des Rindes auf Grand von unganschen Knochenmaterial Zeitscher f. *Tierzuchtg u Zuchtungsbiol*, Hamburg 87, 89-137

May, J, 1976 *Prehistoric Lincolnshire* (Hist Lincolnshire 1, Hist Lincolnshire Comm, Lincoln)

May, J, 1984 The Major Settlements of the Later Iron Age in Lincolnshire *in* Field, N, and White, A, (eds) 1984, *A Prospect of Lincolnshire* (Lincoln), 18-22

May, J, 1987 Absolute Chronology and Possible Conclusions *in* Elsdon, S M, and May, J, *The Iron Age Pottery from Dragonby. A Draft Report* (Nottingham), 67-75

Mellor, J E, 1968-9 Excavations in Leicester 1965-1968 *Trans Leicestershire Archaeol Hist Soc* 44, 1968-9 (1970), 1-10

Mellor, J E, 1975-6 Great Holme Street, Leicester *Trans Leicestershire Archaeol Hist Soc* 51, 1975-6 (1977), 59

Mellor, J E, 1985 Roman Leicester. New light on old problems *East Midlands Archaeol* 1, 29-33

Mellor, J E, forthcoming (a) *Excavations in St. Nicholas Circle, Leicester 1. The Roman Forum*

Mellor, J E, forthcoming (b) *Excavation of a Romano-British Temple in St. Nicholas Circle, Leicester 1969*

Mellor, J E, and Pearce, T, 1981 *The Austin Friars, Leicester* (Counc Brit Archaeol Res Rep 35, London)

Mellor, J E, and Pearce, T, forthcoming *Excavations in St. Nicholas Circle, Leicester 2. Post Roman Occupation*

Miket, R, 1983 *The Roman Fort at South Shields : Excavation of the Defences 1977-81* (Tyne and Wear County Counc Mus, Gateshead)

Miles, D, (ed) 1986 *Archaeology at Barton Court Farm, Abingdon, Oxon* (Oxford Archaeol Unit Rep 3; Counc Brit Archaeol Res Rep 50, Oxford and London)

Millett, M, 1984 Forts and the Origins of Towns: cause or effect? *in* Blagg T F C, and King A C, (eds) *Military and Civilian in Roman Britain* (Brit Archaeol Rep (Brit Ser) 136, Oxford), 65-74

Mocsy, A, 1983 *Nomenclator* (Dissertationes Pannonicae Series III, Vol 1, Budapest)

Monaghan, J, 1982 An Investigation of the Romano-British Pottery Industry on the Upchurch Marshes *Archaeol Cantiana* 98, 1982 (1983), 27-50

Monaghan, J, 1983 The Woodruff Collection *Archaeol Cantiana* 99, 1983 (1984), 199-217

Monaghan, J, 1987 *Upchurch and Thameside Roman Pottery* (Brit Archaeol Rep (Brit Ser) 173, Oxford)

Mossop, H R, 1968 Three New Varieties of Ancient British Coins *Brit Numis J* 37, 1968 (1969), 190

Nash, D E M, 1978 *Settlement and Coinage in Central Gaul c. 200-50 BC* (Brit Archaeol Rep (Supp Ser) 39, Oxford)

Nash, D E M, 1982 Adminius Did Strike Coins *Oxford J Archaeol* 1, 111-14

Nash, D E M, 1987 *Coinage in the Celtic World* (Seaby, London)

Neal, D S, 1974 *The Excavation of the Roman Villa in Gadebridge Park, Hemel Hempstead 1963-8* (Rep Res Com Soc Antiq London 31, Leeds)

Niblett, R, 1985 *Sheepen: an early Roman industrial site at Camulodunum* (Counc Brit Archaeol Res Rep 57, London)

Noel Hume, I, 1954 Romano-British Potteries on the Upchurch Marshes *Archaeol Cantiana* 68, 1954 (1955), 72-90

Oakley, G E, and Hall, A D, 1979 The Spindle Whorls *in* Williams, J H, 1979, 286-99

Oakley, G E, and Harman, M, 1979 The Worked Bone *in* Williams, J H, 1979, 308-18

O'Neil, B H St J, 1928 Excavations at Mancetter, 1927 *Trans Birmingham Archaeol Soc* 53, 1928 (1931), 173-95

Orton, C J, 1975 Quantitative Pottery Studies. Some Progress, Problems and Prospects *Science and Archaeol* 16, 30-35

Orton, C J, 1977a Introduction to the Pottery Reports *in* Blurton, T R, 1977, 28-30

Orton, C J, 1977b Roman Pottery (excluding Samian) *in* Blurton, T R, 1977, 30-53

Oswald, F, 1936-7 *Index of Figure-types on Terra Sigillata ('Samian ware')* (Liverpool Gregg Press reprint, 1964)

Oswald, F, 1948a *The Commandant's House at Margidunum* (Univ College Nottingham)

Oswald, F, 1948b *The Terra Sigillata (Samian Ware) of Margidunum* (Univ College Nottingham)

Oswald, F, and Pryce, T D, 1920 *An introduction to the study of terra sigillata* (London Gregg Press reprint, 1965)

Page, W, (ed) 1907 — *Victoria County History of Leicester Vol 1* (Constable)

Partridge, C R, 1979 — Excavations at Puckeridge and Braughing 1975-79 *Hertfordshire Archaeol* 7, 1979 (1980), 28-132

Partridge, C R, 1981 — *Skeleton Green* (Britannia Monograph Ser 2, Soc Promotion Roman Stud, London)

Peacock, D P S, 1970 — Imported Pottery, Period 1 *in* Rahtz, P, 1970, Excavations on Glastonbury Tor, Somerset 1964-6 *Archaeol J* 127, 1970 (1971), 1-81 (65-7)

Peacock, D P S, 1971 — Roman Amphorae in pre-Roman Britain *in* Hill, M, and Jesson, D, (eds) 1971, *The Iron Age and its Hill-forts* (Univ Southampton Monograph Ser 1), 161-88

Peacock, D P S, 1977a — Roman Amphorae: Typology, Fabric, Origins *Collection de l'Ecole Francaise de Rome* 32 (Rome), 261-78

Peacock, D P S, 1977b — Pompeian Red Ware *in* Peacock, D P S, (ed) 1977, 147-62

Peacock, D P S, (ed) 1977 — *Pottery and Early Commerce* (Academic Press, London)

Peacock, D P S, 1978 — The Rhine and the problem of Gaulish wine in Roman Britain *in* du Plat Taylor, J, and Cleere, H, (eds) 1978, 49-51

Peacock, D P S, and Williams, D F, 1986 — *Amphorae and the Roman economy: an introductory guide* (Longman, London)

Perrin, J R, 1980 — Pottery of 'London Ware' type from the Nene Valley *Durobrivae* 8, 9-10

Perring, D, 1987 — Domestic buildings in Romano-British towns *in* Schofield, J, and Leech, R, (eds) 1987, *Urban Archaeology in Britain* (Counc Brit Archaeol Res Rep 61, London), 147-55

Philp, B J, 1958 — Discoveries at Reculver, 1955 *Archaeol Cantiana* 72, 1958 (1959), 160-66

Pirie, V, 1986 — Three Roman Miniature Axes from Leicestershire *in* Liddle, P, 1986, Archaeology in Leicestershire and Rutland 1985 *Trans Leicestershire Archaeol Hist Soc* 60, 78-95 (84-7)

Platt, C, and Coleman-Smith, R, 1975 — *Excavations in Medieval Southampton 1953-65 Vol II The Finds* (Leicester Univ Press)

Polenz, H, 1982 — Münzen in latènezeitlichen Gräbern Mitteleuropas aus der Zeit zwischen 300 und 50 vor Christi Geburt *Bayer Vorgeschichtsbl* 47, 27-222

Pollard, R J, 1983 — The Coarse Pottery, including the Kiln Products, *in* Catherhall, P D, 1983, A Romano-British Pottery Manufacturing Site at Oakleigh Farm, Higham, Kent *Britannia* 14, 103-41 (121-38)

Pollard, R J, 1987 — The Other Roman Pottery *in* Meates, G W, 1987 *Lullingstone Roman Villa II* (Kent Archaeol Soc Monograph 3, Maidstone)

Pollard, R J, forthcoming (a) — The Roman Pottery *in* Mellor, J E, forthcoming (a)

Pollard, R J, forthcoming (b) — The Roman Pottery *in* Mellor, J E, forthcoming (b)

Pollard, R J, forthcoming (c) — The Roman Pottery *in* Lucas, J N, forthcoming *Excavations in Silver Street, Leicester, 1968: a Roman bath-house(?) and associated features* (provisional title)

Pollard, R J, forthcoming (d) — The Roman Pottery *in* Lucas, J N, forthcoming *Excavations on the Shakespeare's Head site, Leicester, 1968: A Roman cellar and other structures* (provisional title)

Pollard, R J, forthcoming (e) — The Roman Pottery *in* Lucas, J N, forthcoming

Pollard, R J, forthcoming (f) — The Roman Pottery *in* Lucas, J N, forthcoming *Excavations on a Roman extra-mural site on Great Holme Street, Leicester, 1975-76* (provisional title)

Ponsich, M, 1979 — *Implantation Rurale Antique sur le Bas-Guadalquivir Volume II* (Paris)

Potter, T W, 1979 — *Romans in North-west England: Excavations at the Roman*

Forts of Ravenglass, Watercrook and Bowness-on-Solway (Cumberland Westmoreland Antiq Archaeol Soc Res Ser 1)

Rahtz, P A, 1959 — Humberstone Earthwork, Leicester *Trans Leicestershire Archaeol Hist Soc* 35, 1-32

Reece, R, 1979 — Roman Monetary Impact *in* Burnham, B C, and Johnson, H B, (eds) 1979, 211-7

Remesal Rodriguez, J, 1977 — La Economia Oleicola Bética: nuevas formas de análisis *Archivo Español de Arqueologia* 50-1, 1977(1978), 87-142

Remesal Rodriguez, J, 1989 — Tres nuevos centros productores de anforas Dressel 20 y 23. Los Sellos de Lucius Fabius Cilo *Ariadna* 6, 121-153

Richardson, B, and Tyers, P A, 1984 — North Gaulish Pottery in Britain *Britannia* 15, 133-41

Richardson, K M, 1959 — Excavations in Hungate, York *Archaeol J* 116, 1959 (1961), 51-114

Richmond, I A, 1922-3 — The sequence and purpose of the Roman Forts at Castleshaw *Trans Lancashire Cheshire Antiq Soc* 40, 1922-3 (1925), 154-62

Richmond, I A, 1950-1 — Exploratory trenching at the Roman Fort of Cappuck, Roxburghshire in 1949 *Proc Soc Antiq Scot* 85, 1950-1 (1953), 138-45

Richmond, I A, 1968 — *Hod Hill, volume two, Excavations carried out between 1951 and 1958 for the Trustees of the British Museum* (London)

Rigby, V, 1977 — The Gallo-Belgic Pottery from Cirencester, *in* Dore, J, and Greene, K T, (eds) 1977, 37-45

Rigby, V, 1979 — Terra Nigra Stamps *in* Greene, K T, 1979, 127

Rigby, V, 1981a — The Gallo-Belgic Wares *in* Partridge, C R, 1981, 159-95

Rigby, V, 1981b — The Potter Julios - a suitable case for study? *in* Anderson, A C, and Anderson, A S, (eds) 1981, 39-50

Rigby, V, 1982a — The Coarse Pottery *in* Wacher, J S, and McWhirr, A D, 1982, 153-200

Rigby, V, 1982b — The Pottery *in* McWhirr, A D, Viner, L, and Wells, C, 1982 *Cirencester Excavations II: Romano-British Cemeteries at Cirencester* (Cirencester Excavation Comm, Cirencester), 112-25, microfiche 1/5:CO5-G12

Rigby, V, 1985 — Terra Nigra potters' stamps *in* Clay, P, and Mellor J E, 1985, 59

Rigby, V, 1986 — Gaulish Fineware Imports *in* Stead, I M, and Rigby, V, 1986, 223-34

Rigby, V, 1989 — Pottery from the Iron Age Cemetery *in* Stead, I M, and Rigby, V, 1989, 112-210

Rigby, V, and Freestone, I C, 1983 — The Flagons *in* Farley, M, 1983, A Mirror Burial at Dorton, Buckinghamshire *Proc Prehist Soc* 49, 269-302 (291-3)

Rigby, V, and Freestone, I C, 1986 — The Petrology and Typology of the Earliest Identified Central Gaulish Imports *J Roman Pottery Stud* 1, 6-21

Riha, E, 1979 — *Die Romischen Fibeln aus Augst und Kaiseraugst* (Forschungen in Augst, Band 3, Augst, 1979)

Rodwell, K, 1979 — Rome and the Trinovantes *in* Burnham, B C, and Johnson, H C, (eds) 1979, 327-38

Rodwell, W J, 1978 — Stamp-decorated pottery of the early Roman period in Eastern England *in* Arthur, P A, and Marsh, G, (eds) 1978, 225-92

Rogers, G, 1974 — *Potéries sigillées de la Gaule Centrale* (Paris)

St. Joseph, J K, 1953 — Air reconnaissance of southern Britain *J Roman Stud* 43, 81-97

Sawday, D, 1989 — The Post Roman Pottery *in* Lucas, J N, 1989, 28-33

Sawday, D, 1991 — Potters Marston Ware *Trans Leicestershire Archaeol Hist Soc* 65, 34-7

Sawday, D, forthcoming — The Saxo-Norman, Medieval and Post Medieval Pottery *in* Mellor, J E, and Pearce, T, forthcoming

Scheers, S, 1972 Coinage and Currency of the Belgic Tribes during the Gallic War *Brit Numis J* 41, 1972 (1973), 1-6

Scheers, S, 1977 *Traité de numismatique celtique II: la Gaule Belgique* (Ann litt Univ Besançon 195/Centre recherche hist anc 24, ser numis)(Paris)

Scheers, S, 1982 Les imitations celtiques des monnaies romaines en Angleterre et leur signification historique *in* Hackens, T, and Weiller, R, (eds) 1982, *Actes du 9eme congres international de numismatique* (Assoc internat numis professionels pub 6), 587-95

Sealey, P R, 1985 *Amphoras from the 1970 Excavations at Colchester Sheepen* (Brit Archaeol Rep (Brit Ser) 142, Oxford)

Sellwood, L C, 1984a Tribal Boundaries Viewed from the Perspective of Numismatic Evidence *in* Cunliffe, B W, and Miles, D, (eds) 1984, *Aspects of the Iron Age in Central Southern Britain* (Univ Oxford Comm Archaeol Monograph 2), 191-204

Sellwood, L C, 1984b Peripheral Celtic Coinages in Britain: New Research *in* Grasmann, G, Jannssen, W, and Brandt, M (eds) 1984, *Keltische Numismatik und Archäologie/Numismatique celtique et archeologie* (Brit Archaeol Rep (Int Ser) S200, Oxford), 406-19

Sellwood, L C, 1986 Tribal Boundaries Viewed from the Perspective of Numismatic Evidence *Hallstatt Kolloquim Veszprém 1984* (Mitt Arch Inst Bhft 3 (Budapest)) 201-9

Simpson, G, 1968 The Decorated Samian Pottery *in* Cunliffe, B W, (ed) 1968, 148-62

Smith, D J, 1975 Roman mosaics in Britain before the fourth centruy *in* Stern, H, and Le Glay, M (eds) 1975, *La Mosaic Greco-Romaine II* (Paris), 269-90

Smith, D J, 1984a Roman mosaics in Britain: a synthesis *in* Farioli Campeneti, R, (ed) 1984, 357-80

Smith, D J, 1984b Second century traditions in Romano-British mosaics *Mosaic* 11 (Nov), 4-9

Smith, D J, 1985 The Blackfriars Mosaic *in* Clay, P, and Mellor, J E, 1985, 38-40

Stanfield, J A, 1929 Unusual forms of terra sigillata *Archaeol J* 86, 1929 (1930), 113-51

Stanfield, J A, 1937 Romano-Gaulish decorated jugs and work of the potter Sabinus *J Roman Stud* 27, 168-79

Stanfield, J A, and Simpson, G, 1958 *Central Gaulish Potters* (Oxford Univ Press)

Stead, I M, and Rigby, V, 1986 *Baldock. The Excavation of a Roman and pre-Roman Settlement. 1968-72* (Britannia Monograph Ser 7, Soc Promotion Roman Stud, London)

Stead, I M, and Rigby, V, 1989 *Verulamium: the King Harry Lane site* (English Heritage Archaeol Rep 12, English Heritage/British Museum, London)

Stirland, A, 1981 The Human Bones *in* Mellor, J E, and Pearce, T, 1981, 168, Microfiche 1/2

Swan, V G, 1975 *Pottery in Roman Britain* (Shire Archaeol, Princes Risborough)

Swan, V G, 1984 *The Pottery Kilns of Roman Britain* (Roy Commission Hist Monuments Supp Ser 5; HMSO, London)

Symonds, R P, 1980 The Coarse Ware and other Fine Wares *in* Lambrick, G, 1980, Excavations in Park Street, Towcester *Northamptonshire Archaeol* 15, 35-118 (79-98)

Thompson, F H, 1958 A Romano-British pottery kiln at North Hykeham, Lincolnshire; with an appendix on the typology, dating and distribution of 'rustic' ware in Great Britain *Antiq J* 38, 15-51

Thompson, I M, 1982 — *Grog-tempered "Belgic" pottery of South-Eastern England* (Brit Archaeol Rep (Brit Ser) 108, Oxford)

Thornton, J H, 1977 — Leather footwear *in* Blurton, T R, 1977, 14-18

Timby, J, 1982 — *Gallo-Belgic Finewares; a study in characterisation, distribution and development during the First Centuries BC and AD* (unpublished PhD thesis, Univ Southampton)

Timby, J, 1985a — TF 10, Amphorae *in* Hurst, H R, 1985, Kingsholm. Excavations at Kingsholm Close and other sites with a discussion of the archaeology of the area (Gloucester Archaeol Rep 1, Gloucester Archaeol Publ), 72-6

Timby, J, 1985b — The Pottery *in* Fulford, M G, 1985, *Guide to the Silchester Excavations. The Forum Basilica 1982-84* (Univ Reading), 25-8

Timby, J, 1987 — The Distribution of Terra Nigra and Terra Rubra to Britain *Rei Cretariae Romanae Fautorum* 25/26, 291-310

Todd, M, 1968 — The Commoner Late Roman Coarse Wares of the East Midlands *Antiq J* 48, 192-209

Todd, M, 1973 — Coarse Pottery *in* Hebditch, M, and Mellor, J E, 1973, 71-81

Tournaire, J, Buchsenschutz, O, Henderson, J, and Collis, J R, 1982 — Iron Age Coin Moulds from France *Proc Prehist Soc* 48, 417-35

Tucker, W T T, 1899 — On the Discovery of a Roman Tessellated Floor near St. Nicholas Church, Leicester *Reliquary and Illustrated Archaeologist* Jan 1899 1-8

Tyers, P A, 1978 — The poppyhead beakers of Britain and their relationship to the barbotine decorated vesels of the Rhineland and Switzerland *in* Arthur, P A, and Marsh, G, (eds 1978), 61-108

Tyers, P A, 1981 — A Note on the Mica-Dusted vessels *in* Partridge, C R, 1981, 102-3

Ulbert, G, 1959 — *Die römischen Donau-Kastelle Aislingen und Burghofe* (Limesforschungen Band 1)

Ulbricht, I, 1978 — *Die Greweihverarbeitung in Haithabn* (Karl Wachholtz Verlag, Neumunster)

van Arsdell, R D, 1983 — Dumnoc Tigir Seno: A New Reading of a Coritanian Silver Unit *Spink Numis Circ* 91, 154

van Arsdell, R D, 1985 — The Origin and Date of the Silver Coritanian Coinage *Spink Numis Circ* 93, 119

van Arsdell, R D, 1989 — *Celtic Coinage of Britain* (Spink, London)

Vernhet, A, 1976 — Création flavienne de six services de vaisselle à la Graufesenque *Figlina* 1 (Lyons)

Vernhet, A, 1986 — Centre de production de millau atelier de la Graufesenque *in* Bemont, C, and Jacob, J-P, (eds) 1986, *La Terre Sigillee Gallo-Romaine, Documents d'Archeologie Francaise* 6, (Paris), 96-103

Wacher, J S, 1964 — Excavations at Breedon-on-the-Hill, Leicestershire, 1957 *Antiq J* 44, 122-42

Wacher, J S, 1975 — *The Towns of Roman Britain* (Batsford, London)

Wacher, J S, and McWhirr, A D, 1982 — *Cirencester Excavations I: Early Roman Occupation at Cirencester* (Cirencester Excavation Comm, Cirencester), 109-17

Wallace, C, and Webster, P V, 1989 — Jugs and Lids in Black-burnished ware *J Roman Pottery Stud* 2, 88-91

Walthew, C V, 1975 — The Town House and the Villa House in Roman Britain *Britannia* 6, 189-205

Ward, M, 1981 — Terra Nigra-type wares from Chester *in* Anderson, A C, and Anderson, A S, (eds) 1981, 51-68

Ward-Perkins, J B, 1938 — The Roman Villa at Lockleys, Welwyn, *Antiq J* 18, 339-76

Webster, G, 1944 — A Roman Pottery at South Carlton, Lincolnshire *Antiq J*

24, 129-43

Webster, G, 1971-3 Coarse Ware *in* Hobley, B, 1971-3, 55-63

Webster, G, (ed) 1976 *Romano-British Coarse Pottery: a student's guide* (Counc Brit Archaeol Res Rep 6, 3rd edition, London)

Webster, G, 1980 *The Roman Invasion of Britain* (Batsford, London)

Webster, G, 1982 Gazeteer of military objects from Cirencester *in* Wacher, J S, and McWhirr, A D, 1982, 109-17

Webster, G, and Booth, N, 1947 A Romano-British Pottery Kiln at Swanpool, near Lincoln *Antiq J* 27, 61-79

Wedlake, W J, 1982 *The Excavation of the Shrine of Apollo at Nettleton, Wiltshire 1956-1971* (Rep Res Comm Soc Antiq London 40, Dorking)

Wheeler, R E M, and Wheeler, T V, 1936 *Verulamium: A Belgic and Two Roman Cities* (Rep Res Comm Soc Antiq London 11, Oxford)

Whitwell, J B, 1982 *The Coritani. Some Aspects of the Iron Age Tribe and the Roman Civitas* (Brit Archaeol Rep (Brit Ser) 99, Oxford)

Williams, D F, 1981 Petrological examination of a group of Mica-Dusted jars *in* Partridge, C R, 1981, 101-2

Williams, D F, 1987 The Amphorae *in* Sunter, N, and Woodward, P J, 1987, *Romano-British Industries in Purbeck* (Doreset Natural Hist Archaeol Soc Monograph Ser 6), 79-81

Williams, D F, and Peacock, D P S, 1979 The Amphorae *in* Partridge, C R, 1979, 113-6

Williams, D F, and Peacock, D P S, 1983 The importation of olive-oil into Iron Age and Roman Britain *in* Blazquez Martinez, J M, and Remesal Rodriguez, J, (eds) 1983, *Produccion y Comercio del Aceite en la Antiguedad : Segundo Congreso Internacional* (Madrid), 263-80

Williams, J H, 1974 *Two Iron Age Sites in Northampton* (Northampton Development Corporation Archaeol Monograph 1, Northampton)

Williams, J H, 1979 *St. Peter's Street, Northampton Excavations 1973-1976* (Northampton Development Corporation Archaeol Monograph 2, Northampton)

Willis S, in preparation *The arrival and distribution of Roman material culture in the north and east of England during the first century AD* (PhD thesis, Univ Durham)

Wilson, M G, 1972 The Other Pottery *in* Frere, S S, 1972, 263-370

Wilson, M G, 1984 The Other Pottery *in* Frere, S S, 1984b, 200-76

Wilson, R, 1980 *Roman Forts* (Bertson and Boyle Books, London)

Woodfield, C, 1983 The Remainder of the Roman Pottery *in* Brown, A E, and Woodfield, C, 1983 Excavations at Towcester, Northamptonshire: The Alchester Road Suburb *Northamptonshire Archaeol* 18, 43-140 (74-100)

Woodland, R, 1981 The Pottery *in* Mellor, J E, and Pearce, T, 1981, 81-129

Woodland, R, 1987 The Post Roman Pottery *in* Buckley, R J, and Lucas, J N, 1987, 80-99

Woods, P J, 1972 *Brixworth Excavations Vol I The Romano-British Villa, 1965-70 Part I. The Roman Coarse Pottery and Decorated Samian Ware* (Northampton 1972, reprinted from *J Northampton Mus* 8 (1970)), 3-102

Woods, P J, and Hastings, B C, 1984 *Rushden: The Early Fine Wares* (ed and revised by K Brown, Northamptonshire County Counc, Northampton)

Young, C J, 1977 *Oxfordshire Roman Pottery* (Brit Archaeol Rep (Brit Ser) 43, Oxford)

Zalkin, V, 1960 The variation of metapodials and their significance in the study of early cattle *J Moscow Soc Experiments of Nature Biology Sect* 1, 109-27 (in Russian, cited in Driesch, A von den, and Boessneck, J, 1974)

Plate 1 The Peacock Pavement as re-discovered in 1898.

Plate 2 Site 5 Phase 3B. Plaster fillets (F99), beam slot (F85) and *Opus Signinum* floor (V 6).

Plate 3 Site 5 Phase 5A. Features cutting street levels (Phase 3C F64).

Plate 4 Site 6 Phase3B. Daub wall (F19).

Plate 5 Site 6 Phase 7B. Floor joists (F27-F33).

Plate 6 The Peacock Pavement. Site 1 Mosaic 1.

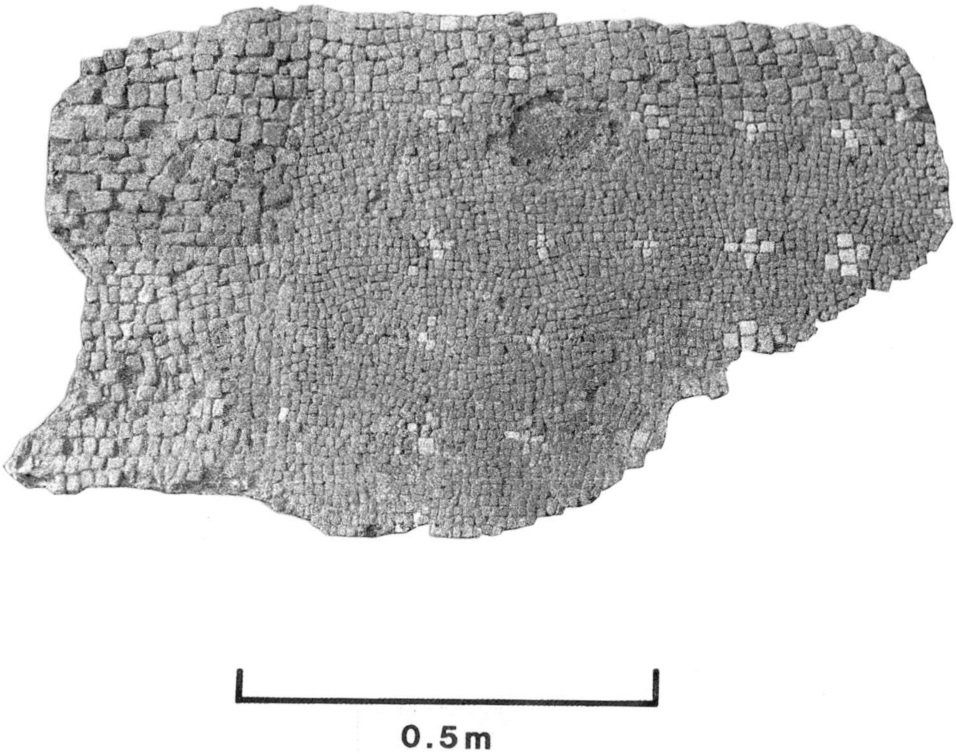

Plate 7 Site 1 Mosaic 2.

Plate 8 Site 1 Mosaic 3.